ILLUSTRATION
VOLUME 9
AMERICAN SHOWCASE

American Showcase, Inc.
New York

CONTENTS

REPRESENTATIVES

continued on next page

continued from previous page

ILLUSTRATION

continued on next page

continued from previous page

VIEWPOINTS

GRAPHIC ARTS ORGANIZATIONS

GREY PAGES

Contents

INDEX

President and Publisher:
Ira Shapiro

Director of Marketing and New Projects:
Chris Curtis
New Projects Manager:
Beth Slone
Book Sales Manager:
Ann Middlebrook
Book Sales Coordinator:
Deborah Lovell

Operations/Credit Manager:
Wendl Kornfeld
Operations Assistant/Mail Service:
Daria Dodds
Accounting Manager:
Cathy Arrigo
Administrative Assistant:
Amy Janello

Production Manager:
Fiona L'Estrange
Production Coordinator:
Kyla Kanz
Grey Pages:
Scott Holden
Production Assistant:
Stephanie Sherman

Distribution and Advertising Sales Manager:
Julia Martin Morris
Sales Representatives:
New York:
Julia Bahr, John Bergstrom, Deborah Darr, Carol Grobman, Donna Levinstone, Barbara Preminger, Wendy Saunders.
Rocky Mountain:
Kate Hoffman
West Coast:
Bob Courtman
Ralph Redpath

Published by:
American Showcase, Inc.
724 Fifth Avenue, 10th Floor
New York, New York 10019
(212) 245-0981

American Illustration Showcase 9
0-931144-35-3 (Softback)
0-931144-36-1 (Hardback)
ISSN 0742-9975 (Hardback and Softback)

©1986. American Showcase, Inc. All Rights Reserved

Book Design and Mechanical Production:
Downey, Weeks + Toomey, Inc., NYC

Typesetting:
Ultra Typographic Service, Inc., NYC
Automatech Graphics Corporation, NYC

Color Separations, Printing and Binding:
Dai Nippon Printing Co. Ltd., Tokyo, Japan

U.S. Book Trade Distribution:
Watson-Guptill Publications
1515 Broadway, New York, New York 10036
(212) 764-7300
Watson-Guptill ISBN: 8230-0185-7

For Sales Outside U.S.:
Rotovision
10, Rue De L'Arqueboise
1211 Geneve 11, Switzerland
Telex 421479 ROVI

continued on next page

REPRESENTATIVES

Notes:

continued from previous page

REPRESENTATIVES

Airstream/Pat Bailey

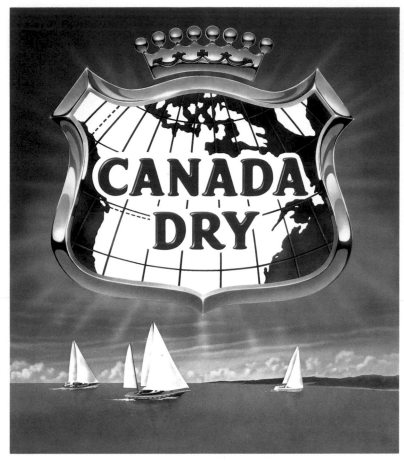

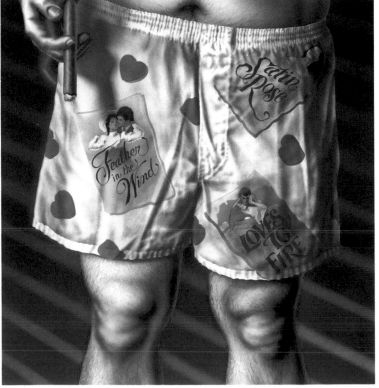

Airstream/Pam Wall

represented by Bernstein & Andriulli, Inc. 60 East 42nd Street New York, N.Y. 10165 (212) 682 1490

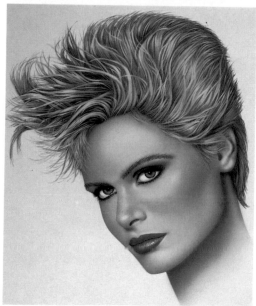

11

Richard Anderson

represented by Bernstein & Andriulli, Inc. 60 East 42nd Street New York, N.Y. 10165 (212) 682-1490

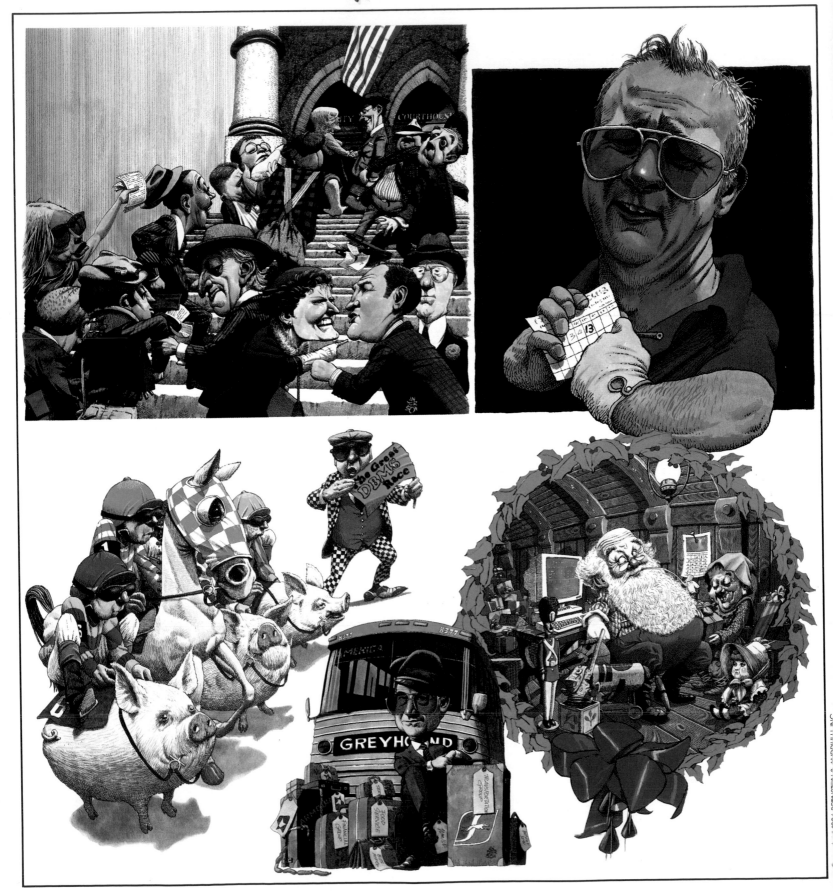

Tony Antonios

represented by Bernstein & Andriulli, Inc. 60 East 42nd Street New York, N.Y. 10165 (212) 682-1490

IS THIS HOW YOUR COMPANY SEES THE GENERAL AGENT?

Some insurance companies think they've reached a higher stage of evolution. So many are replacing the General Agent with their own company managers.

At The Guardian, we consider this a giant step back in time. That's because the General Agency System has always been fundamental to our growth and prosperity. So naturally, we back our Career and Brokerage Agents with a state-of-the-art support system and a highly competitive product line.

So if you think the best days of the General Agent are not in the past, but in the future, talk to a company that feels the same way. Just call us toll-free at 800-648-3434. Because good General Agents don't belong in the museum. They belong at The Guardian.

The Guardian
Life Insurance Company of America

Building on Tradition.

HOW MUCH LONGER ARE YOU GOING TO LET YOUR BANK WALK ALL OVER YOU?

Get absolutely free checking at Palmetto Federal. Per check charges. Monthly service fees. Minimum balance requirements of $250 to $500. Penalty fees when your balance falls below a certain minimum. Did you ever stop to ask yourself if your bank may be treading a little hard? Why not get out from under it all? At Palmetto Federal, we offer free checking that really is free. You pay no per check charges. No monthly service fees. There's no minimum balance to maintain after your initial $100 deposit. And, we don't change the rules the minute you become a customer. Checking is really free. And that's about as good as it gets.

You can sell us your old checks and collect daily interest, too. For a limited time only, we'll make it even more profitable to open a Palmetto Federal checking account by buying up to 200 of your current bank's checks at 3¢ apiece. And, once you open your account, you'll earn 5¼% interest as long as you maintain a $500 balance. Think about what that can add up to when you combine it with the $5 to $10 you'll be saving each month in service charges. Not bad. And, with your new Palmetto Federal account, you don't have to keep up with cancelled checks. We hold them for you, and you always have a duplicate copy right there in your checkbook. So, stand up. Fill out the application and bring your present bank's checks to the nearest Palmetto Federal office. It only takes $100 to open an account. And it could cost you a lot more than that if you don't.

PALMETTO FEDERAL
OF SOUTH CAROLINA
Member FSLIC

If you're over 55, ask us about the advantages of Prime Time Checking.

THE SQUEEZE IS ON!

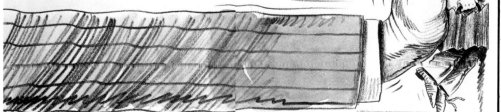

While others find ways to replace the General Agent system, we're finding ways to expand it.

There's a trend in the insurance business that we don't understand. The trend towards replacing the General Agent with company managers. We find it puzzling because at The Guardian, the General Agent has always been indispensable to our success. A success measured by one of the strongest surplus positions of any mutual insurance company. And an investment rate of return that's also one of the best in the industry.

Obviously, we're not going to do anything to alter this kind of performance. Except to do more of the same.

We're looking for outstanding Career and Brokerage General Agents.

Instead of figuring out why some companies are turning their backs on the General Agent, we'd like to figure out ways to get the good ones to join us. So we're making it easy for you to find out more about our General Agency system. Just dial the toll free number

below and we'll tell you all about our superb sales support system, our diversified product line and reinforce what we've said here. That our commitment to the General Agent is unwavering. So pick up the phone and give us a call. You'll see that the place we have for you at The Guardian isn't up against a wall.

Call toll free and let us prove our commitment to the General Agent: 800-648-3434.

The Guardian
Life Insurance Company of America

Building on Tradition.

Per Arnoldi

represented by Bernstein & Andriulli, Inc. 60 East 42nd Street New York, N.Y. 10165 (212) 682-1490

COPENHAGEN

JAZZ

FESTIVAL 1983

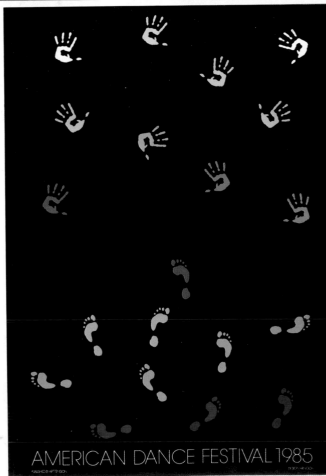

AMERICAN DANCE FESTIVAL 1985

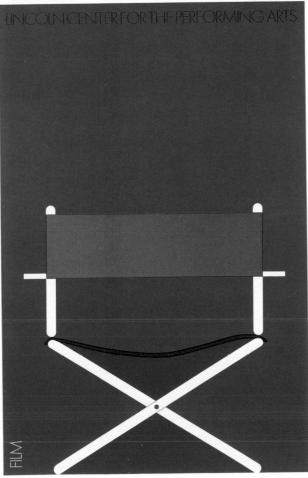

LINCOLN CENTER FOR THE PERFORMING ARTS

FILM

Garin Baker

represented by Bernstein & Andriulli, Inc. 60 East 42nd Street New York, N.Y. 10165 (212) 682-1490

Cathy Deeter

represented by Bernstein & Andriulli, Inc. 60 East 42nd Street New York, N.Y. 10165 (212) 682-1490

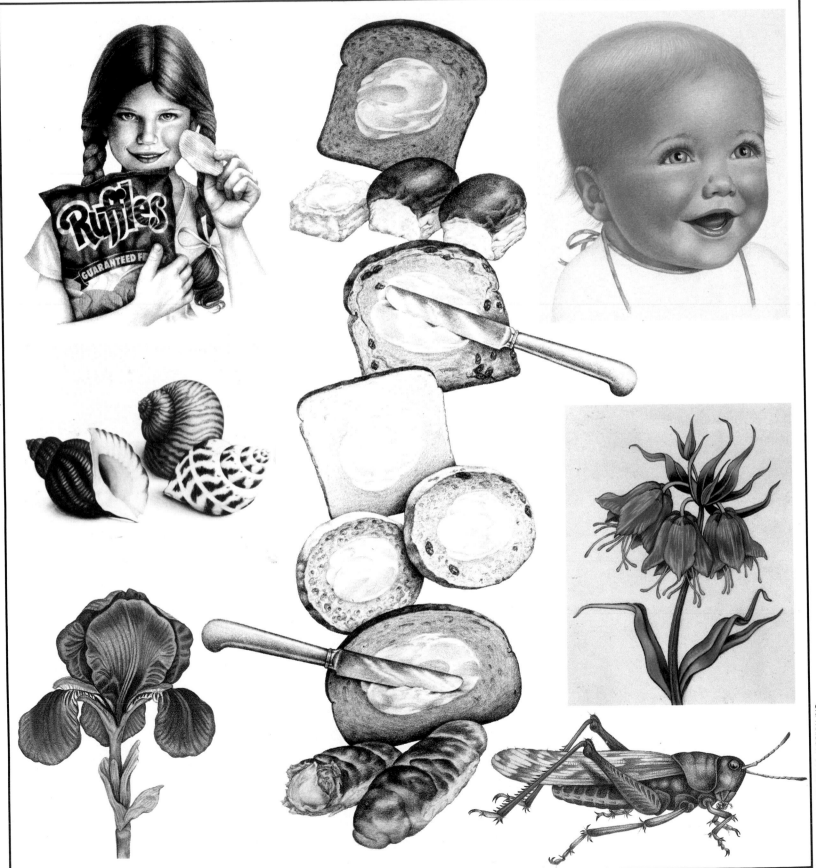

Holly Dickens

represented by Bernstein & Andriulli, Inc. 60 East 42nd Street, New York, N.Y. 10165 (212) 682-1490

Victor Gadino

represented by Bernstein & Andriulli, Inc. 60 East 42nd Street, New York, N.Y. 10165 (212) 682-1490

Joe Genova

represented by Bernstein & Andriulli, Inc. 60 East 42nd Street New York, N.Y. 10165 (212) 682-1490

Ron Fleming/Graphic Associates

represented by Bernstein & Andriulli, Inc. 60 East 42nd Street New York, N.Y. 10165 (212) 682-1490

BERNSTEIN & ANDRIULLI INC

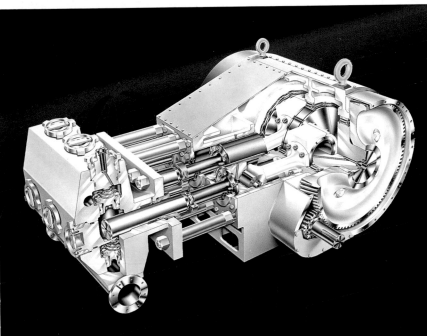

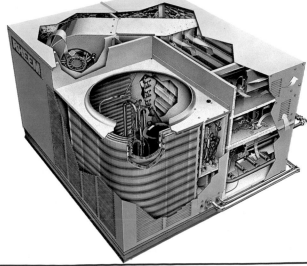

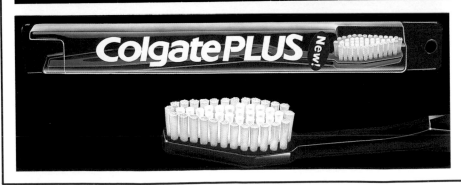

Clay Turner/Graphic Associates

represented by Bernstein & Andriulli, Inc. 60 East 42nd Street New York, N.Y. 10165 (212) 682-1490

Griesbach/Martucci

represented by Bernstein & Andriulli, Inc. 60 East 42nd Street New York, N.Y. 10165 (212) 682-1490

Griesbach/Martucci

represented by Bernstein & Andriulli, Inc. 60 East 42nd Street New York, N.Y. 10165 (212) 682-1490

Kid Kane

represented by Bernstein & Andriulli, Inc. 60 East 42nd Street New York, N.Y. 10165 (212) 682-1490

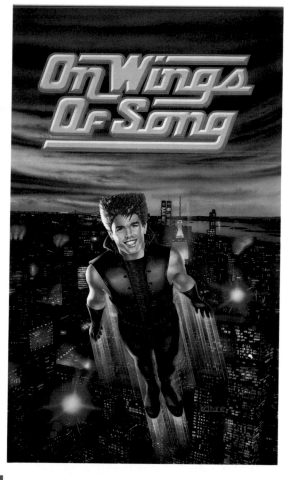

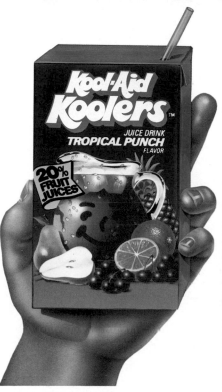

Mary Ann Lasher

represented by Bernstein & Andriulli, Inc. 60 East 42nd Street New York, N.Y. 10165 (212) 682-1490

Bette Levine

represented by Bernstein & Andriulli, Inc. 60 East 42nd Street New York, N.Y. 10165 (212) 682-1490

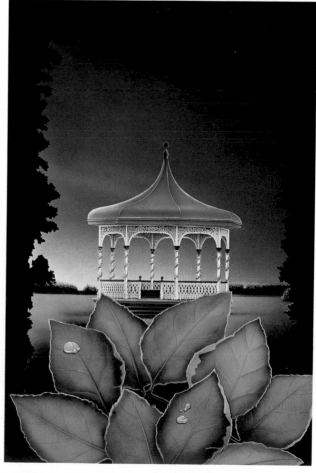

Bill Morse

represented by Bernstein & Andriulli, Inc. 60 East 42nd Street, New York, N.Y. 10165 (212) 682-1490

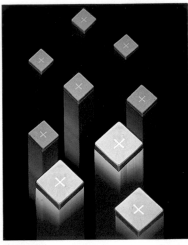

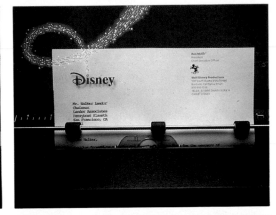

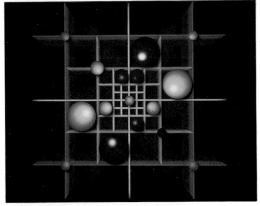

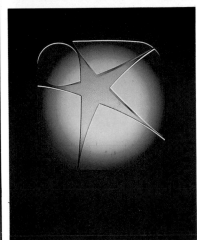

Sharp computer graphics
for print—on 4" x 5" ektachrome
Photographed optically, not
synthesized on a video screen.

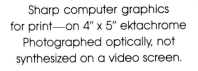

Craig Nelson

represented by Bernstein & Andriulli, Inc. 60 East 42nd Street New York, N.Y. 10165 (212) 682-1490

Joe Salina

represented by Bernstein & Andriulli, Inc. 60 East 42nd Street New York, N.Y. 10165 (212) 682-1490

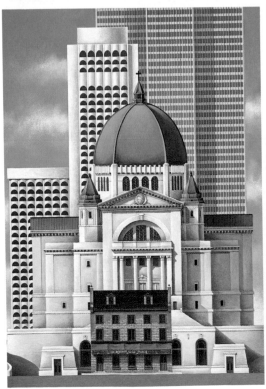

Chuck Slack

represented by Bernstein & Andriulli, Inc. 60 East 42nd Street New York, N.Y. 10165 (212) 682-1490

Peter Stallard

represented by Bernstein & Andriulli, Inc. 60 East 42nd Street New York, N.Y. 10165 (212) 682-1490

J.C. Suares

represented by Bernstein & Andriulli, Inc. 60 East 42nd Street New York, N.Y. 10165 (212) 682-1490

Chuck Wilkinson

represented by Bernstein & Andriulli, Inc. 60 East 42nd Street New York, N.Y. 10165 (212) 682-1490

The New York Times Magazine / March 24, 1985

Russell Cobane

Russell Cobane

Russell Cobane

Russell Cobane

Russell Cobane

Russell Cobane

35

Joe Ovies

Michael Haynes

Sandra Shap

Jim Hunt

Chuck Schmidt

Nighthawk Studio

Ken Graning

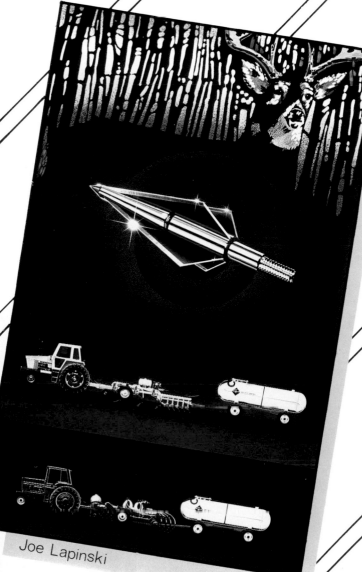

Joe Lapinski

37

D . C
200 WEST 15TH STREET, NEW YORK, NY 10011
(212) 243.4209

DAVID GAMBALE

"It's cash for cars."

ROLL ON
SUNNY
MONEY

The First Greenville Bank

MIKE LESTER

VICKI YIANNIAS

SUSAN HUNT YULE

DENNIS MUKAI

SUSAN HUNT YULE

VICKI YIANNIAS

DENNIS MUKAI

DAVID GAMBALE

MIKE LESTER

DANIELE COLLIGNON
200 WEST 15TH STREET, NEW YORK, NY 10011
(212) 243.4209

RICK JOHNSON

VICTOR VALLA

CLIFF MILLER

RICK JOHNSON

JOHN DAWSON

RALPH BRILLHART

EDWIN HERDER

WALTER RANE

ULDIS KLAVINS

JEFF WALKER

JIM GRIFFIN

JOHN DAWSON

JEFF WALKER

WENDELL MINOR

DAVID GAADT

FRANK STEINER

DWIN HERDER

RICHARD LAUTER

DAN SNEBERGER

RALPH BRILLHART

Greetings from SMALLTOWN USA

JEFF WALKER

HFT

Hankins+Tegenborg

Artist's Representatives
David Hankins Lars Tegenborg
60 E. 42nd Street
New York, N.Y. 10165
(212)867-8092

VICTOR VALLA

Johnson & Johnson

BOB TRAVERS

DAVID GAADT

BOB TRONDSEN

"Careful. It might still be hot."

"IT'S POWER CABLE...
INSULATED WITH UCAR® TR-4202 XL
POLYETHYLENE COMPOUND."

Medium- and high-voltage cable insulated with Union Carbide UCAR polyethylene compound TR-4202 XL will be around underground for a long time to come.

It's a unique, crosslinkable tree-resistant insulation compound that can significantly extend the life of buried cable, especially in a wet underground environment. In accelerated life tests, both full size and miniature cable insulated with UCAR compound TR-4202 XLPE show 3 to 5 times the life of cable insulated with standard XLPE compound. And, UCAR TR-4202 provides heat-resistant properties inherent in a crosslinkable polyethylene for reliability during

peak loading periods.

You know that buried cable failures attributable to treeing are relatively few. You also know that even one cable failure is one too many. So do we.

Specify underground cable with insulation made from Union Carbide UCAR compound TR-4202 XLPE. To be sure.

For detailed information, talk to your cable manufacturer. Or, write to Union Carbide Corporation, Dept. L-2497, Polyolefins Division, Old Ridgebury Road, Danbury, Connecticut, 06817.

And move into the 21st Century right now.

® UCAR is a registered trademark of Union Carbide Corporation.

UNION CARBIDE

POLYOLEFINS DIVISION
Wire & Cable Materials

©1983 Union Carbide Corporation

EDWIN HERDER

FRANK STEINER

DER/KLAVINS

Hankins+Tegenborg

Artist's Representatives

David Hankins Lars Tegenborg
60 E. 42nd Street
New York, N.Y. 10165
(212) 867-8092

LAVATY

See pages 130–149 for more!

Representing

John Berkey, Jim Butcher, Don Daily, Bernard D'Andrea, Roland DesCombes, Chris Duke,
Bruce Emmett, Gervasio Gallardo, Martin Hoffman, Stan Hunter, Chet Jezierski, David McCall Johnston,
Mort Kunstler, Paul Lehr, Lemuel Line, Robert Lo Grippo, Darrel Millsap, Carlos Ochagavia

Frank & Jeff Lavaty & Associates • 50 East 50th Street N.Y. N.Y. 10022 • (212) 355-0910

Wm HARRISON

LARRY WINBORG

TED LODIGENSKY

JOSEPH SELLARS

represented by
BARNEY KANE & FRIENDS
18 East 16 St. NYC 10003
(212) 206·0322

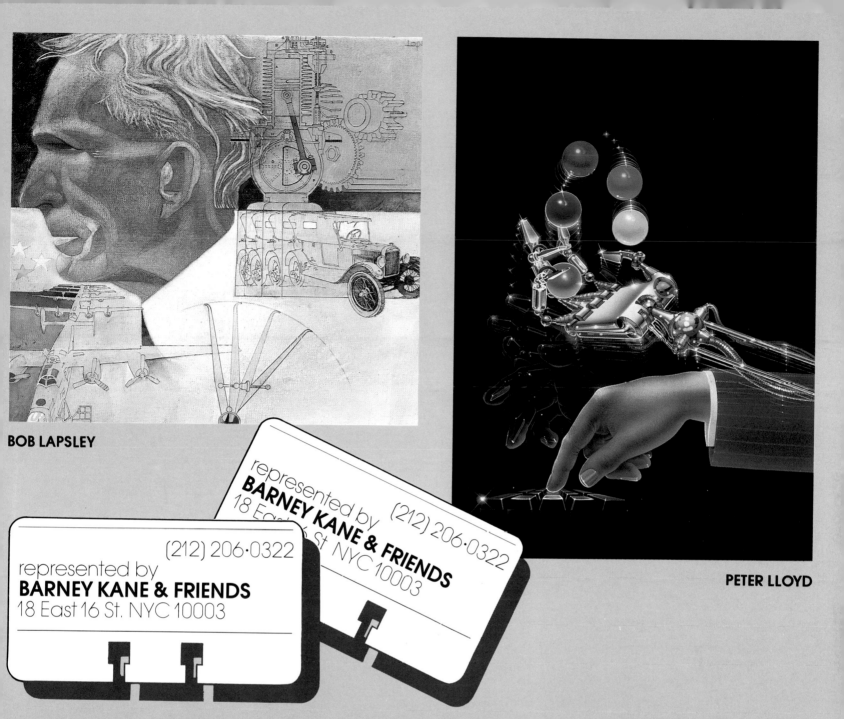

BOB LAPSLEY

PETER LLOYD

represented by
BARNEY KANE & FRIENDS
18 East 16 St. NYC 10003
(212) 206·0322

represented by
BARNEY KANE & FRIENDS
18 East 16 St. NYC 10003
(212) 206·0322

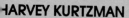
HARVEY KURTZMAN

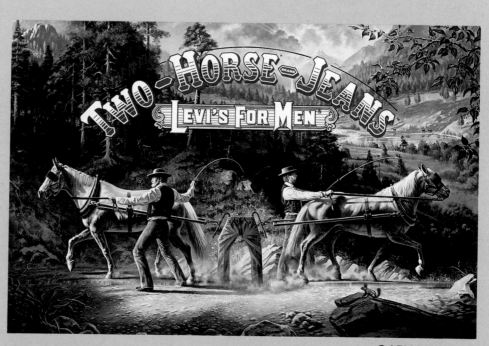

GARY RUDDELL

Illustrators WORLDWIDE

Stephen Berger
Manhattan

Jack Brusca
New York City

Kathy Wyatt
England

Bodhi Wind
Los Angeles

International

Herb Spiers
Agent

S. I. International
43 East 19th Street
New York, NY 10003
(212) 254-4996
Telex: 427539

Sergio Martinez
Madrid

Susi Kilgore
Florida

Vince Perez
San Francisco

Robert Fine
Flushing, NY

Send for our portfolio

Herb Spiers
Agent

S. I. International
43 East 19th Street
New York, NY 10003
(212) 254-4996
Telex: 427539

Modern Muscles

**Messengers
Couriers
Telexes
Teleprinters
Teleposts**

Doug Rosenthal
New York

Artie Ruiz
Jersey City

Ernie Colón
Upper West Side

Paul Tatore
Valhalla

Walt de Rijk
Amsterdam

International

Herb Spiers
Agent

S. I. International
43 East 19th Street
New York, NY 10003
(212) 254-4996
Telex: 427539

Span the Globe

Send for our portfolio

Martin Rigo
Spain

Richard Courtney
Joplin, Missouri

Richard Corben
Kansas City

Allen Davis
Queens

Send for our portfolio

Herb Spiers
Agent

S. I. International
43 East 19th Street
New York, NY 10003
(212) 254-4996
Telex: 427539

51

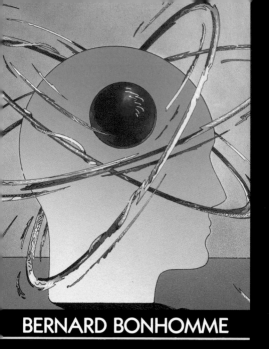

BERNARD BONHOMME

ROBERT BURGER

HOVIK DILAKIAN

AMY HILL

GEORGE MASI

KIRSTEN SODERLIND

KURT VARGÖ

DENNIS ZIEMIENSKI

R O S S

53

121 MADISON AVE., NEW YORK, NY 10016 · (212) 683-1362

par
Rodica Prato

121 MADISON AVE., NEW YORK, NY 10016 · (212) 683-1362

ILLUSTRATORS
200 East 78th Street
Katherine
TISE
212·570·9069
New York, N.Y. 10021
REPRESENTATIVE

JOHN BURGOYNE

ILLUSTRATORS
200 East 75th Street
Katherine
TISE
212·570·9069
New York, N.Y. 10021
REPRESENTATIVE

JOHN BURGOYNE

ILLUSTRATORS
200 East 78th Street
Katherine
TISE
212·570·9069
New York, N.Y. 10021
REPRESENTATIVE

BUNNY CARTER

ILLUSTRATORS
200 East 78th Street
Katherine
TISE
212·570·9069
New York, N.Y. 10021
REPRESENTATIVE

CATHLEEN TOELKE

Art Staff, Inc.

1200 Penobscot Building
Detroit, Michigan 48226
(313) 963-8240

Agents: Ben Jaroslaw
Dick Meissner

The "Worlds Finest" Automotive and Product illustrators
for over twenty five years, serving the worlds most
prestigious clients, add new dimensions to our portfolio.

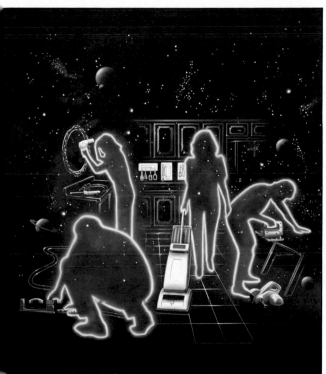

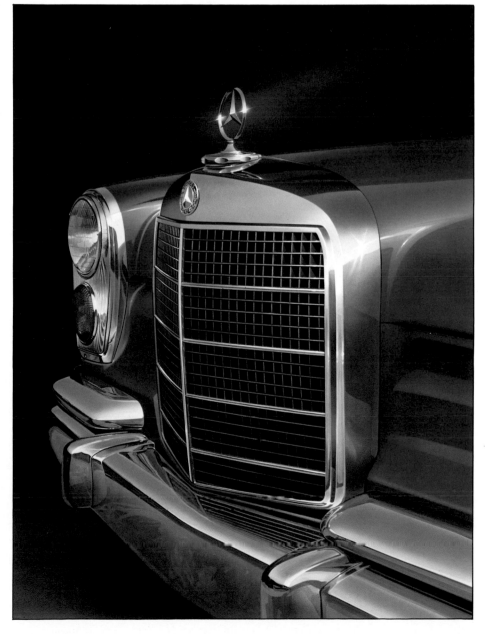

COLOR PAGINATION SYSTEMS

Silicon Valley has invaded the advertising and graphic arts community. From word processors for writers, graphic imagers for comp artists to special effects machines like the Mirage system for T.V., computers are a part of the way we see and develop artwork. Above all, the word Scitex has shaken the print industry, photographers, art directors, color labs, retouchers, and color separators.

The Scitex system was developed by the Israelis to facilitate textile printing. The potential as a stripping and color correction tool for the graphic arts was seen by catalogue houses, magazine publishers and photo plate makers; they started buy-these electronic prepress systems and soon there were several competitors—Hell (Chromacom), Crosfield (Studio) among others. Why? Because these systems are fantastic at pagination. Text and pictorial elements can be combined, moved around, and rescaled almost instantly and once in position converted to screened separations.

These systems can also retouch, and here is where the confusion begins. An original transparency is scanned into the system—converted to digital information—and the image is called up on a monitor. The image is then manipulated by sizing, repositioning, photocomposing, flopping, extending, cloning, changing colors and even airbrushing. Textures and tint areas (in PMS colors) can be added. These changes take place within minutes and show up on the screen as if by magic. Continuous tone prints or transparencies (Chromacom) or polaroids (Scitex) can be output on special peripheral devices for proofing, for archival purposes or as second generation artwork. Screened separations are then made or the data can be transmitted directly to gravure cylinder engraving machines.

This sounds almost too good to be true and when agencies heard about these systems a few years ago, many people rushed their jobs right over to the color separators who had these systems to separate and retouch their artwork, quite a few people were discouraged, as limitation and flaws showed up on these jobs. Even though the systems have the capabilities to perform most retouching functions, the operators running the systems were trained as computer operators or printing technicians and at the time not only had not fully grasped the retouching capabilities but did not understand the retouching language: "Open up the shadow a bit," "The skin looks a little red," or "Clean it up and separate for magazine."

At the same time, dye labs were worried. The color pagination systems meant no more 100% O.T. and no more dyes at all. Retouchers saw the same problem. That situation has not changed. Now photographers feel that the machine is so fantastic that old shots can be combined with new elements and brought back to life. They see the bread disappearing from their tables. May as well hang up the Hasselblad or get into the stock business.

What is this machine that it threatens the people in the industry in this way? With more experience on the systems, art buyers, art directors, and print producers are becoming less threatened. The Chromacom or Scitex can do little more than your friendly retoucher can do as far as its electronic retouching capabilities are concerned. In fact in some cases the system takes three or four times as long to produce an effect as a retoucher can. Many operators do not have the years of experience in retouching or the artistic background that a retoucher has and may treat your directions to a rather crude interpretation. Retouchers may want to get involved with these systems, and are presently exploring this possibility.

On the other hand, these difficulties will be corrected in time and the systems have one great advantage over dye and chrome retouching—speed, and sometimes, money. Some of the best features are cloning and stripping. Position an element same size, enlarged or reduced, on the art and presto! It's done. Not enough art work on top—clone additional sky in less than one hour at half the cost of pulling a dye and extending.

These systems are still relatively new and because we do not fully understand them, they cause controversy. Caution should be taken when considering putting an extensive job through one of the systems. My first experience was a 19-part strip and even though the job turned out well in an incredibly short time period, I wish I had started with something small —such as adding more of a solid background or a color correction. Some jobs can be handled partly by a chrome retoucher and partly by the system. The job should be explained to the technician very carefully and a cost ob-

continued on page 68

Anne Brody

Studio Six
55 Bethune Street
New York, New York 10014
(212) 242-1407

Represents:

Christine Ciesiel

Clients include:
Doubleday Books; J. Wiley & Sons; Savvy Magazine; Conde-Nast; Scholastic Magazines; Johnson & Higgins; Kwasha, Lipton; CTI; BM-E; Restaurant Business Magazine; Frances Denny Inc.

Member Graphic Artists Guild

Creative Freelancers, Inc.

62 West 45th Street
New York, New York 10036
(212) 398-9540

Represents:

Hal Brooks

20 West 87th Street
New York, New York 10024
(212) 595-5980

Clients:
Time-Life Promotions
Dancer-Fitzgerald Sample
  New York, R.C. Cola
McGraw-Hill Publications
Fleet Owner Magazine
Business Week
Trucking Magazine
Corporate Graphics
Harcourt Brace Jovanovich
Home and Auto Magazine
Food Management
Dow Jones and Company, Inc.
Barron's
Institutional Investor Magazine
The American Lawyer
Venture Magazine
Hayden Publications
Computer Decisions
Clarins
Health Magazine
Home Video
Meetings and Conventions
Sportwise, New York, Boston
Your Corporate Look
Cleveland Plain Dealer
Syracuse Post-Standard
Jim Lang Golf Tournament
West-End Games
Guitar Review
Chain Store Executive
Retail Technology
Restaurant News
Pharmaceutical News
Homecenter News
Dewitt Sound Inc.
New York Times
Halcyon Associates

KITCHEN DESIGN

OVERCOMING CHAOS
And Solving Other Back-Of-The-House Woes

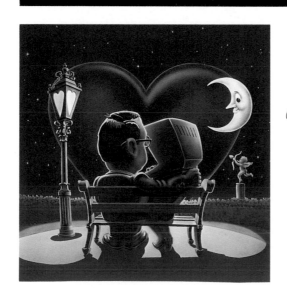

Creative Freelancers, Inc.

62 West 45th Street
New York, New York 10036
(212) 398-9540

Represents:

Howard Darden

Illustration

A partial list of clients includes:
ABC Television; Allied Chemical; American Airlines; American Express; Anheuser-Busch; Bristol Myers; Burlington Mills; Caltex; Congoleum; Diners Club; Dunlop; Exxon; Florsheim; General Electric; Gordon's Gin; NBC Television; Nestlé; Paramount Pictures; J. C. Penney; Rhône-Poulenc; Texaco; Union Camp; U.S. Plywood; Bobbs-Merrill; Field & Stream; Club Magazine; Genesis Magazine; Holt, Rinehart and Winston; J.P. Lippincott; MacMillan Publishing; Penthouse International; Pictura Graphica; Readers Digest; Scholastic Publications; Silver Burdett; Sports Afield.

continued from page 64

tained before starting. Some jobs are best if they are kept off the machine and given to a conventional retoucher.

As for as what color pagination equipment means to the industry, I imagine the answer is simply that it is another, albeit electronic, way to go about retouching a job. Nothing more. Agreed, it is wonderful that there is now a third way to approach a problem, but these systems today are not the answer to all our problems nor a threat to the livelihoods of the photography community. They are, however, of utmost importance in computerizing the entire pre-press area of the printing field and may well be the way most retouching will be performed in the future.

Alistair Gillett
Head Art Buyer
Young & Rubicam Inc.
New York City

Creative Talent

Represented by
Lauren Gelband
62 LeRoy Street
New York, New York 10014
(212) 243-7869

Representing:

Alan Henderson

Marshall Cetlin

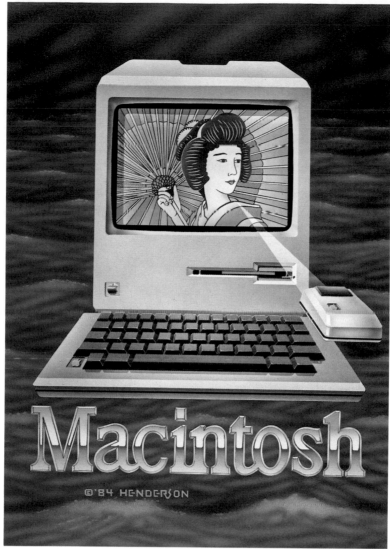

ALAN HENDERSON

Creative
TALENT

Represented By
Lauren Gelband
(212) 243-7869
62 LeRoy St.
N.Y.C., N.Y. 10014

MARSHALL CETLIN

Daniele Deverin

226 East 53rd Street
New York, New York 10022
(212) 755-4945

Member of the Society of
Illustrators and the Graphic
Artists Guild

1. Newsweek
2. Texas Monthly
3. The New York Times
4. Bill Gold Advertising
5. S.S.C.&B.

Jeffrey Smith

1.

2.

3.

Mort Drucker

4.

5.

Daniele Deverin

226 East 53rd Street
New York, New York 10022
(212) 755-4945

Member of the Society of
Illustrators and the Graphic
Artists Guild

Representing:

Don Weller

1. and 2. National Football League
3. Angel Records
4. Star Computer Software
5. Cover for Lodestar Magazine
6. Solutions Magazine

All material © 1986

In San Francisco, call:
Ron Sweet (415) 433-1222

In Los Angeles, call:
Jae Wagoner (213) 392-4877

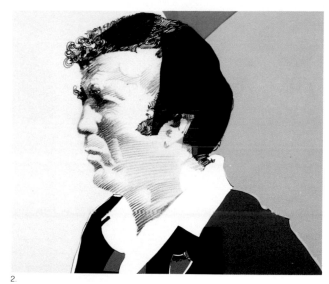

1.

2.

3.

4.

5.

6.

Daniele Deverin

226 East 53rd Street
New York, New York 10022
(212) 755-4945

Member of the Society of
Illustrators and the Graphic
Artists Guild

Representing:

Paul Blakey

1. The Atlanta Magazine
2. Peterson Blyth Cato
   Associates, Inc.
3. Rafshoon Advertising
4. HBM/CREAMER, Inc.

1.

3.

4.

Daniele Deverin

226 East 53rd Street
New York, New York 10022
(212) 755-4945

Member of the Society of
Illustrators and the Graphic
Artists Guild

Representing:

Laszlo Kubinyi

Member of the Graphic Artists
Guild

1. William Douglas McAdams
2. Grey Advertising
3. Klemtner Advertising
4. Business Week
5. Campbell-Ewald Co.

All material © 1986

FAMOUS CONTRACEPTIVE POLICYMAKERS

1.

In that year, Bath Iron Works was born. With a legacy of pride in Maine's shipbuilding tradition, founder General Thomas W. Hyde looked toward a future of promise as the age of sail gave way to a new era of steam and steel.

A legacy of pride... a future of promise. It's as true today as it was a hundred years ago. For without the skill and dedication of generations of Maine shipbuilders, the hallmark Bath-built ® would never have become a synonym for excellence. And without innovative, experienced management, our small shipyard would never have become one of the preeminent names in American shipbuilding.

Maine launched a legend in 1884.

As one U.S. Navy commander put it, "If you asked 80% of the naval officers—the other 20% are new and don't know yet—they'd say the best-built ship is a Bath-built ship."

Thanks, Maine, for a great shipbuilding tradition. From the very beginning, you gave Bath Iron Works a legacy of pride and a future of promise.

BIW
® BATH IRON WORKS CORPORATION
A Congoleum Company, Bath, Maine 04530

2.

3.

CORPORATE SCOREBOARD: FIRST-QUARTER PROFITS OF 875 COMPANIES PAGE 5

BusinessWeek

MAY 16, 1983   A McGraw-HILL PUBLICATION $2.00

A REVOLUTION IN WORK RULES

NEW JOB FLEXIBILITY BOOSTS PRODUCTIVITY PAGE 1
HOW ALLEGHENY IS REBUILDING SUNBEAM PAGE 142

4.

This year, we'll ship over 3½ million pounds of America to South America.

BARRANQUILLA · BOGOTA · ASUNCION · QUITO · SANTIAGO · CALI · EASTERN AIR-FREIGHT · GUAYAQUIL · PANAMA CITY · LA PAZ · LIMA · BUENOS AIRES

Eastern Airlines Air-Freight can now give you more freight service to South American destinations than ever before.

We offer regular freight service to 11 cities in 8 countries in Central and South America.

We'll take your goods from over 90 locations in the U.S., coast to coast, and from Toronto, Montreal and Ottawa in Canada. Service is via our gateway cities: Miami,

Houston, New York, Los Angeles, San Francisco and New Orleans. Then we'll ship your freight to Panama City, Panama; Cali, Barranquilla and Bogota, Colombia; Buenos Aires, Argentina; Guayaquil and Quito, Ecuador; La Paz, Bolivia; Lima, Peru; Santiago, Chile and Asuncion, Paraguay.

Call your local Eastern Air-Freight representative. And let Eastern ship your part of America to South America.

© 1983 Eastern Air Lines, Inc.

EASTERN Air-Freight

5.

Ella
229 Berkeley Street
Boston, Massachusetts 02116
(617) 266-3858

Representing:

Jack Crompton
Susan Dodge
Janet Mager

E·L·L·A

JACK CROMPTON

JANET MAGER

JACK CROMPTON

SUSAN DODGE

SUSAN DODGE

Ella

229 Berkeley Street
Boston, Massachusetts 02116
(617) 266-3858

Representing:

Sharon Drinkwine
Anatoly Dverin
Scott Gordley

E·L·L·A

ANATOLY DVERIN

ANATOLY DVERIN

SHARON DRINKWINE

SCOTT GORDLEY

SCOTT GORDLEY

Ella
229 Berkeley Street
Boston, Massachusetts 02116
(617) 266-3858
Representing:
Rob Cline
Anna Davidian

ROB CLINE

ANNA DAVIDIAN

ROB CLINE

ANNA DAVIDIAN

Ella
229 Berkeley Street
Boston, Massachusetts 02116
(617) 266-3858
Representing:

Roger Leyonmark
Ron Toelke

E·L·L·A

ROGER LEYONMARK

RON TOELKE

ROGER LEYONMARK

RON TOELKE

Ella
229 Berkeley Street
Boston, Massachusetts 02116
(617) 266-3858
Representing:

Bruce Sanders

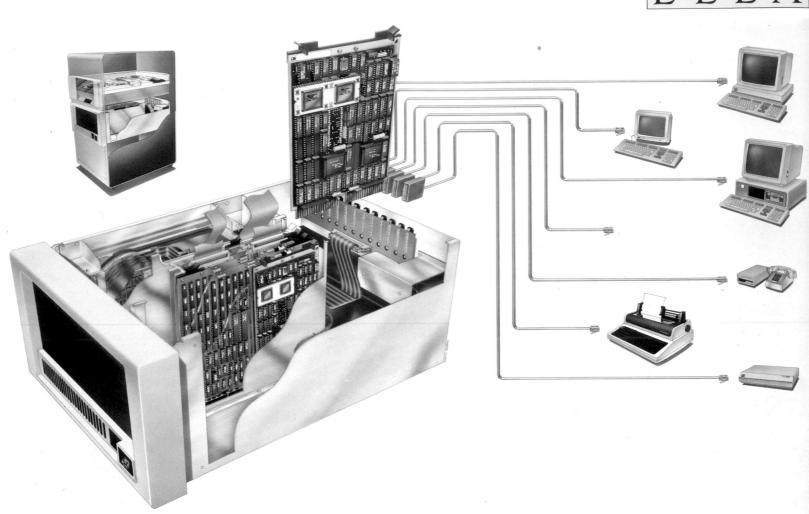

BRUCE SANDERS

BRUCE SANDERS

BRUCE SANDERS

Dennis Godfrey

95 Horatio Street
New York, New York 10014
(212) 807-0840

Representing:

Jeffrey Adams
Joel Nakamura
Greg Ragland

and others

Jeffrey Adams

Joel Nakamura

Greg Ragland

Barbara Gordon
Associates

165 East 32nd Street
New York, New York 10016
(212) 686-3514

Barbara and Elliott Gordon

Barbara Gordon Associates works in all areas of the business, including advertising, paperbacks, movies, industrial, pharmaceutical, fashion, corporate, government, packaging, publishing and television.

Complete portfolios on all artists and photographers represented by the firm are available upon request.

Barbara Gordon
Associates Ltd
165 East 32 Street
New York, N.Y. 10016
212-686-3514

SONJA LAMUT/NENAD JAKESEVIC

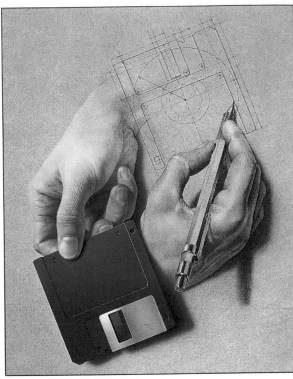

SONJA LAMUT/NENAD JAKESEVIC

JACKIE JASPER

ANDREW NITZBERG, PAPER SCULPTURE

JIM DIETZ

80

Barbara Gordon
Associates

165 East 32nd Street
New York, New York 10016
(212) 686-3514

JACQUIE MARIE VAUX, ANIMAL ILLUSTRATION

RON BARRY

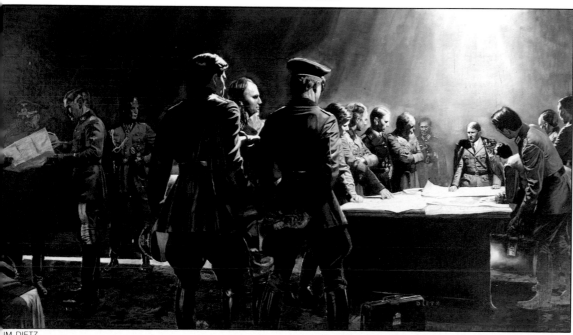

IM DIETZ

JACKIE JASPER

Anita Grien

155 East 38th Street
New York, New York 10016
(212) 697-6170

Hal Just

Illustration and Design

Clients Include: CBS, Franklin Mint, Reader's Digest, Time Inc., Ally & Gargano, BBD&O, Ted Bates, Benton & Bowles, Compton, Dancer Fitzgerald Sample, D'Arcy MacManus Masius, Della Femina Travisano, Wm. Esty, Foote Cone & Belding, Grey, Lord Geller Federico Einstein, Marschalk, O&M, Scali McCabe Sloves, J. Walter Thompson, Y&R.

Alan Reingold

Illustration

Clients Include: ABC, CBS, NBC, PBS, RCA, Burlington Industries, Columbia Pictures, Exxon, Lorimar, Paramount, Universal, Warner Communications; Forbes, G.Q., Nat'l Lampoon, Newsweek, Franklin Library, Reader's Digest· N.W. Ayer, Ted Bates, Grey, O&M, SSC&B, Scali McCabe Sloves, Y&R.

HAL JUST

HAL JUST

SAVING GRACE

ALAN REINGOLD

Family Weekly

ALAN REINGOLD

ALAN REINGOLD

82

Anita Grien

155 East 38th Street
New York, New York 10016
(212) 697-6170

Introducing
Fanny Mellet Berry   Ellen Rixford

Dimensional Illustration, Sculpture, Puppets and Props
in just about every medium.

Clients Include: Exxon, MacNeil Lehrer, Schering
Corp., UJA; Business Week, Fortune, Good
Housekeeping, Psychology Today, Reader's Digest,
U.S. News & World Report; Book-of-the Month Club,
McGraw-Hill, Time Inc.; AC&R, N.W. Ayer, Dancer
Fitzgerald & Sample, Marstellar, O&M, Y&R.

FANNY MELLET BERRY

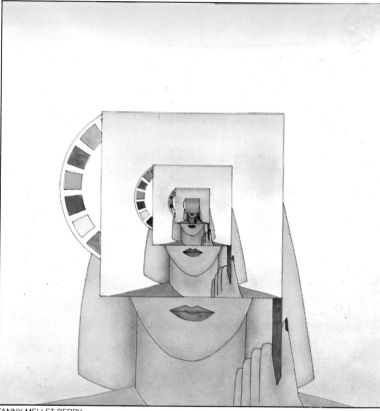

FANNY MELLET BERRY

ELLEN RIXFORD

ELLEN RIXFORD

Anita Grien

155 East 38th Street
New York, New York 10016
(212) 697-6170

Marina Neyman-Levikova

Illustration and Design

Clients Include: ABC, CBS, Arista Records, Epic, Polygram, Vestron Video, Warner Communications; Avon, L'Oréal, Revlon, Sergio Valente, Yves St. Laurent; Cosmopolitan, McGraw-Hill, Omni, Redbook; The Bloom Agency, McCaffrey & McCall, Ogilvy & Mather, Young & Rubicam.

Bill Wilkinson

Technical and Architectural Renderings

Clients Include: Discover Magazine, Franklin Mint, Reader's Digest; BMW, International Paper, Mercedes-Benz, Skidmore Owings & Merrill; Benton & Bowles, Doyle Dane Bernbach, Foote Cone & Belding, Geers Gross, McCaffrey & McCall, Marstellar, Needham Harper & Steers, Young & Rubicam.

MARINA NEYMAN-LEVIKOVA

MARINA NEYMAN-LEVIKOVA

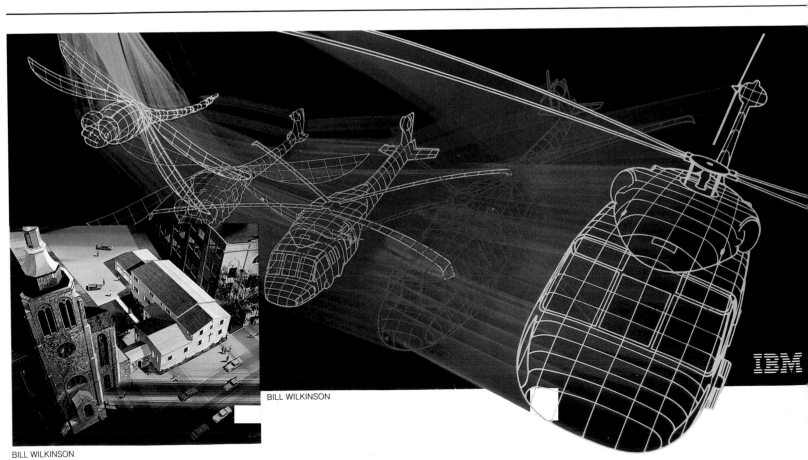

BILL WILKINSON

BILL WILKINSON

84

Anita Grien

155 East 38th Street
New York, New York 10016
(212) 697-6170

Jerry McDaniel

Illustration, Design and Computer Art

Clients Include: Avon, Clairol, Macy's, Mobil Oil, Pan
Am, Philip Morris, NBC, RCA, TWA; Ladies Home Journal,
Reader's Digest, Redbook; McGraw-Hill, Random House,
Time Inc.; Albert Frank Guenther Law, Ally & Gargano,
Ted Bates, Benton & Bowles, Foote Cone & Belding,
McCaffrey & McCall, O&M, Scali McCabe Sloves.

Don Morrison

Illustration

Clients Include: B. Altman, Arrow, Celanese, DuPont,
Greif, Hartmarx, Hathaway, Norman Hilton, Ralph
Lauren, Palm Beach, Springs Industries, Stetson, Paul
Stuart; IBM, L'Oréal; AC&R, Cunningham & Walsh,
Chester Gore, Ogilvy & Mather, Ross Roy, Wells Rich
Greene.

JERRY MCDANIEL—COMPUTER ART

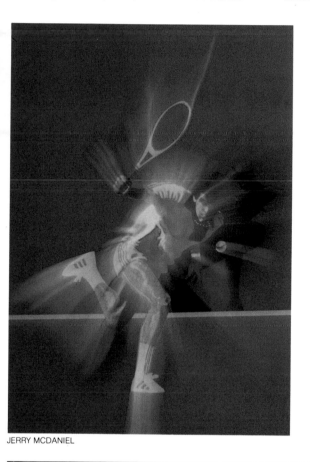

JERRY MCDANIEL

DON MORRISON

DON MORRISON

Irmeli Holmberg

Artist Agent
55 Hudson Street, #3A
New York, New York 10013
(212) 775-1810

Representing:

John Martinez

Clients include: Pantheon Books, RCA, Savvy, Harper
& Row, Graphic de France, New York Times, New York
Magazine, Money, Macy's, Seagrams, Champion Int'l.

Irmeli Holmberg

Artist Agent
55 Hudson Street, #3A
New York, New York 10013
(212) 775-1810

Representing:

Bill Nelson

Clients include: Newsweek, The Washingtonian, Texas
Monthly, TV-Guide, Reader's Digest, AT&T, CBS, Mobil
Oil, The Kennedy Center, Bank America, Beach Boys.

Irmeli Holmberg

Artist Agent
55 Hudson Street #3A
New York, New York 10013
(212) 775-1810

Representing:

Cameron Wasson

Clients include: CBS, Ziff-Davis, Boston Globe, Texas
Monthly, Ladies Home Journal, Chiquita Banana,
Hardee's, Apple Computer, Russ Toggs, 13-30 Corp.

Irmeli Holmberg
Artist Agent
55 Hudson Street #3A
New York, New York 10013
(212) 775-1810

Representing:

Bill Rieser
Clients include:
RCA Records, MCA, Levi's,
Bloomingdale's, Lois
Sportswear, Universal Studios,
Playboy, Y&R, AC&R, Foote
Cone & Belding, Atari.

Irmeli Holmberg

Artist Agent
55 Hudson Street #3A
New York, New York 10013
(212) 775-1810

Representing:

Debbie Pinkney

Clients include:
Macmillan Publishing, Good
Housekeeping, Jello, Heinz,
Food Emporium, Ketchum
Comm., General Nutrition,
Pittsburgh Public Theater,
Pittsburgh Magazine.

HOLMBERG & CO.

Irmeli Holmberg

Artist Agent
55 Hudson Street, #3A
New York, New York 10013
(212) 775-1810

Representing:

Walter Gurbo

Clients include: The New York
Times, Playboy, Village Voice,
Gentleman's Quarterly, Savvy,
New York Magazine, Sesame
Street, Psychology Today,
Atlantic Monthly.

Irmeli Holmberg

Artist Agent
55 Hudson Street #3A
New York, New York 10013
(212) 775-1810

Representing:

Vincent Amicosante

Clients include: Brown & Williamson, CBS Publications,
McGraw-Hill, Scholastic Magazines, Ogilvy & Mather.

Irmeli Holmberg

Artist Agent
55 Hudson Street #3A
New York, New York 10013
(212) 775-1810

Representing:

Bob Radigan

Clients include: PBS, Alcoa, Digital, J & L Steel,
US Steel, Follett Library Book Co., Hammermill
Paper, OTB.

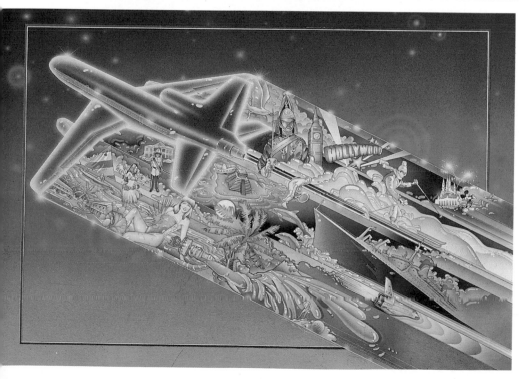

Bud and Evelyne Johnson

201 East 28th Street
New York, New York 10016
(212) 532-0928

representing:

Ilene Astrahan

Bud and Evelyne Johnson
201 East 28th Street
New York, New York 10016
(212) 532-0928

representing:

Tom Tierney

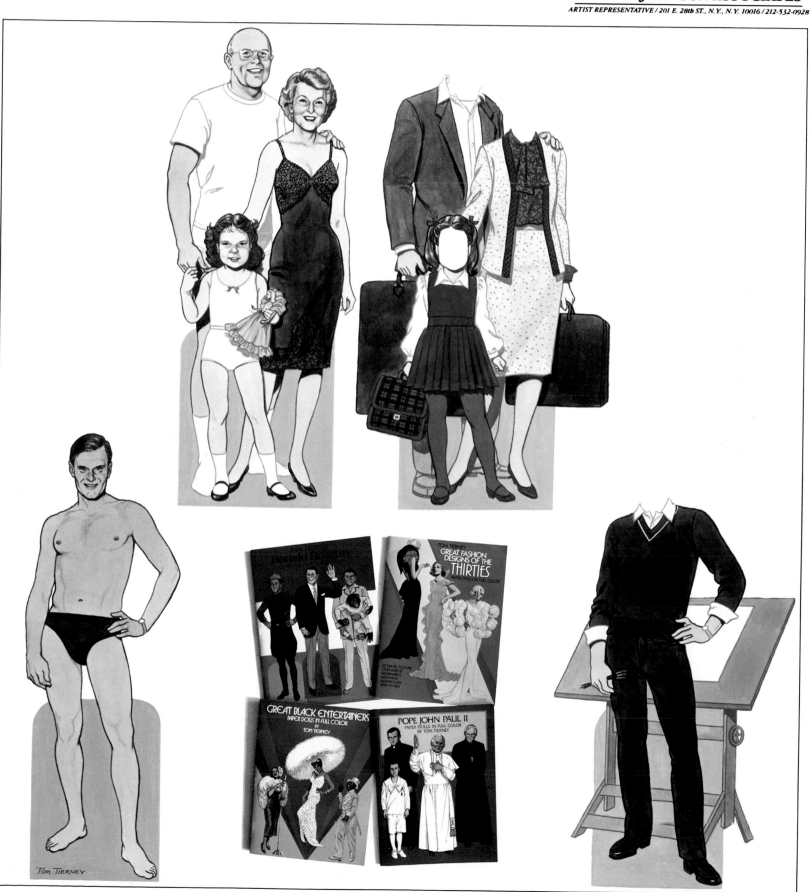

Bud and Evelyne Johnson
201 East 28th Street
New York, New York 10016
(212) 532-0928

representing:

Robert Gunn

EVELYNE JOHNSON ASSOCIATES
ARTIST REPRESENTATIVE / 201 E. 28th ST., N.Y., N.Y. 10016 / 212-532-0928

BUD & EVELYNE JOHNSON
REPRESENT ROBERT GUNN

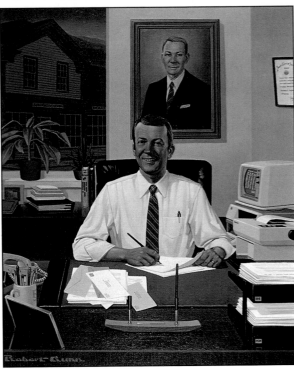

When will my baby recognize me?

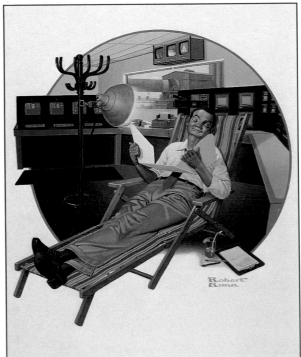

Health-tex
Clothes for boys and girls,
newborn to size 14.

Bud and Evelyne Johnson

201 East 28th Street
New York, New York 10016
(212) 532-0928

representing:

Tricia Zimic

EVELYNE JOHNSON ASSOCIATES

ARTIST REPRESENTATIVE / 201 E. 28th ST., N.Y., N.Y. 10016 / 212-532-0928

Bud and Evelyne Johnson
201 East 28th Street
New York, New York 10016
(212) 532-0928

representing:

Yukio Kondo

EVELYNE JOHNSON ASSOCIATES
ARTIST REPRESENTATIVE / 201 E. 28th ST., N.Y., N.Y. 10016 / 212-532-0928

Bud and Evelyne Johnson
201 East 28th Street
New York, New York 10016
(212) 532-0928

representing:

Mei-Ku Huang MD
Medical Illustration

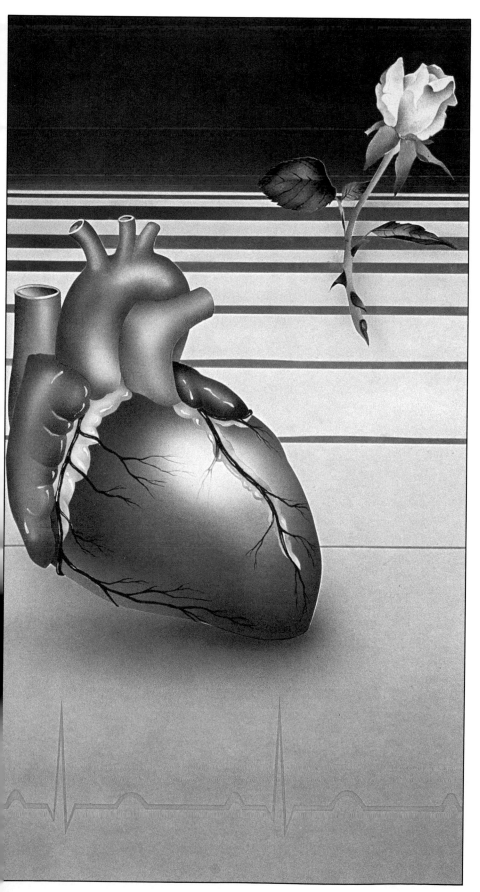

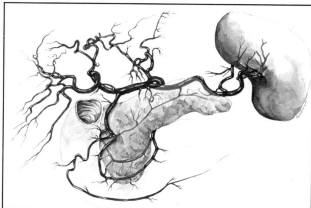

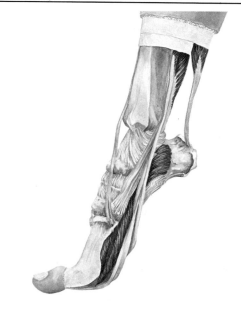

Bud and Evelyne Johnson

201 East 28th Street
New York, New York 10016
(212) 532-0928

representing:

Bill Finewood

Paper Sculpture Illustration

Bud and Evelyne Johnson
201 East 28th Street
New York, New York 10016
(212) 532-0928

representing:

Tom LaPadula

EVELYNE JOHNSON ASSOCIATES
ARTIST REPRESENTATIVE / 201 E. 28th ST., N.Y., N.Y. 10016 / 212-532-0928

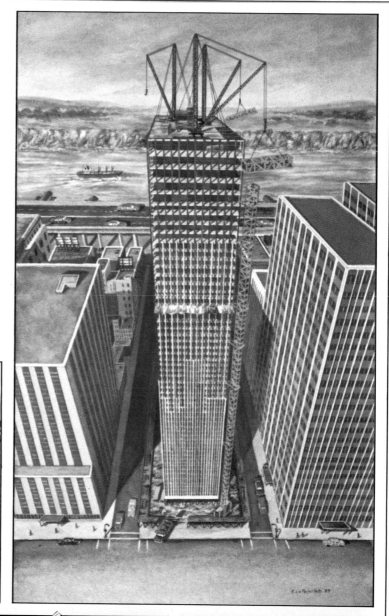

Bud and Evelyne Johnson

201 East 28th Street
New York, New York 10016
(212) 532-0928

representing:

Mitch Rigie

Bud and Evelyne Johnson

201 East 28th Street
New York, New York 10016
(212) 532-0928

representing:

Ted Enik

Bud and Evelyne Johnson

201 East 28th Street
New York, New York 10016
(212) 532-0928

representing:

Frank Daniel

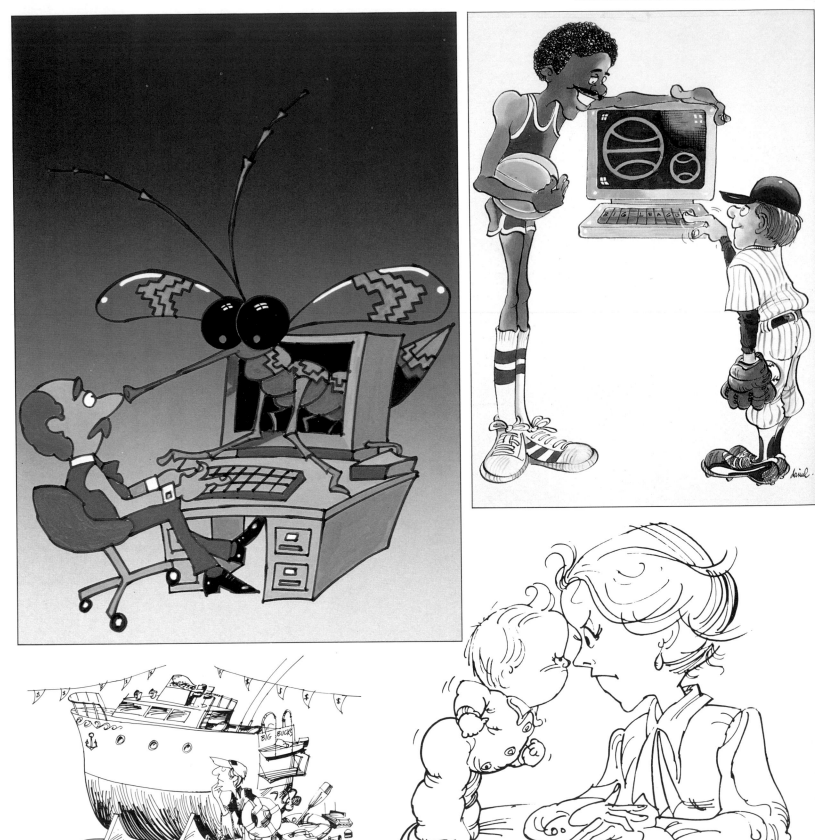

Bud and Evelyne Johnson

201 East 28th Street
New York, New York 10016
(212) 532-0928

representing:

Barbara Steadman

EVELYNE JOHNSON ASSOCIATES

ARTIST REPRESENTATIVE / 201 E. 28th ST., N.Y., N.Y. 10016 / 212-532-0928

Bud and Evelyne Johnson
201 East 28th Street
New York, New York 10016
(212) 532-0928

representing:

Stan Skardinski

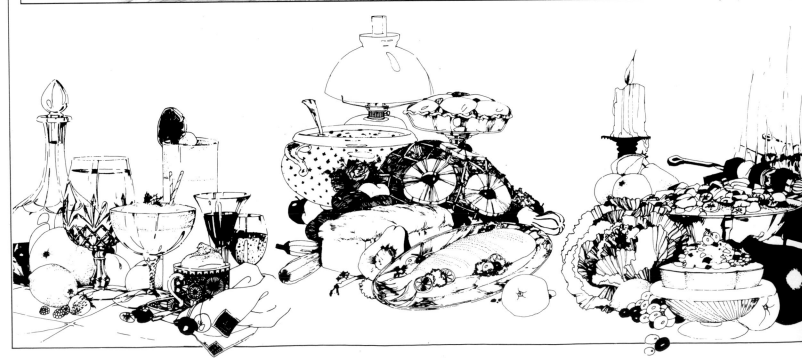

Bud and Evelyne Johnson
201 East 28th Street
New York, New York 10016
(212) 532-0928

representing:

Turi MacCombie

EVELYNE JOHNSON ASSOCIATES
ARTIST REPRESENTATIVE / 201 E. 28th ST., N.Y., N.Y. 10016 / 212-532-0928

Bud and Evelyne Johnson

201 East 28th Street
New York, New York 10016
(212) 532-0928

representing:

Pat Stewart
Kathy Allert

EVELYNE JOHNSON ASSOCIATES

ARTIST REPRESENTATIVE / 201 E. 28th ST., N.Y., N.Y. 10016 / 212-532-0928

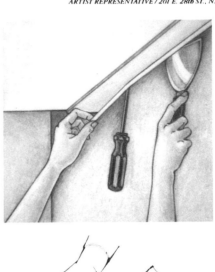

PAT STEWART

KATHY ALLERT

Bud and Evelyne Johnson
201 East 28th Street
New York, New York 10016
(212) 532-0928

representing:

Roberta Collier

EVELYNE JOHNSON ASSOCIATES
ARTIST REPRESENTATIVE / 201 E. 28th ST., N.Y., N.Y. 10016 / 212-532-0928

Bud and Evelyne Johnson

201 East 28th Street
New York, New York 10016
(212) 532-0928

representing:

Carolyn Bracken

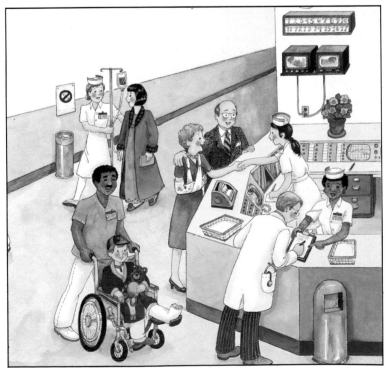

Bud and Evelyne Johnson

201 East 28th Street
New York, New York 10016
(212) 532-0928

representing:

Cathy Beylon

Bud and Evelyne Johnson
201 East 28th Street
New York, New York 10016
(212) 532-0928

representing:

Christopher Santoro

EVELYNE JOHNSON ASSOCIATES
ARTIST REPRESENTATIVE / 201 E. 28th ST., N.Y., N.Y. 10016 / 212-532-0928

Bud and Evelyne Johnson

201 East 28th Street
New York, New York 10016
(212) 532-0928

representing:

Rowan Barnes-Murphy

EVELYNE JOHNSON ASSOCIATES

ARTIST REPRESENTATIVE / 201 E. 28th ST., N.Y., N.Y. 10016 / 212-532-0928

Bud and Evelyne Johnson

201 East 28th Street
New York, New York 10016
(212) 532-0928

representing:

Jane Chambless-Rigie

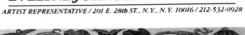

Bud and Evelyne Johnson

201 East 28th Street
New York, New York 10016
(212) 532-0928

representing:

Bruce Lemerise

EVELYNE JOHNSON ASSOCIATES

ARTIST REPRESENTATIVE / 201 E. 28th ST., N.Y., N.Y. 10016 / 212-532-0928

Bud and Evelyne Johnson

201 East 28th Street
New York, New York 10016
(212) 532-0928

representing:

Brookie Maxwell

3-Dimensional Illustration

EVELYNE JOHNSON ASSOCIATES
ARTIST REPRESENTATIVE / 201 E. 28th ST., N.Y., N.Y. 10016 / 212-532-0928

Bud and Evelyne Johnson

201 East 28th Street
New York, New York 10016
(212) 532-0928

representing:

Betty de Araujo
Dee Malan

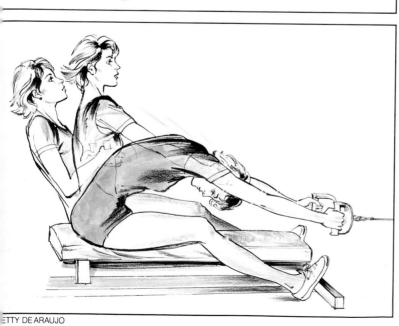

BETTY DE ARAUJO

DEE MALAN

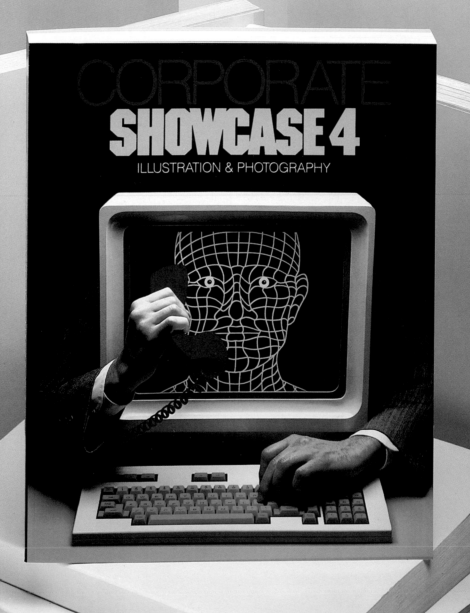

Tania Kimche

470 West 23rd Street
New York, New York 10011
(212) 242-6367

Representing:

Michael Hostovich

Tania Kimche
470 West 23rd Street
New York, New York 10011
(212) 242-6367

Representing:

E.T. Steadman

Tania Kimche

470 West 23rd Street
New York, New York 10011
(212) 242-6367

Representing:

Rafaĺ Olbínski

Bill and Maurine Klimt

15 West 72nd Street
New York, New York 10023
(212) 799-2231

Representing:

Jaime de Jesus
Paul Henry
Steve Huston
Frank Morris
Mark Skolsky
& others

KLIMT

FRANK MORRIS

FRANK MORRIS

FRANK MORRIS

JAIME DE JESUS

JAIME DE JESUS

The RIVER

MARK SKOLSKY

STEVE HUSTON

MARK SKOLSKY

PAUL HENRY

Bill and Maurine Klimt

15 West 72nd Street
New York, New York 10023
(212) 799-2231

Representing:

Bill Purdom

KLIMT

Bill and Maurine Klimt

15 West 72nd Street
New York, New York 10023
(212) 799-2231

Member Graphic Artist Guild

Representing:

Ken Joudrey

Clients:
Ziff-Davis
Landor Associates
Fairchild Publishing
New York Times
Bantam Books
Dell Publications
Berkley Books
McCaffrey & McCall
Foote, Cone & Belding
London Records
Atlantic Records
Rockshots Inc.
International Polygonics Ltd.
SFM Media
Popular Mechanics
Windemere Press
Book-of-the-Month Club

shown here

KLIMT

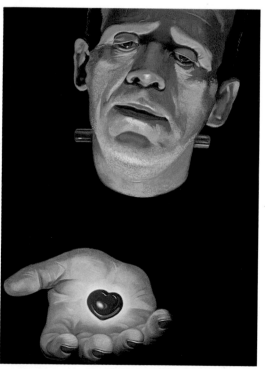

Lander/Osborne

A division of Jane Lander Associates
333 East 30th Street
New York, New York 10016
(212) 679-1358

Contact: Chris Osborne
Bruce Riedner
Jane Lander

Have FAX can zap/(212) 679-1869

Member Joint Ethics Committee
Society of Illustrators

Representing:

Phil Franké

(516) 661-5778

Clients include: AT&T; ABC; CBS; NBC; Paramount Pictures; Warner Brothers; 20th Century Fox; Bill Gold Advertising; Ted Bates Advertising; Burger King; Coleco; Associated Press; Sportschannel; Goodyear; Foote, Cone & Belding; Ogilvy & Mather; Grey Advertising; Geer, Dubois; McCann-Erickson; Doyle Dane Bernbach; BBD&O; Kallir, Philips, Ross; Martin, Sturtevant, Silverman & Marshall; Belmont; MTA; McCaffrey & McCall; Hub Graphics; Playboy Enterprises; Nando Miglio; Avis; Higgins & Associates; Random House; Bradbury Press; Golf Digest; Science Digest; Field & Stream; Popular Mechanics; Financial Executive Magazine.

Lander/Osborne

A division of Jane Lander Associates
333 East 30th Street
New York, New York 10016
(212) 679-1358

Contact: Chris Osborne
Bruce Riedner
Jane Lander

Have FAX can zap/(212) 679-1869

Member Joint Ethics Committee
Society of Illustrators

Representing:

Frank Riley

(201) 423-2659

Clients include: N.W. Ayer, AT&T, Bozell & Jacobs, Backer & Spielvogel, Marschalk Co., Ogilvy & Mather 2, Bloom Agency, Hicks & Greist, Hall Decker McKibbon, Franznick & Cusatis, STG Marketing, AKM Studios, Arista Records, GRP Records, Newsweek, Business Week, Electronic Fun, Wall St. Journal, Working Woman, Working Mother, Venture, Sylvia Porter Personal Finance Mag, K-Power, New York Sport, Lifesavers, Minute Maid, Sony, Stanley Vidmar, Stearns & Foster, Baker Industries, Denby Associates, Roth & Associates.

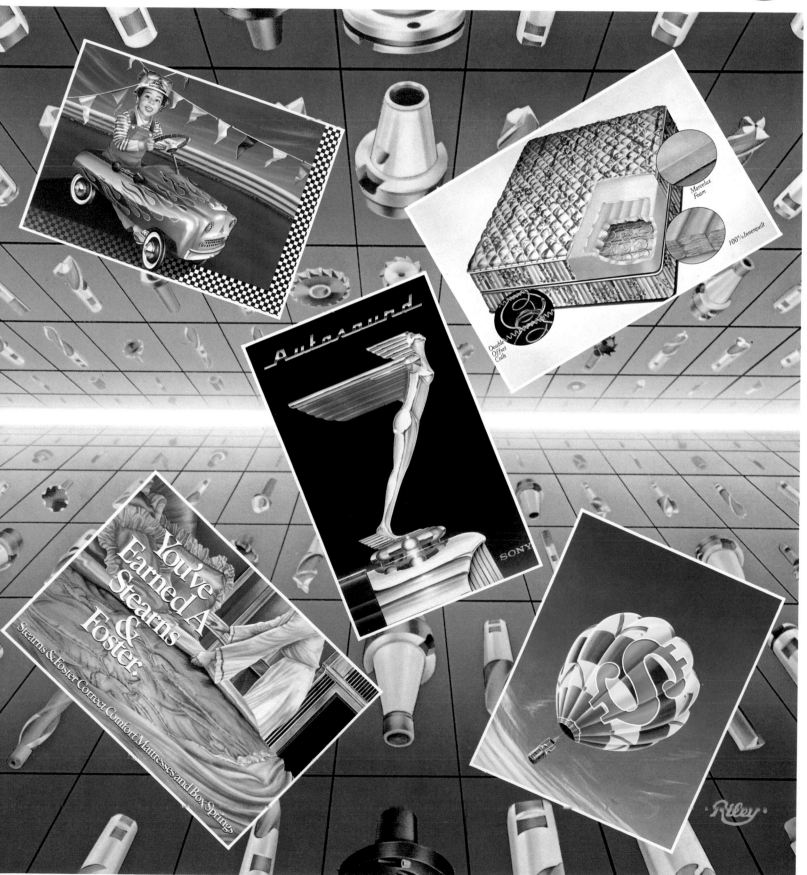

127

Lander/Osborne

A division of Jane Lander Associates
333 East 30th Street
New York, New York 10016
(212) 679-1358

Contact: Chris Osborne
Bruce Riedner
Jane Lander

Have FAX can zap/(212) 679-1869

Member Joint Ethics Committee
Society of Illustrators

Representing:

Mel Furukawa

(212) 349-3225
© 1985 Mel Furukawa
All rights reserved

Clients include: Maxell; AT&T; INA; SW Bell Corp.;
Schiff; IBM; HBO; Merrill Lynch; Van De Kamps;
Wisconsin Power & Light; NY Times; Time Magazine;
J. Walter Thompson; Foote, Cone & Belding; A.C.&R.;
Geer, Dubois; Ogilvy & Mather 2; Rolf Werner Rosenthal;

Geers Gross; Jonson, Pederson, Hinrichs & Shakery;
DANA; Nuciforia Associates; Plapler Russo & Wilvers;
DiIorio Wergeles; Citibank; NYU; GQ; Changing Times
Mag; Signature; Datamation; Video Magazine;
Medical Economics; Sports Illustrated; High Tech
Marketing; A Plus Magazine; Planned Parenthood.

Lander/Osborne

A division of Jane Lander Associates
333 East 30th Street
New York, New York 10016
(212) 679-1358

Contact: Chris Osborne
         Bruce Riedner
         Jane Lander

Have FAX can zap/(212) 679-1869

Member Joint Ethics Committee
         Society of Illustrators

Representing:

Cathy Heck

(915) 686-9343
© 1985 Cathy Heck
All rights reserved

Clients include: Young & Rubicam; Scali, McCabe,
Sloves; Bozell & Jacobs; Grey Advertising; BBD&O;
Benton & Bowles; AT&T; Dowphone; Backer &
Spielvogel; Birkenes & Foreman; DANA; Hertz; Jello;
Mrs. Paul's; Canon; Commodore Computers; Drakes'
Cakes; Bambergers; Scholastic Magazine; Woman's
Day; Pocket Books; Banbury Books; A Plus Magazine;
Texas International.

LAVATY

Chris Duke
John Berkey
David McCall Johnston
Jim Butcher
Don Daily
Mort Kunstler
Stan Hunter
Carlos Ochagavia
Roland DesCombes
Lemuel Line
Robert Lo Grippo
Martin Hoffman
Darrel Millsap
Gervasio Gallardo
Bernard D'Andrea
Bruce Emmett
Paul Lehr
Chet Jezierski

Represented by
Frank Lavaty
Jeff Lavaty
Mike Mascendaro

Frank & Jeff Lavaty & Associates • 50 East 50th Street N.Y. N.Y. 10022 • (212) 355-0910

Frank and Jeff Lavaty
& Associates
50 East 50th Street
New York, New York 10022
(212) 355-0910

Representing:

Chris Duke

LAVATY

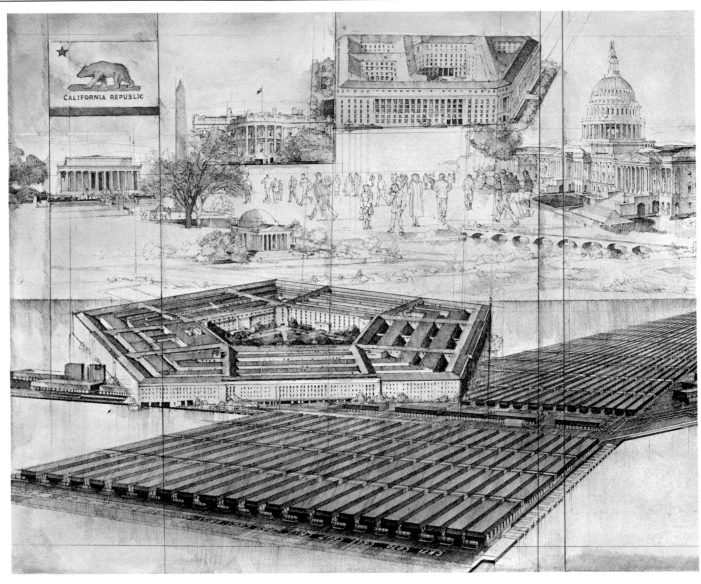

**Frank and Jeff Lavaty
& Associates**
50 East 50th Street
New York, New York 10022
(212) 355-0910
Representing:

John Berkey

LAVATY

Frank and Jeff Lavaty
& Associates

50 East 50th Street
New York, New York 10022
(212) 355-0910

Representing:

David McCall Johnston

**Frank and Jeff Lavaty
& Associates**
50 East 50th Street
New York, New York 10022
(212) 355-0910
Representing:
Jim Butcher

**Frank and Jeff Lavaty
& Associates**

50 East 50th Street
New York, New York 10022
(212) 355-0910

Representing:

Don Daily

LAVATY

**Frank and Jeff Lavaty
& Associates**

50 East 50th Street
New York, New York 10022
(212) 355-0910

Representing:

Mort Kunstler

LAVATY

**Frank and Jeff Lavaty
& Associates**

50 East 50th Street
New York, New York 10022
(212) 355-0910

Representing:

Stan Hunter

LAVATY

**Frank and Jeff Lavaty
& Associates**

50 East 50th Street
New York, New York 10022
(212) 355-0910

Representing:

Carlos Ochagavia

LAVATY

Frank and Jeff Lavaty
& Associates

50 East 50th Street
New York, New York 10022
(212) 355-0910

Representing:

Roland Descombes

LAVATY

**Frank and Jeff Lavaty
& Associates**

50 East 50th Street
New York, New York 10022
(212) 355-0910

Representing:

Lemuel Line

LAVATY

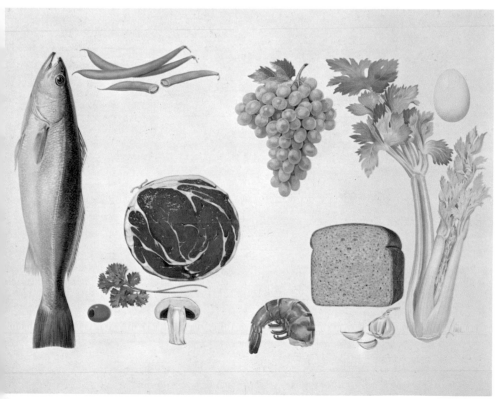

**Frank and Jeff Lavaty
& Associates**

50 East 50th Street
New York, New York 10022
(212) 355-0910

Representing:

Robert Logrippo

LAVATY

**Frank and Jeff Lavaty
& Associates**
50 East 50th Street
New York, New York 10022
(212) 355-0910

Representing:

Martin Hoffman

LAVATY

Frank and Jeff Lavaty
& Associates
50 East 50th Street
New York, New York 10022
(212) 355-0910

Representing:

Darrel Millsap

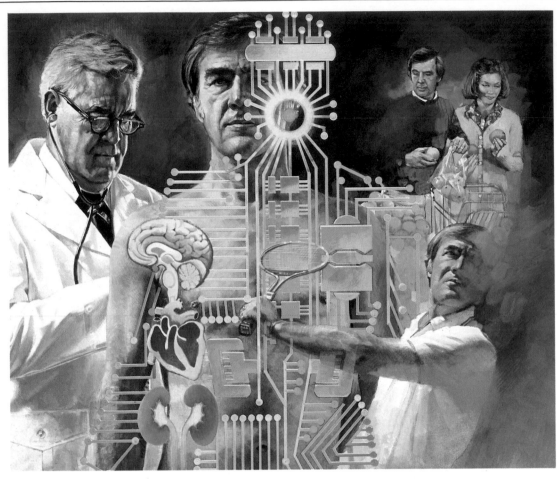

DARREL MILLSAP

Frank and Jeff Lavaty
& Associates

50 East 50th Street
New York, New York 10022
(212) 355-0910

Representing:

Gervasio Gallardo

LAVATY

**Frank and Jeff Lavaty
& Associates**

50 East 50th Street
New York, New York 10022
(212) 355-0910

Representing:

Bernard D'Andrea

LAVATY

Frank and Jeff Lavaty
& Associates
50 East 50th Street
New York, New York 10022
(212) 355-0910

Representing:

Bruce Emmett

**Frank and Jeff Lavaty
& Associates**
50 East 50th Street
New York, New York 10022
(212) 355-0910

Representing:

Paul Lehr

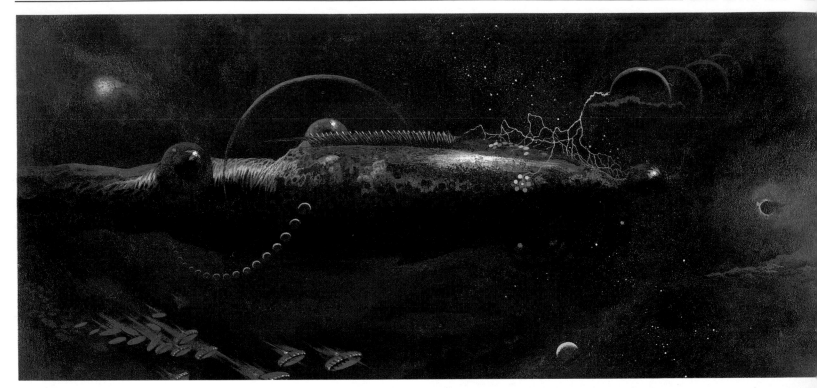

Frank and Jeff Lavaty
& Associates
50 East 50th Street
New York, New York 10022
(212) 355-0910

Representing:

Chet Jezierski

LAVATY

WHO WAS HERB LUBALIN?

THE FACE BEHIND THE FACES.

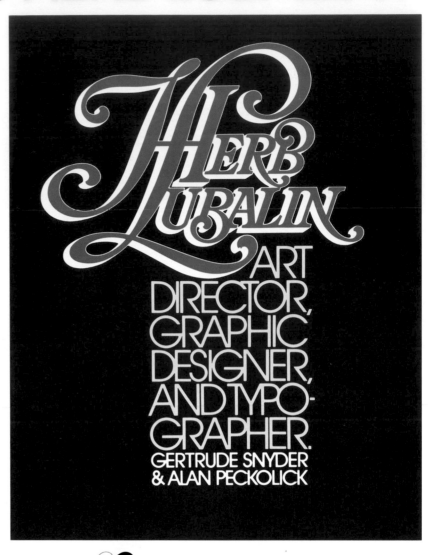

He was a skinny, colorblind, left-handed artist, known to friends and colleagues as a deafeningly silent man. But through his typography-based and editorial designs, he created bold new forms for communication and changed the dimensions of advertising and graphics.

Herb Lubalin is the definitive book about the typographic impresario and design master of our time. It is illustrated with more than 360 extraordinary examples of Lubalin's award-winning work, including: ■ Logos and Letterheads ■ Editorial and Book Design ■ Packaging ■ Advertising and Sales Promotion ■ Annual Reports ■ Best of *U&lc,* and more.

"The magnitude of Herb Lubalin's achievements will be felt for a long time to come....I think he was probably the greatest graphic designer ever."
—Lou Dorfsman, Vice President, Creative Director, Advertising and Design, CBS Inc.

184 pages, Color throughout, 9" x 11⅞"
Clothbound, Retail Value: $39.95
SPECIAL OFFER
Send for your copy of **Herb Lubalin** today and pay only $35.00.* Postage and handling are FREE within the U.S. and Canada. To order, **call 212-245-0981** and charge your AMEX, Visa or Mastercard. Or send your check or money order to:
AMERICAN SHOWCASE, INC.
724 Fifth Avenue, New York, NY 10019
*New York residents, please add appropriate sales tax.

Tamara Linden
Artists' Representative
3500 Piedmont Road
Suite 430
Atlanta, Georgia 30305
(404) 262-1209

CHARLES A. PASSARELLI

CHARLES A. PASSARELLI

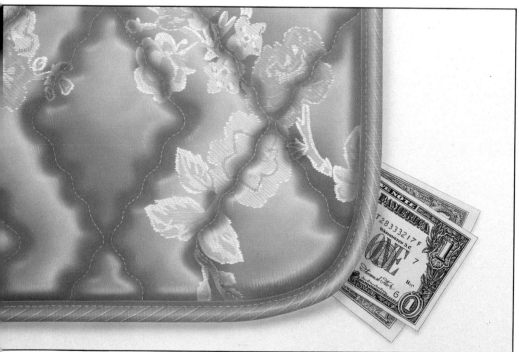

OM FLECK

JOSEPH M. OVIES

TAMARA
INCORPORATED

LA ILLUS
HAVE SO
NO ONE

RITA MARI
ARTIST

Gene Allison	Aleta Jenks	Paul Roge
Chris Consani	Hiro Kimura	Greg Row
Jim Endicott	Gary Pierazzi	Gary Rude
Marla Frazee	Robert Pryor	Dick Saka

TRATORS
METHING
ELSE HAS.

AND FRIENDS

PRESENTATIVES

6376 West 5th Street, Los Angeles, California 90048.

West Coast	Chicago-Midwest
Rita Marie	Rodney Ray
Office: (213) 934-3395	Office: (312) 222-0337
Messages: (213) 936-2757	Messages: (312) 472-6550

Telecopier in Office.

Rita Marie & Friends

Rita Marie
Office Tel: (213) 934-3395
Messages Tel: (213) 936-2757

Rodney Ray
Office Tel: (312) 222-0337
Messages Tel: (312) 472-6550

Representing:

Hiro Kimura

Rita Marie & Friends

Representing:

Dick Sakahara

28826 Cedarbluff Drive
Rancho Palos Verdes,
California 90274
(213) 541-8187

Rita Marie
Office Tel: (213) 934-3395
Messages Tel: (213) 936-2757

Rodney Ray
Office Tel: (312) 222-0337
Messages Tel: (312) 472-6550

Tokyo Representative:
Tim Okamoto
Ko-Po-Ai #202
2-24-17 Takaido
Higashi, Suginami-ku
Tokyo 168 Japan

Rita Marie & Friends

Rita Marie
Office Tel: (213) 934-3395
Messages Tel: (213) 936-2757

Rodney Ray
Office Tel: (312) 222-0337
Messages Tel: (312) 472-6550

Representing:

Paul Rogers

Rita Marie
& Friends

Rita Marie
Office Tel: (213) 934-3395
Messages Tel: (213) 936-2757

Rodney Ray
Office Tel: (312) 222-0337
Messages Tel: (312) 472-6550

Representing:

Paul Rogers

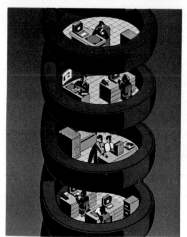

**Rita Marie
& Friends**

Rita Marie
Office Tel: (213) 934-3395
Messages Tel: (213) 936-2757

Rodney Ray
Office Tel: (312) 222-0337
Messages Tel: (312) 472-6550

Representing:

Chris Consani

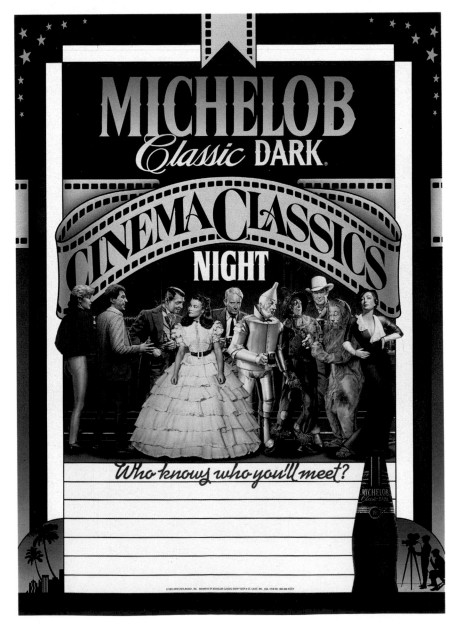

Rita Marie & Friends

Rita Marie
Office Tel: (213) 934-3395
Messages Tel: (213) 936-2757

Rodney Ray
Office Tel: (312) 222-0337
Messages Tel: (312) 472-6550

Representing:

Marla Frazee

CHARLES OF THE RITZ

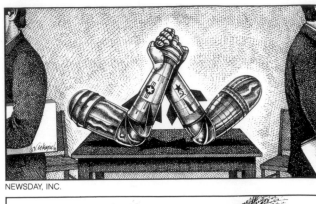

NEWSDAY, INC.

ZIFF-DAVIS PUBLISHING CO.

TOWERS, PERRIN, FORSTER & CROSBY

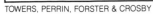

Judy Mattelson
Mattelson Associates, Ltd.
(212) 684-2974

Representing:

Karen Kluglein

Watercolor paintings

Member Graphic Artists Guild

M&M/MARS

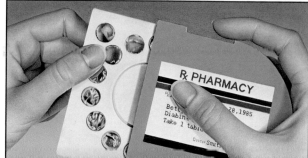

PFIZER

HEARST PUBLICATIONS

SELF PROMOTION

RALSTON PURINA

HEARST PUBLICATIONS

Judy Mattelson
Artist's Representative

BARNSTEAD

HENNESSEY

IBM

CANNES FILM FESTIVAL PROGRAM 1984

GEFFEN FILMS

AMD ANNUAL REPORT

IBM

194 THIRD AVENUE NEW YORK NY 10003

VICKI MORGAN ASSOCIATES

(212) 475·0440

REPRESENTING

JOHN ALCORN

RAY CRUZ

VIVIENNE FLESHER

JOE & KATHY HEINER

TIM LEWIS

RICHARD MANTEL

WAYNE McLOUGHLIN

EMANUEL SCHONGUT

NANCY STAHL

WILLARDSON+ASSOCIATES

BRUCE WOLFE

WENDY WRAY

BRIAN ZICK

PHOTOGRAPHY
JIM KOZYRA

Vicki Morgan Associates

(212) 475-0440

Representing:

John Alcorn

Member of Graphic Artists Guild
© 1985 John Alcorn
all rights reserved

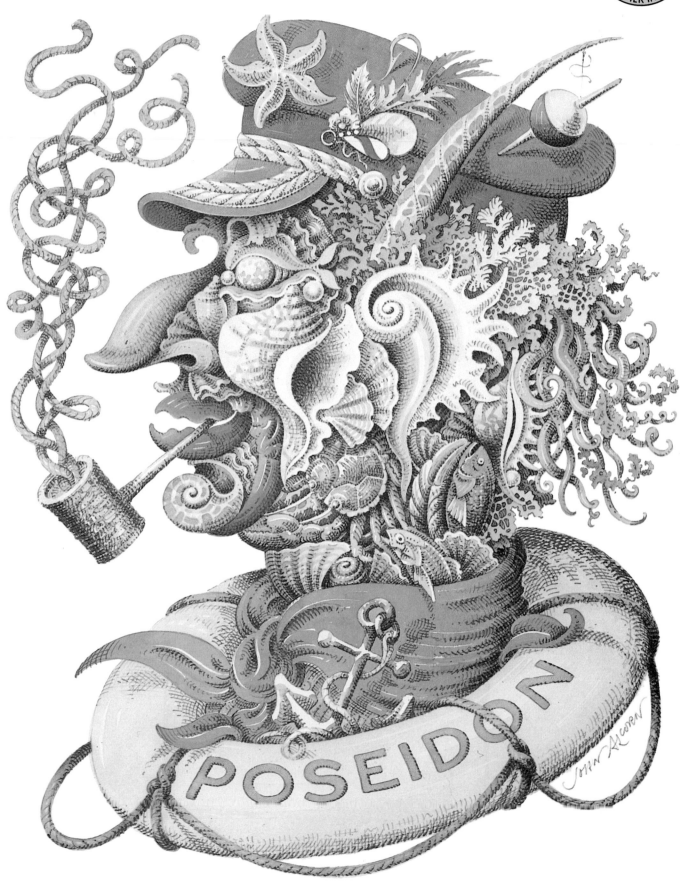

Vicki Morgan Associates
(212) 475-0440

Representing:

Richard Mantel

Member of Graphic Artists Guild

Vicki Morgan Associates

(212) 475-0440

Representing:

Nancy Stahl

Top row: Viking Press; Maxwell House.
Bottom row: Miller Beer; Sports Illustrated.

Vicki Morgan Associates

(212) 475-0440

Representing:

Tim Lewis

Member of Graphic Artists Guild
© 1985 Tim Lewis
all rights reserved

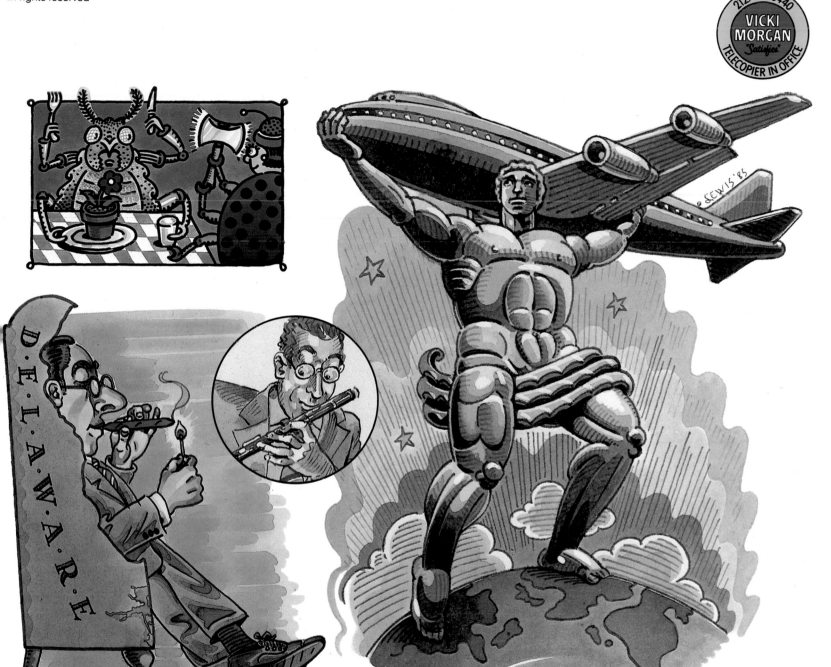

Vicki Morgan Associates

(212) 475-0440

Representing:

Ray Cruz

Member of Graphic Artists Guild

MOTHER'S DAY MAY 12

Vicki Morgan Associates

(212) 475-0440

Representing:

Wendy Wray

Member of Graphic Artists Guild
© 1985 Wendy Wray
all rights reserved

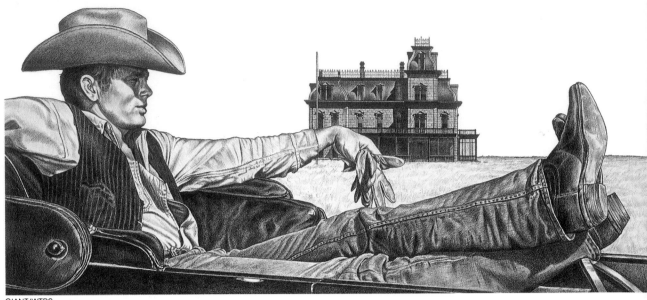

GIANT/WTBS

DAVID T. KEARNS/PRESIDENT XEROX CORPORATION/
NEEDHAM HARPER WORLDWIDE

DALE MURPHY/WTBS

212/475-0440
VICKI
MORGAN
"Satisfies"
TELECOPIER IN OFFICE

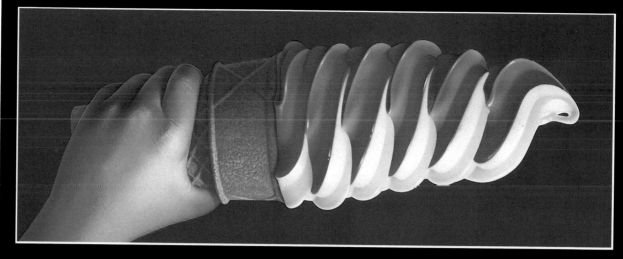

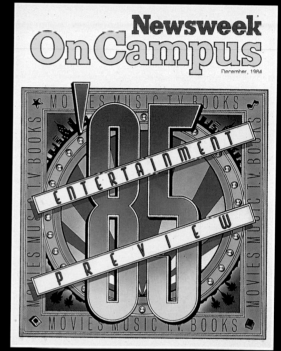

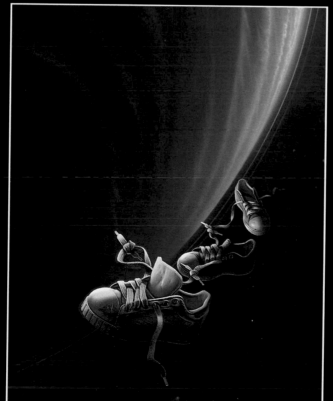

Vicki Morgan Associates

(212) 475-0440

Representing:

Joe and Kathy Heiner

Studio: (801) 756-6444

Other Representatives:

Mary Vandamme (San Francisco)
(415) 433-1292

Ellen Knable (Los Angeles)
(213) 855-8855

Vicki Morgan Associates

(212) 475-0440

representing:

Brian Zick

Pamela R. Neail Associates

27 Bleecker Street
New York, New York 10012
(212) 673-1600

Represents:

Sean Daly

Pamela R. Neail Associates
27 Bleecker Street
New York, New York 10012
(212) 673-1600
Represents:

Linda Richards

MOTIVATION

"**N**ow I know I'm crazy," an art director said to me as I was on my way to a meeting. "I passed up a nice lunch because I just had to follow through on this idea." I replied, "You aren't crazy... you have what it takes to make it in advertising."

Another art director I enjoyed working with very much never got home early enough to see his son before bedtime. Night after night he would slave away at the drawing board, developing one idea after another to present the next day. (Crazy, you say! He has since left to become head art director at another well-respected direct marketing agency!)

If fact, most evenings in our agency you'll find art directors and writers taxing their brains, pushing themselves to the absolute limit to come up with that one breakthrough idea that will beat the control ad. (In direct marketing the ad that pulls the most orders becomes the control and all other ads are tested against it.)

I always ask myself, "Why?" Why are these talented, sensitive, intelligent people cancelling dinner dates, missing trains, disappointing friends (PTA meetings I can understand!) to come up with a fresh creative approach that no one's ever seen before? Is it for the glory? Or out of fear of failure? Or is it just plain dedication? The truth is that the creative process is all consuming. Nothing else seems to matter until that fabulous idea has flowed from the right side of the brain, where the imagination flourishes, to that blank piece of paper in front of you. Meetings are time consuming, paperwork is tiresome, dealing with people is grueling, but creating—that's something else. People outside of advertising find that unstoppable drive to create difficult to understand, and think of us as insecure, workaholics, or just plain crazy.

If you love advertising as much as I do you know that money, success and status are important. But is that motivation enough to take ourselves to the brink, to work until midnight, to neglect our families and friends?

There must be something else, beyond material reward, something magical you are born with, to choose the creative end of this business, something that makes us a bit irritable when we must strive hour after hour to "create," and something that can change our mood instantly when we hear, "The client loved your idea!"

In direct marketing those five little words: "Your ad beat the control" will make any creative person jump for joy and forget all the pain.

Chances are you become more valuable when you can do that and monetary rewards surely follow. But what really counts is that you dug deep and toiled hard for the idea and it paid off.

Ego, maybe? Satisfaction, yes! Do we dare to compare giving birth to an idea with the paradox of agony and ecstasy a mother must feel at the birth of a child? You answer that. I must get back to the drawing board.

Fernando E. Rola
Senior Vice President/
Executive Art Director
Rapp & Collins, Inc.
New York City

No Coast Graphics

Joe Malone
2629 18th Street
Denver, Colorado 80211
(303) 458-7086

Represents

John Cuneo

No Coast Graphics

No Coast Graphics

Joe Malone
2629 18th Street
Denver, Colorado 80211
(303) 458-7086

Represents

Cindy Enright

Joanne Palulian
18 McKinley Street
Rowayton, Connecticut 06853
(203) 866-3734

New York Office:
(212) 581-8338

Representing:

David Lesh

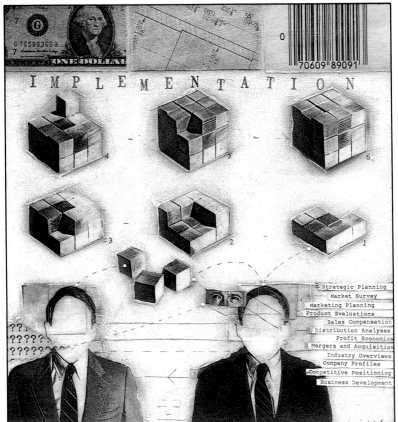

Joanne Palulian

18 McKinley Street
Rowayton, Connecticut 06853
(203) 866-3734

New York Office:
(212) 581-8338

Representing:

Dickran Palulian

The Penny & Stermer Group

A division of:
Barbara Penny Associates, Inc.
48 West 21 Street
New York, New York 10010
(212) 243-4412

Representing:

Michael Kanarek

THE
PENNY &
STERMER
GROUP

The Penny & Stermer Group

A division of:
Barbara Penny Associates, Inc.
48 West 21 Street
New York, New York 10010
(212) 243-4412

Representing:

Rich Grote

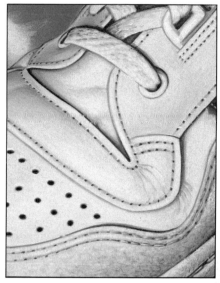

The Penny & Stermer Group

A division of:
Barbara Penny Associates, Inc.
48 West 21 Street
New York, New York 10010
(212) 243-4412

Representing:

Julia Noonan

The Penny & Stermer Group

A division of:
Barbara Penny Associates, Inc.
48 West 21 Street
New York, New York 10010
(212) 243-4412

Representing:

Bob Alcorn

THE
PENNY &
STERMER
GROUP

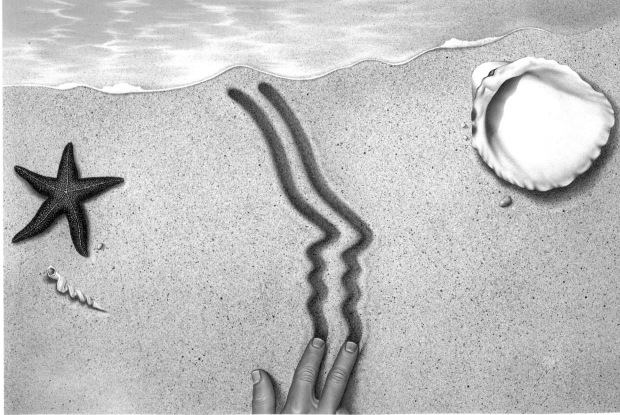

The Penny & Stermer Group

A division of:
Barbara Penny Associates, Inc.
48 West 21 Street
New York, New York 10010
(212) 243-4412

Representing:

Deborah Bazzel

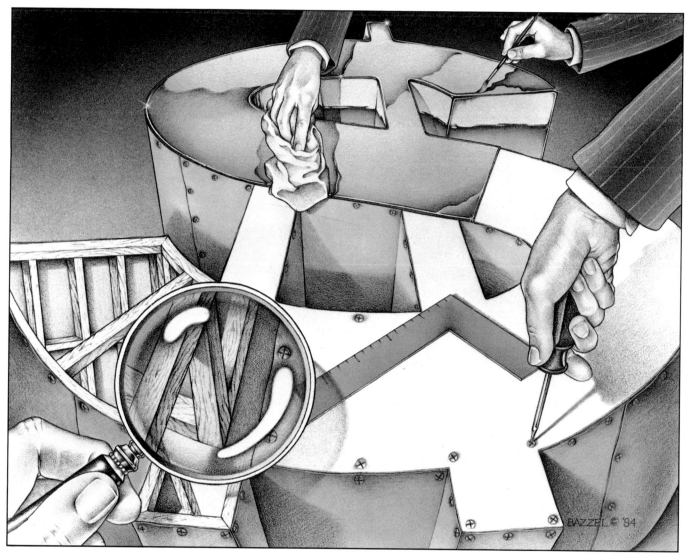

The Penny & Stermer Group

A division of:
Barbara Penny Associates, Inc.
48 West 21 Street
New York, New York 10010
(212) 243-4412

Representing:

Jane Clark

STORYBOARDS AND COMPS

Illustration portfolio available on request

THE
PENNY &
STERMER
GROUP

The Penny & Stermer Group

A division of:
Barbara Penny Associates, Inc.
48 West 21 Street
New York, New York 10010
(212) 243-4412

Representing:

Gary Smith

THE
PENNY &
STERMER
GROUP

Madeline Renard

Renard Represents Inc.
501 Fifth Avenue
New York, New York 10017
(212) 490-2450

Madeline Renard

JOHN COLLIER

STEVE BJÖRKMAN

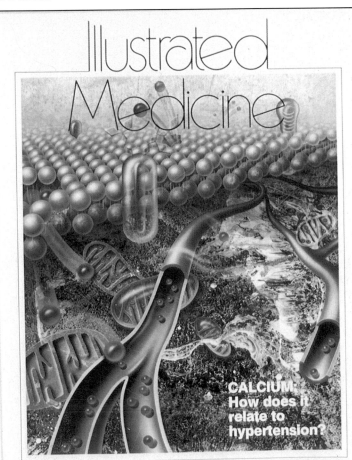

AUDRA GERAS

BART FORBES

Madeline Renard

Renard Represents Inc.
501 Fifth Avenue
New York, New York 10017
(212) 490-2450

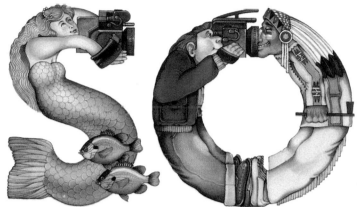

JÓZEF SUMICHRAST © 1985, SONY CORPORATION OF AMERICA.

ROBERT RODRIGUEZ

MILES HARDIMAN

JOHN MARTIN

193

Karen Sims Ridgeway

1466 Broadway
New York, New York 10036
(212) 921-1919
(201) 746-7131

Solving your visual assignments through talent and
creative technology:

- collage/mixed media
- colored pencil/pastels
- line art
- line art with color washes

- oil painting
- photo/airbrush combination
- photography with computer graphics

Portfolios upon request

MARILYN JONES

DAVID RICKERD

DAVID RICKERD

DAVID RICKERD

RON MORECRAFT

Karen Sims Ridgeway

1466 Broadway
New York, New York 10036
(212) 921-1919
(201) 746-7131

Solving your visual assignments through talent and creative technology:

- collage/mixed media
- colored pencil/pastels
- line art
- line art with color washes

- oil painting
- photo/airbrush combination
- photography with computer graphics

Portfolios upon request

RON RIDGEWAY

SCOTT BRICHER

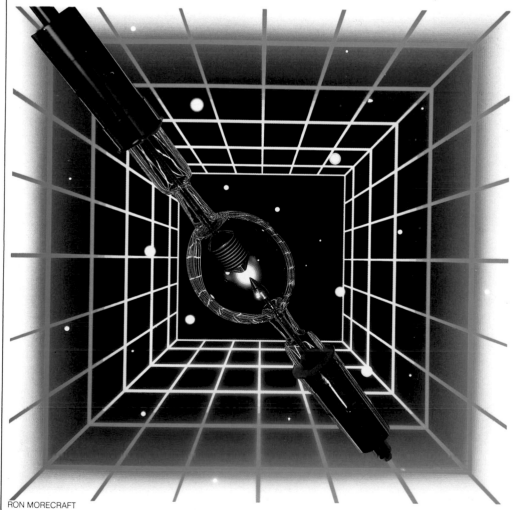

RON MORECRAFT

YEMI

Edward T. Riley, Inc.

81 Greene Street, (PO Box 51)
New York, New York 10012
(212) 925-3053

Whit Stillman
Managing Director

Representing
Elliott Banfield
Quentin Blake
Zevi Blum
William Bramhall
Cesc
Paul Degen
Chris Demarest
David Gothard
Carolyn Gowdy
Paul Hogarth
Pierre Le-Tan
Robert Andrew Parker
Cheryl Peterson
J. J. Sempé
Philippe Weisbecker
& Other Artists

ROBERT ANDREW PARKER

CHERYL PETERSON

PIERRE LE-TAN

ELLIOTT BANFIELD

CHRIS DEMAREST

Every message is at the mercy
of its environment.

J. J. SEMPE

CAROLYN GOWDY

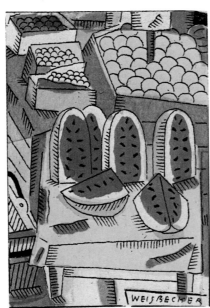

PHILIPPE WEISBECKER

WILLIAM BRAMHALL

DAVID GOTHARD

196

Richard W. Salzman
Artist Representative

·EVERETT PECK·

RICHARD ·W· SALZMAN
ARTIST·REPRESENTATIVE

619 · 272 · 8147

·—·DENISE HILTON·PUTNAM·—·

ARTIST·REPRESENTATIVE

6 1 9 · 2 7 2 · 8 1 4 7

JOYCE KITCHELL

·DANIELS·

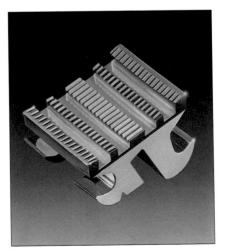

·RUBEN DE ANDA·   ·MANUEL GARCIA·

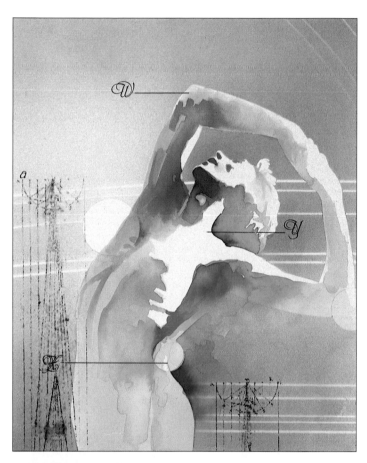

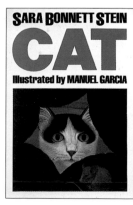

RICHARD·W·SALZMAN

ARTIST·REPRESENTATIVE

619 · 272 · 8147

Fran Seigel

515 Madison Avenue
New York, New York 10022
(212) 486-9644

Representing:

Kinuko Y. Craft

Do you have a special job with an unusual point of view? Kinuko Craft's eclectic approach to illustration communicates these messages precisely on target.

Kinuko's work for advertising and editorial clients has received numerous awards and was recently exhibited at the Society of Illustrators in a one-woman show. Her work has also been featured consistently in Grafis, CA, American Illustration, and the Society of Illustrators annuals.

Top row: Citibank/Bernhardt Fudyma Design, Science Digest.

Bottom: European Travel, Family Weekly, Infodata/Grafik Communications.

KINUKO Y. CRAFT

Fran Seigel
515 Madison Aveue
New York, New York 10022
(212) 486-9644

Representing:

Earl Keleny

Earl Keleny's paintings for advertising offer new alternatives to photoreal illustration or photography. Contemporary unique visuals which will stand out from the crowd but capture its attention.

Recognition includes: American Illustration 4, Society of Illustrators 25, Society of Publication Designers Portfolio Show (1985), Graphis Annual 84-85.

Top row: CBS Entertainment, Leroux Schnapps/Warwick Advtg.

Middle: Daewoo/
J. Walter Thompson

Bottom: Games Magazine,
Carroll & Graf

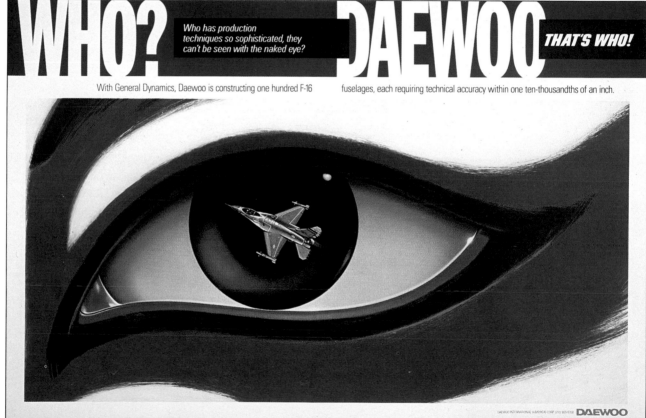

WHO? Who has production techniques so sophisticated, they can't be seen with the naked eye? DAEWOO THAT'S WHO!

With General Dynamics, Daewoo is constructing one hundred F-16 fuselages, each requiring technical accuracy within one ten-thousandths of an inch.

EARL KELENY

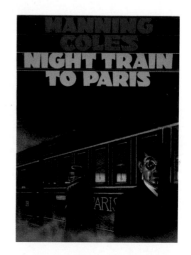

Joan Sigman
336 East 54th Street
New York, New York 10022
(212) 421-0050
(212) 832-7980

Represents:

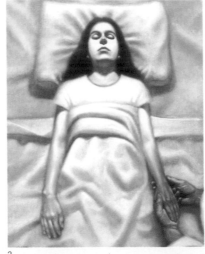

1.   2.   3.

James E. Tennison
117 Ironworks Road
Clinton, Connecticut 06413

1. "Strutting Chicken"
2. Discipleship Journal
   "His Life-giving Touch"
3. Fort Worth Symphony
   Orchestra "Pops In The Dark"
4. Dallas Opera "1985 Fall
   Season Line-up"

4.

2.

John H. Howard
(212) 832-7980

1. Simon & Schuster "The Bass
   Saxophone"
2. Literary Cavalcade
   "E.M. Forster"
3. PC Magazine "Remote
   Computing"

1.   3.

Joan Sigman

Joan Sigman
336 East 54th Street
New York, New York 10022
(212) 421-0050
(212) 832-7980

Represents:

Robert Goldstrom
471 Fifth Street
Brooklyn, New York 11215
(718) 768-7367

1. Emergency Medicine—Magazine cover and spread
2. Pantheon Books—book cover, "The Artful Egg"
3. Agena Business Systems—consumer magazine ad.
   and poster

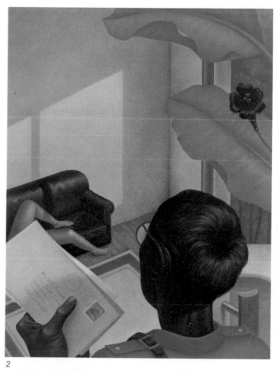

2

Joan Sigman
336 East 54th Street
New York, New York 10022
(212) 421-0050
(212) 832-7980

Represents:

Daniel Kirk
85 South Street
New York, New York 10038
(212) 825-0190

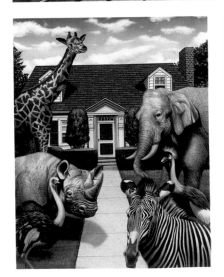

Free fertilizer for ideas.

One of the first steps in developing your advertising campaign is finding out what's being done in the same area —food, automobile, travel, cosmetics, or whatever.

You don't want to do something that's been done, or worse yet, that's being done.

And, unless you know what's being done, it's very difficult to stand out.

So you need to know what's going on. Both in the US, and internationally.

And you need to know on a continuing basis.

The ways to get this kind of information are either expensive or inefficient, or both. Clipping services charge a lot, don't organize the stuff very well, and generally don't edit out the chaff.

So someone in your company winds up getting a pile of tearsheets with no rhyme or reason to them.

That's not worth much.

Archive solves the problem.

Archive magazine is the solution to this state of affairs.

Archive is an internationally famous advertising magazine which is edited by the equally internationally famous Walter Lürzer, of West Germany.

When you subscribe to Archive, you get an in-depth overview of what's happening in, say, the fashion or liquor industry, *all over the world*.

The material is organized by category, is easy to read, and easy to understand. A careful study of Archive will reap big dividends for anyone involved in the creation, selling, or commissioning of advertising.

That means you.

For only $35 a year (less than the price of a lunch, and a discount off the cover price) you can get Archive com-

ing to you every two months.

One copy free.

To introduce you to Archive, we'll send you one copy free for the asking. At the same time, we'll enter an Archive subscription in your name at the special rate of $35.00 for 5 more issues (6 in all). That's a savings of 22% off the cover price.

If, for any reason, you are not completely satisfied, simply return the bill marked "cancel" and owe nothing. The first issue is yours to keep with our compliments.

For fast subscription service, call (212) 245-0981. Or write, Archive, c/o American Showcase, 724 Fifth Avenue, New York, NY 10019.

Susan Trimpe
(206) 728-1300

Don Baker
1822 N.E. Ravenna Boulevard
Seattle, Washington 98105
(206) 522-8133

Partial client list includes:
Alaska Airlines, Alaska Seafood
Commission, Blue Cross, First
Interstate Bank, McDonald's,
Microsoft, Rainier Bank, Tree
Top, Washington State Apple
Commission, Washington Dairy
Products Commission,
Weyerhaeuser.

Susan Trimpe

2717 Western Avenue
Seattle, Washington 98121
(206) 728-1300

Represents:

**Stephen
Peringer**

Partial client list includes:
Alascom, Bantam Books,
Capital Records, Hanes,
Hawaiian Punch, John Fluke
Mfg. Co., Macmillan Publishing,
McDonald's, Microsoft, Nike,
Nintendo, O'Brien International,
Olympic Stain, Washington
State Lottery.

Susan Trimpe

2717 Western Avenue
Seattle, Washington 98121
(206) 728-1300

Represents:

Wendy Edelson

Partial client list includes: Darigold, Eddie Bauer,
Flakey Jakes, Houghton Mifflin, Macmillan Publishing,
Parents Magazine, Roman Meal, Safeco, Scholastic,
Sunrise Publications, Tree Top, Washington Magazine.

SEASON'S GREETINGS

December
1 2 3 4 5 6 7 8 9 10 11 12 13 14 15 16 17 18 19 20 21 22 23 24 25 26 27 28 29 30 31
January
1 2 3 4 5 6 7 8 9 10 11 12 13 14 15 16 17 18 19 20 21 22 23 24 25 26 27 28 29 30 31

SOLZER
HAIL

Deborah Wolfe Ltd

731 North 24th Street
Philadelphia, Pennsylvania 19130
(215) 232-6666

HARRY DAVIS

STEVE CUSANO

Outrageous Opinions Welcome

We hope you've enjoyed reading the VIEWPOINTS in American Showcase Volume 9. This popular feature is designed to be enlightening as well as entertaining, providing unique insights and comments on the current state of advertising.

We'd like to take this opportunity to invite you to share your own thoughts, opinions and memories with thousands of your colleagues the world over. Please write for editorial guidelines:

Wendl Kornfeld
Operations Manager
American Showcase, Inc.
724 Fifth Avenue
10th Floor
New York, N.Y. 10019

Please include your name, title, company, address and phone number. We cannot, of course, guarantee inclusion of your article in our next edition; however, we will acknowledge and read each submission.

Thanks. We're looking forward to hearing from you. Hope to see you in <u>VOLUME 10</u>!

American Showcase, Inc.

Wooden Reps

(now doing business as).

Grubbs/Bate & Associates

1151 West Peachtree Street, N.W.
Atlanta, Georgia 30309
(404) 892-6303

Telecopier in office.

Representing:

Bob August

GRUBBS/BATE
& ASSOCIATES
1151 WEST PEACHTREE ST.
ATLANTA, GEORGIA 30309
(404) 892-6303

Wooden Reps

(now doing business as)

Grubbs/Bate & Associates

1151 West Peachtree Street, N.W.
Atlanta, Georgia 30309
(404) 892-6303

Telecopier in office.

Representing:

Mike Hodges

Telecopier in studio.

Clients include:

ABC Television, Air Canada, American Journal of
Nursing, Booze-Allen, Hartford Insurance,
Manufacturers Hanover Trust, Newsweek, Norelco,
Pfizer, RCA Records, Science Digest, Southern
Company, Sports Illustrated, TDK Tapes.

Wooden Reps

(now doing business as)

Grubbs/Bate & Associates

1151 West Peachtree Street, N.W.
Atlanta, Georgia 30309
(404) 892-6303

Telecopier in office.

Representing:

Johnna Hogenkamp

Paper illustration

Clients include:

Business Week Magazine, Dole Pineapple, Hallmark Cards, John Deere & Co., Kimberly Clark, Kraft, Maytag, McDonalds, Pickwick Records, Pillsbury, Red Lobster, Sheaffer Pen, 3M, Toro, Visa, Zales.

KIMBERLY CLARK

BOOTH NEWSPAPER

U.S. ARMY

Wooden Reps

(now doing business as)

Grubbs/Bate & Associates
1151 West Peachtree Street, N.W.
Atlanta, Georgia 30309
(404) 892-6303

Telecopier in office.
Representing:

Kevin Hulsey

Technical, Photo-real, & Architectural illustration.

Telecopier in studio.

KEVIN HULSEY

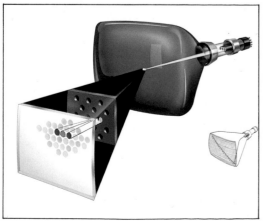

Kevin Hulsey

Wooden Reps

(now doing business as)

Grubbs/Bate & Associates

1151 West Peachtree Street, N.W.
Atlanta, Georgia 30309
(404) 892-6303

Telecopier in office.

Representing:

Image Electronic, Inc.

ie. computer-aided design/illustration   a/v · print · video

218

Wooden Reps

(now doing business as)

Grubbs/Bate & Associates

1151 West Peachtree Street, N.W.
Atlanta, Georgia 30309
(404) 892-6303

Telecopier in office.

Representing:

Chris Lewis

Clients include:

American Express, AT&T, BDA/BBDO, Bozell & Jacobs, CBI Equifax, Coca Cola, Contel, Cooper Leder, Georgia Pacific, Henderson Advertising, Jartran, John Harland Co., J. Walter Thompson, McCann Erickson, Ogilvy & Mather, Spartan Express, Taco Bell.

CHRIS LEWIS

Wooden Reps

(now doing business as)

Grubbs/Bate & Associates

1151 West Peachtree Street, N.W.
Atlanta, Georgia 30309
(404) 892-6303

Telecopier in office.

Representing:

Theo Rudnak

Telecopier in studio.

Clients include:

Anheuser Busch, Atlantic Monthly, B.F. Goodrich, Baldwin Pianos, Delta, Eastern, H.J. Heinz, Hanes, Holiday Inn, IBM, Kimberly-Clark, Kraft, McDonalds, New Age, Newsweek, Oldsmobile, Pabst Blue Ribbon, Playboy, Procter and Gamble, Sherwin Williams, Standard Oil, U.S. Government, United.

220

Wooden Reps

(now doing business as)

Grubbs/Bate & Associates

1151 West Peachtree Street, N.W.
Atlanta, Georgia 30309
(404) 892-6303

Telecopier in office.

Representing:

Joe Saffold

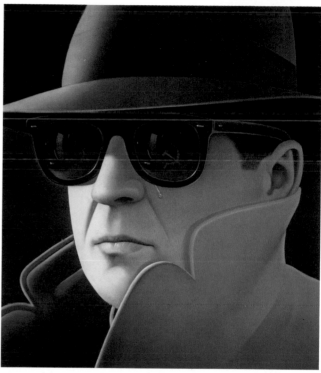

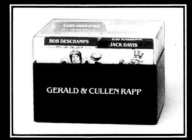

INDEX Representatives

continued on next page

ILLUSTRATION

Notes:

continued from previous page

...and girls on the grass,
laughing, lying, musicking.
Let's meet ardors under arbors.
But hurry please, sometime soon.
'Girls in flower,' *he* would say.
I say they must stay this way.
Through the summer, anyway.

Steven Simpson

*Bruce Leslie Wolfe is represented
in the Northwest by Ron Sweet.
In the Southwest by France Aline.
In the Midwest by Joel Harlib.
And in the East by Vicki Morgan.*

*The Studio address is:
206 El Cerrito Avenue
Piedmont, California 94611
Telephone 415/655-7871.*

Wolfe

Tim Girvin Design, Inc.

911 Western Avenue
Suite 408
Seattle, WA 98104

206.623.7808/7918
Telecopier 206.623.7816

In New York call
Madeline Renard
212.490.2450

Different design.

American Express, Bloomingdale's, Ciba-Geigy, Dayton Hudson, Disney Studios, Embassy Pictures, Estee Lauder, Foxmoor, BF Goodrich, Harper & Row, Hoffman-LaRoche, IBM, L'Oreal, Herman Miller, Nordstrom, PBS, Pennzoil, Polaroid, Revlon, Sheraton Hotels, Simpson Paper Co., Time, Westin Hotels, Zales.

Relevant samples will be sent with a project description on your letterhead.

STEWART BROTHERS COFFEE

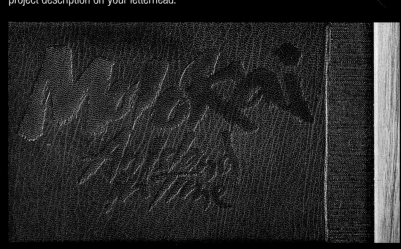

Bloomingdale's BY MAIL LTD.

CORPORATE GIFTS

THE LEGEND of Billie Jean

VIET NAM

PERFORMA '87
A FESTIVAL OF NEW WORKS

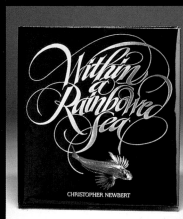

Within a Rainbowed Sea

CHRISTOPHER NEWBERT

Dilettante Chocolates

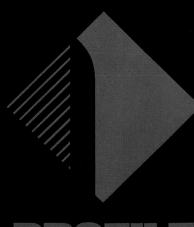

PROFILE

ECCO L'ITALIA

bloomingdale's

IAE
INTERNATIONAL AERO ENGINES

Joszis

CAMPBELL·MITHUN ADVERTISING

LADY STETSON

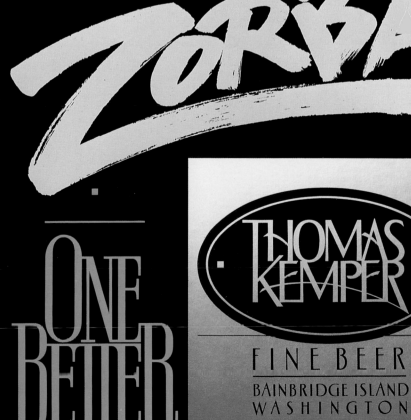

ZORBA

ONE BETTER

THOMAS KEMPER

FINE BEER

BAINBRIDGE ISLAND WASHINGTON

J·O·N
R·A·W·S·O·N
illustration

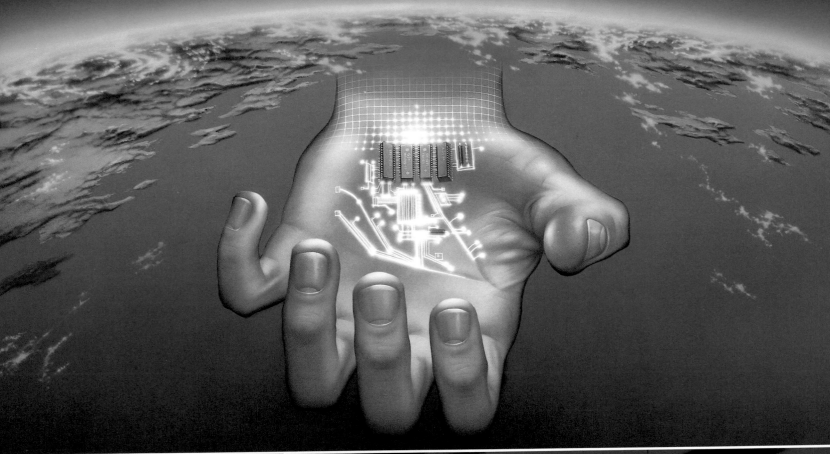

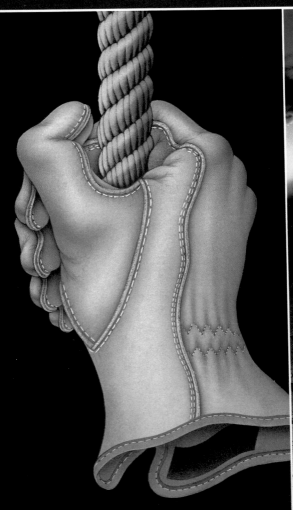

PIE in the SKY

WRAPPING PAPER
GAME©

MARK · WATTS
ILLUSTRATION · TYPE · DESIGN

STUDIO 215 · 945 · 9422   NEW YORK 212 · 986 · 5680

DREAMER
53

Corvette

ANDREA BROOKS

99 Bank Street/3G, New York City 10014

(212) 924-3085

Marlies
Merk Najaka
241 Central Park W.
N.Y.C., N.Y. 10024
(212) 580-0058

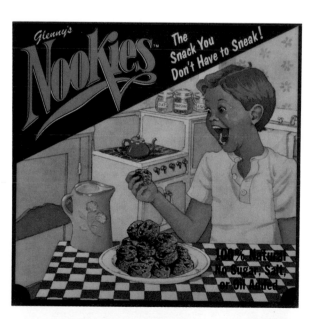

DAVID CAIN
ILLUSTRATION
212/691-5783

200 WEST 20 STREET, #607
NEW YORK, NEW YORK 10011

Acquisitions and Mergers, © David Cain 1986

Doubleday & Company

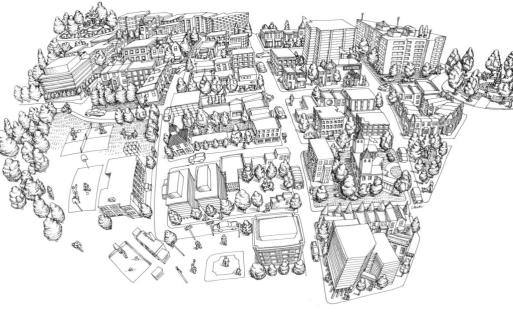

Member of G.A.G., A.I.G.A.
Clients include: Cosmair, D'Arcy MacManus Masius,
The New York Times, Henri Bendel, Estee Lauder,
The Washington Post, John Wiley Publishing

SANDRA FILIPPUCCI
270 park avenue south, new york ny 10010
212 • 477•8732

REPRESENTATION: DALE ELDRIDGE & ASSOCIATES, INC. 314•773•2242

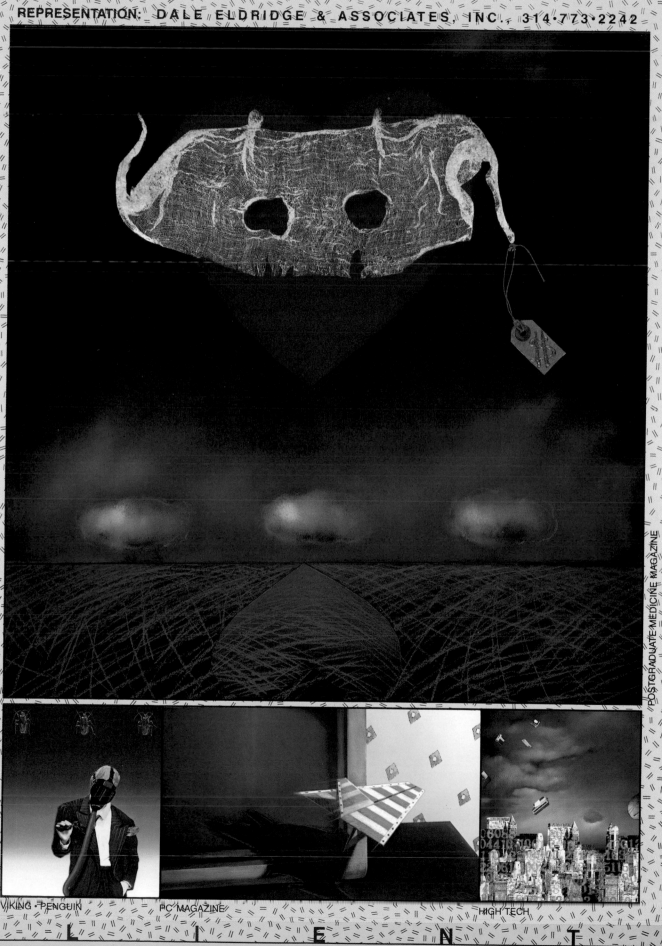

VIKING•PENGUIN   PC MAGAZINE   HIGH TECH

POSTGRADUATE MEDICINE MAGAZINE

C L I E N T S

time magazine, sports illustrated, newsday magazine, n.y. times, science '85, p.c. magazine, consumer electronics, video magazine, sports medicine magazine, satellite marketing magazine, viking-penguin books, benton & bowles, dancer-fitzgerald, geer dubois.

MEMBER SOCIETY OF ILLUSTRATORS

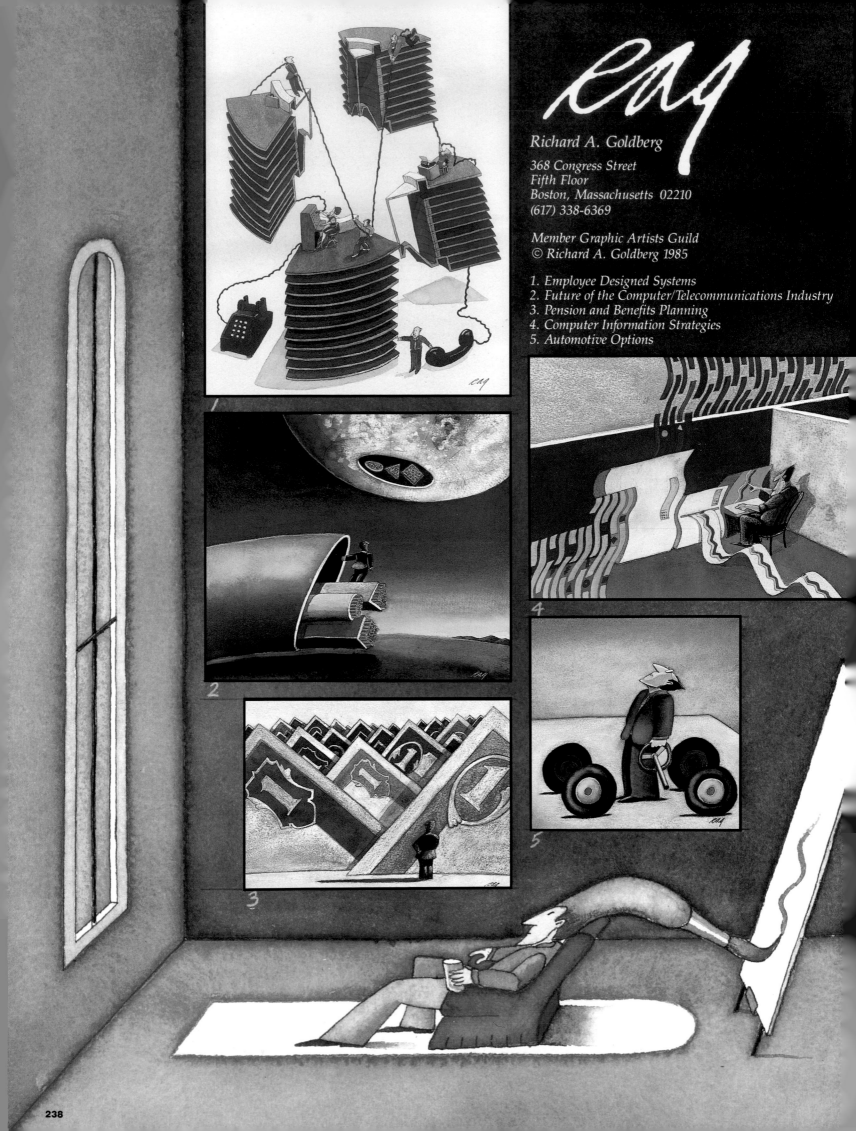

Richard A. Goldberg

368 Congress Street
Fifth Floor
Boston, Massachusetts 02210
(617) 338-6369

Member Graphic Artists Guild
© Richard A. Goldberg 1985

1. Employee Designed Systems
2. Future of the Computer/Telecommunications Industry
3. Pension and Benefits Planning
4. Computer Information Strategies
5. Automotive Options

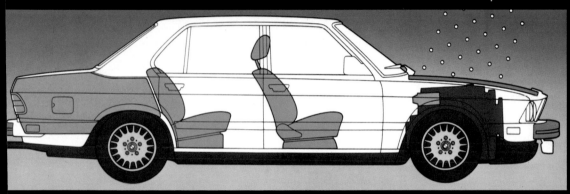

GERARD HUERTA DESIGN, INC·

45 Corbin Drive Darien, CT O6820

(2O3) 656·O5O5

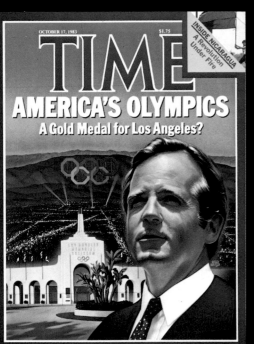

ROGER
HUYSSEN

45 Corbin Drive
Darien, CT 06820
(203) 656-0200

LES KATZ

Represented by: Sharon Drexler
451 Westminster Rd.
Brooklyn, New York 11218
(718) 284-4779

1985 wheat thins

MAYOR'S CUP
SERIES

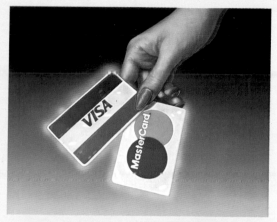

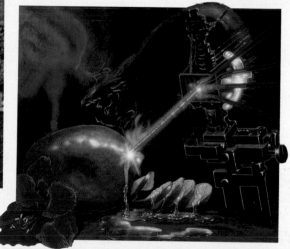

SWEET NOTHINGS
WHISPERED OVERNIGHT.

EXPRESS MAIL
NEXT DAY SERVICE

BEN LUCE
5 EAST 17TH STREET, 6TH FL.
NEW YORK, NEW YORK 10003
212-255-8193

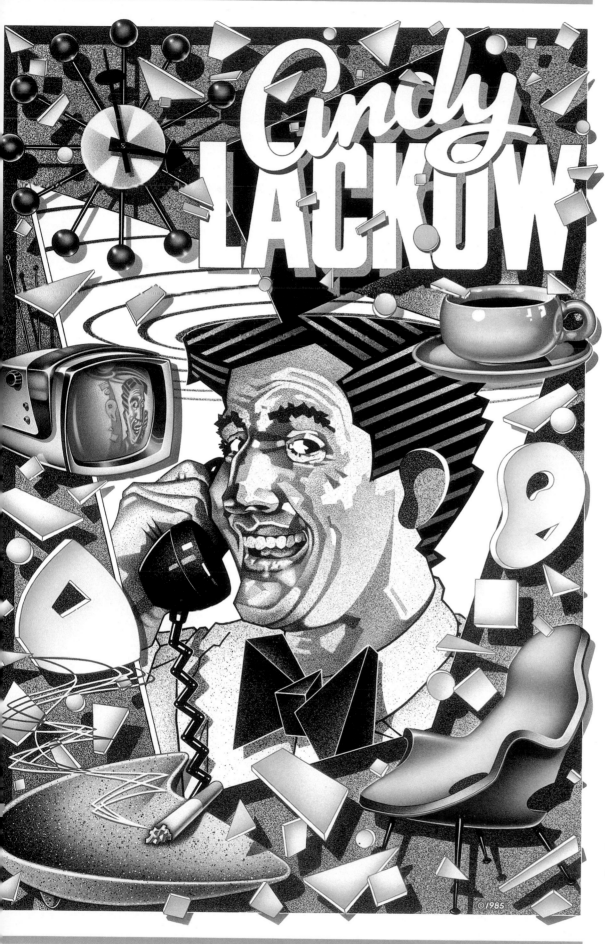

DESIGN · ILLUSTRATION

TONY MASCIO

SUPER BOWL XIX

4 Teton Court, Voorhees, New Jersey 08043
1 (609) 424-5278   Service (215) 567-1585

Represented by Pamela R. Neail Associates
27-31 Bleecker Street, New York, N.Y. 10012
1 (212) 673-1600

ANDREA MISTRETTA

ILLUSTRATION • LETTERING • DESIGN
TELECOPIER AVAILABLE

(201) 652-5325

5 BOHNERT PLACE WALDWICK, N.J. 07463

PARTIAL CLIENT ROSTER:

ABC-TV
BEST FOODS
BORDEN
CIBA GEIGY
CONOCO
COLUMBIA PICTURES
EXPRESS MAIL
FORBES MAGAZINE
GIANETTINO & MEREDITH
GREY ADVERTISING
JOHNSON SIMPSON
KWASHA LIPTON
LINGER ASSOCIATES
MEDICAL ECONOMICS
1330 CORPORATION
3M
SAAB SCANIA OF AMERICA
WILLIAM ESTY

AWARDS:

SOCIETY OF ILLUSTRATORS
23, 25
ART DIRECTORS CLUB OF N.J.
18, 19, 20, 21, 22
BRONZE MEDAL, 21
DESI, '84

FBI RECORDS

GIANETTINO & MEREDITH

HOWARD SAVINGS BANK

COLUMBIA PICTURES

BORDEN

LINGER ASSOCIATES

D E N N I S
M U K A I

LOS ANGELES
Joanne Hedge
213 . 874 . 1661

SAN FRANCISCO
Mary Vandamme
415 . 433 . 1292

NEW YORK
Daniele Collignon
212 . 243 . 4209

CHICAGO
Joel Harlib
312 . 329 . 1370

Mark Samuels

NYC • 212 • 777 • 8580 / 718 • 447 • 8536

THE CASTING SESSION

THE BUSINESS LUNCH

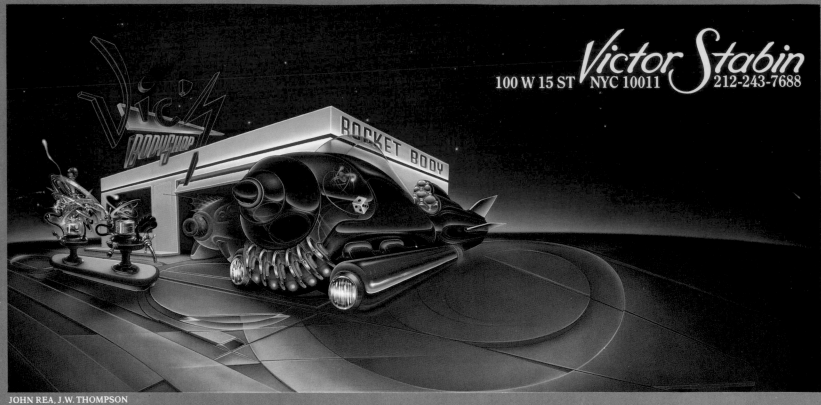

Victor Stabin
100 W 15 ST   NYC 10011   212-243-7688

JOHN REA, J.W. THOMPSON

MY DENTIST, 212 477 0430

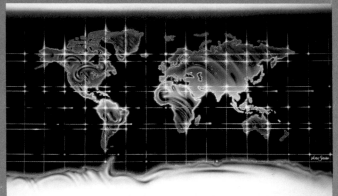

VISUAL IMAGES, LEE STRAUSLAND

McCAFFREY McCALL , STEVE BERNSTEIN

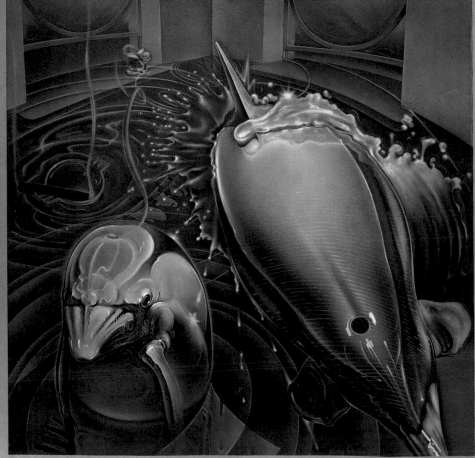

LAVEY WOLFF SWIFT, DAN SMITH

BLOOMINGDALES, GERRY ORANATO

DUGALD STERMER

Represented in San Francisco by Jim Lilie:

[415] 921-8281

[415] 441-4384

GHOST
VISION

A NOVEL BY JEANIE KORTUM

Please take
car

249

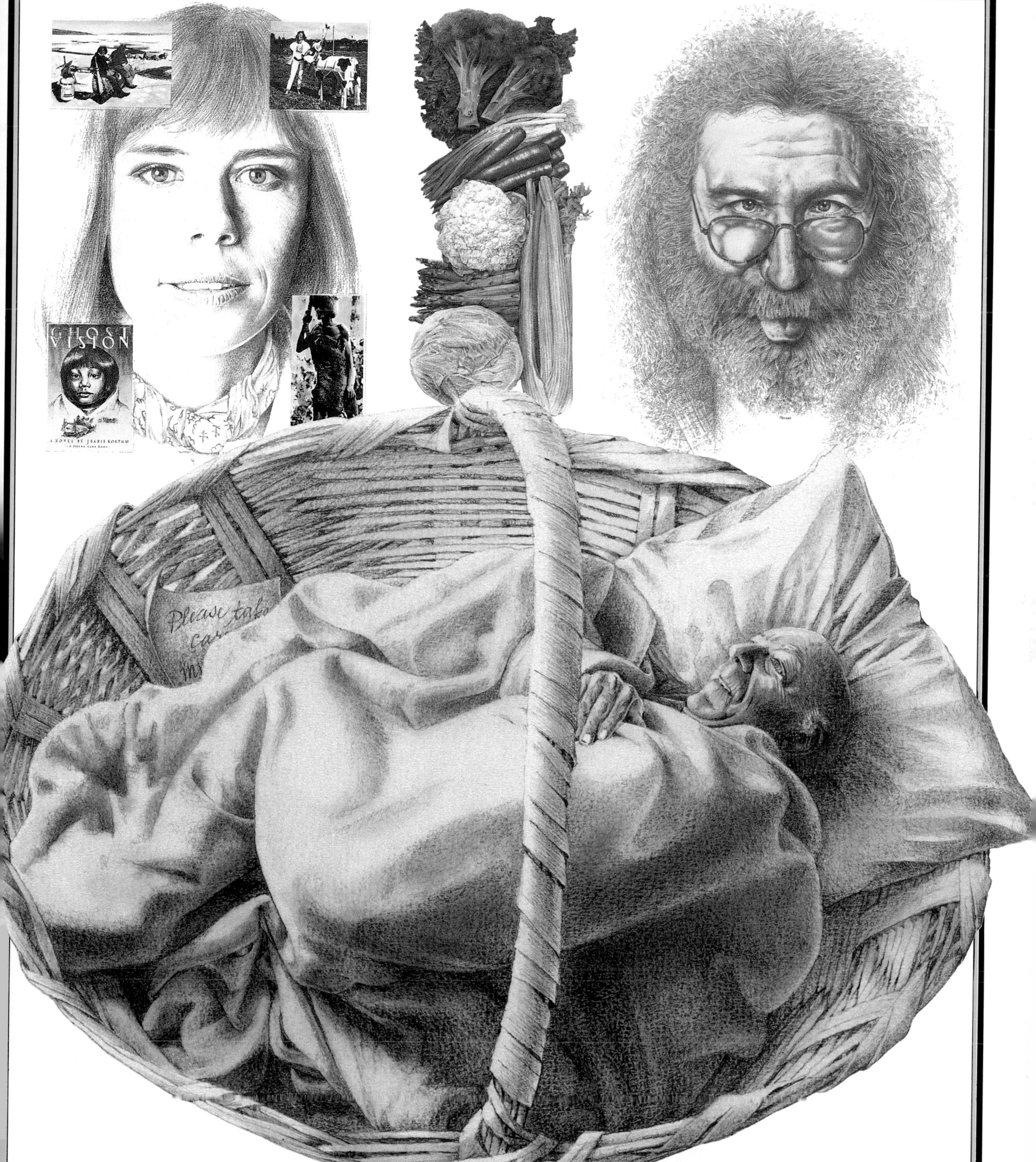

MICHAEL
TROSSMAN

411 West End Avenue
New York, New York 10024
(212) 799-6852
Telex: 668359
Cable: TURTLES NEW YORK
Chicago: Vincent J. Kamin
(312) 787-8834

Clients include:
The New York Times
Mobil
Time
Esquire
Rolling Stone
Vanity Fair
Playboy

Workman Publishing
Self
MS
New York Magazine
Inside Sports
National Lampoon
RCA Records
Lincoln Center

JAMES TURGEON ILLUSTRATION · LETTERING · DESIGN 233 EAST WACKER CHICAGO, ILLINOIS 60601 (312) 861-1039

CLIENTS NOW INCLUDE LIZARD BREWERY

Neil Waldman   47 Woodlands Avenue White Plains, New York 10607   (914) 693-2782

K E N **W** A L K E R

6 W. 3RD ST.
ANSAS CITY
ISSOURI
4 1 0 5
6 · 474 · 3922

DESIGN Jim Costa

CLIENTS INCLUDE:

American Family Physician
Sunrise Publications, Inc.
Meredith Publishing Co.
Phillips Petroleum Co.
Marion Laboratories
United States Army
The Getty Corp.
Purina, Elanco
U.S. Telecom

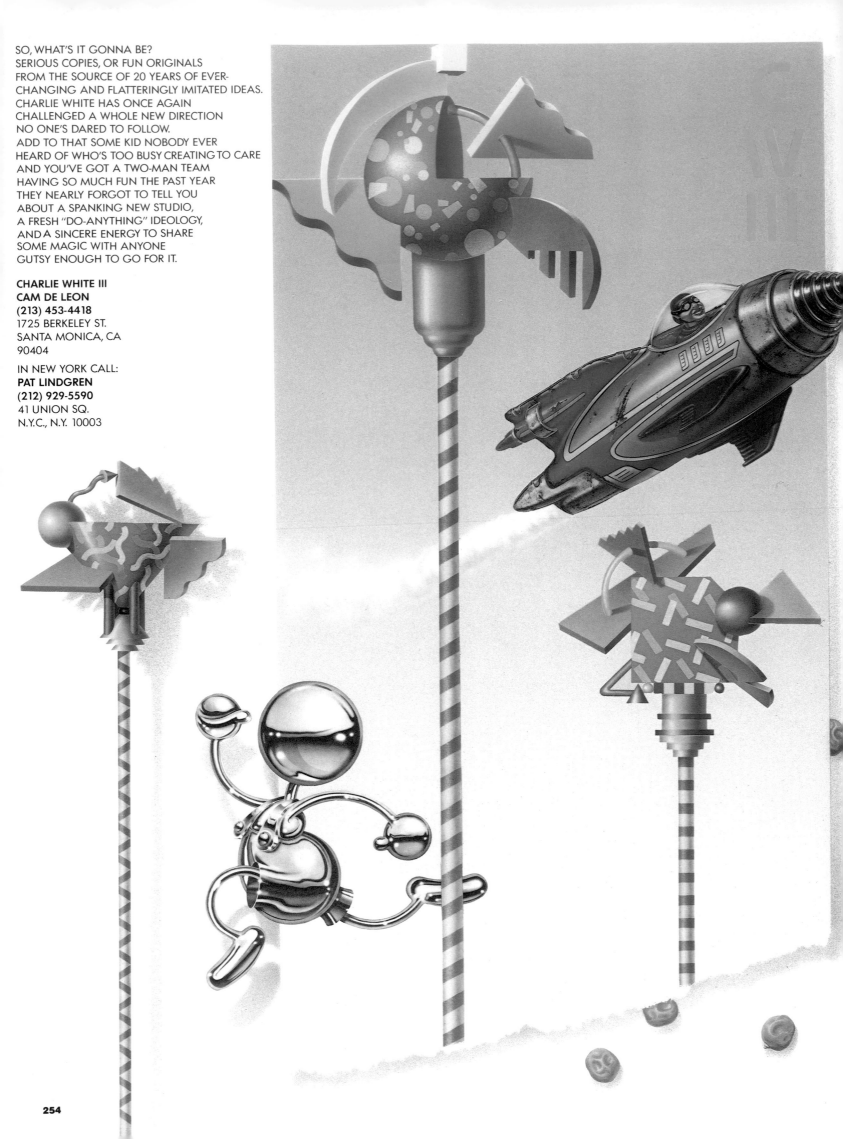

SO, WHAT'S IT GONNA BE?
SERIOUS COPIES, OR FUN ORIGINALS
FROM THE SOURCE OF 20 YEARS OF EVER-
CHANGING AND FLATTERINGLY IMITATED IDEAS.
CHARLIE WHITE HAS ONCE AGAIN
CHALLENGED A WHOLE NEW DIRECTION
NO ONE'S DARED TO FOLLOW.
ADD TO THAT SOME KID NOBODY EVER
HEARD OF WHO'S TOO BUSY CREATING TO CARE
AND YOU'VE GOT A TWO-MAN TEAM
HAVING SO MUCH FUN THE PAST YEAR
THEY NEARLY FORGOT TO TELL YOU
ABOUT A SPANKING NEW STUDIO,
A FRESH "DO-ANYTHING" IDEOLOGY,
AND A SINCERE ENERGY TO SHARE
SOME MAGIC WITH ANYONE
GUTSY ENOUGH TO GO FOR IT.

CHARLIE WHITE III
CAM DE LEON
(213) 453-4418
1725 BERKELEY ST.
SANTA MONICA, CA
90404

IN NEW YORK CALL:
PAT LINDGREN
(212) 929-5590
41 UNION SQ.
N.Y.C., N.Y. 10003

254

PUNZ WOLFF

EAST 20 ST. N.Y.C. 10003

212-254-5705

255

Kathie Abrams

41 Union Square West
Room 1001
New York, New York 10003
(212) 741-1333

Humorous illustration for advertising, corporate, publishing and audio-visual clients, including:

American Express; *American Health;* American Symphony Orchestra; AT&T; Bose Audio; Burson-Marsteller; Business Times; Chase Manhattan Bank; Dodd, Mead & Co.; Farrar, Straus & Giroux; Harper & Row; Hermes; Ibis Media; Leutwyler Associates;

Marine Midland Bank; McGraw-Hill; Midco Pipe & Tube; Newsweek; Ogilvy & Mather; 1001 Home Ideas; Random House; RFE Industries; Rumrill-Hoyt; Scholastic; Simon & Schuster; Sports Illustrated; Frederick Warne; Ziff-Davis.

Illustrations, from top to bottom:

Left: Chase Manhattan Bank/Robert Meyer Design; *American Health;* 1001 Home Ideas/Rumrill-Hoyt. Center: AT&T/Leutwyler Associates; *The Physician and Sportsmedicine.* At right, a series for Business Times cable television and a spot for the American Symphony Orchestra through Ogilvy & Mather.

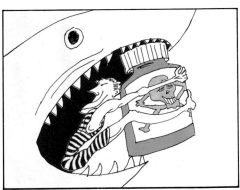

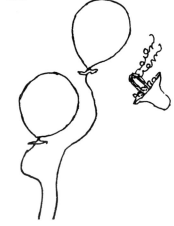

256

Jeanette Adams
261 Broadway
New York, New York 10007
(212) 732-3878
(603) 835-2984

Concept, Design and Illustration
in Mixed Media.

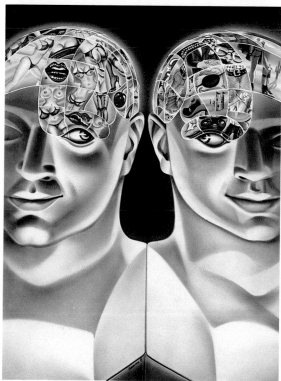

Brian Ajhar

321 East 12th Street #30
New York, New York 10003
(212) 254-0694

Client list:

Forbes; Dun's Business Month;
Money; Sports Illustrated;
Reader's Digest; The New York
Times; Barrons; World Tennis;
Success; Datamation; Viking
Penguin Inc.; Gallery; Field
and Stream; Psychology Today;
Investment Dealers Digest;
Frequent Flyer; Business Week;
The Nation; Ziff-Davis Publications;
Fairchild Publications; East West
Network; McCall's Working
Mother; Mechanics Illustrated;
Health; Working Woman;
Games; American Lawyer;
Travel and Leisure; Parents;
American Photographer; Print;
Art Direction; Chemical
Business; Witan Associates
(Japan); Herman Associates;
Harcourt Brace Jovanovich;
Slater, Hanfit, Martin.

Top:
Client: Money Magazine
Center left:
Client: Money Magazine
Center right:
Artist Portfolio
Bottom:
Client: Success Magazine

Susan Aldrich

Represented by:
Wendy Morgan
Network Studios
5 Logan Hill Road
Northport, New York 11768
(516) 757-5609

Advertising, Editorial and
Corporate Illustration

Paul R. Alexander

37 Pine Mountain Road
Redding, Connecticut 06896
(203) 544-9293

Clients represented on this page, from top down and bottom left to right; Playboy Magazine, General Electric Company, Ace Books, and South Bend Lathe Inc.

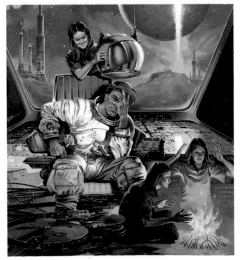

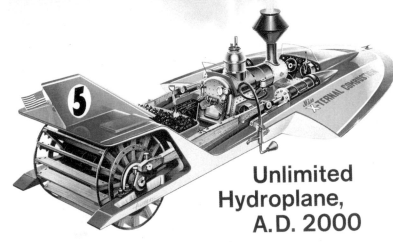

Unlimited
Hydroplane,
A.D. 2000

Roger Bergendorff, Inc.

17106 Sims Street, Suite A
Huntington Beach, California 92649
(714) 840-7665

Clients include:
Yamaha, CBS, Apple Computers, Corning Glass,
Della Femina Travisano, Warner Bros., Armor All,
Fisher, Grey Advertising, Orion Pictures, National
Football League, Foote Cone Belding, Paper Moon
Graphics, Normark Skis, Dynastar Skis, Mazda, Izuzu,
Scott USA, Alitalia Airlines, Doubleday Inc., MCA
Records, O'Neill, AMF, National Park Service, TRW,
Treesweet Products, Caterpillar, Fairchild Industries.   Member Graphic Artists Guild

269

GRAPHIC ARTS ORGANIZATIONS

Arizona:

Phoenix Society of Visual Arts
P.O. Box 469
Phoenix, AZ 85001

California:

Advertising Club of Los Angeles
514 Shatto Pl., Rm. 328
Los Angeles, CA 90020
(213) 382-1228

APA
Advertising Photographers of America, Inc.
823 North La Brea Blvd.
Los Angeles, CA 90038
(213) 935-7283

APA
Advertising Photographers of America, Inc.
1061 Folsom Street
San Francisco, CA 94103
(415) 332-8831

Art Directors and Artists Club
2791 24th St.
Sacramento, CA 95818
(916) 731-8802

Art Directors Club
633 Masonic
San Francisco, CA 94117
(415) 387-4040

Book Club of California
312 Sutter St., Ste. 510
San Francisco, CA 94108
(415) 781-7532

Graphic Artists Guild of Los Angeles
5971 W. 3rd
Los Angeles, CA 90036
(213) 938-0009

Los Angeles Advertising Women
5301 Laurel Canyon Blvd. #219
North Hollywood, CA 91607
(818) 762-4669

Society of Illustrators of Los Angeles
5000 Van Nuys #400
Sherman Oaks, CA 91403
(818) 784-0588

Society of Motion Picture & TV Art Directors
14724 Ventura Blvd.
Sherman Oaks, CA 91403
(818) 905-0599

Western Art Directors Club
P.O. Box 966
Palo Alto, CA 94302
(415) 321-4196

Women in Design
P.O. Box 2607
San Francisco, CA 94126
(415) 397-1748

Women's Graphic Center
The Woman's Building
1727 N. Spring St.
Los Angeles, CA 90012
(213) 222-5101

Colorado:

International Design Conference at Aspen
1000 N. 3rd
Aspen, CO 81612
(303) 925-2257

Connecticut:

Connecticut Art Directors Club
P.O. Box 1974
New Haven, CT 06521

District of Columbia:

American Advertising Federation
1400 K. St. N.W., Ste. 1000
Washington, DC 20005
(202) 898-0089

American Institute of Architects
1735 New York Avenue, N.W.
Washington, DC 20006
(202) 626-7300

Art Directors Club of Washington, DC
655 15th St., N.W.
Washington, DC 20005
(202) 347-5900

Federal Design Council
P.O. Box 7537
Washington, DC 20044

International Copyright Information Center, A.A.D.
1707 L Street, N.W.
Washington, DC 20036

NEA: Design Arts Program
1100 Pennsylvania Ave., N.W. Rm #625
Washington, DC 20506
(202) 682-5437

Georgia:

Atlanta Art Papers, Inc.
P.O. Box 77348
Atlanta, GA 30357
(404) 885-1273

Graphics Artists Guild
3158 Maple Drive, N.E., Ste. 46
Atlanta, GA 30305
(404) 262-8077

Illinois:

APA
Advertising Photographers of America, Inc.
100 West Erie
Chicago, IL 60610
(312) 642-0937

Institute of Business Designers
National
1155 Merchandise Mart
Chicago, IL 60654
(312) 467-1950

Society of Environmental Graphic Designers
228 N. LaSalle St., Ste. 1205
Chicago, IL 60601

STA
233 East Ontario St.
Chicago, IL 60611
(312) 787-2018

Women in Design
2 N. Riverside Plaza
Chicago, IL 60606
(312) 648-1874

Kansas:

Wichita Art Directors Club
P.O. Box 562
Wichita, KS 67202

Maryland:

Council of Communications Societies
P.O. Box 1074
Silver Springs, MD 20910

Massachusetts:

Art Directors Club of Boston
50 Commonwealth Ave.
Boston, MA 02116
(617) 536-8999

Center for Design of Industrial Schedules
221 Longwood Ave.
Boston, MA 02115
(617) 734-2163

Graphic Artists Guild
P.O. Box 1454-GMF
Boston, MA 02205
(617) 451-5362

Michigan:

Creative Advertising Club of Detroit
c/o Rhoda Parkin
30400 Van Dyke
Warren, MI 48093

Minnesota:

Minnesota Graphic Designers Association
314 Clifton Ave.
Minneapolis, MN 55403
(612) 870-4156

Missouri:

Advertising Club of Greater St. Louis
440 Mansion House Center
St. Louis, MO 63102
(314) 231-4185

Advertising Club of Kansas City
1 Ward Parkway Center, Ste. 102
Kansas City, MO 64112
(816) 753-4088

New Jersey:

Point-of-Purchase Advertising Institute
2 Executive Dr.
Fort Lee, NJ 07024
(201) 585-8400

New York:

The Advertising Club of New York
Roosevelt Hotel, Rm. 310 (45 E. 45th)
New York, NY 10017
(212) 697-0877

The Advertising Council, Inc.
825 Third Ave., 25th Floor
New York, NY 10022
(212) 758-0400

APA
Advertising Photographers of America, Inc.
45 E. 20th Street
New York, NY 10003
(212) 254-5500

Advertising Typographers Association of America, Inc.
5 Penn Plaza, 12th Fl.
New York, NY 10001
(212) 594-0685

continued on page 27

Semyon Bilmes
15-69 Ocean Avenue
Brooklyn, New York 11230
(718) 338-4268

Jerry Blank
1048 Lincoln Avenue
San Jose, California 95125
(408) 289-9095

Computer Illustration
High Technology look for ads,
brochures, posters, point of
purchase and publishing.

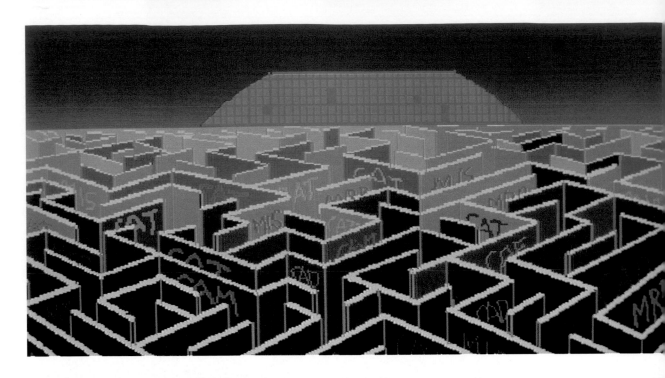

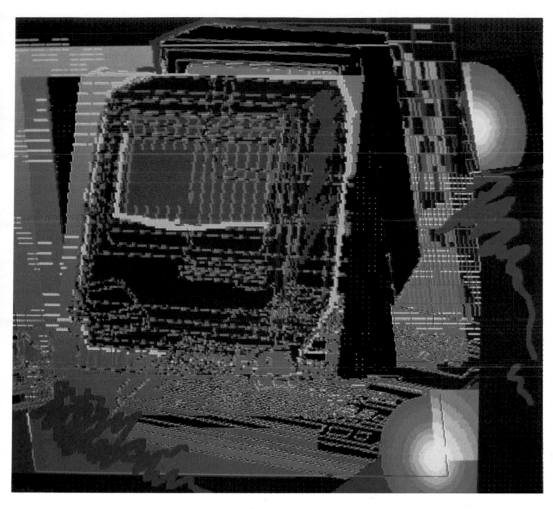

Tom Bloom
235 East 84th Street
New York, New York 10028
(212) 628-6861

Represented by Patricia Lindgren & Audrey Lavine
(212) 929-5590

Tom Bloom

235 East 84th Street
New York, New York 10028
(212) 628-6861

Represented by Patricia Lindgren & Audrey Lavine
(212) 929-5590

Peter Bono

59 Van Houten Avenue
Passaic, New Jersey 07055
(201) 778-5489

I can come up with original concepts or work with your design.

Clients include:
Dancer Fitzgerald Sample; Scali, McCabe, Sloves; Ogilvy & Mather Direct; Durfee & Solow Advertising; Manufacturers Hanover; American Express; 13-30 Corporation; PSE&G of N.J.

McGraw-Hill; Ziff-Davis; Bill Communications; Fairchild Publications; Penthouse Publications; Playboy Publications; Business Week; Family Circle; Barron's; New York Times; Changing Times; Redbook.

Exhibited at the Society of Illustrators Annual Show.

Lee Lee Brazeal

4212 San Felipe
Houston, Texas 77027

Represented by:

Dallas
Art Rep, Inc.
Linda Smith
(214) 521-5156

Partial list of clients include:

Allen & Dorward
American Airlines
Bloom Adv.
Bozell & Jacobs
Coca-Cola
Continental Airlines
Dennard Creative
Dominion Bancshares Corp.
Gulf Coast Symphony
Haggar Slacks
Holiday Inn
Horchow Collection
Houston Symphony
Loucks Atelier
Minute Maid
Ogilvy & Mather
Shell Oil
Texas Instruments
Texas Monthly
Tracey-Locke Adv.
Woody Pirtle Design

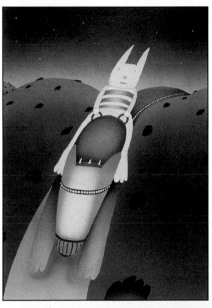

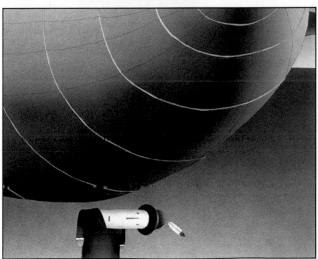

continued from page 270

Advertising Women of New York Foundation, Inc.
153 E. 57th St.
New York, NY 10022
(212) 593-1950

American Association of Advertising Agencies
666 Third Ave.
New York, NY 10017
(212) 682-2500

American Booksellers Association, Inc.
122 E. 42nd St.
New York, NY 10168
(212) 867-9060

The Public Relations Society of America, Inc.
845 Third Ave.
New York, NY 10022
(212) 826-1750

American Council for the Arts
570 Seventh Ave.
New York, NY 10018
(212) 354-6655

The American Institute of Graphic Arts
1059 Third Ave.
New York, NY 10021
(212) 752-0813

American Society of Interior Designers
National Headquarters
1430 Broadway
New York, NY 10018
(212) 944-9220

New York Chapter
200 Lexington Ave.
New York, NY 10016
(212) 685-3480

American Society of Magazine Photographers
205 Lexington Ave.
New York, NY 10016
(212) 889-9144

Art Directors Club of New York
488 Madison Ave.
New York, NY 10022
(212) 838-8140

Association of American Publishers, Inc.
220 E. 23rd, 2nd Floor
New York, NY 10010
(212) 689-8920

Association of the Graphic Arts
5 Penn Plaza
New York, NY 10001
(212) 279-2100

Center for Arts Information
625 Broadway
New York, NY 10012
(212) 677-7548

The Children's Book Council, Inc.
67 Irving Place
New York, NY 10003
(212) 254-2666

CLIO
336 E. 59th St.
New York, NY 10022
(212) 593-1900

Foundation for the Community of Artists
280 Broadway, Ste. 412
New York, NY 10007
(212) 227-3770

Graphic Artists Guild
30 E. 20th St., Rm. 405
New York, NY 10003
(212) 777-7353

Guild of Book Workers
521 Fifth Ave.
New York, NY 10175
(212) 757-6454

Institute of Outdoor Advertising
342 Madison Ave.
New York, NY 10173
(212) 986-5920

International Advertising Association, Inc.
475 Fifth Ave.
New York, NY 10017
(212) 684-1583

The One Club
251 E. 50th St.
New York, NY 10022
(212) 935-0121

Society of Illustrators
128 E. 63rd St.
New York, NY 10021
(212) 838-2560

Society of Photographers and Artists Representatives
1123 Broadway #914
New York, NY 10010
(212) 924-6023

Society of Publication Designers
25 W. 43rd St., Ste. 711
New York, NY 10036
(212) 354-8585

Television Bureau of Advertising
477 Madison Ave.
New York, NY 10022
(212) 486-1111

Type Directors Club of New York
545 W. 45th St.
New York, NY 10036
(212) 245-6300

U.S. Trademark Association
6 E. 45th St.
New York, NY 10017
(212) 986-5880

Volunteer Lawyers for the Arts
1560 Broadway, Ste. 711
New York, NY 10036
(212) 575-1150

Women in the Arts
325 Spring St.
New York, NY 10013
(212) 691-0988

Women in Design
P.O. Box 5315
FDR Station
New York, NY 10022

Ohio:

Advertising Club of Cincinnati
2228 Gilbert
Cincinnati, OH 45206
(513) 281-6877

Cleveland Society of Communicating Arts
812 Huron Rd., S.E.
Cleveland, OH 44115
(216) 621-5139

Columbus Society of Communicating Arts
c/o Salvato & Coe
2015 West Fifth Ave.
Columbus, OH 43221
(614) 488-3131

Design Collective
D.F. Cooke
131 North High St.
Columbus, OH 43215
(614) 464-2880

Pennsylvania:

Art Directors Club of Philadelphia
2017 Walnut St.
Philadelphia, PA 19103
(215) 569-3650

Tennessee:

Engraved Stationery Manufacturers Association
c/o Printing Industries Association of the South
1000 17th Ave. South
Nashville, TN 37212
(615) 327-4444

Texas:

Advertising Artists of Fort Worth
3424 Falcon Dr.
Fort Worth, TX 76119

Art Directors Club of Houston
2029 So. Blvd.
Houston, TX 77098
(713) 523-1019

Dallas Society of Visual Communication
3530 High Mesa Dr.
Dallas, TX 75234
(214) 241-2017

Virginia:

Industrial Designers Society of America
1360 Beverly Rd., Ste. 303
McLean, VA 22101
(703) 556-0919

Tidewater Society of Communicating Arts
P.O. Box 153
Norfolk, VA 23501

Washington:

Seattle Design Association
P.O. Box 1097
Main Office Station
Seattle, WA 98111
(206) 285-6725
(Formerly Seattle Women in Design)

Seattle Women in Advertising
219 First Avenue N., Ste. 300
Seattle, WA 98109
(206) 285-0919

Society of Professional Graphic Artists
c/o Steve Chin, Pres.
85 S. Washington Street, Ste. 204
Seattle, WA 98104

Wisconsin:

The Advertising Club
231 W. Wisconsin #404
Milwaukee, WI 53203
(414) 271-7351

Illustrators & Designers of Milwaukee
c/o Don Berg
207 E. Michigan
Milwaukee, WI 53202
(414) 276-7828

Alice Brickner

4720 Grosvenor Avenue
Bronx, New York 10471
(212) 549-5909

Watercolor illustration for advertising, promotion, pharmaceutical and packaging use.

Clients include: American Airlines, AT&T, Robert A. Becker, Inc.; Boehringer Ingelheim Ltd., Carrafiello, Diehl & Associates, Caswell-Massey, Chesebrough-Pond's, Inc.; Ciba-Geigy, Cook and Shanosky Assoc., Corporate Graphics, Dancer-Fitzgerald-Sample, Inc.; Dolphin Productions, Games Magazine, General Foods, Gross, Townsend, Frank; Fortune, Harcourt Brace Jovanovich, IBM, Johnson & Simpson, KPR, Lavey/Wolff/Swift, Inc.; London Records, William Douglas McAdams, McGraw-Hill, Merck & Co., Miles Laboratories, Nabisco, Nonesuch Records, Ogilvy & Mather, Anthony Russell, Inc.; Self Magazine, Shareholders Reports, Inc.; Sieber & McIntyre, SmithKline Corp., Sports Illustrated, Sudler & Hennessy, Vogue, John Wiley & Sons.

Work appeared in: Graphis Annuals, Society of Illustrators Annuals, NY Art Director's Club Exhibitions, New Jersey Art Director's Club Exhibitions, Creativity Exhibitions, Communication Arts Magazine, and Print Magazine.

Member Graphic Artists Guild

© Alice Brickner 1985

CONDE NAST: SELF MAGAZINE

TIME/LIFE: DISCOVER MAGAZINE

MEAD ANNUAL REPORT: PAPER AND THE ELECTRONIC CONNECTION

ALLIED CORP.: OMNI MAGAZINE

CORNING MEDICAL

Lou Brooks

415 West 55th Street
New York, New York 10019
(212) 245-3632

Illustration, Design and
Lettering

First page, top to bottom:

Illustration and lettering for a
soft drink campaign.
Parody of pop art with movie
popcorn theme announcing
Showtime and The Movie
Channel.
Illustration for Playboy Germany
depicting aggression in
businessmen.

Second page, left side, top to
bottom:

Logo redesign for the game of
Monopoly.
Illustration for ice cream
campaign.
Fiftieth Anniversary
Commemorative Edition tin
box for game of Monopoly.
Illustration about television
advertising and the
consumer.
Illustration for Chunky
Chocolate.

Second page, right side, top to
bottom:

Pictures 1-4: Art for animated
network promo for MTV.
Picture 5: Art for animated tv
commercial for CBS Records.
Pictures 6-7: Art for animated tv
commercial for Scripto Pens.
Sample reel available.

Member Graphic Artists Guild

Great Balls Of Fun!

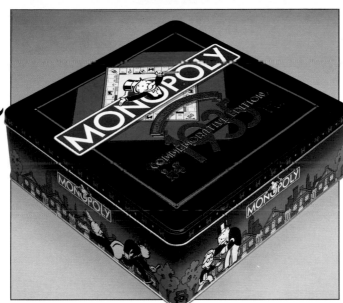

Brooks

RICH, THICK CHOCOLATE IN EVERY BITE...

Chunky's Back!

Chunky's Back!

Chunky's Better!

stlé Foods Corporation, 1985

Don Brown
129 East 29th Street
New York, New York 10016
(212) 532-1705
(718) 816-6260

Clients include: Doremus &
Company, Griffin Bacal,
McCaffrey & McCall, Ogilvy
Mather Direct, *Diversion, Dun's
Business Month, Fortune, PC
Week, Scholastic,* Harcourt
Brace Jovanovich, Houghton
Mifflin, Mobil, Peat Marwick, and
Pitney Bowes.

Member Graphic Artists Guild

© 1985 Don Brown

Rick Brown

Illustration
1502 North Maple Street
Burbank, California 91505
(818) 842-0726

Client List

Universal Studios
Walt Disney Productions
NFL Properties, Inc.
Paper Moon Graphics
MCA Records, Inc.
Piedmont Airlines
Hang Ten
Nickelodeon

Diana Bryan

Director of:

The Bryan Group

200 East 16th Street #1D
New York, New York 10003
(212) 475-7927

THE BRYAN GROUP produces computer animation/video, illustration and computer graphics for advertising, exhibits, posters, packaging, audio-visuals, editorial and manufacturing.

Ads have also appeared in the 1981 Black Book, the American Showcase, Volumes 7 and 8

Clients include: Datsun, American Express, Chiquita Banana, Ogilvy and Mather, Young and Rubicam, Connoisseur Magazine, Business Week, Time Magazine, Travel and Leisure, The New York Times, The Washington Post, Time-Life Publications, Ziff-Davis Publications, Glamour, Mademoiselle, Savvy, Sports Illustrated, Working Woman, Rolling Stone, Workman Publications, The New York Shakespeare Festival, The A.I.G.A.

Works exhibited in: the Graphis Annual, Print Magazine, the Society of Illustrator's Annual, Art Direction, Creativity '77, the New York Art Director's Club, The Society of Publication Designers, the A.I.G.A., the A.C.U.C.A.A. Graphics Competition, the Library of Congress.

COMPUTER GRAPHICS
Bottom right image: Success Magazine, AD/Louis Cruz
Computer courtesy Studio Tech, Secaucus, New Jersey

ILLUSTRATIONS
Top right and left for American Express
Top center for the A.I.G.A.
    Art Director Elton Robinson
Bottom center for Chiquita Banana
    Art Director Nancy Babcock
Bottom left for the St. Ann's Theater
    Designer Hilaire Dubourcq
Member Graphic Artists Guild and S.I.G.G.R.A.P.H.

For further samples, ask for a mini-portfolio.

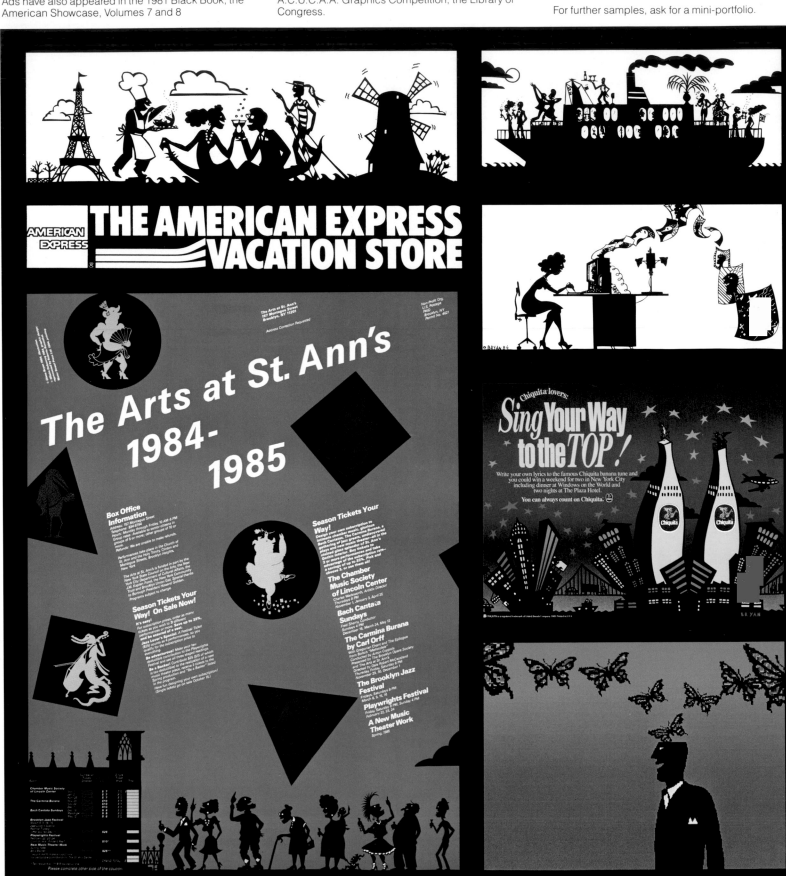

Yvonne
Buchanan

411 14th Street
Brooklyn, New York 11215
(718) 965-3021

Clients include: AT&T; Ford
Foundation; J.P. Martin
Associates; Cato-Johnson;
N.W. Ayer; Specht Gilbert &
Partners; Sachs and Rosen;
Steve Phillips Design; Hearst
Publications; Conde Nast;
Fairchild Publications; Ziff-Davis;
Montcom Publications; Grey
Communications; T.V. Guide;
McGraw-Hill; Black Enterprise;
New York Times; Village Voice;
McCaffery and Ratner; Dancer,
Fitzgerald; Gannett Publications;
Jonson Pedersen Hinrichs &
Shakery; Peat Marwick; Chase
Manhattan.

Color portfolio available upon
request.

© 1985 Yvonne Buchanan

Leslie Cabarga

258 West Tulpehocken Street
Philadelphia, Pennsylvania 19144
(215) 438-9954

Once again and forevermore
representing himself! After
fifteen years, still providing
creative solutions to your design
problems, still making your
deadlines, still avoiding meat
and dairy products!

286

Daryl Cagle

17 Forest Lawn Avenue
Stamford, Connecticut 06905
(203) 359-3780

FAX/Telecopier service.

Clients include: Avon Products;
Ballantine Books; *Fortune;
Forbes; Family Circle; Sesame
Street; Electric Company;*
Scholastic Publications; *Muppet
Magazine;* Childrens Television
Workshop; Henson Associates;
Keds; Hasbro-Bradley;
McDonalds; Libby Glass;
Anchor Hocking; Thermos;
Union Underwear; Playskool;
Binney and Smith; CBS Toys;
Armitron; Timex.

Member: Graphic Artists Guild;
          Society of Illustrators.

Wende L. Caporale

Studio Hill Farm
Route 116
North Salem, New York 10560
(914) 669-5653

Clients:

Reader's Digest, Guideposts, Tennis Magazine/
Tennis Buyer's Guide, St. Martin's Press,
Doubleday/The Literary Guild, Connecticut
Magazine.

Member Graphic Artists Guild

Kye Carbone

241 Union Street
Brooklyn, New York 11231
(718) 802-9143

From left to right, top to bottom:

1. Japanese Samurai. The New Age Journal.

2. Chapter Opener for Computer Annual. John Wiley and Sons.

3. Portrait of Charles Darwin. Unpublished.

4. Portrait of Franz Kafka. Chelsea House Publishers.

5. Portrait of Robert Browning. Chelsea House Publishers.

6. Krakatoa Earthquake of 1883. M.D. Magazine.

7. Portrait of Nancy. Unpublished.

Other credits include:

The New York Times, Newsday, Business Week, Forbes, Simon & Schuster, Harper & Row

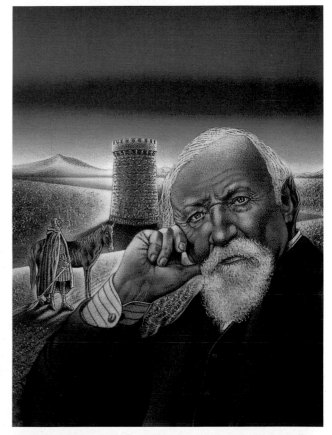

Peter Cascio

317 East 18th Street (5C)
New York, New York 10003
(212) 228-6876

Illustration and design

Member Graphic Artists Guild

Margo Chase
Design

120 South Sycamore Avenue
Los Angeles, California 90036
(213) 937-4421

Lettering and Design

Clients Include:
Bullock's
Bullock's Wilshire
CBS Entertainment
Dailey and Associates
Dancer, Fitzgerald, Sample, Inc.
Fattal & Collins
Hakuhodo Advertising, Inc.
Herald Examiner
J. Walter Thompson
Motown Records
NBC
Snyder Advertising
UCLA Extension
UCLA Medical Center
Warner Bros. Records
Wells, Rich, Greene/West

Anatoly Chernishov

3967 Sedgwick Avenue, #20F
Riverdale, New York 10463
(212) 884-8122

Partial Client List: AT&T, Bantam Books, Equitable Life
Assurance Soc., Home Insurance, Mercedes-Benz,
Merrill Lynch, Metropolitan Life Insurance, New York
Magazine, Panasonic, Philip Morris.

Member Graphic Artists Guild.

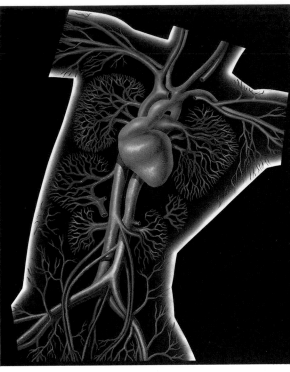

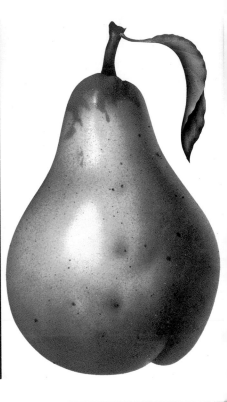

Joseph Ciardiello

2182 Clove Road
Staten Island, New York 10305
(718) 727-4757

Clients include: A.B.C., Fortune, McCaffrey & McCall,
Sports Illustrated, Exxon, Business Week, Atlantic,
Franklin Library, Psychology Today, New York Magazine,
Ziff-Davis, C.B.S. Publications, Science '85, Changing
Times, Steve Phillips Design, Random House,
Datamation, Signature, Reader's Digest Books.

Work Exhibited: Society of Illustrators Annuals, Print
Magazine, Graphis Annual, Society of Publication
Designers, Art Directors Annual Exhibit, American
Illustration 3

Member: Graphic Artists Guild
Society of Illustrators

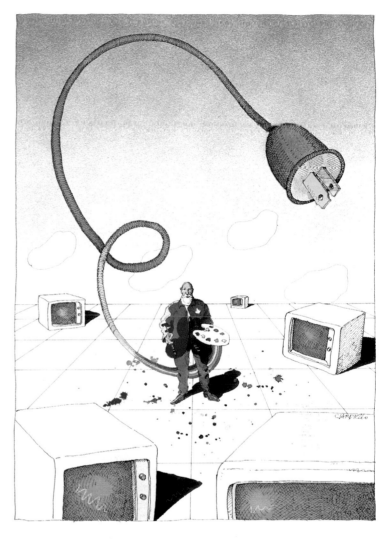

UP FROM DOWN UNDER

You are, perhaps, familiar with the problem: the color that was a perfect match when it was surrounded by white paper now looks absolutely WRONG because it is surrounded by another color that changes it completely…

This is annoying when it happens to a printed piece, but interesting when it happens to people. It happened to me. In another country, I've discovered (although I'm the same person I always was), the background I'm now in makes apparent those things that weren't apparent before.

I come from Australia. (Please, no jokes. Besides, I tell some of my own…later.) In Australia, I never thought that I was particularly Australian (I don't play tennis, I've given up swimming, and I don't drink beer: it's a wonder I wasn't <u>deported</u>.) But living in New York, I realize that I'm a lot more Australian than I thought.

Take pencil holders, for example. You won't believe this, but it's true: Americans store your pencils in a completely different way than Australians do, with a whole different <u>attitude</u> than Australian artists. While a coffee tin will suffice for an Australian, Americans put pencils in specially designed pencil holders.

I think of art departments at home: the too-short-and-stubby-to-use pencils and paint-stiffened brushes in old treacle tins, the cow-gum erasers added to in many idle moments so that they are now obscene lumps, the two-mile hike to the nearest xerox machine, the way half-finished projects have built up around the edges of the rooms until you can hardly see the <u>walls</u>, let alone the fading Milton Glaser poster.

I am generalizing with such confidence because I have done what might be termed "research." When I first hit these shores I registered at a freelance agency as a freelance artist, and it turned out to be an excellent way of seeing firsthand the way art departments work over here.

I was surprised at the difference. These art departments were <u>neat</u>. They were <u>organized</u>. Things got done quickly, efficiently. I love the way Americans say: "We <u>deliver</u>," meaning not pizza or Chinese takeout, but rather, "We're upright, noble, and trustworthy. We do what we say we're going to do."

Australians tend to chuckle at such things as electric erasers, electric staplers, sonic pen cleaners, and high-density plastic sheets to cut on. That's not to say that you couldn't go into an art supply shop over there and stock up on a whole lot of high-tech goodies. It's just that the Australian <u>mentality</u> is not high-tech.

I think this is partly because (do I dare bring our convict beginnings into this?) we have this vision of ourselves as people who <u>make do</u>, who <u>cope</u> with whatever adversity sets in front of us—be it drought or flood or clogged rapidograph—with that tough, pioneer fighting spirit that got us where we are today.

The feeling is that it's a bit sissy to have to rely on anything other than your own two hands and native wit. An example from our folklore: A Cobb & Co. (famous Australian stagecoach company) driver was once asked by a lady passenger if he'd ever been caught in a bushfire. Yes, he had. Horrified, the lady asked him how he'd escaped alive.

"Well, ma'am," the driver replied, "I tied a billy full of water to the back axle. Then I drove like 'ell through the fire. When I reached the safety of the boundary gate, that billy was on the boil and ready for tea!"

Maybe the myth is true, maybe we do come through when the going gets tough. But since most of the time, for Australians, the going isn't at <u>all</u> tough, no one knows.

Unfortunately, though, this national heritage is coupled with a less harmless trait—apathy. This is the famous "she'll be right" attitude; a glorious, reckless laziness that extends even beyond personal safety:

Passerby (seeing a tiger snake moving periously close to the foot of a resting sundowner): "Hey there, mate, look out! There's a snake near your foot!"
Weary sundowner (continuing to lie at rest): "Which foot, mate?"

Australia is like a delinquent child—you both love it and despair over it. I firmly believe that these national failings I've mentioned numb creative people and are the reason so many of them leave. And once they are away, once they are in the real world, there are no excuses any more. No more: "Well, it's good—for us."

Don't get me wrong. I love Australia dearly—so much that I hate to admit that it has any failings

continued on page 306

Bill Cigliano

Represented by:

Eileen Moss
333 East 49th Street
New York, New York 10017
(212) 980-8061

In Chicago call: (312) 878-1659

Clients include: Abbott Laboratories, AG Becker, Arista Records, Ballantine Books, Beatrice Foods, Borg-Warner, Burry, Canteen Corporation, Chicago Magazine, Gerber, Kraft Foods, Lanier, MacMillan Publishers, Mazola, Miller Breweries, Morton Salt, International Harvester, New York Art Director's Club, Procter & Gamble, Rockwell International, Seagrams Distilleries, Seven-Up, Standard Oil, Stanley Hardware, Strohs Breweries, Success Magazine, United Airlines, US Gypsum, Viking Penguin Books.

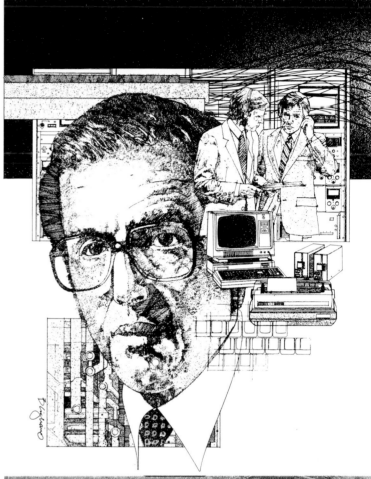

Bob Clarke

46 Washburn Park
Rochester, New York 14620
(716) 442-8686

No sizzle, slogans, or hype—Just a top quality job
on time.

Clients:

ABC, NBC, Showtime, Allied Corporation, Kodak, Mobil Corporation, Grey Advertising, Hutchins Young & Rubicam, McCann-Erickson, Rumrill-Hoyt, J. Walter Thompson, Good Housekeeping Magazine, Mechanix Illustrated, Outdoor Life, Parade, Reader's Digest, Rolling Stone, Avon Books, Dell, Dodd-Mead, Doubleday, The Literary Guild, McGraw-Hill, Warner Books, Calhoun Collectors' Society, The International Museum, Atlantic Records, London Records

Member Graphic Artists Guild

© 1985 Bob Clarke

Bob Clarke

46 Washburn Park
Rochester, New York 14620
(716) 442-8686

No sizzle, slogans, or hype—Just a top quality job on time.

Clients:

ABC, NBC, Showtime, Allied Corporation, Kodak, Mobil Corporation, Grey Advertising, Hutchins Young & Rubicam, McCann-Erickson, Rumrill-Hoyt, J. Walter Thompson, Good Housekeeping Magazine, Mechanix Illustrated, Outdoor Life, Parade, Reader's Digest, Rolling Stone, Avon Books, Dell, Dodd-Mead, Doubleday, The Literary Guild, McGraw-Hill, Warner Books, Calhoun Collectors' Society, The International Museum, Atlantic Records, London Records

Member Graphic Artists Guild

Bob Conge
28 Harper Street
Rochester, New York 14607
(716) 473-0291

Michael K. Conway

316 East 93rd Street
New York, New York 10128
(212) 369-0019

Illustration and design

Clients include:

Grey Direct
McCaffrey & McCall
Muir Cornelius Moore
R. Greenberg and Associates
Serino, Coyne and Nappi
NBC Local Graphics
Chicago International
  Film Festival
Logos
Scholastic Inc.
James Smith Studio
Campus Life
Scott Foresman Publishing Inc.
Advertising Age
Crain's Chicago Business

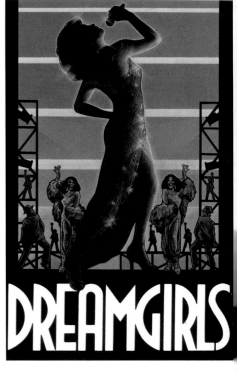

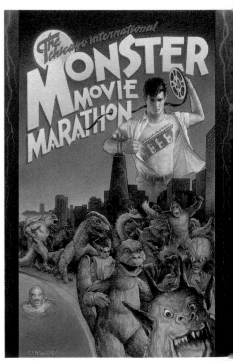

MICHAEL
CONWAY
ILLUSTRATION

316 EAST 93ᴿᴰ ST.
N.Y.C., NEW YORK 10128
[212] 369-0019

Laura Cornell

118 East 93rd Street
New York, New York 10128
(212) 534-0596

Clients have included:
TRW; Price Waterhouse; The
Franklin Library; New York
Magazine; Savvy; Seventeen;
Redbook; Parents; Cuisine;
Houghton Mifflin; Dodd, Mead;
D.C. Heath; Macmillan.

Art credits, clockwise from top:
Vogue Knitting Magazine
Sports Illustrated
Splendid Tours Corporation
Gannett
Money Magazine

Member Graphic Artists Guild

Dan Cosgrove

405 North Wabash
Chicago, Illinois 60611
(312) 527-0375

Illustration and Graphic Design

Clients include: Culligan, Kraft,
Busch Gardens, McDonald's,
Shasta, Beatrice, Seven-Up,
Playboy, Time, Nashville
Magazine, Pillsbury, S.C.
Johnson, Kellogg's, Star-Kist,
Sears, Baskin-Robbins, Adolph
Coors, Anheuser-Busch, United
Airlines, G.D. Searle, Northern
Telecom, Heileman Brewing,
Household Finance, and Allstate.

Member Graphic Artists Guild.

Greg Couch

112 Willow Street, #5A
Brooklyn Heights, New York
11201
(718) 625-1298

Clients have included: Time
Inc., Ziff-Davis Publishing,
Forbes, Paper Moon Graphics,
Games Magazine, Viking-
Penguin, Hearst Publishing,
Scholastic, New York Times
Promotion, RCA Records,
McGraw-Hill, Dorritie & Lyons,
Pfizer, Avis, McCaffery-McCall,
Sandoz, Rolf Werner Rosenthal.

Member Graphic Artists Guild

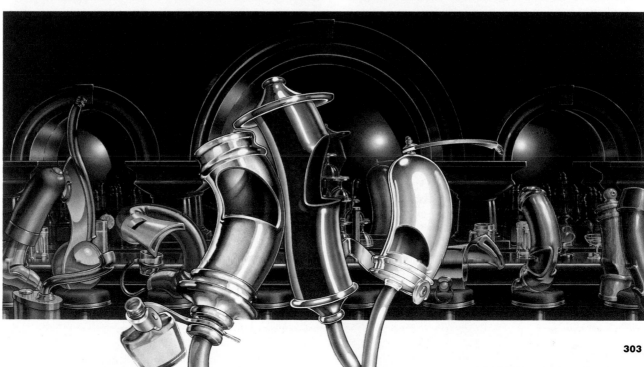

303

John Craig

Route 2, Box 81
Soldiers Grove,
Wisconsin 54655
(608) 872-2371

Telecopier Available.

Represented by:
Carolyn Potts
& Associates
(312) 935-1707

Collage

Clients include: *Advertising Age; American Way; A+;* Anheuser Busch; *AT&T;* Bell & Howell; *Better Homes;* Cenergy Corp.; *Chicago;* Cracker Jack; *Cuisine; Datamation; 80 Micro;* Encyclopedia Britannica; Franklin Mint; *Games;* Henry Weinhards; *Horizon;* Jonson, Pederson, Hinrichs & Shakery; *Inc.; Money; Moviegoer; Minnesota Monthly;* Natural Light; *New Age; Newsday;* Pantheon Books; *PC World; Philadelphia; Playboy; Popular Computing;* Ruby Street Cards; *Runner;* Scott, Foresman & Co.; *Sesame Street;* Sheraton; Sieber McIntire; *Success;* 7-UP; *Sunshine; Texas Monthly;* 13-30 Corporation; *Time; TWA Ambassador.*

Member Graphic Artists Guild. For additional samples in different techniques, see American Showcase #7 & #8.

D.L. Cramer Ph.D.

Medical/Biological Illustration
10 Beechwood Drive
Wayne, New Jersey 07470
(201) 628-8793

Illustrations for. Time, Sports Illustrated, Reader's Digest, Natural History, Runner, Science Digest, Med. Publishing, Modern Medicine, Hospital Medicine, RN, Cardiovascular Medicine, Drug Therapy, The Journal of Respiratory Diseases, Crown Publishing, McGraw-Hill, S. Karger, Grolier, CIBA, Hoffman-LaRoche, Searle, Bristol-Myers, Winthrop Labs, Pfizer, Schering,

Burroughs Wellcome, Mead Johnson, William Douglas McAdams, Lawrence Charles and Free, Chiat Day, Chedd Angier, Benton and Bowles, N.W. Ayer.

Teaching: Currently Director of the Human Anatomy Labs NYU School of Medicine.

Exhibitions: Society of Illustrators Invitational, AIGA. Graphic Artists Guild Show.

Affiliations: Society of Illustrators (Past President) Graphic Artists Guild, AAAS, New York Academy of Sciences, USPF, ADFPA.

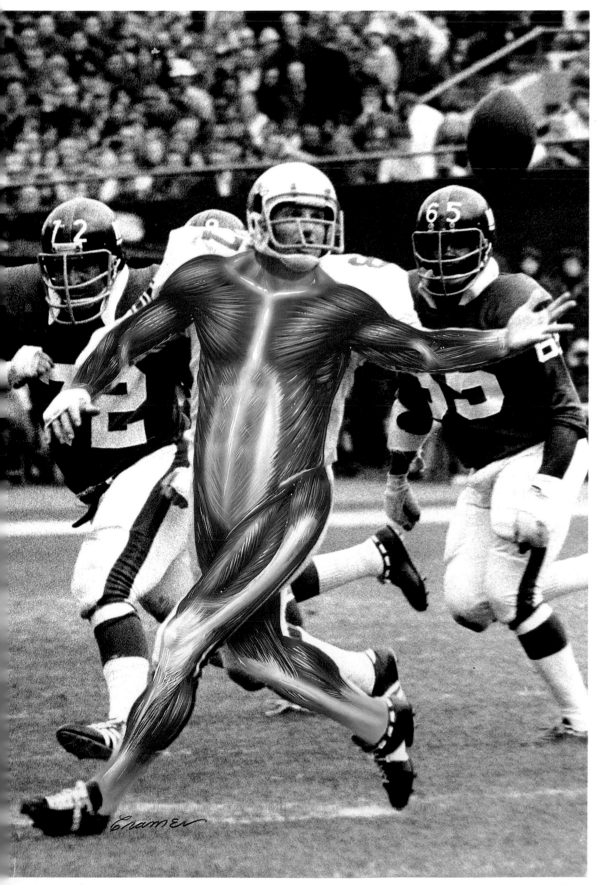

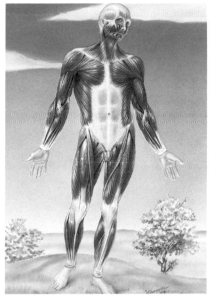

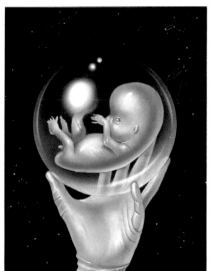

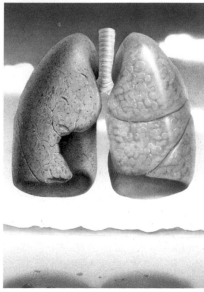

continued from page 294

at all. But it has, and it is when one is out of the country that one can see them most clearly.

If I didn't have a certain crazy, naive Australian optimism, I would never have taken on a haphazardly designed magazine on the condition I keep it exactly the way it was and expect to keep any integrity as a designer. On the other hand, there's a certain pride that, as the first person on the new staff, I was able to produce anything at <u>all</u> while setting up the whole art department.

In Australia, I'd be given some sort of consolation prize for that. But I don't want any consolation prizes. Here in New York one is constantly aware of—exhilarated by—so much excellence and striving after excellence. And that's what I want to be part of, what I came to this country for.

Jane Eldershaw
Art Director
New Woman Magazine
New York City

Glossary:

BILLY— tin can with handle used in the bush to boil water and to do other cooking, over an open fire.

SUNDOWNER— tramp who travels the outback, sometimes looking for work, more often simply showing up at the end of the day at a station (ranch) to ask for food and perhaps shelter, hence the name.

Gary Crane
Illustration/Design
523 West 24th Street
Norfolk, Virginia 23517
(804) 627-0717

Represented by:
Elizabeth A. Sheehan
Philadelphia, Washington
Baltimore, Richmond
(301) 233-7511

Clients include:
J. Walter Thompson
Doremus
Lawler Ballard
Barker Campbell & Farley
Davis & Phillips
Group III
Scholastic
Virginia Stage Co.
Vansant Dugdale
Earle Palmer Brown
RCA Records, Du Pont
Virginia Opera Assoc.
General Electric

John Hickey
Illustration/Design
523 West 24th Street
Norfolk, Virginia 23517
(804) 627-0717

Represented by:
Elizabeth A. Sheehan
Philadelphia, Washington
Baltimore, Richmond
(301) 233-7511

Clients include:
Lawler Ballard
Barker Campbell & Farley
Davis & Phillips
Seamark Inc.
Gordon & Michealson
Hahnemann University
Wasserman Studio
Gurdarian Assoc.
Red Cross
Boghigian & Macuga

Bob Crofut

225 Peaceable Street
Ridgefield, Connecticut 06877
(203) 431-4304

Clients have included:

The Franklin Library, The Reader's Digest, N.B.C., Ballantine Books, M.G.M., Outdoor Life, Avon Books, New American Library, Field and Stream, Seventeen, The Easton Press, Guideposts, Prentice-Hall, Pocket Books, M.B.I., The International Chiropractors Association, N.Y.U. Medical Center, Viking Penguin, The Heritage Press, Minwax Corporation, Geer DuBois, Hoechst Pharmaceutical, Yankee Magazine, Medical Economics, N.M.S. Pharmaceutical Co., The Medical Laboratory Observer, Science 83, William Douglas McAdams, Bristol Babcock Corporation, The Exxon Corporation, and I.B.M.

Collections:
New Britain Museum of American Art
Permanent Museum of American Illustration of
The Society of Illustrators
New York University Medical Center

Awards:
16 Society of Illustrators
Award of Excellence from the New Jersey
Art Directors Club

Member:
Society of Illustrators

Bob Crofut

225 Peaceable Street
Ridgefield, Connecticut 06877
(203) 431-4304

Books:
Society of Illustrators Annuals 21, 22, 23, 25, 26 and 27
Art Directors Index Volume 10
American Showcase Volumes 7, 8 and 9
A Treasury of Outdoor Life
100 Years of American Illustration
Contemporary Graphic Artists

Please call for large format color brochure. Next day
portfolio service to most U.S. cities.

"The most beautiful thing we can experience is the
mysterious. It is the source of all true art and science."
Albert Einstein

Howard Cruse

88-11 34th Avenue
Apartment 5-D
Jackson Heights, New York 11372
(718) 639-4951

Top left:
Client: South Central Bell
Agency: Luckie & Forney Inc.

Top right:
Client: Blue Cross/Blue Shield of Alabama
Agency: Luckie & Forney Inc.

Bottom left:
Editorial illustration
Heavy Metal Magazine

Bottom right:
Editorial illustration
Starlog Magazine

Tom Curry

In Austin: (512) 443-8427

N.Y. Rep: Eileen Moss &
Associates
333 East 49th Street
New York, New York
10017
(212) 980-8061

Southwest Rep: Art Rep Inc.
(214) 521-5156

Chicago Rep: Skillicorn &
Associates
(312) 856-1626

Partial client list includes:
Adweek, American Airlines,
Anheuser-Busch, Apple
Computer, Boy's Life, California
Dreamers, Continental Airlines,
Del Taco, Dr. Pepper, Emergency
Medicine, Exxon, Financial World,
Frito-Lay, Holiday Inn, Holt
Caterpillar, IBM, M Bank, Murine,
Newsweek, Northwest Mall,
Paul Broadhead & Associates,
Random House, Selsun Blue,
Southwest Airlines, Steak & Ale,
Stroh's Brewing Co., Texas
Instruments, Texas Monthly,
The Cleveland Plain Dealer,
The Dallas Times Herald.

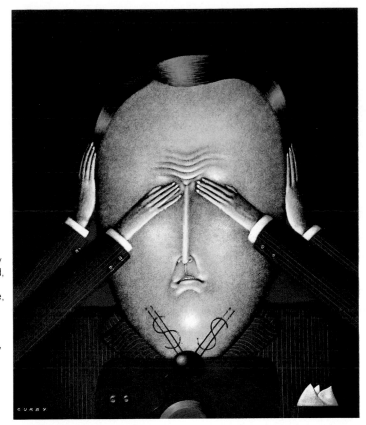

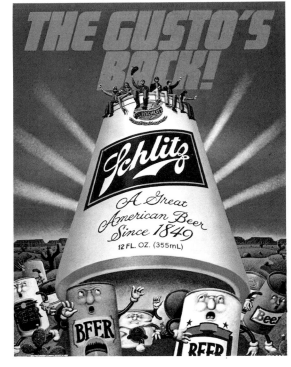
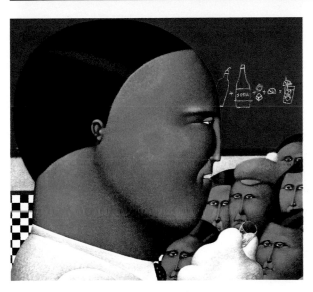

Margaret Cusack

Margaret & Frank & Friends, Inc.
124 Hoyt Street in Boerum Hill
Brooklyn, New York 11217
(718) 237-0145

Margaret Cusack has been creating fabric illustrations and props since 1972. Hand-stitched samplers and soft sculpture are also an important part of her award-winning portfolio. Timing and pricing are comparable to other more conventional illustration styles. Given normal time, pencil sketches and a fabric paste-up of the work are shown before the final sewing begins. A 4″ × 5″ transparency of the artwork is included in the one fee.

Having worked as an art director and graphic designer herself, Cusack is aware that extra-tight deadlines are often the norm. Most assignments are completed within two weeks, although there have been one-week and even overnight deadlines.

Clients include: American Express, Howard Johnson's, Peek Freans, Singer, Perrier, Texaco, Mobil, Thai Airlines, Shenandoah Musical, The New York Times, Reader's Digest, HBJ, RCA, Ortho, Ciba-Geigy.

AMERICAN EXPRESS

HOWARD JOHNSON'S

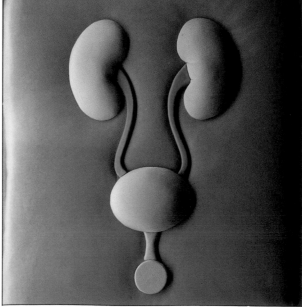

EMERGENCY MEDICINE MAGAZINE

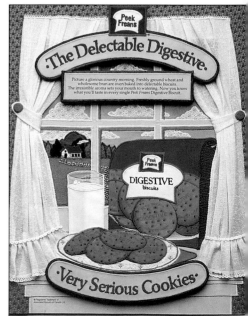

ASSOCIATED BISCUITS

Tom Cushwa

303 Park Avenue South
Apartment 511
New York, New York 10010
(212) 228-2615

Clockwise from top left:
Cover illustration for Family Weekly for an article on
   cosmetic dentistry.
Illustration for American Diabetes Association.
Illustration for Business Week.
Self Promotion.
Illustration for Business Week.
Book cover for John Wiley Publishers.

Other Clients include: New York Times, Ad Forum,
Calderhead & Phin Advertising, Dell Publishing,
Financial World, Games Magazine, Grove Press,
Medical Economics, Scholastic, Harcourt Brace
Jovanovich, Pinnacle Books, Workman Press.

Member Graphic Artists Guild.

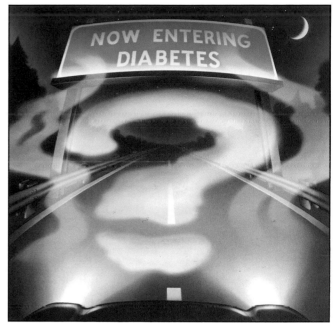

Sid Daniels

12 East 22nd Street #11B
New York, New York 10010
(212) 673-6520

Acrylic Paintings

Clients have included:
Ann Taylor
Arista Records
Audio Times
Burke Foods Ltd.
Fiorucci Inc.
Gross Townsend Frank Inc.
Harbor Publishing Inc.
Hospitality Investment Inc.

Jacqueline Cochran Inc.
Marshall Fields
Rockshots Inc.
Video Business

Works exhibited in:
The New Illustration, a publication from the exhibition
 held at the Society of Illustrators, 1982
Featured illustration on this page seen in movie *Tootsie*
'Elan' Warwick Hotel Philadelphia
Eddington and Worth New York

Inspiration 122
Creativity 10
Desi Graphics Design USA 1981
Art Directors Club 60th Annual 1981
Art Direction Magazine 1979
Look Magazine 1979

Member Graphic Artists Guild

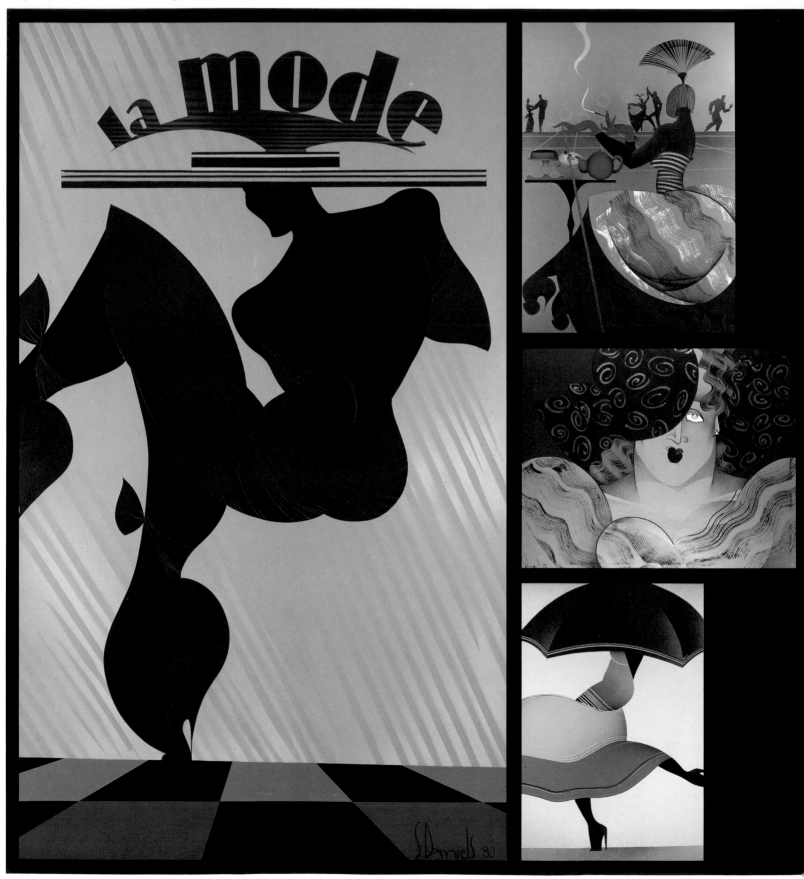

Michael Davis

1461 Rock Springs Circle
Atlanta, Georgia 30306
(404) 872-5525

Member Graphic Artists Guild

PARTIAL CLIENT LIST:

Ally & Gargano
American Express
N W Ayer
Backer & Spielvogel
BBDO
Louis Benito Advertising
Dunkin' Donuts
Ensslin & Hall Advertising
Ford Motor Company
HBO
IBM
ITT
McDonald & Little
Nikon
Ogilvy & Mather
Pringle Dixon Pringle
Sawyer Riley Compton
Searle & Company
Six Flags
J. Walter Thompson, USA
Walker & Associates
Young & Rubicam

EXHIBITED:
Permanent Collection
Grand Central Galleries

CREDITS:
Wynton Marsalis reference from
a photograph by David Leifer.

Sally Ride reference from a
photograph by Bob Cerri.

Represented by:

Sheryle Propst

P.O. Box 1583
Norcross, Georgia 30091
(404) 263-9296

Member SPAR

Telecopier Service Available

Dazzeland Studios

Visual Music!

Studio Hotline: (801) 355-8555

Reps:

Los Angeles: Joanne Hedge (213) 874-1661

San Francisco: Mary Van Damme (415) 433-1292

Chicago: Joel Harlib (312) 329-1370

New York: Jerry Leff Associates, Inc. (212) 697-8525

Atlanta: The Williams Group (404) 873-2287

DOD ELECTRONICS

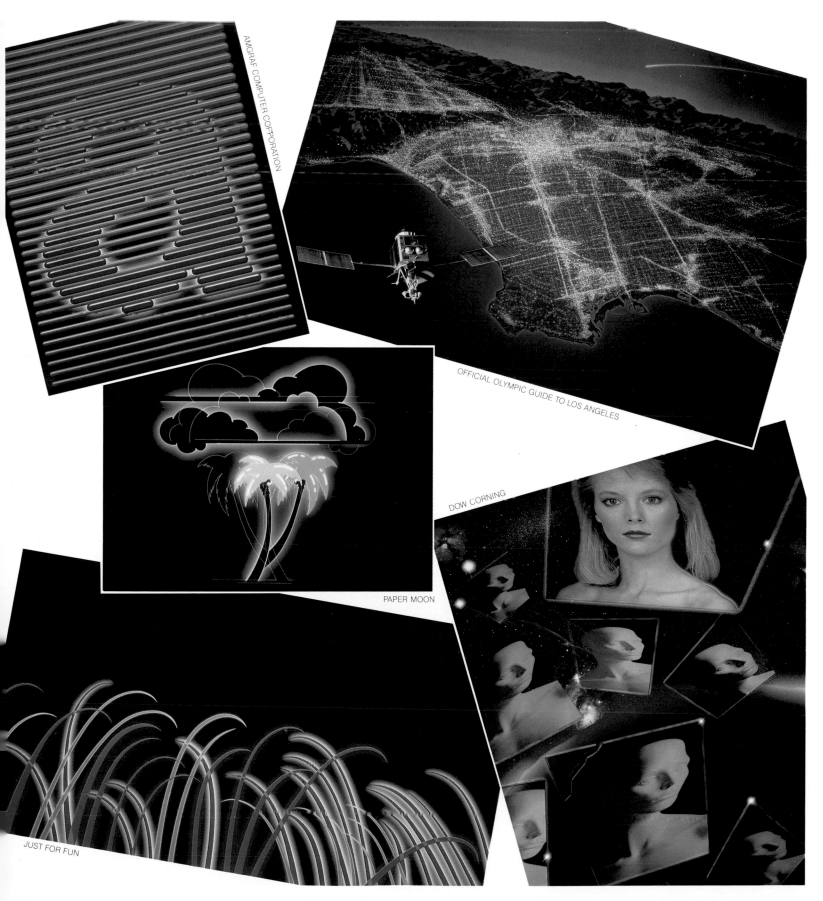

AMGRAF COMPUTER CORPORATION

OFFICIAL OLYMPIC GUIDE TO LOS ANGELES

DOW CORNING

PAPER MOON

JUST FOR FUN

Michael Dean

5512 Chaucer
Houston, Texas 77005
(713) 527-0295

Clients include: Shell, Exxon, Pennzoil, Pepsi, Pizza
Hut, Drilco, Texas Monthly, Houston City Magazine,
Outside Magazine, Astroworld, Waterworld,
Southwestern Bell, Houston Natural Gas, Goldlance,
First City Bank, U.S. Home, Gemcraft Homes,
Houston Gamblers, Republic Bank, ComputerCraft,
13-30 Corporation and Gulf Oil Corp.

Telecopier available.

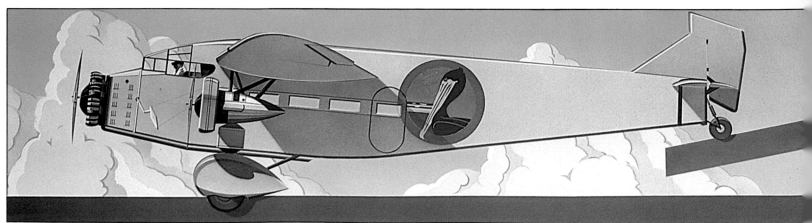

Roger T. De Muth

2627 De Groff Road
Nunda, New York 14517
(716) 468-2685 or
Office (315) 423-4075

Represented in western NY state by:
Linda Oreman:
(716) 244-6956

Work has appeared: American Showcase volume 8, Page 90. Society of Illustrator's #23, 27. American Illustration #4.

Clients have included:
American Greetings, Chase-Lincoln First Bank, Doubleday, Eastman Kodak; Harcourt-Brace Jovanovich; Gould's Pumps; Instructor Magazine; Itek; Fay's Drugs; Organic Gardening Magazine; Rochester Telephone; Hutchins Y&R; Rubbermaid; Gannett Newspapers, First Federal Banks, Xerox.

Illustrations, clockwise from top right: Logo for peanut butter company; Cover for Newcomer's Guide to Rochester; Logo image for Food Co-op; "Litigator," and Top left- "My ant in Florida," from visual pun series.

Glenn Dodds
392 Central Park West
New York, New York 10025
(212) 679-3630

Clients include: New York Telephone, MCA, Radio
Shack, AT&T, Avis, IBM, Borg-Warner, Intercontinental
Hotels, Hush Puppies, Selchow & Righter, TIE, Heinz
Publications: New Woman, Forbes, American
Heritage, Glamour, MD, Venture, Woman's Day,
Datamation, New American Library, U.S. News,
Reader's Digest.

Glenn Dodds

392 Central Park West
New York, New York 10025
(212) 679-3630

Clients include: New York Telephone, MCA, Radio
Shack, AT&T, Avis, IBM, Borg-Warner, Intercontinental
Hotels, Hush Puppies, Selchow & Righter, TIE, Heinz
Publications: New Woman, Forbes, American
Heritage, Glamour, MD, Venture, Woman's Day,
Datamation, New American Library, U.S. News,
Reader's Digest.

Doret/Smith Studios

12 East 14th Street #4D
New York, New York 10003

Michael Doret

(212) 929-1688

Specializing in the design and integration of letter and image—from trademarks and logotypes to posters.

Additional work may also be seen in American Showcase #s 4-8.

Michael Doret and Laura Smith are independent artists. They do, however, work together as a studio on larger scale projects.

Represented in the Southwest by:
Liz McCann
(214) 871-0353

Clockwise from top right:
Cover for TIME Magazine
Book covers for Vintage Books
   and Pinnacle Books
Logo for Red Rock Records
Illustration for Sweepstakes ad
   for Time-Life Books
Cruise poster for Royal
   Carribean Lines
Cover of Morgan State
   University publication

Member Graphic Artists Guild

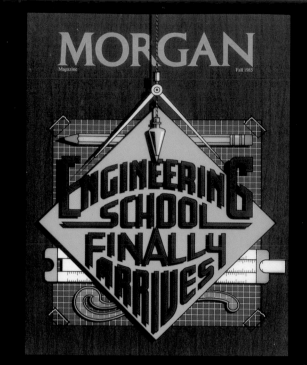

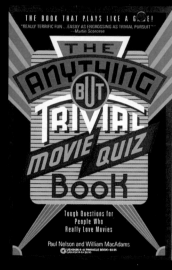

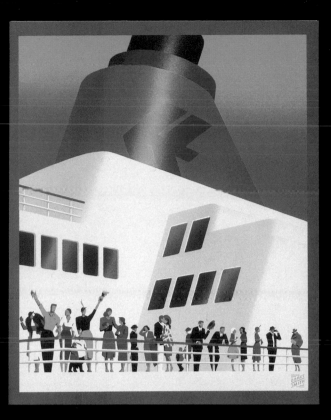

Doret/Smith Studios
12 East 14th Street #4D
New York, New York 10003

Laura Smith
(212) 206-9162

Specializing in designed, graphic illustration.

Additional work may also be seen in American Showcase #s 7 and 8.

Laura Smith and Michael Doret are independent artists. They do, however, work together as a studio on larger scale projects.

Clockwise from top right:
Poster for the cruise liner Europa
Illustration for advertisement for
    SunQuenchers sunglasses
Illustration for book cover,
    "VOICES" for Stein & Day
Cover of promotional publication
    for The Wall Street Journal
Double page spread in
    Manhattan Inc. magazine
Full page illustration for Meetings
    & Conventions magazine

Member Graphic Artists Guild

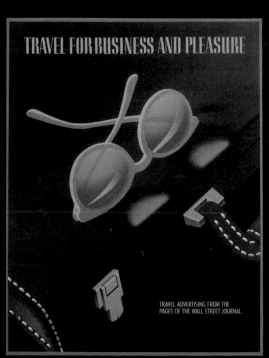

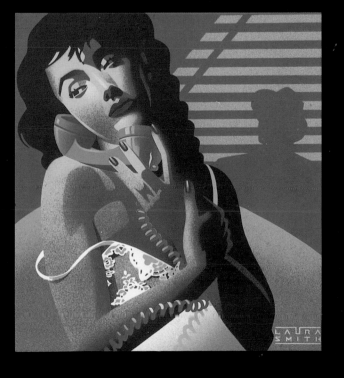

LAURA SMITH

Lawrence W. Duke

Star Route Box 93
Woodside, California 94062

Studio:
1258 Folsom Street
San Francisco, California 94103
(415) 861-0941

Regan Dunnick

110 Lovett #202
Houston, Texas 77006
(713) 523-6590

Representatives:

Dallas—Debbie Bozeman
  (214) 526-3117
Northeast—Patricia Lindgren &
  Audrey Lavine (212) 929-5590
Houston—Diana Diorio
  (713) 266-9390

A partial client list:
Continental Airlines
N.C.A.A.
Frito-Lay
American Airlines
Southwestern Bell
Taco Bell
Texas Monthly
Macy's
Dai Nippon—Japan
Simpson Paper
St. Louis Museum of Fine Arts
G.E.
Nashville Network

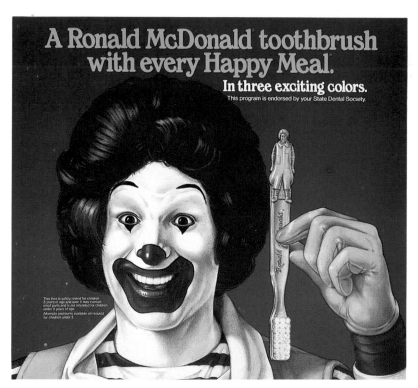

Eaton & Iwen, Inc.

307 North Michigan Avenue
Chicago, Illinois 60601
(312) 332-3256

Represented in New England by Ella (617) 266-3858

Represented in the South by Dale Eldridge
(314) 361-6360

Gil Eisner

310 West 86th Street
New York, New York 10024
(212) 595-2023

Partial client list:

Adweek, American Heritage,
AT&T, East/West Network,
Forbes, Newsweek, The New
York Times, Personal Computing,
Popular Computing, Science
Digest, Time-Life, The
Washington Post, WBMG
(Walter Bernard/Milton Glaser)
Video Review, W. B. Grace
Company.

**Carmela
Emerson**
110-20 71st Avenue, #519
Forest Hills, New York 11375
(718) 793-2113
Illustration/Design

Pegasus poster available at
Bruce McGaw Graphics 1-800-221-4813.

Bill Farnsworth
P.O. Box 653
New Milford, Connecticut 06776
(203) 355-1649

Marybeth Farrell

320 West 76th Street, Apartment 2G
New York, New York 10023
(212) 799-7486

Graphic Artists Guild member.

Matt Faulkner
435 Clinton Street
Brooklyn, New York 11231
(718) 858-1724

Member of the
Graphic Artists Guild

Jeff Feinen

Represented by Andy Badin
and Associates
246 East 46th Street
New York, New York 10017
(212) 986-8833

Clients include: Grey
Advertising; Snow's Soups;
Holly Farms; Wyler Foods;
Robert Towers Advertising; U.S.
Open; Margeotes-Fertita &
Weiss; Godiva Chocolates;
Estée Lauder; Wyse Advertising;
Smuckers; Mary Ellen Preserves;
Ogilvy and Mather; Chemlawn;
Denton and Dowles; Proctor and
Gamble; McCaffrey & McCall;
Hartford Insurance; Fisher-Price
Toys; Bolling-Peterson; Goldome
Bank for Savings; Manufacturers'
and Traders' Trust Company;
Marine Midland Bank; Wilson
Farms; Agway Insurance;
J.C. Penney; Faller, Klenk and
Quinlin; Lockport Savings Bank;
The Permanent Savings Bank;
Kobs & Brady; Glen Grant Scotch
Whiskey; Sudler & Hennessey;
Parke-Davis; William Estee;
Nissan Trucks; William Douglas
McAdams; Roche
Pharmaceuticals; Hausman
Productions; IBM; Doremus and
Company; The Atlantic Group;
First Eastern Securities;
Marschalk; Citibank; Robert
Becker Advertising; Mead-
Johnson; Leber-Katz Partners;
Campbell's Soups; Longman
Publishing.

Member Affiliations:
Graphic Artists Guild
Society Of Illustrators

**Stanislaw
Fernandes**

(212) 533-2648

Art and Design for
advertising, editorial
and corporate assignments

"THE SHOCK APPEAL
Stanislaw Fernandes takes
realism and turns it into
the surreal, often in a
bizarre and shocking manner.
Illustrations from highly
detailed medical subjects
to far out science fiction
all somehow accommodate
themselves to his dramatic,
eye-popping style.

Fernandes approaches his
subjects with hard-edged,
literal, realistic terms.
From his formal training in
architecture and the fine
arts, he achieved a
discipline that he
transforms to graphic design
and illustration. But it
is his creative eye and
natural talent that elevates
a craft to an art form.

Fernandes was way ahead of
the current trend toward
visual shock appeal in
advertising and illustration.
For some time he has been
creating high-tech,
futuristic impressions of
everyday subjects for major
advertising agencies,
magazines and other highly
visible clients."
COMMUNICATION WORLD

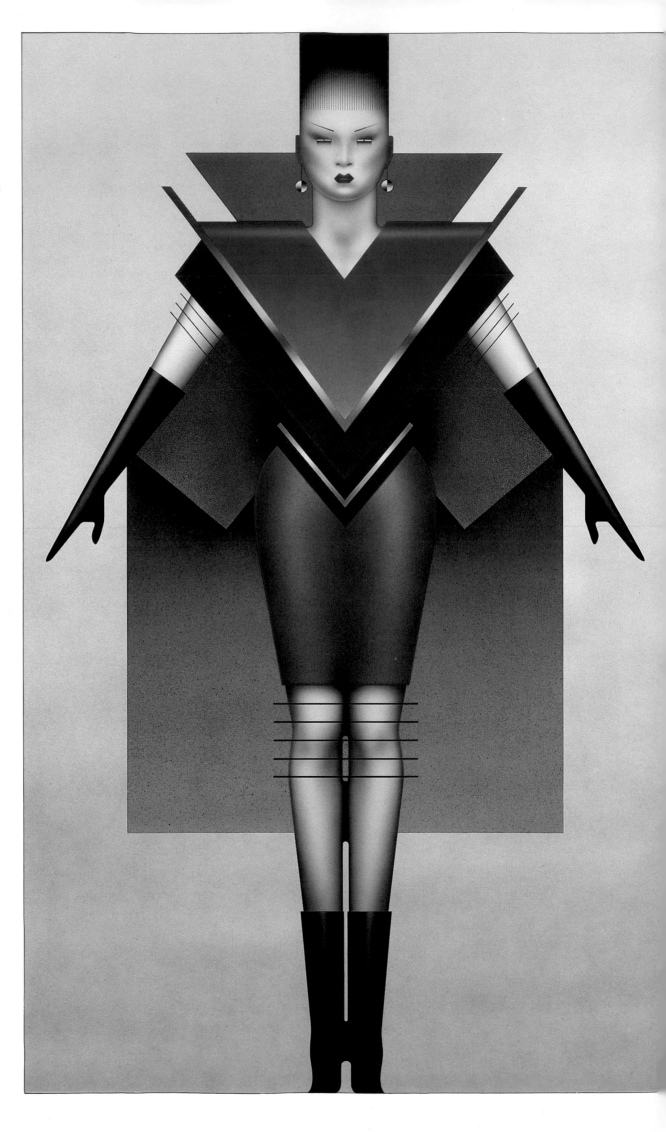

Mike Fisher

3811 General Pershing Street
New Orleans, Louisiana 70125
(504) 827-0382

Illustrator and designer

Black and white illustration (right) achieves two goals.
An all purpose one color usage, plus a rich full color
look when hand-dyed.

Color slide portfolio available upon request.

Irving Freeman

145 Fourth Avenue
New York, New York 10003
(212) 674-6705

A complete graphic studio specializing
in Typographic & Packaging Design.

Member Graphic Artists Guild.

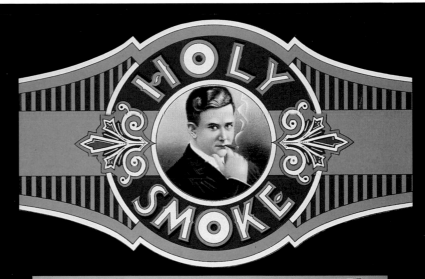

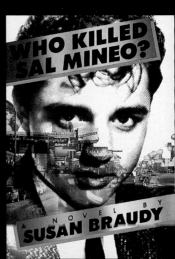

Funtastic Studios

Michael Waldman

Illustrator-Designer
506 West 42nd Street
New York, New York 10036
(212) 239-8245

Clients include:
King Features syndicate
Warner Communications
Clairol
NCR
Goodyear
Digital Effects
Kron Chocolate
Blimpie
The United States Department
  of Agriculture
Hasbro
Romulus Productions
EcuMed
Planet Publications
Peter Pan Industries
Digital Review Magazine
Video Games Magazine
Cannon Mills
Acme United
Danceskin
Mortgage Banking Magazine
Harrison Communications
Public Relations Journal

Member Graphic Artists Guild.

Cynthia Gale

229 East 88th Street
New York, New York 10128
(212) 860-5429

Cut paper & collage illustration.

Clients include: Leber Katz Partners Advertising,
Chemical Business, Chemical Engineering, Savvy,
and Travel Weekly magazines, WLIB radio,
Mummenschanz show posters and Social Education
Journal.

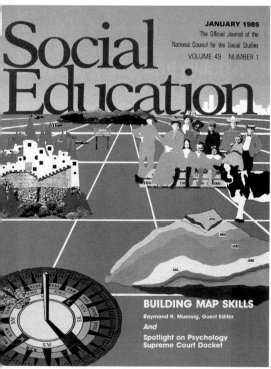

Michael Garland

78 Columbia Avenue
Hartsdale, New York 10530
(914) 946-4536

Clients include:
J. Walter Thompson, AT&T,
Hartford Insurance, IBM,
General Electric, The United
States Marines, Forbes
Magazine, Ladies' Home
Journal, Estée Lauder,
Macmillan Press, Ziff-Davis,
Muir Cornelius Moore, Frequent
Flyer, Cosmopolitan, Parents
Magazine, Putnam Publishing
Group, Games Magazine, Avon,
McGraw-Hill, Industry Week,
Runner's World Magazine,
Ashe/LeDonne, Crown
Publishers, Scribner/Atheneum
Publishers, Fawcett
Publications, Bantam Books,
Ballantine Books, Random
House, ABC, N W Ayer, NBC,
Emergency Medicine
Magazine, Woman's Day,
Lederle Drugs.

Work Exhibited in
Illustrators 23, 24, 25, 26, 27
Communication Design Show 1983
The Original Art Show 1981, 1983
Pratt Alumni Show 1985
American Artist Magazine
National Competition 1985

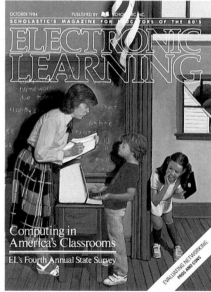

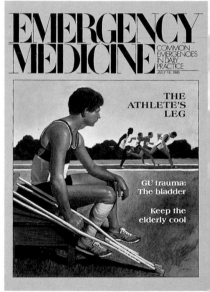

Carol Gillot

62 West 13th Street
New York, New York 10011
(212) 243-6448

Represented by:
Milton Newborn & Associates
135 East 54th Street
New York, New York 10022
(212) 421-0050

Clients Include:
AT&T; Sony; Lederle Labs;
Marion Labs; Pfizer; Ortho;
Popular Computing; Time;
Fortune; Science Digest; PC;
Warner Communications; Smith,
Klein, Beckman; OUP; Merck;
Squibb.

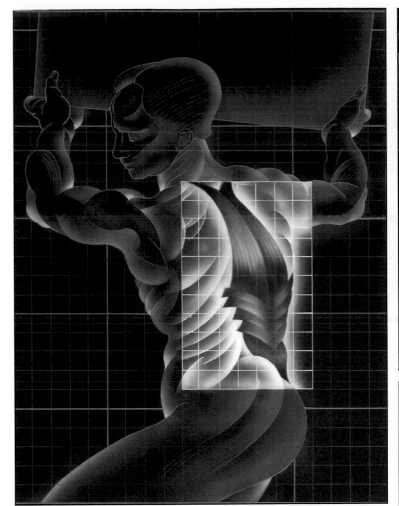

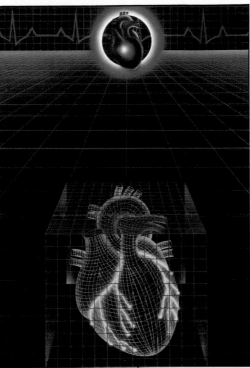

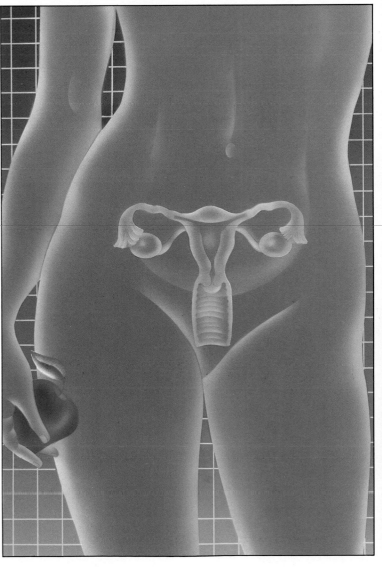

Susan Gray

42 West 12th Street
New York, New York 10011
(212) 675-2243/(212) 787-5400

Clients include:
Young & Rubicam; J. Walter Thompson; McCann-Erickson;
D'Arcy-MacManus Masius; Grey Advertising; Milton
Glaser Inc.; Johnson & Johnson; Grand Union;
Elizabeth Arden; Oil of Olay; New American Library;
Simon & Schuster; Doubleday; Harcourt Brace
Jovanovich; Forbes; Business Week; Fortune.

Member Graphic Artists Guild
Member Joint Ethics Committee   Susan Gray © '86

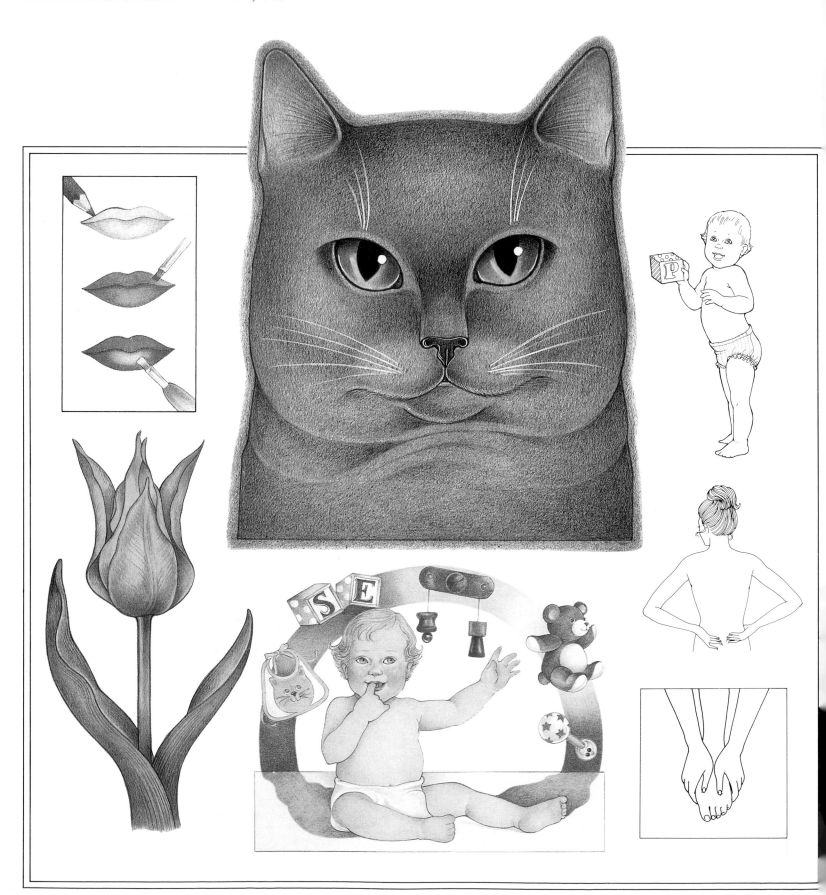

**Don Grimes
Design, Inc.**

3514 Oak Grove
Dallas, Texas 75204
(214) 526-0040

When carefully conceived,
properly designed and skillfully
executed, a word can be worth
a thousand pictures.

Here are a few choice words
from the vocabulary of Don
Grimes.

Marika Hahn

11 Riverside Drive
New York, New York 10023
(212) 580-7896

Clients include:
Benton & Bowles, Inc.
Ted Bates
Ogilvy & Mather
Revlon
Avon
Estée Lauder
Simon & Schuster
Bloomingdale's

Cosmopolitan
Family Circle
Glamour

Member of the Graphic Artists Guild

Deborah Ann Hall

05-28 65th Avenue
Studio 6B
Forest Hills, New York 11375
(718) 896-3152

American Broadcasting Company
National Broadcasting Company
Home Box Office
T.V. Guide
MGM/UA
Grey Advertising, Inc.
McCaffery and McCall, Inc.
Marino, Coyne & Nappi
Pearlman/Rowe/Kolomatsky

Van Brunt Co.
Polydor Records
WNEW-TV
Circle In The Square Theatre
The New York Times
The Village Voice
Discover
Fifth House Productions, Inc.

Member of
The Society of Illustrators, AIGA,
and The Graphic Artists Guild

Joan Hall

155 Bank Street
Studio H954
New York, New York 10014
(212) 243-6059

Two and Three Dimensional Collage Illustration

Clients include: IBM, Remy Martin, Baileys, Estée
Lauder, NYNEX, Warner Bros., International Paper
Company, WPLJ, Hoechst Fibers Industries, RCA, The
New York Times, Omni, Time, L'Express, Vogue,
Gourmet, Popular Computing, Video Pro, New York,
Seventeen, Redbook, McCalls, T.V. Guide, Psychology
Today, Emergency Medicine, Book-of-the-Month Club,
Warner Books, Avon Books, Random House, Simon &
Schuster, Dell Publications.

Publications and Exhibitions:
Print Magazine, Art Direction, The Society of Illustrators,
The New York Art Directors Club, The Society of
Publication Designers, The A.I.G.A., Graphis.

Instructor of "Collage & Assemblage"
The School of Visual Arts, New York

Member Graphic Artists Guild.

RACTER

NEW YORK MAGAZINE

FOOD & WINE MAGAZINE

TORTILLA FLATS

Tom Hallman
8 South 17th Street
Allentown, Pennsylvania 18104
(215) 776-1144

Art credits, clockwise from top left:
Series for Diagnostics Design, a research and development firm.
One of fourteen covers in DRAGONTALES series, Signet Books.
PERSONAL DEMON, Signet Books.
Cover story on global terrorism, Inside Magazine.
Article on rape, Nursing Magazine.
Series for Diagnostics Design, a research and development firm.

Clients have included: Avon Books, Ballantine, Berkley,
Dell, New American Library, Fortune, Nursing
Magazine, Playboy, Rodale Press, Arm & Hammer,
Armstrong, Commodore Computers, Lewis & Gilman,
Rorer Pharmaceutical, SmithKline Corp., W.R. Grace,
CA Annual, Society of Illustrators Annual.

hallman.

Glenn
Harrington

Represented by

Barbara Gordon
Associates

165 East 32nd Street
New York, New York 10016
(212) 686-3514

Barbara Gordon
Associates Ltd
165 East 32 Street
New York, N.Y. 10016
212-686-3514

Laurel Harwood

239 Broadway · Suite 1350
New York, New York 10001
(212) 689-3515

Clients include: Johnson & Johnson; International
Games For The Disabled, St. Martin's Press, Walker
Publications; Simmon Boardman; Visual Information
Services; Carl Byoir.

Member of the Graphic Artists Guild

Bryan Haynes
1733 Ellincourt Drive
South Pasadena, California
91030
(818) 799-7989

Represented by:

Eldridge/Skillicorn & Associates
St. Louis: (314) 773-2242
Chicago: (312) 856-1626

Member of the Graphic Artist's
Guild

Steve Heimann

P.O. Box 406
Oradell, New Jersey 07649
(201) 345-9132

Clients include: AT&T; Bendix Corp.; Book-of-the-Month Club; Dominica Postal Service; DuCair Bioessence; Inter-Governmental Philatelic Corp.; Letraset; Life Styles Cosmetics; Medical Economics; Prentice-Hall Publishing; Prime Designs, Procter and Gamble; Random House; R.N. Magazine; S.C. Johnson and Son; Silver Burdett; Uganda Postal Service; Video Corp. of America.

Member Graphic Artists Guild

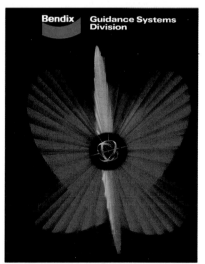

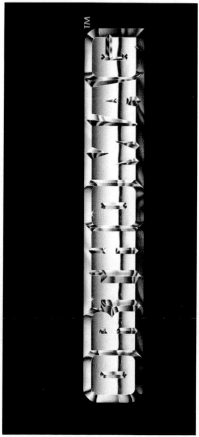

Richard High Design

4500 Montrose Suite D
Houston, Texas 77006
(713) 521-2772

Richard High creates typographic
solutions for architects, art
directors, graphic designers, and
direct corporate clients.

Our clients have included American
Express, Delan Int., Exxon USA,
Hewitt Associates, Interface Corp.
Original Appalachian Artworks,
Shell Oil Co., Steak & Ale, Steck
Vaughn, Tenneco, Texas Commerce
Banks, Texas Instruments, Texas
State Optical, 13-30 Corporation,
Wellcraft and Whataburger.

Additional samples or slides are
available upon request and refer
to American Showcase 7 and 8.
Call Richard High Design for unique
approaches to advertising, design,
packaging and corporate identity.

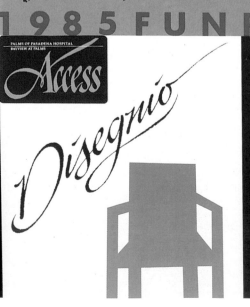

Christopher Hopkins
Illustration

2932 Wilshire Boulevard, Suite 202
Santa Monica, California 90403
(213) 828-6455

Represented by:
Chicago—Joni Tuke
(312) 787-6826

New York—American Artists
(212) 682-2462

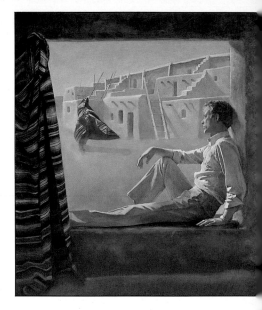

Mitch Hyatt

WINDTUNNEL
4171 Buckingham Court
Marietta, Georgia 30066
(404) 924-1241

Clients Include:
Anheuser-Busch Inc.
Audio-Technica USA Inc.
Bloomingdale's
Burger King Inc.
Ciba-Geigy
Dole
Gold Bond Building Products
Grit
Hardees
Letraset USA Inc.
Maxwell House
Mattel Toys Inc.
Mountain Dew
Nestlés
New Jersey Bell
Pepsi
Peachtree Software
Special Olympics
Stride Rite
TDK
Union Carbide
Wang Computers
Welch's Foods Inc.

Izumi Inoue

311 East 12th Street
New York, New York 10003
(212) 473-1614

From left to right, top to bottom

1. Business Week: Collision Course
2. Science Digest: Food for Thought
3. Self-Promotion: High Voltage
4. WABC-TV New York: 1984 Fall Party Invitation
5. HBO: Quick Sketch
6. HBO: Quick Sketch

Other clients include:
PolyGram Records, Fortune, New York Times, St. Martin's Press, Macmillan, AT&T, Southern New England Telephone Co. and U.S. News.

Member Graphic Artists Guild.

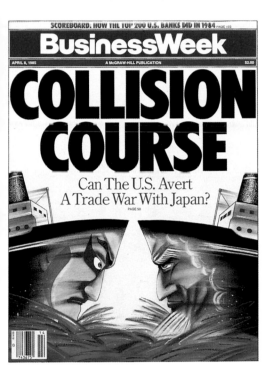

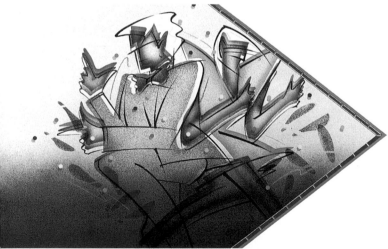

Seth Jaben

New York City
(212) 260-7859

Clients include:

Time Inc.
IBM
Random House
New York Times
Peat-Marwick Corporation
McGraw-Hill
Muir Cornelius Moore
Cognitive Systems
Adweek
Webb Company

13-30 Corporation
E.G. Smith Inc.
Psychology Today
Scholastic Publishers
Dish Is It Tile Inc.
New York Magazine
Penthouse
Playboy
Science Digest
Optima Design Inc.
Rodale Press

COGNITIVE SYSTEMS INC.

COGNITIVE SYSTEMS INC.

COMPUTER WIDOW

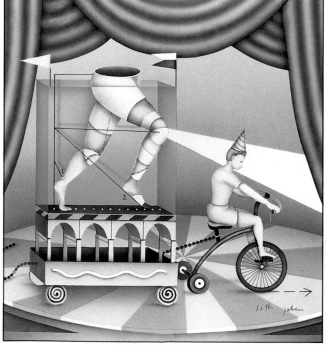

POSTGRADUATE MEDICINE

Jay
17858 Rose Street
Lansing, Illinois 60438

(312) 849-5676

Represented by:

Chicago: Steven Edsey
& Sons, Inc.
(312) 474-9704

Atlanta: McLean Represents
(404) 221-0798

Dallas: Trudy Sands
(214) 634-9538

B.E. Johnson/Concept One

366 Oxford Street
Rochester, New York 14607
(716) 461-4240

Los Angeles:
Robert Jones
10889 Wilshire Boulevard
Los Angeles, California 90024
(213) 208-5093

Technical and Astronomical Art, Optical and
Mechanical Effects, Industrial Design.

© 1985 B.E. Johnson

Realities…Illusions…Intensities…
Subtleties…Sensations…Perceptions…
The elements of any image.

The illustrator's advantage is in the combination.

To obtain a photograph where none can be had—
to evoke a feeling where none has existed.

For, in illustration, the impossible *is* attainable…
it just takes a little longer.

Member: Graphic Artists Guild, IAAA,
Society of Illustrators

James A. Michener's "SPACE"
CBS/Paramount/Random House
AD Marie-Christine Lawrence

Grumman X-29A
Greenstone & Rabasca
AD Stephen Bartholomew

RCA "Our Space Program"
Needham Harper Worldwide
AD Steve Singer

Gentex Helmets
Lewis Keegan & Straus
AD Hugh Keegan

Spread:
NASA Fine Art Collection
Director: Bob Schulman

Technology
and the art to understand it.

Nature
and the art to appreciate it.

The unknown
and the art to experience it.

DESIGNERS
ILLUSTRATORS
CONSTRUCTORS

Randy Jones

323 East 10th Street
New York, New York 10009
(212) 677-5387

Clients Include: Ogilvy & Mather, The New York Times,
Bantam Books, Inx Syndicate/United Features,
Playboy Magazine, Discover Magazine, National
Lampoon, Business Week, Beverage Media,
International Herald Tribune, Hartford Courant, Heavy
Metal, Regents Publishing, Market & Med Decisions,
Twilight Zone Magazine.

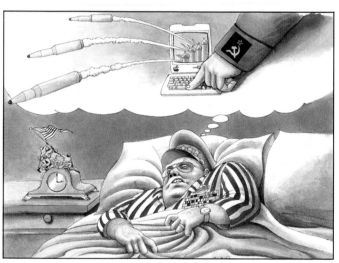

Paula Joseph

147 West 13th Street
New York, New York 10011
(212) 242-6137

Member Graphic Artists Guild

Barbara Kelley

555 10th Street
Brooklyn, New York 11215
(718) 788-2465

Represented in San Francisco
by: Janice Stefanski
(415) 928-0457

Credits: Society of Illustrators
Science Fiction/Fantasy Art
Show, Creativity 14, Creativity
15, The Portfolio Show '85.

Clients Include: The Wall Street
Journal, New York Times,
Business Week, Forbes,
Chronicle Books, Reader's
Digest Books, Audio Magazine,
Success Magazine, American
Express, New York Life
Insurance, Bank America, Dow
Jones, Conrans, Diamond
Shamrock Corp., Dun &
Bradstreet Inc., Woody Pirtle,
McCann Erickson, Ogilvy &
Mather.

Bonnie S. Knabel

Berkeley Court
Brookline, Massachusetts 02146
(Boston)
(617) 232-1291

Illustration and Design

Clients include: W.R. Grace Co., New England Life Insurance Co., Boy Scouts of America, Cahners Publishing Co.: Electronic Business Magazine and Purchasing Magazine, Bernard Hodes Adv., Codex Corporation, A.V. (Audio Visual) Design Associates, California Museum of Science and Industry: Kinsey Museum of Health and The Aerospace Museum,

Peckham Corporation, Florida Bureau of Real Estate and Retirement, J. Makowski Associates, Inc. (energy consultants).

Slide portfolio available upon request.

Member: Graphic Artists Guild

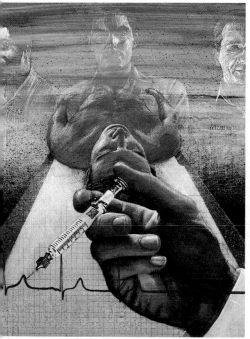

367

Vladimir Kordic

35351 Grovewood Drive
Eastlake, Ohio 44094
(216) 951-4026

Agents:

Woody Coleman
(216) 621-1771

Joel Harlib
(312) 329-1370

4x5 Portfolio available.

Terry Kovalcik

48 West 20th Street
New York, New York 10011
(212) 620-7772   (201) 345-2155

Are your teeth older than you are?

Your teeth should be the most durable part of your entire body.

Anthropologists have found human teeth millions of years old which have survived just about everything nature could throw at them. Yet millions of Americans are walking around with teeth that are literally on their last legs, in bodies which are in relatively good shape.

Once the teeth age prematurely, the likelihood is that the rest of the body will not be far behind.

Doctors have known for a very long time that healthy teeth are essential to good general health. Not only do healthy teeth facilitate chewing and good digestion; unhealthy teeth undermine your health by pumping toxins and bacteria into your entire system.

Dr. Charles Mayo, one of the founders of the internationally famous Mayo Clinic, knew the definite connection between bodily health and oral health when he stated, "Preventive dentistry can extend human life ten years."

He might also have mentioned something about the quality of that extended life. It's no fun not being able to bite into a piece of fruit or an inch-thick sirloin for the rest of your life. Or to hold back a smile because you're ashamed of the way your teeth look. Or be afraid to kiss someone you love because your breath won't convey the intended message.

A second chance for your teeth.

It doesn't have to be that way.

It may surprise you to know that there are people well into their eighties with almost perfect teeth and gums. Some of these were endowed by nature, and by their mouth chemistry, with stronger teeth than you have. Others, if the truth be told, spent a lot of time caring for their teeth, and have done so since childhood. In some cases, it's a little bit of both.

But if you weren't lucky, and you feel that nature short-changed you, take heart. It's not too late. There are a lot of things that modern dentistry can do to put your mouth back in good shape.

Bleeding gums and loose teeth.

Puffy, bleeding gums and loose teeth are part of a condition commonly known as pyorrhea, now called gum disease or periodontal disease, which is responsible for most of the teeth lost after adolescence. The good news is: it is preventable. Its progress can be arrested, and if it's not too far gone, it can even be reversed with proper treatment and care. When that happens the teeth not only look younger, they are in fact healthier, and stronger. They can do more work, so you chew better. Your gums don't bleed, and your breath smells sweeter.

Our hygienists and periodontists use modern techniques which actually promote firm healthy gums and bones. They are very understanding, and can teach you how to care for your teeth, and keep them healthy and beautiful.

The important thing is that you do something about the condition as soon as possible, before surgery becomes necessary, or you lose teeth.

It's never too late.

If you have lost teeth, you may be inclined to think that the game's over, and you are relegated to removable dentures for the rest of your life.

Maybe not.

It's possible you may be a good candidate for dental implants. The American Dental Association recognizes modern dental implants as a viable alternative to dentures. We specialize in implants here at Omnicare, and many patients who used to wear dentures are now enjoying beautiful, permanent, natural-looking, natural-feeling teeth.

Implants are not indicated for everybody, but they may turn out to be just right for you.

Remember, when you lose a tooth, the teeth on either side lose support. With the loss of even a single tooth, certain changes occur in the mouth. The teeth on either side of the extracted tooth may drift and become mobile.

On the other hand, the tooth opposite the missing tooth may grow into the created space. Both changes result in the alteration of the way you bite and chew.

Thus, a tooth that is not replaced can cause havoc on one whole side of your mouth. An implant could solve the problem. A number of excellent modern bridges could, too. It's important—not to let the problem drag on. The sooner we can help you, the happier you are going to be.

Fear is the enemy.

And don't be afraid, whatever you do.

There are many ways for us to help you control pain, anxiety, and stress. Stress kills. It not only destroys teeth through clenching and grinding. It also causes heart attacks.

Cosmetic dentistry.

Even if your teeth are healthy, you may not feel they are your best asset, aesthetically speaking. Discoloration, stains, chips, shape and profile deficiencies, gaps, and so on may be making you unhappy. If so, you will be delighted to hear that new space-age materials and new techniques make it possible to improve the appearance of your teeth.

We have specialists at Omnicare who are expert in these techniques. When treatment is completed, you will have a hard time remembering how your teeth used to look. And people won't know what has happened, they'll just notice that you look more attractive.

A team of specialists under one roof.

One of the nice things about Omnicare is that you don't get shunted around the city from one specialist to the next. Our specialists are all located in what you might think of as a medical center for the mouth and teeth.

More different specialties are represented here than you—or anyone—are ever likely to need. Our staff is trained to use the latest in modern dental equipment—including a panoramic x-ray machine which does the job while cutting down on approximately 95% of the radiation.

Orthodontics and Orthognathics.

Omnicare can provide a wide spectrum of services, from easy prevention techniques and nutritional counseling to complex reconstructions requiring implants, crowns and fixed bridges. In addition to orthodontics (straightening teeth) for adults and children, we offer orthognathics (correction of jaw and facial deformities). We have a special team, consisting of an orthodontist, oral surgeon, and reconstructionist, who work together to rebuild mouths with severe problems.

House calls.

In special situations, when patients are bedridden or housebound, we extend ourselves to make house calls. We say "Omnicare." We mean it.

The next step.

The next step is up to you.

Whatever the condition of your teeth, a great deal can now be done to beautify, strengthen, and support them. The ravages of time can be repaired. So don't think you have to go on living with a mouth full of superannuated teeth that are on a downhill spiral.

You don't have to settle for a future of periodontitis, bone atrophy, loose and missing teeth and the kind of problems your grandparents had no choice but to put up with.

The kind of modern dentistry we practice is not inexpensive, but it represents the best investment you can make in the health of your mouth, and your entire body.

So call for an appointment for a consultation or second opinion, or send in the coupon.

Don't think of it as an ordinary visit to the dentist. This is special. Think of it as time invested in your health and future well-being. You're going to like it here.

So will your mouth.

OMNICARE
A second chance for your teeth.
745 Fifth Avenue, New York, N.Y. 10151 (212) 355-6122
☐ Please send me your informative booklet. ☐ Please call me.

Name _____
Address _____
City _____ State or County ____ Zip ____
Telephone _____

Karin Kretschmann

323 West 75th Street
New York, New York 10023
(212) 724-5001

Clients include: General Foods,
Seagrams, Time Inc.,
Manufacturer's Hanover Trust,
CBS, Bozell & Jacobs Inc., Grey
Advertising, Smucker's, Saatchi
& Saatchi Compton, AT&T,
Ogilvy & Mather, American
Express, TWA, TV Guide.

Member: Graphic Artists Guild
Society of Illustrators

Shannon Kriegshauser

Represented by:

Ceci Bartels Associates

11 Jefferson Road
St. Louis, Missouri 63119
(314) 961-1670
Telecopier:
(314) 961-1859

Studio:
(309) 565-7110
Studio Telecopier:
(309) 565-4339

Peter Kuper
250 West 99th Street, #9C
New York, New York 10025
(212) 864-5729

Partial Client List:
Revlon
Forbes
Venture
Village Voice
New York Times
Plain Dealer
Viking/Penguin
Holt, Rinehart and Winston
Travel and Leisure
Games Magazine
P.C. Week
GEO
New York Magazine

Member: Graphic Artists Guild

Joan Landis

(PRIMITIVE)

represented by:

Darwin Bahm
6 Jane Street
New York, New York 10014
(212) 989-7074

Bob Bahm
(216) 398-1338

Bruce Langton

53145 Kinglet Lane
South Bend, Indiana 46637
(219) 277-6137

Advertising, editorial and product illustration with versatility in concept and technique.

Clients have included: Gulton Electra-Voice, Inc.; International Harvester; Lowe's, Inc.; Coachmen Industries, Inc.; Holiday Rambler; Miles Laboratories, Inc.; Saturdays in California; Mastic Corporation; Wheel Horse; United States Auto Club; Crown International, Inc.; Audio-Technica.

Member Graphic Artists Guild

James A. Lebbad

1133 Broadway, Room 1229
New York, New York 10010
(212) 645-5260

Typography and Design

Clients include:
Arista Records; Ballantine Books; Berkley Publishing
Group; Grey Advertising; Home Box Office; McCaffrey
& McCall; NBC; Ogilvy & Mather; Saatchi & Saatchi
Compton; Scholastic; Wunderman, Ricotta & Kline;
Young & Rubicam.

Clockwise from Upper Right:
Logo for Berkley Publishing, Title treatment for ABC
Movie, Type illustration for Reader's Digest, Illustrated
logo for Guest Quarters Hotels, Logo for MGM/UA
Video, Title treatment for Ballantine Books, Title
treatment for Berkley Publishing.

© James A. Lebbad 1986

Member Graphic Artists Guild

Jared D. Lee
2942 Hamilton Road
Lebanon, Ohio 45036
(513) 932-2154

Telecopier Service

Animation Reel Available.

Brad Pallas, *Woman's Day Magazine*
"Anyone who can draw woman for *Woman's Day* and make the Editor, Art Director and reader all laugh out loud has got to be great!"

Judy Purvis, Young & Rubicam
"Jared is a real pro, even though he does live in a place like Ohio."

Peter Marcionetti, Duffy & Shanley
"Jared brings something to the party."

Phil Kimmelman, KCMP Productions Ltd.
"Having Jared Lee design for animation has not only produced some of the best animated spots I have worked on, but his contributions beyond the call of duty in continuity and concept have made working with him a unique and delightful experience!"

Larry Corey, RM&D, Inc.
"Jared seems to know exactly what I'm thinking. I can't even do that!"

Member Graphic Artists Guild.

1. McGraw-Hill
2. Wells Rich Greene
3. Arbitron Ratings Co.
4. *National Wildlife Magazine*
© Jared D. Lee Studio, Inc. 1986

JARED LEE

PHOTO: KRAMER PHOTOGRAPHY

1.

2.

3.

4.

Robert S. Levy

(212) 986-8833

Represented by:
Ann & Andy Badin
835 Third Avenue
New York, New York 10022

Clients: DDB, O&M, B&B,
Marsteller, IBM, GTE, Digital
Equipment Corporation,
Armstrong.

Howard B. Lewis

140 West 22nd Street
New York, New York 10011
(212) 243-3954
(718) 875-2762

Member Graphic Artists Guild

Clients include: Avon Books;
Business Week; Dancer,
Fitzgerald & Sample;
D'Arcy, McManus & Masius;
Diversions Mag.; Dun's
Business Month; Eastern
Review; High Tech Mktg.;
Ketchum Adv.; Metropolitan
Life Ins. Co.; Metropolitan
Transit Authority; Money Mag.;
New York Mag.; New York
Times; Scholastic; Successful
Meetings Mag.; 13·30 Corp.;
W. B. Doner & Co.; Working
Mother; U.S. Air; Ziff Davis

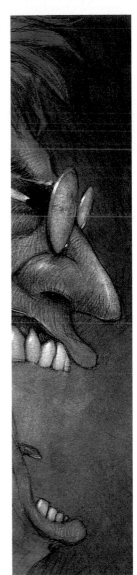

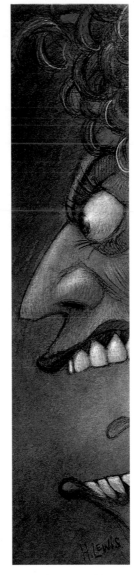

Little Apple Art

Marshall & Richie Moseley
409 Sixth Avenue
Brooklyn, New York 11215
(718) 499-7045

Illustration, graphic design and lettering.

The studio of Marshall and Richie Moseley provides services to advertising agencies, corporations and publishers. Clients have included: Polaroid; National Airlines; American Airlines; Coca-Cola; Parker Brothers; International Paper; Sheraton International; IBM; Continental Insurance; Ralston Purina; Holiday Inn; Thomas Cook; General Foods; NBC; CBS Records; WABC; GAB; Proctor & Gamble; Maxwell House; Dun & Bradstreet; Colgate-Palmolive; LILCO; Hearst Corporation; Independence Savings Bank; Union Savings Bank;

Random House; Dell; Ballantine; Harper & Row; *Parents* Magazine; *Changing Times; The New York Times*; Scholastic Publications; Book-of-the-month Club; Cloverdale Press; *National Wildlife* Magazine; *Independent Agent* Magazine; *Business Meetings* Magazine; Marvel Books; Doyle Dane Bernbach; N.W. Ayer; BBDO; Scali, McCabe, Sloves; Cunningham & Walsh; McCann-Erickson; Ted Bates; Compton Advertising; William Esty; Ogilvy & Mather; Dancer Fitzgerald Sample; Hutchins/Y&R; Doremus; Pearlman, Rowe, Kolomatsky; and others.

Additional samples available on request.

Member Graphic Artists Guild.

Al Lorenz

(203) 226-7674

Represented by: Carol Bancroft & Friends
185 Goodhill Road
Weston, Connecticut 06883

Clients include
Barton & Gillette; Batten, Barton, Durstine & Osborne,
Inc.; Benton & Bowles, Inc.; Charles F. Noyes;
Compton Advertising; Doremus & Company; Doyle
Dane Bernbach; Edward Larabee Barnes; Elton

Design; I.M. Pei & Partners; J. Walter Thompson; John
Carl Warnecke; Johnson-Burgee; Kenyon & Eckhardt;
Loucks/Atelier; Marcel Breuer Associates; Ogilvy &
Mather; Olympia & York; Perkins & Will; Scali, McCabe,
Sloves, Inc.; Skidmore, Owings & Merrill; Soskin/
Thompson Associates; Ted Bates Advertising; Wells,
Rich, Green, Inc.; Williamson, Picket, Gross Inc.;
Young & Rubicam.

Awards:
1983 Society of Illustrators—Certificate of Merit
1983 AIGA: Certificate of Excellence—Communication
  Graphics
1983 Silver Award: Advertising Club of Fairfield County
1983 Communication Arts Magazine: Award of Excellence

1984 Society of Illustrators—
  Certificate of Merit
1985 Art Directors Show—
  Silver Award

Author of:
Illustrating Architecture, 1985
Van Nostrand Reinhold Company, Inc.

Professor School of Architecture
Pratt Institute
Brooklyn, New York 11205

ROCKEFELLER CENTER MANAGEMENT CORPORATION   SOSKIN/THOMPSON ASSOCIATES

© Al Lorenz

381

Hal Lōse
designer & illustrator
533 West Hortter Street
Philadelphia, Pennsylvania 19119
(215) 849-7635

©1985

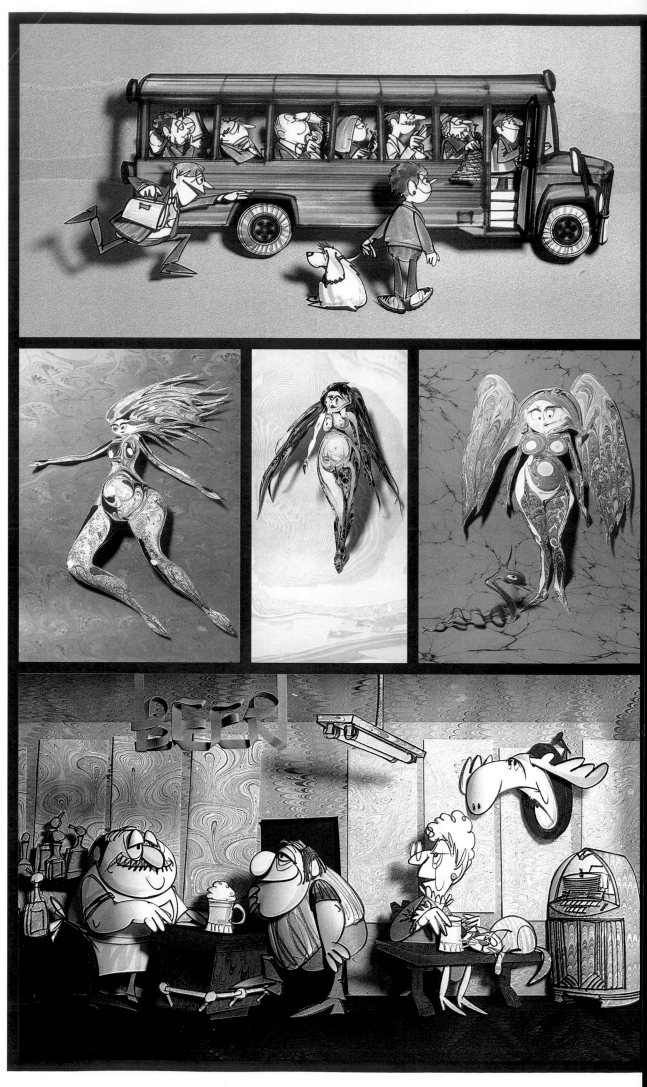

Rick Lovell, Inc.

860 Lakewind Court
Alpharetta, Georgia 30201
(404) 442-3943

Representatives:
Atlanta; The Williams Group
         (404) 873-2287
New York; Tricia Weber
         (212) 370-4486
Chicago: Tom Owen
         (312) 664-1665

Member Graphic Artists Guild

Telecopier in Studio
© 1985 Rick Lovell, Inc.
All Rights Reserved

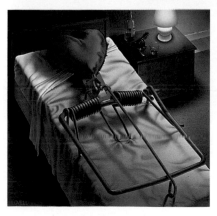

Dick Lubey

726 Harvard Street
Rochester, New York 14610
(716) 442-6075

Clients have included:

Bausch & Lomb
Blair/BBDO
Canandaigua Wine
The Doral-Eastern
The Dunlop-Phoenix
Executive Sports
Fader Jones & Zakardis
The Franklin Mint
Gannett
Georgia Pacific/Atlanta Golf
    Classic
The Honda Classic
Keystone Foods
Kodak
LPGA
Lady Keystone Open
Mazda Hall of Fame
    Championship
McDonald's Kids' Classic
Muscular Dystrophy Assoc.
Niagara Mohawk Power Corp.
NFL Properties
Oak Hill Country Club
Outdoor Life
PGA Championship
The Rochester International
Rochester Automobile Dealers
    Assoc.
Rochester Telephone
Rochester Gas & Electric
Rumrill-Hoyt
U. of R. Medical Center
Via Volvo
Westinghouse Communities Inc.
Xerox

Works exhibited in Illustrators
19, 20, 21, 22, 24, 25, 27.

Member Society of Illustrators.

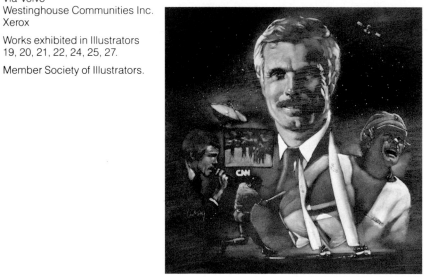

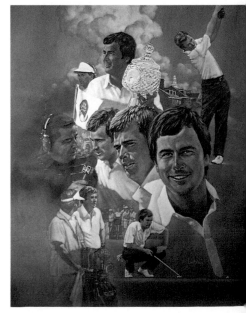

Dennis Luzak

Box 342
Redding Ridge,
Connecticut 06876
(203) 938-3158

Clients:

Time, Inc.
Ford Motor Company
Chrysler Corporation
General Motors Corporation
NBC
CBS
ABC
Burroughs Wellcome Corp.
McCall's Magazine
Ladies' Home Journal
Good Housekeeping Magazine
Redbook
Playboy
Sports Illustrated
Fortune Magazine
Forbes
Yankee Magazine
Changing Times
Random House
Reader's Digest Corporation
Simon & Schuster
New American Library
National Geographic Society
Franklin Mint
Xerox Corporation
Eli Lilly Corporation
Outboard Marine Corporation
International Paper Corporation
Consolidated Paper Corp.
Universal City Studios
Columbia Pictures Industries
Paramount Pictures Corporation
Time-Life Records
Warner Communications
Institutional Investor
Randolph Computer Corp.
General Electric
Air Canada
Borden Company
Lederle Pharmaceutical
Manufacturers Hanover Trust
First National Bank of Chicago
First National Bank of Boston
McGraw-Hill Publishers
Renault Corporation
RCA
United States Postal Service
ABI
Beechnut
Ayerst Pharmaceutical
Westwood Pharmaceutical
Ciba-Geigy
AmTrak
Schweppes
Colgate-Palmolive
Coca-Cola
Levi Strauss
Foote, Cone & Belding
DuPont Corporation
McCaffrey and McCall
Dancer Fitzgerald Sample
William Douglas McAdams
Grey Advertising
AGK/NY

Member:
Society of Illustrators
Graphic Artists Guild

ANNUAL REPORT/STEVEN JACOBS, FULTON & GREEN

385

Greg MacNair

Represented by:

Ceci Bartels Associates

111 Jefferson Road
St. Louis, Missouri 63119
(314) 961-1670

Telecopier:
(314) 961-1859

Studio: (314) 721-3781

Clients include: Anheuser Busch; Brown Shoe, Inc.;
Ralston Purina; Six Flags; Southwestern Bell; 7-Up;
D'Arcy-MacManus Masius; Tatham-Laird & Kudner;
NW Ayer; Leo Burnett; Bartels & Carstens; Doyle
Dane Bernbach.

Work appeared in: Graphis Annuals 83/84, 84/85;
Print Regional Annuals 83, 84; Print Magazine
May/June 85.

Benton Mahan

P.O. Box 66
Chesterville, Ohio 43317
(419) 768-2204

Partial Client List

J. Walter Thompson, McGraw-Hill, Doubleday
Publishing, Borden, Good Housekeeping, ITT,
American Airlines, Diebolt Co. and many others.

1. Ohio Magazine
2. Central Mutual Insurance
3. Living Single Magazine
4. Peabody Galion—Truck Division
5. Lord, Sullivan and Yorder
6. Yankee Magazine

1.

2.

3.

5.

Don Martin
Miami, Florida
(305) 665-2376

(A), (C) ©E.C. Publications, Inc. 1984
(B), (D), (E) © Don Martin 1984
Member Graphic Artists Guild

A

B

C

D

E

R. Martin

Richard Martin
485 Hilda Street
East Meadow, New York 11554
(516) 221-3630

Member Graphic Artists Guild
See previous ad in Art Directors Index, Volume 11

Claude Martinot

145 Second Avenue
New York, New York 10003
(212) 473-3137

Member of the Graphic Artists Guild

Clients have included: Burson-Marsteller, Cunard
Lines, Cunningham & Walsh, Doyle Dane Bernbach,
The Bronx Zoo, Federal Reserve Bank of New York,
McGraw-Hill, Mother's Today, Ogilvy & Mather, Parents
Magazine, Rolf Werner Rosenthal, Ted Bates.

Barbara Maslen
Tower Gallery
45 West 18th Street
New York, New York 10011
(212) 645-5325

Clients: American Express,
ABC, Avon, Burlington, CBS,
Condé Nast, Estée Lauder,
Frances Denney, Hearst,
McGraw-Hill, Nabisco, New York
Magazine, New York Times,
Revlon, Rolling Stone, Simon &
Schuster, Time, WWD, Xerox,
Ziff-Davis.

Member Graphic Artists Guild

Akio Matsuyoshi

165 Perry Street, #1B
New York, New York 10014
(212) 242-7043

Represented by:

Jose Iglesias
1123 Broadway Suite 714
New York, New York 10010
(212) 929-7962

Client List: CBS Publications, Ziff Davis, AT&T,
Businessweek, J. Walter Thompson, Home Box Office,
Scholastic Press.

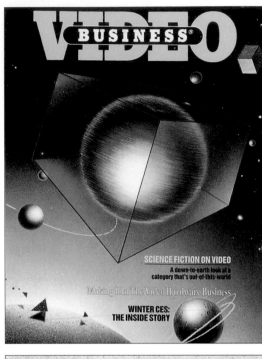

Bill Mayer
428 Sycamore Street
Decatur, Georgia 30030
(404) 378-0686
(404) 373-0284

Gary L. McElhaney

Mirror Image Productions
5205 Airport Boulevard, Suite 201
Austin, Texas 78751
(512) 451-3986

Video Portfolio available upon request

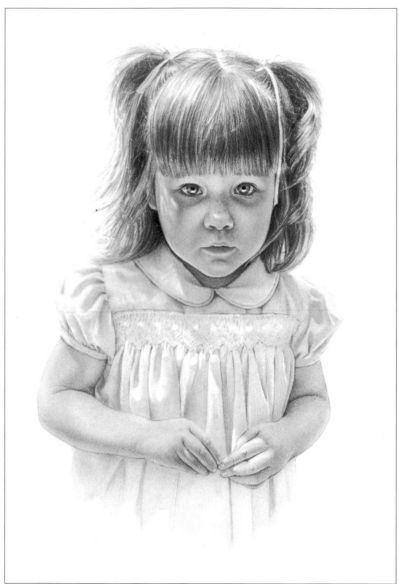

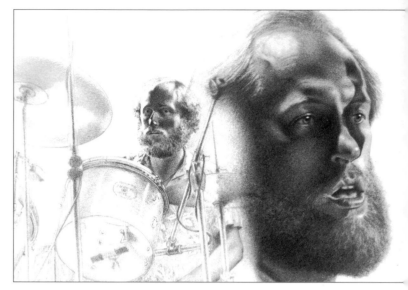

David McKelvey

Illustrator
1022 Huntshire Place
Atlanta, Georgia 30340
(404) 938-1949

Represented by The Williams Group
Contact Phillip Williams or Richard Coveny
(404) 873-2287

New York contact Tricia Weber
(212) 370-4486

Telecopier Available

See ad in American Showcase Volume 7, page 150,
and in Volume 8, page 218.

**Neal
McPheeters**

16 West 71st Street
New York, New York 10023
(212) 799-7021

Member:
Graphic Artists Guild
Society of Illustrators

Paul Meisel

Hudson Street, 5E
New York, New York 10013
(212) 226-5463

Bottom left:
New York Times Book Review

Other images:
TWA Ambassador Magazine

Patrick Merrell

48 West 20th Street
New York, New York 10011
(212) 620-7777

Illustration, Design, Puzzles,
Lettering.

Clients include:
Xerox
Dancer Fitzgerald Sample
McGraw-Hill
Burger King
Gray Strayton
McCaffrey & McCall
Fortune Computers
Parachute Press
Fisher-Price
Macmillan Publishing
Westinghouse
Popular Science
CTW
Venture Magazine
Marvel Comics
DC Comics
Ketchum Advertising
The Gadzooks! Gazette
RC Cola
Scholastic
Columbia Marketing
Reeves Communications
Dell

Member Graphic Artists Guild

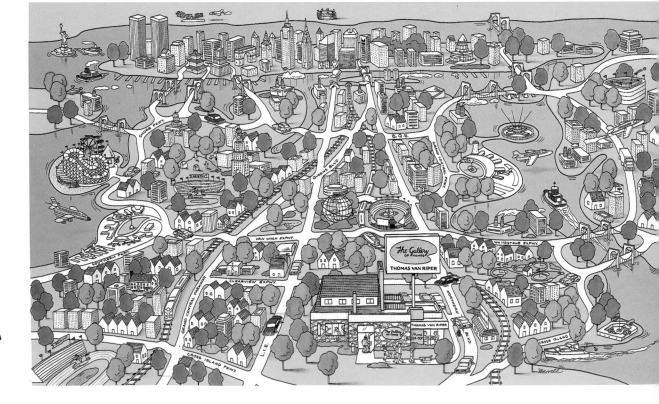

Gary Meyer

227 West Channel Road
Santa Monica, California 90402
(213) 454-2174

Member of the Society of
Illustrators and the Society of
Illustrators of Los Angeles.

Awards:
CA Magazine Award of
Excellence

Illustration West 22:
Best of Show
Best of Category
Special Judges Award

Illustration West 21:
Two Special Judges awards

Illustration West 19:
Best of Category

Twelfth Annual Key Arts Awards:
First Place

Tima X, Color Illustration:
First Place
Third Place

Tima 11, Color Illustration:
First Place

North American Sculpture
    Exhibition, 1983:
The Beyond Bronze Award

North American Sculpture
    Exhibition, 1981:
Art Castings of Colorado Award

Clients:
Universal Studios, Columbia
Pictures, Twentieth Century Fox,
Paramount Studios, Levi's,
Tomy Toys, Hughes Helicopters,
Litton Ship Systems, Garrett
Corporation, Popular Mechanics,
Apple Computers, Blitz Weinhard,
Western Microtechnology,
Visicorp, MGM, CBS Records,
A&M Records, Lionhart
Productions, Ogilvy & Mather,
Geiniger Advertising, Jeff Bacon
Design Inc., Foote, Cone &
Belding/Honig, Salisbury
Communications, Warner Bros.,
Wells, Rich, Green; Steinhilber
Deutsch & Gard.

Rick Meyerowitz

is represented by
Darwin Bahm
6 Jane Street
New York, New York 10014
(212) 989-7074

Bob Bahm
(216) 398-1338
and
Martine Mollard
32 Rue du Mont Thabor
Paris 75001, France
260-3348

Call to see his portfolio and
animation reel

Celia Mitchell

361 Washington Avenue
Brooklyn, New York 11238
(718) 783-0847
(814) 765-6339

Clients include:
Avis, Bill Communication, Restaurant Business
Magazine, Hellman's Best Foods, Nynex, Mobile
Communications, Paco Rabbane Parfums,
Reader's Digest, St. Martin's Press, Sandoz Health
Care Products, Pepsi International, T.W.A.

Comp. Art and finished Illustration.

Avis welcomes you to Hawaii

HELLMANN'S
REAL
MAYONNAISE

David Montiel

115 West 16th Street, #211
New York, New York 10011
(212) 989-7426

Illustrations:

From left to right, top to bottom

1. Kennex Corp.:
   advertising poster
2. Random House:
   "Something to be Desired"
3. Random House:
   "A Fan's Notes"
4. NAL: "Deadheads"
5. Random House:
   "You Know Me Al"

Other Clients include:

Young & Rubicam; Exxon Corp.;
Jonson, Pederson, Hinrichs &
Shakery; Geer DuBois; HCM;
Ciba-Geigy Pharmaceuticals;
Playboy; Time.

IF THE LORD HAD MEANT FOR ART DIRECTORS TO DRAW, HE WOULDN'T HAVE CREATED PURCHASE ORDERS

Probably no one ever wanted to be able to draw more than I did. And still do.

But by the time I got into the business, I faced reality. I can't draw. (Technically speaking, of course, I can draw. Even an account executive can draw. I just can't draw very well.)

I like to watch people draw. It fascinates me to watch someone's hand move a pencil over a sheet of paper and see an image appear. It's almost as if their hand is being guided, or as if they're tracing something I can't see. How do they do it?

When I was a kid, I loved to draw. I drew with crayons and pencils and color pens. I even drew in 3-D using red and blue pencils. And, at that time, I drew better than anyone else I knew.

That was to change.

Like many others, I followed a circuitous route to becoming an art director. My path led through two years of pre-med and one year of a variety-pack of courses in college, trying to discover what I wanted to do with the rest of my life.

My father, himself a doctor, didn't really object to my not following in his footsteps, as long as I'd become a lawyer or something professional like that. But when he learned I wanted to become an artist and go into advertising art, it was hard for him to take.

"Whoever heard of a male artist!" he asked loudly.

"Well, dear, just think of Michelangelo," my mother said to him. "There are lots of very famous male artists."

That was the only time in my life I've ever been compared to Michelangelo. Thanks, Mom.

And so Dad acquiesced reluctantly, but still expressed concern that I would spend my life on street corners trying to sell my paintings. If he'd only known how mediocre my drawing skills were, I think he would have withdrawn school funding right then and there.

But he didn't. And so here I am, some twenty years later. In an office, not on a street corner.

Being an art director, I could never come close to explaining my job function to my parents, or to anyone else for that matter. In school I did my own lettering and my own illustrations and my own photo indications and my own layouts to execute my own concepts. Parents can understand that.

"My son did this ad."

But the real world is different.

I do my own layout and share concept with a writer.

And I sign purchase orders to the people I decide can do the best job for the money on everything else.

Oh, sure, there's that occasional job with no money and no time that's just right for me. I get to do an illustration. It's always a little crude (unpolished, not distasteful), so I design around it. Sometimes I draw on a paper towel. Sometimes I stat it up. Sometimes I stat it down. It can never be mistaken for a photograph, but can sometimes be mistaken for an illustration. It's fun to do, and it works just fine.

But that's the exception to the rule, to say the least.

At one time I worked with a writer who used to be an art director. She had to become a writer because she drew too well to be an art director. She drew much better than I did, or than any of our other art directors did. It was a little embarrassing not to be able to draw as well as a writer, but I like to think that maybe I wrote a couple of headlines that were better than hers. At least that way I can live with myself.

I know one other ex-art director who can draw. He's now a full-time illustrator, and a very good one. I guess he had to do that because he can't write.

And so it goes.

I'm sure there are bound to be some art directors out there who can draw. That's okay. Don't feel bad about it. It happens.

As for me, I have my purchase orders. With them I can vicariously draw wonderful illustrations and even shoot wonderful photographs. I can do things I never dreamed I could do in school. It's great!

Thank You, Lord, for creating the purchase order.

Amen.

Steve Stanley
Vice President/
Associate Creative Director
Penny & Pengra Inc.
Houston, Texas

Jack Moore

Jack Moore Studio
131 Cedar Lake West
Denville, New Jersey 07834
(201) 627-6931

Member Graphic Artists Guild

Manuel Morales

East Coast Representative
CAROL BANCROFT & FRIENDS
185 Goodhill Road
Weston, Connecticut 06883
(203) 226-7674

Midwest Representative
WOODY COLEMAN PRESENTS
490 Rockside Road
Cleveland, Ohio 44131
(216) 661-4222

You have seen Manny's work and face on a recent Budweiser commercial entitled "Painters." You have seen his covers on everything from Science Fiction to Modern Romance. You have seen his illustrations on software packages, brochures, and advertisements.

Manny's style is distinctive. His versatility is remarkable. He combines his freehand airbrushing skills with oils to achieve the three dimensional look as seen in these images.

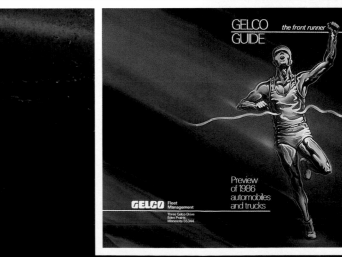

Alan Neider

51 Penn Common
Milford, Connecticut 06460
(203) 878-9260

Represented in New York by:

Bill and Maurine Klimt
15 West 72nd Street
New York, New York 10023
(212) 799 2231

Represented in Connecticut and Massachusetts by:
Bernadette Ayer
P.O. Box 415
59 Lakeside Drive
Granby, Connecticut 06035
(203) 653-3085

Meredith Nemirov

110 Kent Street
Brooklyn, New York 11222
(718) 389-5972

Watercolor

Three Dimensional Portraits—Commercial and Private Commissions.

Slides and Resume available upon request.

Clients include: Avon, Revlon, Book-of-the-Month Club, The New York Times, Success Magazine, Good Housekeeping, Home Magazine, Macmillan, Ziff-Davis, Kraft, Inc.

Exhibited: American Museum of Immigration, NYC., The Brooklyn Museum, The Queens Museum, Tuscon Museum of Fine Arts, Palm Springs Dessert Museum.

Publications: Society of Illustrators 25th Annual, American Illustration 82/83, Outstanding American Illustrators Today, 1984 and 1985.

Member Graphic Artists Guild

Robert Neubecker

395 Broadway
New York, New York 10013
(212) 219-8435

Conceptual illustration
Creating a visual language for such clients as:
The New York Times, The Washington Post, Newsweek,
Time, Sports Illustrated, Business Week, Barron's,
Forbes, Fortune, Mellon Bank, Dime Savings Bank,
Roche Chemical, Union Carbide, United Airlines,
NY Port Authority and many others.

Michael Ng

58-35 155th Street
Flushing, New York 11355
(718) 461-8264

Clients include: New York Times, Business Week, PC Magazine, Redbook, American Booksellers, Video Magazine, Sports Illustrated, Anthony Russell Design, Becker/Hockfield Design Associates, Ziff-Davis Advertising, CBS Records, Grey Advertising, Leslie Evans Graphics.

Editorial and Corporate Illustration, Black and White, Line Work and Water Color.

Work Appearing in Society of Illustrators 21st and 22nd Annuals.

1. One of twenty-five album covers for CBS Masterwork Series.

2. One of three bookmarkers for Doubleday & Co.

1.

2.

Larry Nichols

449 North Pennsylvania Street
Indianapolis, Indiana 46202
(317) 637-0250

Clients include: Mayflower
Corporation, Blue Cross/Blue
Shield, Firestone, American
Legion, RCA, Kiwanis
Magazine, Steak n Shake
Restaurants, Stokley Van-Camp,
McDonald's, Endless Vacation
Magazine.

Member Graphic Artists Guild

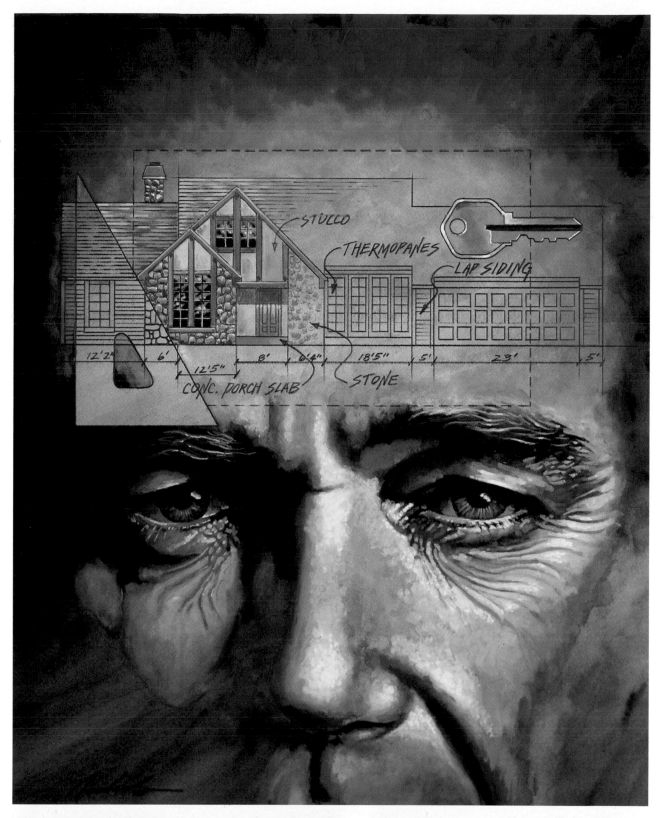

Pamela Noftsinger
New York City
(212) 316-4241

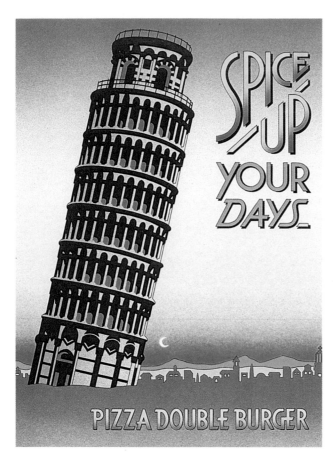

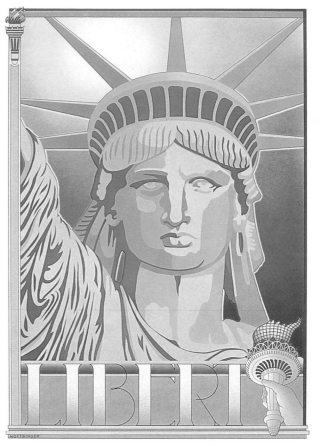

Denis Orloff

382 Carroll Street
Brooklyn, New York 11215
(718) 965-0385

Clients include:

ABC
Time
Reader's Digest   Forbes
Fortune   McGraw-Hill
New York Times   Nadler & Larimer
Connoisseur   Townscape Institute
Ogilvy & Mather
McCann Erickson   Member Graphic Artists Guild
Arista Records   Slide portfolio available upon request.

Jacqueline Osborn

101 Middlefield Road
Palo Alto, California 94301
(415) 326-2276

418

Ed Parker

9 Carlisle Street
Andover, Massachusetts 01810
(617) 475-2659

Represented by:
Kirchoff/Wohlberg, Inc.
866 United Nations Plaza
New York, New York 10017
(212) 644-2020

Clients include: NYNEX, Parker Brothers, Boston Globe, Infocom, Polaroid, Houghton Mifflin, Wang, Simon & Schuster, New Balance, Massachusetts State Lottery, Lotus, Massport, Little Brown, Kendall, Atlantic Press.

Member: Society of Illustrators

Pamela H. Patrick

Represented by:

Nancy Bruck
315 East 69th Street
New York, New York 10021
(212) 288-6023

Daniel Pelavin
46 Commerce Street
New York, New York 10014
(212) 929-2706

Illustration, Design
and Lettering.

Clients include:
AT&T
Adweek
American Express
Anthony Russell Inc.
Bernhardt Fudyma Design
The Boston Globe
Business Week
CBS
The Economist
Fortune
IBM
Inc.
Jonson Pedersen Hinrichs
  & Shakery
Landor Associates
McCaffery & McCall
McCall's
McCann Ericson
Muir Cornelius Moore
New York Magazine
The New York Times
Ogilvy & Mather
Psychology Today
Random House
Scali McCabe Sloves
Simon & Schuster
Sports Illustrated
Time Inc.

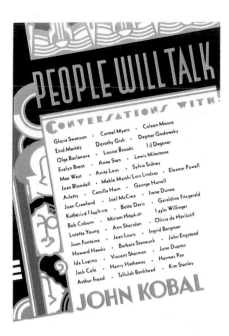

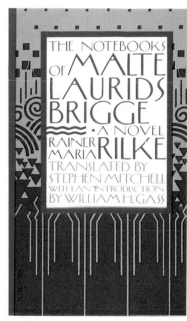

Gary Penca

3184 N.W. 39th Court
Fort Lauderdale, Florida 33309
(305) 733-5847

Represented by:
New York—Bill & Maurine Klimt
(212) 799-2231

Chicago—Joni Tuke
(312) 787-6826

Atlanta—Naomi Silva
(404) 892-8314

Specializing in:
• Advertising
• Medical
• Editorial
• Technical
• Product Illustration

Telecopier available

Member Graphic Artists Guild

R.T. Percivalle

140 West 15th Street
New York, New York 10011
(212) 243-6589

ILLUSTRATION,
CONCEPT & DESIGN

Clients Include:

Atlantic Records
ABC News Graphics
Audio Times Magazine
Business Week
CBS Entertainment
Home Satellite Magazine
J. Walter Thompson
Newsweek
People Magazine
RCA Records
Times Books
William Esty Advertising
Ziff-Davis

Top Left:
Poster for Statue of Liberty's
"100 YEARS"
Client: Nestlé's
Agency: Jordon, Case &
McGrath

Top Right:
Self Promotion

Middle:
Editorial about Detroit's car
industry meeting stereo
manufacturers. Client:
Audio Times/CES Publications

Bottom:
Book Jacket for "The World of
New York."
Client: The New York Times
Publisher: Times Books

Member Graphic Artists Guild

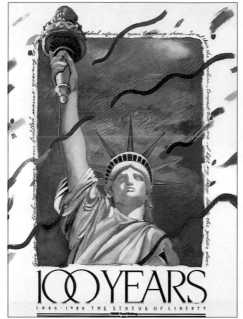

**Winslow Pinney
Pels**

Hack Green Road
Pound Ridge, New York 10576
New York City: (212) 570-7087
Westchester: (914) 764-8470

OF MICE AND MEN

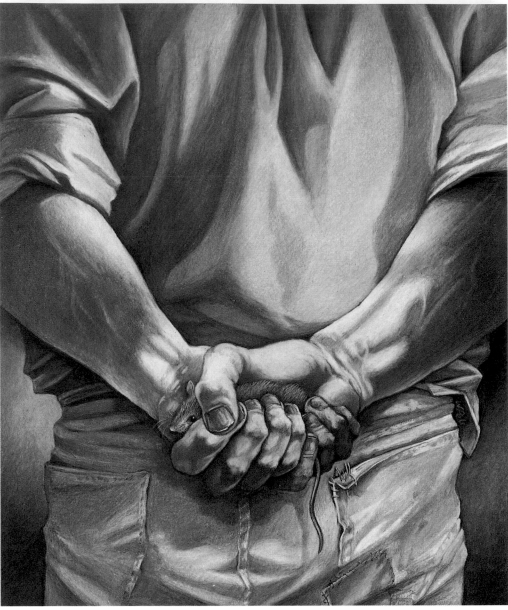

TEXAS OPERA THEATER, OGILVY AND MATHER/AD: AL CHINCHAR

EXXON/PBS, MCCAFFREY AND MCCALL/AD: PEGGY PETTUS

EVITA, ASH LEDONNE/AD: DAVID TRIEGER

424

Al Pisano
21 Skyline Drive
Upper Saddle River
New Jersey 07458
(201) 327-6716
(212) 944-8320

Al Pisano is a Multi-award-winning, Three-dimensional Artist/Designer. He services a wide variety of clients world-wide, and has received recognition for his talents both in Design and Typography, as well as in Illustration.

Clients include: American Express, Avon, Exxon, Seagram's National Distillers, Citicorp, Reader's Digest, Bantam Books, Dell Books, Berkeley Publishing Group, Time-Life, Newsweek, General Foods Corporation, and many others.

Girair Poladian
130 Gale Place
New York, New York 10463
(212) 601-2520

Scott Pollack

represented by:

**Eileen Moss &
Associates**

33 East 49th Street
New York, New York 10017
(212) 980-8061

Animatic Reel Available upon
request

Partial Client List:

AT&T, Ally & Gargano, N.W. Ayer,
Ted Bates, BBD&O, Backer &
Spielvogel, Darron's, Boston
Gas, N.Y. Daily News, Dancer
Fitzgerald Sample, Grey,
Emerson Lane Fortuna,
Madison Avenue Magazine,
Michigan State Lottery, Money
Magazine, Nabisco, Outdoor
Life, Peat Marwick Mitchell,
Prudential Life, Rumrill Hoyt,
Saatchi & Saatchi Compton,
SBS Skyline Systems (IBM),
Ski, Texaco, Video Magazine,
W.B. Doner, William Douglas
McAdams, Working Mother
Magazine, Needham Harper
Steers, Union Carbide.

427

Mike Quon
Design Office,
Inc.

568 Broadway
Suite 703
New York, New York 10012
(212) 226-6024

Los Angeles Representative
Milton Quon
(213) 293-0706

Design/Illustration

Some recent clients have
included: American Express,
AT&T, Club Med, Merrill Lynch,
Polaroid, Time Inc.

© Mike Quon 1986

BURLINGTON INDUSTRIES

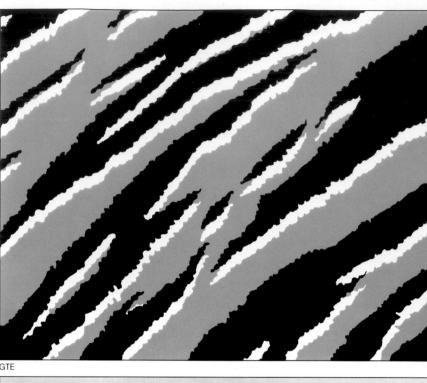

GTE

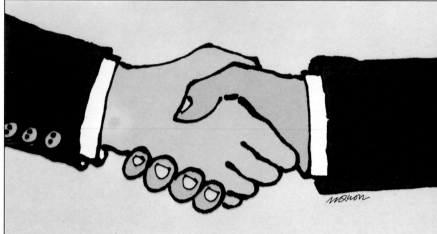

MERRILL LYNCH

WALL STREET JOURNAL

Radiomayonnaise

12A Appleton Street
Boston, Massachusetts 02116
(617) 536-5440

Michael G. Cobb
Dianne De Lancey

Illustration, Lettering and Design

Clockwise from top left:

Cover illustration and logo for MCA Records
Cover illustration for MCA Records
Cover illustration for Houghton Mifflin, Inc.

Self Promotion
Cover illustration, lettering and design for
The Berkeley Beacon

Members Graphic Artist's Guild

Scott Reynolds

308 West 30th Street
New York, New York 10001
(212) 239-0009

Portfolio available upon request

Chicago Representative
Joel Harlib
(312) 329-1370

Japan Representative–in
New York
Media Space, Inc.
(212) 206-9233

Anna Rich
777 Saint Mark's Avenue
Brooklyn, New York 11213
(718) 604-0121

Mike Rodericks

129 Lounsbury Road
Trumbull, Connecticut 06611
(203) 268-1551

Clients Include:

NBC TV, Seventeen Magazine, CBS Toys Inc., Mechanix Illustrated, Guinness Book of World Records Pavilions, McGraw-Hill Publishing, Timex Watch Inc., Ogilvy & Mather, SFM/Metromedia Stations, Book-of-the-Month Club, Yankee Magazine, Hilti Manufacturing, Golf Digest Magazine, Easton Press, Postal Commemorative Society, Macmillan Books, Patient Care Magazine, Scholastic Publications, View Magazine, Business & Commercial Aviation, Emergency Medicine Magazine, Guideposts Magazine.

432

Lilla Rogers

255 Clinton Street
Brooklyn, New York 11201
(718) 624-6862

Represented in the Southeast by:
Phelps & Jones
(404) 264-0264

Barbara Roman
48-53 205th Street
Bayside, New York 11364
(718) 229-6393

1. Advertisement for Audio
   Activations, Inc.
   Lee Epstein Advertising
   Art Director: Lee Epstein

2. East West Journal
   Art Directors:
   Louise Sandhaus Madnick
   Deborah Bowman

3. East West Journal
   Art Director:
   Deborah Bowman

4. After Christmas Card
   Self Promotion

5. Phi Delta Kappa
   Art Director: Kris Herzog
   New York Art Directors Club

Other Clients include:
   Atlantic Records
   Book of the Month Club
   Davis Publications
   Success Magazine
   Gallery Magazine
   FW Publications
   New Woman Magazine

Examples of work sent upon
request

Member Graphic Artists Guild

YOUR SUBCONSCIOUS CAN HELP WIN THE BATTLE AT NIGHT.

1.

2.

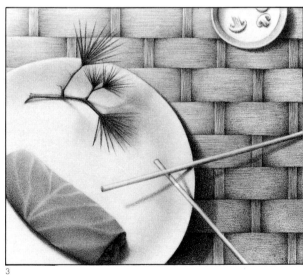

3.

4.

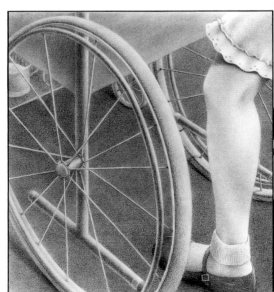

5.

Javier Romero

327 West 21st Street
New York, New York 10011
(212) 206-9175

Illustration and Graphic Design

Clients have included:

Alitalia, American Express, BBDO, Bloomingdale's, Elizabeth Arden, Foot, Cone & Belding, Fortune, GQ, Grey Advertising, Hertz, IBM, J. Walter Thompson, Kenyon Eckhardt, Macy's, Mademoiselle, Nestle, New York Magazine, Self, Showtime, The New York Times, Time, Inc., Vanity Fair, Vanguard Records, Wrangler

Works appeared in:

Art Directors Club, 61, 64
Creativity 13, 14, 15
Society of Illustrators 23, 25, 26
Print New York Design
Print Regional Design 84, 85

Larry Ross

53 Fairview Avenue
Madison, New Jersey 07940
(201) 377-6859

Clients have included:

The New York Times
Time Magazine
The Washington Post
Scali, McCabe, & Sloves
Young & Rubicam
Wells, Rich, & Green
Children's Television Workshop
CBS
ABC
Changing Times Magazine
E. P. Dutton
Doubleday
Scholastic Magazines
Volkswagen
Eastern Airlines

Richard Ross

704 West 20th Street
New York, New York 10010
(212) 675-8800

Clients include:
Newsweek; Random House,
Inc.; International Paper
Corporation; The McCalls
Publishing Co.; Avon Books; The
Viking Press; St. Martin's Press;
Cycle Guide Publications;
Penguin Books; Olympic
Records; Jonella Records; The
Baltimore Sun; The Hartford
Courant; Newsday; Notre Dame
University

Published in:
Print Magazine, American
Illustration Volume 2 & 4,
Illustrators 27

Member Graphic Artists Guild

Donna Ruff

595 West End Avenue
New York, New York 10024
(212) 255-1635
(212) 580-9056

Illustrations in mixed media.

Member Graphic Artists Guild

Tom Schaller
2255 Broadway, #303
New York, New York 10024
(212) 362-5524

Clients/Accounts

Bay Banks
Best Western Hotels
Cable Vision
G.T.E. Sylvania
George Kovacs
Hilton Hotels
I.B.M.
Pacific Shores Hotel

T.A.C.
Cambridge Seven Associates
The Gruzen Partnership
Hardy, Holzman, Pfeiffer
Hill Holiday
Patrick Nugent & Co.
Swanke, Hayden & Connell

Member Graphic Artists Guild

Roy Schlemme

585 Centre Street
Oradell, New Jersey 07649
(212) 921-9732 or (201) 265-2991

Complete advertising and promotional services including art direction, design, copy and mechanical preparation also available.

Over 75 national and international awards, shows and publications.

Partial client list:

McCann-Erickson
J. Walter Thompson
Benton & Bowles
Young & Rubicam
Ogilvy & Mather
Doremus & Co.
Tatham, Laird & Kudner
McGraw-Hill
Time, Inc.
E.P. Dutton
Harper & Row
The New York Times
Harcourt Brace Jovanovich
Xerox Educational Publications
Bill Communications
Ziff Davis
Gannett Newspapers
Times Mirror Magazines
Martin Marietta
Mead Paper
Borden
Warner Communications
NBC (WNBC-TV, WRC-TV)
Canadian Nat'l Railways
Texaco
CIBA/Geigy
Fisher-Price Toys
Scott Paper
Lufthansa
Westinghouse
Goodyear

Roy Schlemme
(Graphics with a twist.)

440

Glen A.
Schofield

Hillside Avenue
Roseland, New Jersey 07068
(201) 226-5597

Clients include:

IBM; Digital Learning Systems,
Inc.; Everest Manufacturing;
Cougar Electronics; Dolphin
Productions; Aqua Meter
Instrument Corp.; Omni
Magazine; Royal Silk, Ltd.;
American Institute of Aerospace
and Aeronautics; M/G
Architects; Atlantic Records;
Warner Communications;
Intercontinental Greetings;
AT&T; Allen Bennington
Publishers; Rose Art Industries;
Molson Ale; Turchette
Advertising Agency.

Exhibits Include:

Society of Illustrators Science
 Fiction Show
Worcester Science Center
New Jersey State Museum

Member:

A.S.F.A.
Graphic Artists Guild

M. Schottland

Represented by:

Tania Kimche

470 West 23rd Street
New York, New York 10011
(212) 242-6367

T A N I A
TANIA KIMCHE ARTISTS REPRESENTATIVE 470 West 23rd St., N.Y. N.Y. 100
(212) 242-6367

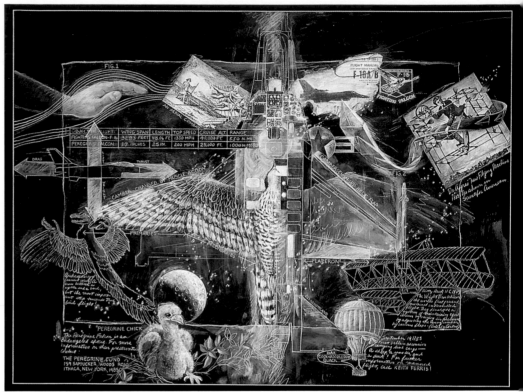

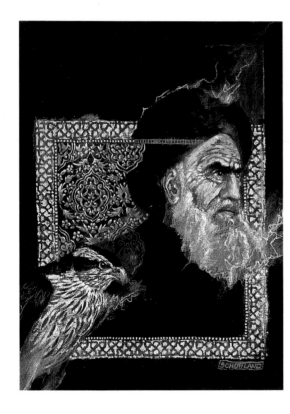

John Schreck

371 Beacon Street, Suite 2
Boston, Massachusetts 02116
(617) 236-0350

Clients Include:
Kodak
Xerox
Parker Brothers
Corning Glass Co.
New England Telephone
Acushnet (Golf Division)
S.D. Warren (Plate Div.)
Converse (Shoes)
Commercial Union
Red Cross
Rochester Telephone
A & W Root Beer
Dexter Shoes
Nap Shoes
Rockport Shoes
Bausch & Lomb
Nat'l. Inst. for the Deaf
Rochester Inst. of Tech.
Emerson College
Art Institute of Boston
Taconic Telephone
Marine Bus. Magazine
Boston Magazine
Inc. Magazine
Docktor Pet
Howard Johnson
Union Warren Bank
Shawmut Bank & Trust Co.
New England Life
Etc.

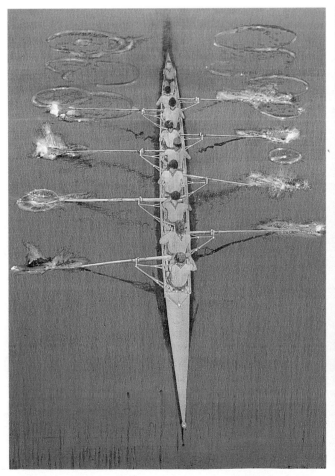

Joshua Schreier

466 Washington Street
New York, New York 10013
(212) 925-0472

Clients include:
New York Times
Carnegie Hall
IBM
Travel and Leisure
Geo
American Health

Jill Karla Schwarz

30 North Moore Street
New York, New York 10013
(212) 227-2444

Clients include:

Time Inc.; The New York Times;
Ally & Gargano; Germain
Monteil; Colgate Palmolive;
Grey Advertising; NBC;
Time-Life Books; Doubleday;
Cunningham & Walsh; RCA;
McCall's; Macy's; American
Artist; Macmillan; Franklin
Library; Ms.; Harpers;
Emergency Medicine; House
Beautiful; Psychology Today;
Stewart, Tabori & Chang.

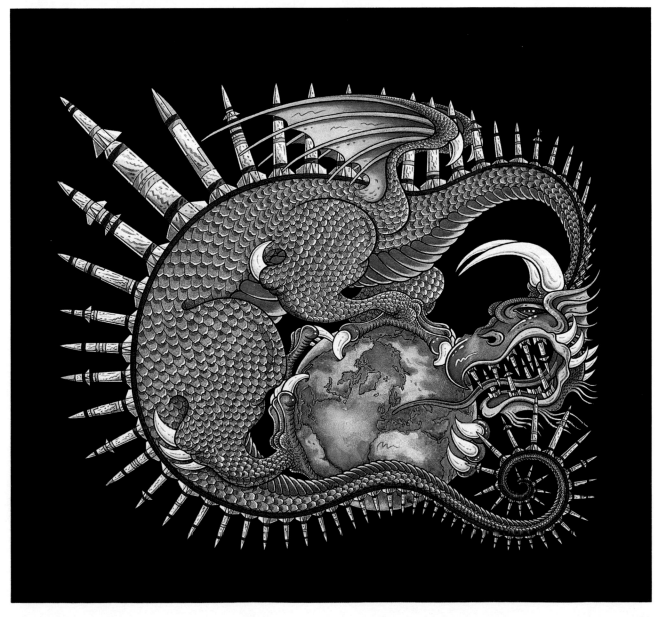

CREATIVE MEANING

"I hold myself indebted to anyone from whose enlightened understanding another ray of knowledge communicates to mine. Really to inform the mind is to correct and enlarge the heart." —*Junius*

I was just musing the other day about what provides the biggest challenge in the advertising business. If you've grown up on the creative side you'd probably say creating an award-winning campaign or, if account management, helping a particular client achieve a greater share of market.

But one of my most rewarding experiences was related to people, and the discovery of some things about myself I thought I'd lost in the rush to fame and fortune, amidst the politics of big, big business.

It involved moving from a large agency, where I supervised creative work on major accounts, to a small agency established by a well-known publishing company as a non-house profit center.

That was ten years ago. The large agency was Kenyon & Eckhardt, where I worked on the Ford Corporate account doing for Lee Iaccoca what now *giant* Kenyon & Eckhardt (having been bought by Lorimar and subsequently merged with Bozell & Jacobs) is still doing for him at Chrysler. The small agency was Doubleday Advertising, owned by the publishing company of the same name.

I was hired as Creative Director and was eager to accept the job of molding this organization into a top-flight advertising agency that could compete with the best. Of course, my first job would be to replace all of the staff (who must be burnt-out hacks —the flotsam and jetsam of the agency business). Replace them with up and coming DDB types. Isn't that standard procedure? After all, who in their right mind would be working on the fringes of this glamorous business when they could be scribbling at the feet of advertising's living hall of famers, enshrined at the many megalopolises on Madison Avenue?

However, I'm glad I waited to give everyone a chance to prove themselves. And then I remembered something a lot of us have forgotten in this business, that it's a Creative Director's job to provide direction, to inspire, to lead, and to bring out the best in the people who work to create the agency's product. Instead of treating them as producers of assembly line ads and TV campaigns, I found out the kind of art they liked, the books they read, and learned of their hopes and fears. I related to them in the lost art of human communication. I discovered that many of these people hadn't been given the opportunity to show the depths of their talents and, not only in the creative department, but in media and account management as well. Before long we were working as a well-integrated team that turned out more exciting work than many agencies ten times the size.

The recognition soon came, with creative and marketing awards and increased sales, followed by new clients.

But the best part was that I not only got to understand what motivates creative people but what's really important in human relations. In doing so, I discovered some interesting things about myself. In fact, if we're ever so fortunate to run into each other some day, I'd be happy to tell you about them over a long, cool drink.

Don Turner
Executive Vice President
Firestone And Associates, Inc.
New York City

eff Seaver

0 West 24th Street, #4B
w York, New York 10011
2) 741-2279

ents: ABC; Ally & Gargano; American Express;
&T; Backer & Spielvogel; BBD&O; Ted Bates;
ok-of-the-Month; *Business Week;* Dow Jones; Doyle
ne Bernbach; Dunkin' Donuts; *Fortune;* GE; Grey;
E; Hertz; IBM; Lever Bros.; Marshalk; McCaffrey &
Call; McCann-Erickson; Merrill Lynch; *National*
mpoon; New York; The New York Times; Ogilvy &
ther; Pfizer; Sandoz; Scali, McCabe & Sloves;
ence Digest; Science 85; Sony; *Sports Afield;*
kaco; J. Walter Thompson; Touche-Ross; Wells,
h & Greene; Workman.

Works exhibited in: *Illustrators 19, 20, 23, 24;*
Communications Art Annual; Outstanding American
Illustrators Today; Art Direction; Art Directors Annual;
New York Art Directors Club; Western Art Directors
Show; *National Lampoon Art Poster Book* and
Exhibition; American Humorous Illustrators Exhibition,
Tokyo, Japan; Museum of Art & Science, Chicago.

Member Graphic Artists Guild

Oren Sherman
30 Ipswich Street
Studio 301
Boston, Massachusetts 02215
(617) 437-7368

Hatch Shell
Coca Cola Company/MDC

Oren Sherman

30 Ipswich Street
Studio 301
Boston, Massachusetts 02215
(617) 437-7368

Clockwise from top.

San Francisco
Britannia Corporation/Grand Cayman Island, BWI
South Shore Bank
Britannia Corporation/Grand Cayman Island, BWI
Air Rendezvous

William A. Sloan

Represented by THREE
Contact: John Husak
568 Broadway
Suite 405
New York, New York 10012
(212) 226-8110

Clients Include: *Adweek;*
American Express; *American
Heritage;* Ash LeDonne Fisher;
Citicorp; Four Winds Travel;
Gross Townsend Frank, Inc.;
MacMillan Publishing; *Money;*
Rolf Werner Rosenthal, Inc.;
Serino, Coyne & Nappi;
St. Martin's Press; Tamotsu;
Viking Penguin Publishing;
Wolff Whitehill, Inc.

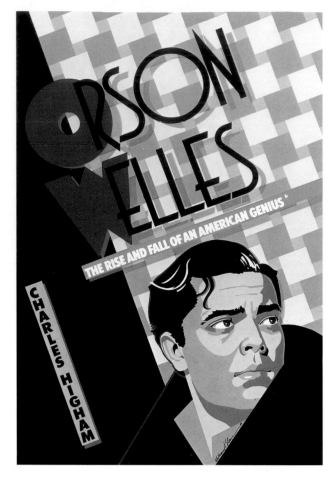

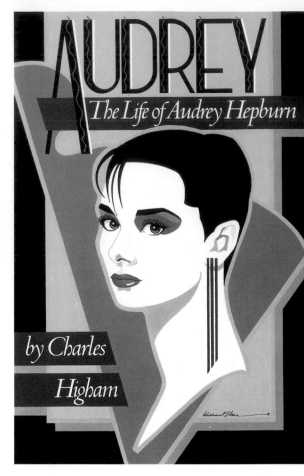

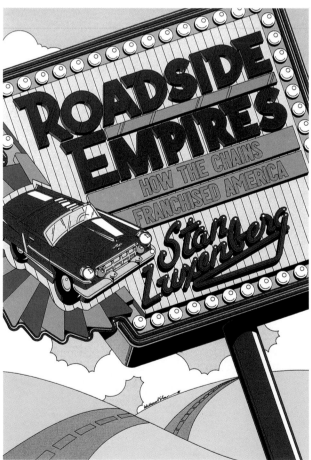

450

Guy Smalley

Represented by:
Smallkaps Associates Inc.
83 Madison Avenue
New York, New York 10016
(212) 683-0339

Stylized illustration

Partial Client List:
ABC Television, American Cancer Society, Corning
Glass, Family Circle Magazine, Foote, Cone & Belding,
General Foods, Harcourt Brace Jovanovich, Ideal Toys,
Macmillan Publishing, McGraw-Hill Book Co., Parents
Magazine, Scholastic Magazine, Stroh Brewery, Y&R.

SMALLEY
ILLUSTRATOR

Elwood H. Smith
2 Locust Grove Road
Rhinebeck, New York 12572

Represented by:
Maggie Pickard
(914) 876-2358

Marcia Smith

112 Linden Street
Rochester, New York 14620
(716) 461-9348

Clients include:
Avon Books
Borden
Chase Lincoln First Bank
D.C. Heath, Canada, Ltd.
Harper & Row
Houghton Mifflin Co.
Hutchins/Young & Rubicam
Nalge/Sybron Corp.
Michigan Fruit Canners/
    Curtice-Burns, Inc.
Singer
Xerox Corp.

Mouse: courtesy Nalge Co., Div.
of Sybon Corp.

©MARCIA SMITH

Hodges Soileau

350 Flax Hill Road
Norwalk, Connecticut 06854
(203) 852-0751

Clients include: Outdoor Life, ITT, Air Canada, Boy's Life, Aetna Life, RCA, Wamsutta, Meredith Corp., Unicover Corp., Hoechst Fibers, Sony, Spaulding, Reichold Chemicals, Milton Bradley, Corporate Annual Reports, Benton & Bowles, Bozell & Jacobs, Golf Digest, Ladies Home Journal, Seventeen, Good Housekeeping, Fortune, Flying Magazine, Field & Stream, Runner Magazine, R. J. Reynolds Tobacco Co., Book Publishers: Macmillan Publishing Co., New American Library, Avon, Bantam, Viking Penquin, Ballantine, Fawcett, Berkley, Banbury, Reader's Digest, Doubleday, Coronado, Harper & Row, Harlequin, and Franklin Library.

Member: Society of Illustrators
American Portrait Society

Pat Soper
214 Stephens St.
Lafayette, Louisiana 70506
(318) 233-1635
Illustrators 27

James Soukup
Route 1
Seward, Nebraska 68434
(402) 643-2339

Represented by:
Kiki Pollard
848 Greenwood Avenue, N. E.
Atlanta, Georgia 30306
(404) 875-1363
Tampa, Florida 33572
(813) 725-4438

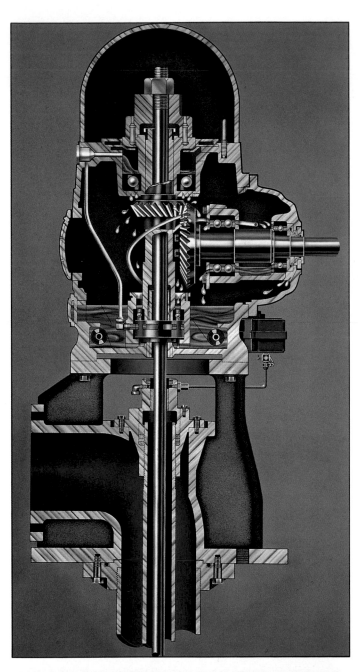

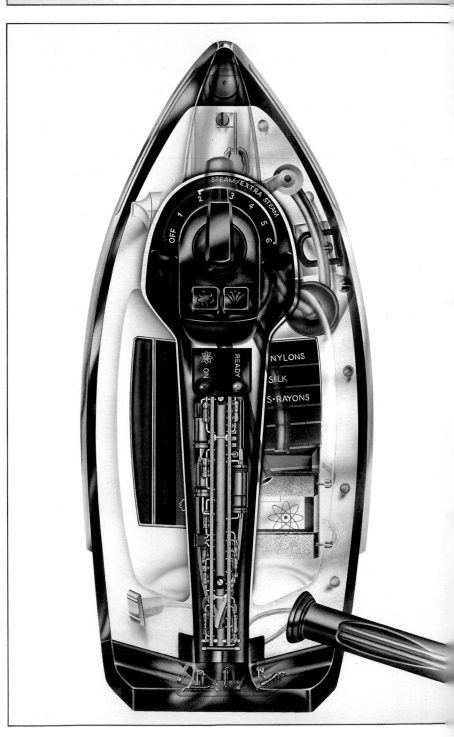

Chris Spollen
Moonlight Press
High Contrast Illustration
(718) 979-9695

Clients:
Stanley Tool Company
International Paper
Bell South Company
Mutual Life Insurance
20th Century Fox
Chubb Group Insurance
Digital Computer Co.
Home Box Office
McCaffrey and McCall
MacLean Hunter Media, Inc.
Franklin Library
Consumer Report Magazine
Warner Brothers Pubs.
Benton & Bowels
Ziff-Davis
CBS Publishing
Medical Economics Company
Barron's
Popular Mechanics Magazine
Hayden Publishing Company
Datamation Magazine
Compton Advertising
Acute Care Medicine
Avis
Working Woman Magazine
Atlantic Recording
Travel & Leisure Magazine
ABC
Milton Bradley Co.
Rodale Press
Glamor Magazine
Science 85 Magazine
Ogilvy & Mather Advertising

Member:
Graphic Artists Guild
Society of Illustrators

A mini portfolio of samples
sent upon request.

John Sposato
43 East 22nd Street
New York, New York 10010
(212) 477-3909

Illustration, Graphic Design, Concepts and Lettering.

CLIENTS:—Magazines: Newsweek; New York; Town and Country; Institutional Investor; Emergency Medicine; Physician's Weekly; Scholastic. Television: NBC; HBO; ABC. Publishers: Random House; Simon & Schuster, Macmillan; Harcourt Brace Jovanovich; Harper & Row; Holt, Reinhart & Winston; G P Putnam; E P Dutton; Dell; Crown; Doubleday; McGraw-Hill; Bobbs-Merrill; Atheneum. Also: Calvert Distillers;

Strathmore Paper; Key Pharmaceuticals; Paramount Pictures; Alcoholics Anonymous; Young & Rubicam; Ted Bates; Geers-Gross; MGM; Polydor; RCA Records.

AWARDS— Society of Illustrators 18, 19, 21 and 26; Art Directors Club; Graphis Annual; Graphis Posters; American Institute of Graphic Arts; CA Annual; Art Direction's Creativity; Type Directors Club; Advertising Club of New York (Andy Awards).

ILLUSTRATIONS IN

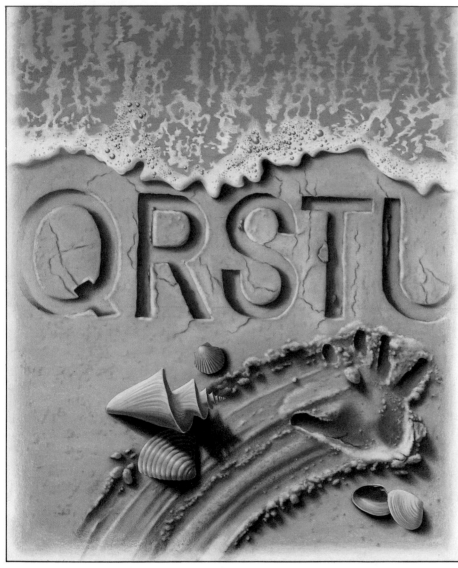

Craig Sprovach

604 Fairfield Avenue
Stamford, Connecticut 06902
(203) 327-2529
(203) 357-7370

Illustration and Design

As an airbrush artist, I specialize in advertising, magazine, book and album cover illustration.

A partial list of clients include: Thames Talent, Ltd., Graphic Designers Inc., Great Southern Company Merchandising, Break Through Graphic Design & The Graphic Spectrum. My portfolio is also available upon request.

Michael Steirnagle
4141 Pinnacle Suite 132
El Paso, Texas 79902
(915) 533-9295

Telecopier in studio

Represented in the Southwest by:
Melanie Spiegel, Photocom, Inc.
(214) 428-8781

Represented in the West by:
Ivy Glick
(415) 543-6056

Jane Sterrett

160 Fifth Avenue
New York, New York 10010
(212) 929-2566

Electrographics
Photography
Collage

Clients include:
Newsweek
Fortune
Business Week
Barnwell Industries
Page America/RCA
The Runner
P.C. Magazine
Games Magazine
Video Review
Frequent Flyer
MCA/TV
Newsday
The Daily News
High Tech Marketing
Datamation
Consumer Electronics
M.D. Computing
John Wiley & Sons
Emergency Medicine
Book-of-the-Month Club
M.I.T. Press
Macmillan
The New York Times

Susan Stillman

126 West 71st Street 5A
New York, New York 10023
(212) 724-5634

Clients include: Pfizer Inc.,
Sudler and Hennessey, RCA
Records, New York Magazine,
E. P. Dutton, St. Martin's Press,
Crown, New York Times, Rolf
Werner Rosenthal, Book-of-
the-Month, Life, Fortune,
Gentleman's Quarterly.

Work featured in: Art Direction
Magazine, Society of Illustrators
22, 23, 25, 26, Communication
Arts Art Annual, Creativity
Annuals.

Member Graphic Artists Guild

Stephen Sweny

217 East 29th Street
New York, New York 10016
(212) 532-4072

WHAT WOULD YOU PAY TO LIVE FOREVER?

These days, the costs of things like medical research, artificial transplants and kidney dialysis are putting our entire health-care system on the critical list.

The question is, just how much can we afford to spend to save someone's life? Turn to Channel 7 every night this week at 5, and take a look at the different ways we're paying for our health problems.

5 PM EYEWITNESS NEWS ⑦

IS GENETIC ENGINEERING BREEDING SOME UGLY TRAITS IN THE MEDICAL PROFESSION?

"WHAT WOULD YOU PAY TO LIVE FOREVER?"

And also tonight, call in and make your voice heard on Newsline ⑦. The topic:

Rent Stabilization: Good Or Bad?

EYEWITNESS NEWS AT 5 PM ⑦

463

David Taylor

1449 North Pennsylvania Street
Indianapolis, Indiana 46202
(317) 634-2728

Clients include: R.C.A., Sears, Reader's Digest,
Outdoor Life, Field & Stream, Sheraton Hotels,
Saturday Evening Post, Lilly, World Book, NBC,
American Legion Magazine, Gatorade, International
Harvester, Burger Chef, McDonald's, Southwest
Forest, Coke and Firestone.

Illustrators Annual 27

Member Graphic Artists Guild

Torpedo Studios

Explosive Imagery,
Streamlined Design!

350 East 89 Street
New York, New York 10128
(212) 502-3976

Clients:
Alley Cards, Audio, Buster
Brown, Cannon Mills, Children's
Television Workshop, Computer
Games, Fabri-Graphics, Fisher-
Price, H. Bailey Int., Healthtex,
Intercontinental Greetings,
Jetsetters, Inc.; Madison
Avenue, Medical Tribune, The
Movies, New Body, New York
Magazine, Rockshots,
Sportswise, Tables and Video
Games.

Also Published in:

Art Direction, Print and Society
of Illustrators 26th Annual.

Member Graphic Artists Guild

MELISSA RUSSELL

MIKE PANTUSO

GEORGE BLUME

George Tsui

2250 Elliot Street
Merrick, New York 11566
(516) 223-8474

Advertising and editorial illustration.

Clients have included: ABC; CBS; NBC; Film Rite; Universal; Showtime; Creative Alliance; Grey Advertising; J. Walter Thompson; Ogilvy & Mather; Benton & Bowles; McCaffery & McCall; Siebel-Mohr, Corp.; Marsteller Inc.; Warwick Advertising, Inc.; BBDO; Kobs & Brady; Young & Rubicam; Smith, Connelly & Smollen, Inc.; Jove Books; Bantam Books; Signet; Avon; Dell Books; Reader's Digest; Nelson Doubleday, Inc.; etc.

Awards:
1977 Emmy Award for Outstanding Individual Craft—The National Academy of Television Arts and Sciences.
1978 Certificate of Distinction—Art Direction Magazine.
Award of Excellence—1982 Communications Awards Program.

Works exhibited in "Outstanding American Illustrators Today" 1985, published by Graphic-Sha Publishing Co., Japan.

Member Graphic Artists Guild.

Lauren Uram

251 Washington Avenue
Brooklyn, New York 11205
(718) 789-7717

Clients include:

Ziff-Davis, Dell Publishing, Ballantine Books, Simon and Schuster, Hayden Publishing Company, Facts on File Publications, NBC, MIT, East/West Network, British American Tobacco, American International Pictures, The United States International Communications Agency, Biomedical Information Corporation, Consco, The New York Times, Teradyne Inc., The Daily News, The Village Voice, The Washington Post, The City Sun, Rupert Jensen Associates, Bernhardt Fudyma Design, Graphic Promotions, Emergency Medicine, Policy Review Magazine, National Review, Video Magazine, Life Magazine, Financial World Magazine, Music and Sound Output, Institutional Investor, Health Magazine, Changing Times Magazine, Redbook Magazine, Business Week Magazine, N.W. Ayer, Cole and Weber, Cunningham and Walsh, Ketchum Advertising.

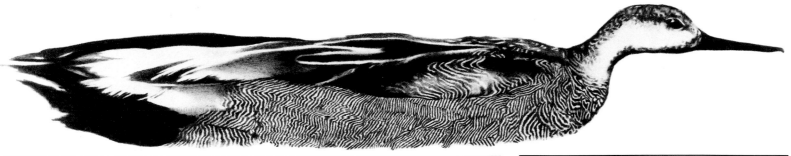

ABA · 1985

MAY · 25-28 · SAN FRANCISCO · CALIFORNIA

THE COAST-TO-COAST BESTSELLERS OF
BALLANTINE · DEL REY · FAWCETT

Dana Ventura
134 West 32nd Street, Suite 602
New York, New York 10001
(212) 244-4270
Studio (215) 949-1337

Illustration, lettering and design

Clients:
Digital Computers
Pepsi-Cola
LJN Toys
Alka Seltzer
Elliotts Apple Juice
Billboard Magazine
Spring House Publications

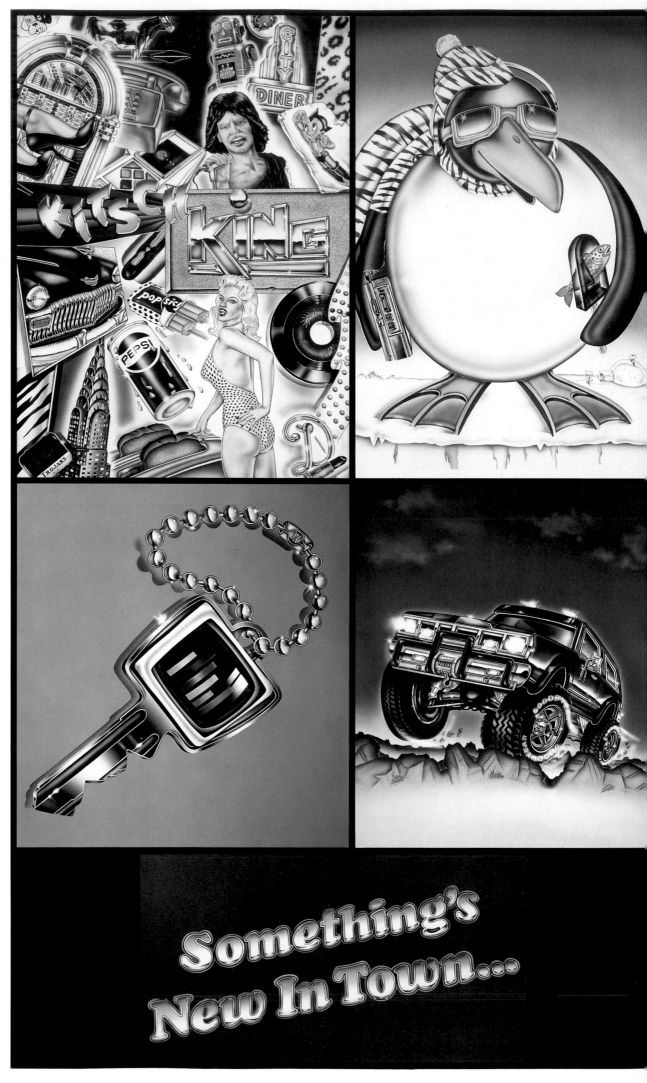

Hillary Vermont

218 East 17th Street
New York, New York 10003
(212) 674-3845

Creator of conceptual colorful
illustrations and graphic
solutions for all aspects of
design plus innovative images
for product lines including
stationery and gift items, fashion
and accessories, bath and
kitchen products such as
greeting cards, posters,
tote-bags, mugs, towels,
sunglasses, t-shirts and more.

Clients include:
Avon
Brastex-Gramercy
Burlington Industries
E-M Trading Corp.
Fiorucci
Laurel Entertainment
Museum of Modern Art
Murjani International
New Humor Mfg. Co.
NYC Card Company
Paper Moon Graphics
Playboy Publications
Rainboworld
Scholastic Magazines
Versatility T-Shirts
Weight Watcher's Magazine

All designs © Hillary Vermont
Member of Graphic Artists Guild

Sam Viviano

25 West 13th Street
New York, New York 10011
(212) 242-1471

Cartoon, caricature and humorous illustration.

Clients: ABC, Amtrak, BBD&O, CBS, CTW, Citibank, *Crain's New York Business*, Cunningham & Walsh, Diener/Hauser/Bates, Doyle Dane Bernbach, *Family Weekly, Field & Stream, Golf Digest*, IBM, *Institutional Investor, Mad Magazine*, McCaffrey & McCall, McCann-Erickson, Metromedia, NBC, N.W. Ayer, *National Lampoon*, New American Library, Ogilvy & Mather, PBS, *People*, RCA, *Redbook, Rolling Stone*, Scholastic, Showtime, *Tennis*, United Artists, Ziff-Davis.

Member Graphic Artists Guild

© Sam Viviano 1985

470

Larry Walczak

803 Park Avenue
Hoboken, New Jersey 07030
(201) 798-6176

Advertising and Editorial illustration in silhouette and stipple and in combinations thereof. Black and white and in color.

Clients include: Sawdon & Bess; Einson & Freeman; Harper & Row; NBC/WYNY; Best Foods; Harcourt Brace Jovanovich; McLean-Hunter; Letraset, Inc.; Diet-Pepsi; *New York Times;* McGraw-Hill; Scholastic; Garland Publishing; *American Artist* magazine; and Flax Advertising.

Member: Graphic Artists Guild

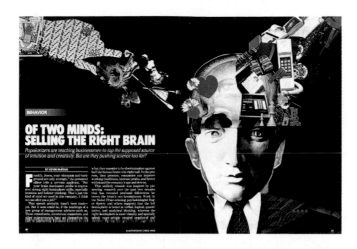

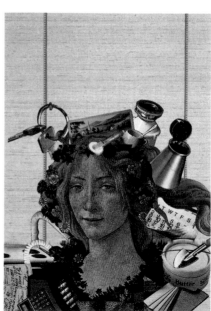

Charles Waller
Design Inc.

Penthouse C
35 Bethune Street
New York, New York 10014
(212) 752-4392

Client List:
Allied Corporation
American Express
AT&T
Business Week
Chase Manhattan Bank
Forbes
IBM
INX Syndicate
New York Times
Sony Corporation of America
Time Inc.
Ziff Davis Publications
13-30 Corporation
Ally/Gargano Advertising
BBD&O Advertising
Chiat/Day Advertising
Doremus Advertising
Janklow & Bender Advertising
Ogilvy & Mather Advertising

Jo Ann
Wanamaker

225 West 86th Street
New York, New York 10024
(212) 724-1786

Client List

American Home Magazine
AT&T
Austin Knight Adv.
Ballantine Books
Bloomingdale's
Business Images
DiFranza, Williamson
Fisher Camuto
Footwear News
George Gotlib Design
Hammond, Inc.
Harcourt, Brace, Jovanovich
Levy, Flaxman
Macy's
Modern Bride
Nordica Inc.
Sawdon and Bess Inc.
The New York Times
Vogue Magazine
Women's Wear Daily
Working Mother Magazine

Footwear Council Ad Award
Winner

Member Graphic Artists Guild

GLOVE AFFAIR Try on these gloves by La Crasia from our spring collection. Styles in either pastel hand-made silk-crochet in pink, lilac, white, ivory; or nylon Lycra® spandex stretch lace in fuchsia, aqua, red, white, and black. Both styles, wrist length. $18

macy's

Women's Gloves (D.017) Herald Square and your Macy's. Sorry, no mail and phone
Use your Macy's charge.

Richard Jesse Watson

P.O. Box 1470
Murphys, California 95247
(209) 728-2701

Member Graphic Artists Guild.

Carl Weisser

8 Livingston Street #33
Brooklyn Heights, New York 11201
(718) 834-0952

Paper silhouettes cut with scissors. Featured at the
Museum of American Folk Art and in New York
Magazine's "Best Bets."

Clients include:

AT&T	Scholastic
Dow Jones	Gruner + Jahl
Koala Technologies	Yankee Magazine
Bloomingdales	Marquardt & Roche
Bantam Books	Middleberg Middleton
Rodale Press	The Bloom Agency

SILHOUETTES

cut with scissors

by

Carl Weisser

Kim Whitesides

P.O. Box 2189
Park City, Utah 84060
(801) 649-0490

Represented by:

New York: Madeline Renard
(212) 490-2450

Chicago: Joel Harlib & Assoc.
(312) 329-1370

Dallas: Linda Smith/Linda Ryan
(214) 521-5156

San Francisco: Mary VanDamme
(415) 433-1292

Los Angeles: France Aline
(213) 383-0498

Simple Clean, Exciting Design, Illustration

Mel Williges

2 Hepworth Court
West Orange, New Jersey 07052
(201) 731-4086

Clients include:
The New York Times, Time-Life Inc., Houghton-Mifflin
Company, Little, Brown and Company, ABC, Playboy
Enterprises Inc.

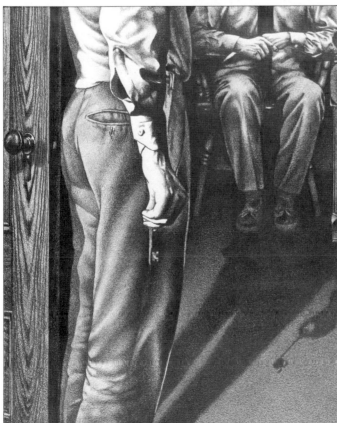

Edward Witus Design

2932 Wilshire Boulevard
Suite 202
Santa Monica, California 90403
(213) 828-6521

Design and Lettering for
Advertising and Entertainment

Represented by:
Marni Hall & Associates
(213) 934-9420

Paul Yalowitz
598 Freeman Avenue
Brentwood, New York 11717
(516) 273-7782

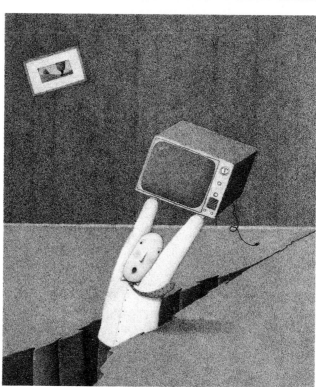

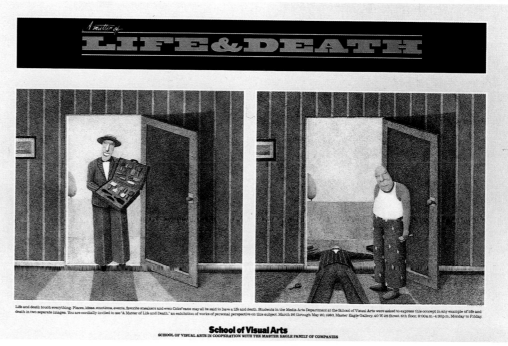

Cartoons Sell

Cartoons. They humor, charm, satirize, exaggerate. Cartoons add impact! They make ordinary situations bigger than life. Whether you're marketing financial services, food, travel, entertainment or anything else, for that matter, you'll find cartoons are a powerful communicator. Cartoons sell.

Lee Lorenz

Jack Davis

Bob Deschamps

Lionel Kalish

Lou Myers

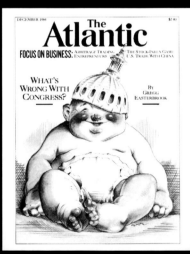

Michael Witte

AMERICA'S PREMIER CARTOONISTS ARE REPRESENTED BY:

GERALD & CULLEN RAPP, INC.
108 E. 35 St. (1-C)
New York City 10016
Phone (212) 889-3337

FREE FILE BOX: Write to us
on your company letterhead
and we will send you our filebox.
It's packed with miniature color
portfolios of all 22 illustrators
we represent.

GERALD & CULLEN RAPP

Free fertilizer for ideas.

One of the first steps in developing your advertising campaign is finding out what's being done in the same area —food, automobile, travel, cosmetics, or whatever.

You don't want to do something that's been done, or worse yet, that's being done.

And, unless you know what's being done, it's very difficult to stand out.

So you need to know what's going on. Both in the US, and internationally.

And you need to know on a continuing basis.

The ways to get this kind of information are either expensive or inefficient, or both. Clipping services charge a lot, don't organize the stuff very well, and generally don't edit out the chaff.

So someone in your company winds up getting a pile of tearsheets with no rhyme or reason to them.

That's not worth much.

Archive solves the problem.

Archive magazine is the solution to this state of affairs.

Archive is an internationally famous advertising magazine which is edited by the equally internationally famous Walter Lurzer, of West Germany.

When you subscribe to Archive, you get an in-depth overview of what's happening in, say, the fashion or liquor industry, *all over the world.*

The material is organized by category, is easy to read, and easy to understand. A careful study of Archive will reap big dividends for anyone involved in the creation, selling, or commissioning of advertising.

That means you.

For only $35 a year (less than the price of a lunch, and a discount off the cover price) you can get Archive com-

ing to you every two months.

One copy free.

To introduce you to Archive, we'll send you one copy free for the asking. At the same time, we'll enter an Archive subscription in your name at the special rate of $35.00 for 5 more issues (6 in all). That's a savings of 22% off the cover price.

If, for any reason, you are not completely satisfied, simply return the bill marked "cancel" and owe nothing. The first issue is yours to keep with our compliments.

For fast subscription service, call (212) 245-0981. Or write, Archive, c/o American Showcase, 724 Fifth Avenue, New York, NY 10019.

WHO WAS HERB LUBALIN?

THE FACE BEHIND THE FACES.

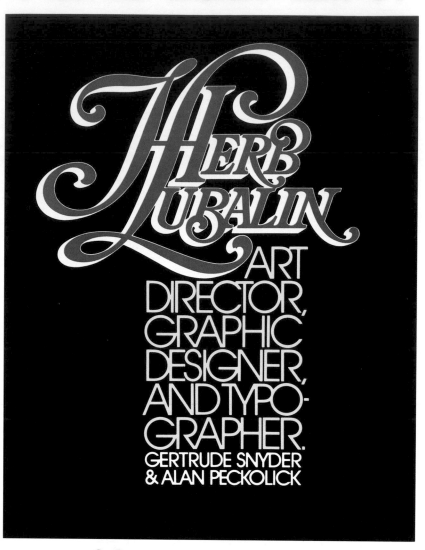

He was a skinny, colorblind, left-handed artist, known to friends and colleagues as a deafeningly silent man. But through his typography-based and editorial designs, he created bold new forms for communication and changed the dimensions of advertising and graphics.
Herb Lubalin is the definitive book about the typographic impresario and design master of our time. It is illustrated with more than 360 extraordinary examples of Lubalin's award-winning work, including: ■ Logos and Letterheads ■ Editorial and Book Design ■ Packaging ■ Advertising and Sales Promotion ■ Annual Reports ■ Best of *U&lc,* and more.
"The magnitude of Herb Lubalin's achievements will be felt for a long time to come....I think he was probably the greatest graphic designer ever."
—Lou Dorfsman, Vice President, Creative Director, Advertising and Design, CBS Inc.

184 pages, Color throughout, 9" x 11⅞"
Clothbound, Retail Value: $39.95
SPECIAL OFFER
Send for your copy of **Herb Lubalin** today and pay only $35.00.* Postage and handling are FREE within the U.S. and Canada. To order, **call 212-245-0981** and charge your AMEX, Visa or Mastercard. Or send your check or money order to:
AMERICAN SHOWCASE, INC.
724 Fifth Avenue, New York, NY 10019
*New York residents, please add appropriate sales tax.

INDEX Representatives & Illustrators

continued on next page

INDEX Representatives & Illustrators

INDEX

continued on next page

INDEX

continued from previous page

PHONE LISTINGS & ADDRESSES OF REPRESENTATIVES & VISUAL ARTISTS

Contents

Regions

New York City

Northeast
Connecticut
Delaware
Maine
Maryland
Massachusetts
New Hampshire
New Jersey
New York State
Pennsylvania
Rhode Island
Vermont
Washington, D.C.
West Virginia

Southeast
Alabama
Florida
Georgia
Kentucky
Louisiana
Mississippi
North Carolina
South Carolina
Tennessee
Virginia

Midwest
Illinois
Indiana
Iowa
Kansas
Michigan
Minnesota
Missouri
Nebraska
North Dakota
Ohio
South Dakota
Wisconsin

Southwest
Arizona
Arkansas
New Mexico
Oklahoma
Texas

Rocky Mountain
Colorado
Idaho
Montana
Utah
Wyoming

West Coast
Alaska
British Columbia
California
Hawaii
Nevada
Oregon
Washington

GREY PAGES

REPRESENTATIVES

Legend
A = Animator
AV = Audio Visual
C = Cartoonist
D = Director
F = Film
G = Graphic Designer
H & MU = Hair & Make-up
I = Illustrator
L = Lettering
M = Music
P = Photographer
R = Retoucher
TV = Television
S = Stylist

NEW YORK CITY

A

Abbey, Ken & Assoc/421 Seventh Ave, New York, NY   212-758-5259
  David Greenberg, (P), Hal Oringer, (P), Ted Pobiner, (P), A
  J Sandone, (P)
Acevedo, Alba/257 Windsor Pl, Brooklyn, NY   718-788-1818
  David G Klein, (I)
Adams, Kristine/62 W 45th St, New York, NY   212-869-4170
Adams, Ray/22 W 38th St, New York, NY   212-719-5514
Adler, Phil/35 W 38th St, New York, NY   212-354-0456
  Walter Auster, (P)
American Artists/353 W 53rd St #1W, New York, NY   212-682-2462
  Ed Acuna, (I), Don Almquist, (I), Joyce Ballantyne, (I), Keith
  Batcheller, (I), Frank Bolle, (I), Dan Bridy, (I), Rick Brown,
  (I), Bob Byrd, (I), Rob Cage, (I), Gary Ciccarelli, (I), Gary
  Ciccati, (I), Hank Connelly, (I), Jim Deigan, (I), Norm
  Doherty, (I), Alfred D'Ortenzio, (I), Lane DuPont, (I), Russell
  Farrell, (I), John Freas, (P), George Gaadt, (I), Jackie
  Geyer, (I), Michael Goodwin, (I), John Hamagami, (I), Karel
  Havileck, (I), Doug Henry, (I), John Holm, (I), Chris Hopkins,
  (I), Sandy Huffaker, (I), Todd Kat, (I), Richard Kriegler, (I),
  Diane LaRoja, (I), Kaaren Lewis, (I), Ed Lindlof, (I), Ron
  Mahoney, (I), Julia Manya, (I), Mick McGinty, (I), Steve
  Miller, (I), Richard Nelsen, (I), Jim Owens, (I), George
  Poladian, (I), Tony Randazzo, (I), Ed Renfro, (I), Paul
  Rogers, (I), Mike Ruland, (I), Jan Sawka, (I), Todd Schorr,
  (I), Victor Scocozza, (I), Joe Scrofani, (I), Mary Sherman,
  (I), Vince Streano, (I), Rudy Tesa, (I), Ron Wolin, (I), Andy
  Zito, (I), Craig Zuckerman, (I)
Anton, Jerry/107 E 38th St #5A, New York, NY   212-679-4562
  Bobbye Cochran, (I), Abe Echevarria, (I), Norman Green,
  (I), Aaron Rezny, (P), Bob Ziering, (I)
Arnold, Peter Inc/1466 Broadway #1405, New York, NY   212-840-6928
  Fred Bavendam, (P), Bob Evans, (P), Jacques Jangoux, (P),
  Manfred Kage, (P), Stephen Krasemann, (P), Hans
  Pfletschinger, (P), David Scharf, (P), Erika Stone, (P), Bruno
  Zehnder, (P)
Artists Associates/211 E 51st St #5F, New York, NY   212-755-1365
  Norman Adams, (I), Don Braupigam, (I), Michael Deas, (I),
  Mark English, (I), Alex Gnidziejko, (I), Robert Heindel, (I),
  Steve Karchin, (I), Dick Krepel, (I), Skip Liepky, (I), Rick
  McCollum, (I), Fred Otnes, (I), Daniel Schwartz, (I)
Artists International/225 Lafayette St, New York, NY   212-334-9310
Arton Associates/216 E 45th St, New York, NY   212-661-0850
  Paul Giovanopoulis, (I), Jacob Knight, (I), Carveth Kramer,
  (I), Michelle Laporte, (I), Karen Laurence, (I)
Asciutto, Mary Anne/99 Madison Ave, New York, NY   212-679-8660
  Anthony Accardo, (I), Alex Bloch, (I), Helen Cogancherry,
  (I), Olivia Cole, (I), Jill Dublin, (I), Simon Galkin, (I), Meryl
  Henderson, (I), Morissa Lipstein, (I), Loretta Lustig, (I), Sal
  Murdocca, (I), Jan Pyk, (I)
Ash, Michael/5 W 19th St, New York, NY   212-741-0015
Azzara, Louise/131 E 17th St, New York, NY   212-674-8114

B

Backer, Vic/30 W 26th St, New York, NY   212-620-0944
Badin, Andy/835 Third Ave 4th Fl, New York, NY   212-986-8833
  Jeff Feinen, (I), Vera, (I), Brad Guice, (P), Robert S Levy,
  (I), George Tsui, (I)
Bahm, Darwin/6 Jane St, New York, NY   212-989-7074
  Joan Landis, (I), Rick Meyerowitz, (I), Arno Sternglass, (I),
  Sketch Pad Studio, (I), John Thompson, (I), Robert Weaver,
  (I)
Barboza, Ken Assoc/853 Broadway #1603, New York, NY   212-505-8635
Barclay, R Francis/5 W 19th St, New York, NY   212-255-3440
Basile, Ron/1328 Broadway PH, New York, NY   212-244-5511
Becker, Noel/150 W 55th St, New York, NY   212-757-8987
  Howard Tangye, (P), Sy Vinopoll, (P)
Beckerman, Ann/50 W 29th St, New York, NY   212-684-0496
Beilin, Frank/405 E 56th St, New York, NY   212-751-3074
Benedict, Brinker/6 W 20th St, New York, NY   212-675-8067

BERNSTEIN & ANDRIULLI/60 E 42ND ST #505,
NEW YORK, NY (P 10-34)   212-682-149
  Tony Antonios, (I), Graphic Assoc, (I), Garin Baker, (I),
  Garie Blackwell, (I), Airstream, (I), Melinda Bordelon, (I),
  Everett Davidson, (I), Cathy Deeter, (I), Griesbach/Martucci,
  (I), Victor Gadino, (I), Veronika Hart, (I), Catherine Huerta,
  (I), Cathy Johnson, (I), Kid Kane, (I), Mary Ann Lasher, (I),
  Bette Levine, (I), Michael Molkenthin, (P), Frank Moscati,
  (P), Simpson/Flint, (P), Marla Shega, (I), Chuck Slack, (I),
  Murray Tinkelman, (I), Clay Turner, (I), Chuck Wilkinson, (I),
  James B. Wood, (P), Richard Anderson, (I), Per Arnoldi, (I),
  Holly Dickens, (I), Joe Genova, (I), Bill Morse, (I),
  Craig Nelson, (I), Joe Salina, (I), Peter Stallard, (I),
  J C Suares, (I)
Bishop, Lynn/134 E 24th St, New York, NY   212-254-573
  Irene Stern, (P)
Black Star/450 Park Ave S, New York, NY   212-679-328
  John W. Alexanders, (P), Nancy Rica Schiff, (P), Arnold
  Zann, (P)
Bloncourt, Nelson/308 W 30th St, New York, NY   212-594-367
Blum, Felice S/79 W 12th St, New York, NY   212-929-216
Boghosian, Marty/1123 Broadway #412, New York, NY   212-242-125
  James Salzano, (P)
Booth, Tom Inc/425 W 23rd St #17A, New York, NY   212-243-275
  Mike Datoli, (P), Joshua Green, (P), David Hartman, (P),
  Bob Hiemstra, (I), Patrick Russell, (P), John Stember, (P),
  Mike VanHorn, (I)
Brackman, Henrietta/415 E 52nd St, New York, NY   212-753-648
Brackman, Selma/251 Park Ave S, New York, NY   212-777-421
Brennan, Dan/32 E 38th St, New York, NY   212-889-655
  Tom Biondo, (P), Knut Bry, (P), Francois Deconnick, (P),
  Renato Grignaschi, (P), Bob Krieger, (P), Michel Momy, (P)
Brindle, Carolyn/203 E 89th St #3D, New York, NY   212-534-417
BRODY, ANNE/55 BETHUNE ST STUDIO 6,
NEW YORK, NY (P 65)   212-242-140
  Anatoly Chernishov, (I), Christine Ciesiel, (I), John
  Jamilkowski, (I), Claude Martinot, (I), Harold Pattek, (G),
  Debora Whitehouse, (I)
Brody, Sam/230 E 44th St #2F, New York, NY   212-758-064
  Robert Butler, (P), Linda Clenney, (I), Fred Hilliard, (I), Gary
  Kufner, (P), Stanford Smilow, (P), Steen Svenson, (P), Rudi
  Tesa, (P)
Brown Ink Assoc/267 Fifth Ave #1004, New York, NY   212-686-557
  Deborah Albena, (I), Paulette Bogan, (I), Bob Brown, (I),
  Lisa Campbell, (I), Virginia Curtin, (I), Darrel Kanyok, (I),
  Richard Kushner, (I), Kurt Merkel, (I), John Reiner, (I),
  Christine Roose, (I), Jody Silver, (I), Conrad Weiss, (I)
Brown, Doug/400 Madison Ave, New York, NY   212-980-49
  Andrew Unangst, (P)
Browne, Pema Ltd/185 E 85th St, New York, NY   212-369-192
  George Angelini, (I), Joe Burleson, (I), Peter Catalanotto, (I),
  Ted Enik, (I), Ron Jones, (I), Glee LoScalzo, (I), David
  Plourde, (I), Paul Reott, (I), John Rush, (I), John Sandford,
  (I)
Bruck, J S/157 W 57th St, New York, NY   212-247-113
  Richard Anderson, (I), Peter Caras, (I), Eva Cellini, (I),
  Joseph Cellini, (I), Michael Dudash, (I), Tom Freeman, (I),
  Donald Hedlin, (I), Jim Mathewuse, (I), Richard Newton, (I),
  Victoria Vebell, (I), Sally Jo Vitsky, (I), Gary Watson, (I)
BRUCK, NANCY/315 E 69TH ST #2B,
NEW YORK, NY (P 420)   212-288-60
  Gary Feinstein, (P), Pamela Patrick, (I)
Bruml, Kathy/262 West End Ave, New York, NY   212-874-56
  Charles Folds, (P), Michael Skott, (P)
Byrnes, Charles/5 E 19th St, New York, NY   212-473-33
  Steve Steigman, (P)

C

Cafiano, Charles/140 Fifth Ave, New York, NY   212-777-26
  Stan Fellerman, (P), Kenro Izu, (P)
Cahill, Joe/135 E 50th St, New York, NY   212-751-05
  Shig Ikeda, (P), Brad Miller, (P), Howard Sochurek, (P)

Camera 5 Inc/6 W 20th St, New York, NY   212-989-2004
   Bob Bishop, (P), Peter Calvin, (P), Karin Epstein, (P), Curt
   Gunther, (P), Boyd Hagen, (P), Ralph Lewin, (P), Michael
   Marks, (P), Ralph Pabst, (P), Neal Preston, (P), Ken Regan,
   (P), Bob Sherman, (P), Ben Weaver, (P), Bob Wiley, (P)
Camp, Woodfin & Assoc/415 Madison Ave, New York, NY   212-750-1020
   Kip Brundage, (P)
Caputo, Elise & Assoc/305 Madison #1805, New York, NY   212-949-2440
   Ric Cohn, (P), Donald Penny, (P), Joe Toto, (P)
Carleo, Teresa/1328 Broadway PH, New York, NY   212-244-5515
   Steve Chenn, (P)
Carmel/69 Mercer St, New York, NY   212-925-6216
   Guy Powers, (P)
Carp, Stan/11 E 48th St, New York, NY   212-759-8880
   Nick Samardge, (P), Allen Vogel, (P)
Casey, Judy/200 W 54th St #3C, New York, NY   212-757-6144
   Michael Doster, (I), Torkil Gudnason, (P), Michael O Brien,
   (P), Taolo Roversi, (P)
Casey, Marge/245 E 63rd St, New York, NY   212-486-9575
Cedeno, Lucy/10 W 18th St, New York, NY   212-255-9212
Celnick, Manny/36 E 12th St, New York, NY   212-473-4455
Chapnick, Ben/450 Park Ave S, New York, NY   212-679-3288
   Arnold Zann, (P)
Chie/15 E 11th St #2M, New York, NY   212-243-2353
CHISLOVSKY, CAROL/420 MADISON AVE #401,
NEW YORK, NY (P 35-37)   **212-980-3510**
   Randal Birkey, (I), Russell Cobane, (I), Robert Cooper, (I),
   Ken Graning, (I), John Gray, (I), Michael Haynes, (I),
   Hubert, (I), Tim Herman, (I), William Hosner, (I), Jim Hunt,
   (I), Joe Lapinski, (I), Felix Marich, (I), Joe Ovies, (I), Vincent
   Petragnani, (I), Chuck Schmidt, (I), Sandra Shap, (I), Danny
   Smythe, (I), Nighthawk Studios, (I), Bob Thomas, (I)
COLLIGNON, DANIELE/200 W 15TH ST,
NEW YORK, NY (P 38,39)   **212-243-4209**
   Bob Aiese, (I), David Gambale, (I), Mel Greifinger, (I),
   Richard Hughes, (P), Mike Lester, (I), Dennis Mukai, (I),
   Fran Oelbaum, (I), Vicki Yiannias, (I), Susan Hunt Yule, (I),
   Varlet-Martinelli, (I)
Conroy, Chris/124 E 24th St, New York, NY   212-598-9766
   Howard Alt, (P), David Kennedy, (P)
Crawford, Janice/340 E 93rd St #9I, New York, NY   212-722-4964
   Bob Crawford, (I)
CREATIVE FREELANCERS/62 W 45TH ST,
NEW YORK, NY (P 66,67)   **212-398-9540**
   Harold Brooks, (I), Howard Darden, (I), Claudia Fouse, (I),
   Arie Haas, (I), Rosanne Percivalle, (I), Alex Tiani, (I)
CREATIVE TALENT/62 LEROY ST, NEW YORK, NY (P 69)   **212-243-7869**
   Marshall Cetlin, (I), Alan Henderson, (I), Guy Smalley, (I)
Crecco, Michael/342 Madison Ave, New York, NY   212-682-5663
Cullom, Ellen/55 E 9th St, New York, NY   212-777-1749

D P I/521 Madison Ave, New York, NY   212-752-3930
   Shorty Wilcox, (P)
Dagrosa, Terry/374 Eighth Ave 2nd Fl, New York, NY   212-868-1676
Davies, Nora/370 E 76th St, New York, NY   212-628-6657
DeBacker, Clo/29 E 19th St, New York, NY   212-420-1276
   Bob Kiss, (P)
Dedell, Jacqueline/58 W 15th St, New York, NY   212-741-2539
   Teresa Fasolino, (I), Chermayeff and Geismar, (I), Ivan
   Powell, (I), Barry Root, (I), Richard Williams, (I), Henry Wolf,
   (P)
DellaCroce, Julia/120 W 81st St, New York, NY   212-580-1321
   Bob Bender, (P)
des Verges, Diana/73 Fifth Ave, New York, NY   212-691-8674
DEVERIN, DANIELE/226 E 53RD ST,
NEW YORK, NY (P 70-73)   **212-755-4945**
   Paul Blakey, (I), Greg Couch, (I), Mort Drucker, (I), Lazlo
   Kubinyi, (I), Charles Shields, (I), Jeff Smith, (I), Don Weller,
   (I)
DeVito, Kitty/43 E 30th St 14th Fl, New York, NY   212-889-9670
   Bart DeVito, (P)
DeVlieger, Mary/2109 Broadway, New York, NY   212-903-4321

DeWan, Michael/250 Cabrini Blvd #2E, New York, NY   212-927-9458
   Nancy Bundt, (P), Don Sparks, (P)
Dewey, Frank & Assoc/420 Lexington Ave, New York, NY   212-986-1249
DiCarlo, Barbara/500 E 85th St, New York, NY   212-734-2509
   Bob Wolfson, (P)
Dickinson, Alexis/175 Fifth Ave #1112, New York, NY   212-473-8020
   Jim Allen, (P), Robert Cohen, (P), Richard Dunkley, (P),
   Laura Ferguson, (S), Gregory King, (I), Jonathon Nix, (I),
   Eleanor Thompson, (P)
DiMartino, Joseph/200 E 58th St, New York, NY   **212-935-9522**
   Mark Blanton, (I), Sid Evans, (I), Don Rogers, (I),
   Graphicsgroup, (I), Whistl'n-Dixie, (I)
Dorman, Paul/419 E 57th St, New York, NY   212-826-6737
   Studio DGM, (P)
Drexler, Sharon/451 Westminster Rd, Brooklyn, NY   718-284-4779
   Les Katz, (I)
Droske, Diane/300 E 40th St #19R, New York, NY   212-867-2383
   Tom Hollyman, (P), Nancy LeVine, (P), Tobey Sanford, (P)
DuBane, J J/130 W 17th St, New York, NY   212-696-0274
Dubner, Logan/342 Madison Ave, New York, NY   212-883-0242
   Charles Kemper, (P), Siorenzo Niccoli, (P)

Eagles, Betsy/130 W 57th St, New York, NY   212-582-1501
   Ron Nicolaysen, (P), Lance Steadler, (P)
East Village Enterprises/231 W 29th St #807, New York, NY   212-563-5722
   Kevin Henigan, (I), David Jehn, (G), Carlos Torres, (I)
Edlitz, Ann/230 E 79th St #14F, New York, NY   212-744-7945
Ellis, Mirjana/176 Westminster Rd, Brooklyn, NY   718-282-6449
   Ray Ellis, (P)
Eng, Barbara/110 E 23rd St, New York, NY   212-254-8334
Englert, Tim/305 W 84th St #313, New York, NY   212-496-2074
Erlacher, Bill/211 E 51st St, New York, NY   212-755-1365
Everly, Bart/156 Fifth Ave #327, New York, NY   212-924-1510
Eyre, Susan/292 Marlboro Rd, Brooklyn, NY   718-282-5034
   Robert Phillips, (P)

Feldman, Robert/358 W 18th St, New York, NY   212-741-7254
   Alen MacWeeney, (P), Terry Niefield, (P)
Fischer, Bob/135 E 54th St, New York, NY   212-755-2131
   Bill Siliano, (P)
Fishback, Lee/350 W 21st St, New York, NY   212-929-2951
Flesher, Lex/194 Third Ave, New York, NY   212-475-0440
Flood, Phyllis Rich/67 Irving Pl, New York, NY   212-674-8080
   Istvan Banyai, (I), Christoph Blumrich, (I), Seymour Chwast,
   (I), Jose Cruz, (I), Elizabeth Koda-Callan, (I), Sarah Moon,
   (P), Elwood H Smith, (I), Stanislaw Zagorski, (I)
Folickman, Gary/399 E 72nd St, New York, NY   212-288-4198
Foster, Peter/870 UN Plaza, New York, NY   212-593-0793
   Charles Tracey, (P)
Friess, Susan/36 W 20th St, New York, NY   212-675-3021
   Richard Goldman, (P)
Friscia, Salmon/20 W 10th St, New York, NY   212-228-4134
Furst, Franz/420 E 55th St, New York, NY   212-753-3148
   Greg Pease, (P)

Gamma-Liaison/150 E 58th St, New York, NY   212-888-7272
   Bruce McAllister, (P)
Gargagliano, Tony/216 E 45th St, New York, NY   212-661-0850
Gaynin, Gail/241 Central Park West, New York, NY   212-255-3040
   Terry Clough, (P)
Gebbia, Doreen/156 Fifth Ave, New York, NY   212-807-0588
Gelb, Elizabeth/856 West End Ave, New York, NY   212-222-1215
Gelband, Lauren/62 Leroy St, New York, NY   212-243-7869
Giraldi, Tina/54 W 39th St, New York, NY   212-840-8225
Godes, Lauren/32 Union Sq E #414, New York, NY   212-674-3725
   Jeffrey Krein, (P), Ellen Smith, (I)
GODFREY, DENNIS/95 HORATIO ST #203,
NEW YORK, NY (P 79)   **212-807-0840**
   Jeffrey Adams, (I), Joel Nakamura, (I), Karen Payne, (I),
   Morgan Pickard, (I), Greg Ragland, (I), Lane Smith (I)
Goldman, David/18 E 17th St, New York, NY   212-807-6627

REPRESENTATIVES CONT'D.
Please send us your additions and updates.

REPRESENTATIVES

Norm Bendell, (I), Jay Brenner, (P), Jim Kingston, (I), Joe Marvullo, (P)

Goldstein, Michael L/107 W 69th St, New York, NY   212-874-6933
Carla Bauer, (I), Fred Schulze, (P)

Gomberg, Susan/145 E 22nd St, New York, NY   212-473-8747
Richard Fried, (P), Ron Lieberman, (I), Janeart Limited, (P), Kathy S Schorr, (I)

Goodman, Barbara L/435 E 79th St, New York, NY   212-288-3076

Goodwin, Phyllis A/10 E 81st St, New York, NY   212-570-6021
Carl Furuta, (P), Howard Menkin, (P)

GORDON, BARBARA ASSOC/165 E 32ND ST, NEW YORK, NY (P 80,81)   **212-686-3514**
Ron Barry, (I), Bob Clarke, (I), Keita Colton, (I), James Dietz, (I), Glenn Harrington, (I), Robert Hunt, (I), Nenad Jakesevic, (I), Jackie Jasper, (I), Sonja Lamut, (I), April Lawton, (I), Andrew Nitzberg, (I), Sharleen Pederson, (I), Jas Szygiel, (I), Jackie Vaux, (I)

Gordon, Fran/1654 E 13th St #5A, Brooklyn, NY   718-339-4277

Green, Anita/160 E 26th St, New York, NY   212-674-4788
Alan Dolgins, (P), Stuart Peltz, (P)

Greenblatt, Eunice N/370 E 76th St, New York, NY   212-772-1776
Bob Brody, (P)

GRIEN, ANITA/155 E 38TH ST, NEW YORK, NY (P 82-85)   **212-697-6170**
Dolores Bego, (I), Fanny M Berry, (I), Hal Just, (I), Jerry McDaniel, (I), Don Morrison, (I), Marina Neyman-Levikova, (I), Alan Reingold, (I), Ellen Rixford, (I), Bill Wilkinson, (I)

Griffith, Valerie/10 Sheridan Square, New York, NY   212-675-2089

Groves, Michael/220 E 57th St #18D, New York, NY   212-532-2074
Ulf Skogsbergh, (P)

H Hajjar, Rene/220 Park Ave S, New York, NY   212-777-5361
Chris Jones, (P)

HANKINS + TEGENBORG LTD/310 MADISON AVE, NEW YORK, NY (P 40-43)   **212-867-8092**
Peter Attard, (I), Ralph Brillhart, (I), John Cernak, (I), Jim Cherry, (I), Mac Conner, (I), David Cook, (I), John Dawson, (I), Guy Deel, (I), Ron DiScensa, (I), John Dismukes, (I), John Ennis, (I), George Fernandez, (I), David Gaadt, (I), Sergio Giovine, (I), James Griffin, (I), Tom Hall, (I), Edwin Herder, (I), Michael Herring, (I), Aleta Jenks, (I), Rick Johnson, (I), Mike Kane, (I), Uldis Klavins, (I), Richard Lauter, (I), Cliff Miller, (I), Wendell Minor, (I), Greg Olanoff, (I), Walter Rane, (I), Robert Sabin, (I), Harry Schaare, (I), Bill Schmidt, (I), Dan Sneberger, (I), Frank Steiner, (I), Ludmilla Strugatsky, (I), Robert Travers, (I), Bob Trondsen, (I), Victor Valla, (I), Jeff Walker, (I)

Hansen, Wendy/126 Madison Ave, New York, NY   212-684-7139
Minh, (P)

Hare, Fran/126 W 23rd St, New York, NY   212-794-0043
Peter B Kaplan, (P)

Harmon, Rod/254 W 51st St, New York, NY   212-245-8935
Brian Hennessey, (P), Al Rubin, (P), Michael Sabanosh, (I), David Spagnolo, (I)

Henry, John/237 E 31st St, New York, NY   212-686-6883
Gregory Cannon, (P), Kerry Hayes, (P), Rosemary Howard, (P)

Herron, Pat/829 Park Ave, New York, NY   212-753-0462
Larry Dale Gordon, (P), Malcolm Kirk, (P)

Heyl, Fran/230 Park Ave #2525, New York, NY   212-687-8930

Hoeye, Michael/120 W 70th St, New York, NY   212-362-9546
Leland Neff, (P), Lilo Raymond, (P), Richie Williamson, (P)

HOLMBERG, IRMELI/55 HUDSON ST #3A, NEW YORK, NY (P 86-93)   **212-775-1810**
Vincent Amicosante, (I), Rainbow Grinder, (I), Walter Gurbo, (I), Mitchell Hyatt, (I), John Martinez, (I), Bill Nelson, (I), Debbie Pinkney, (I), Bob Radigan, (I), Bill Rieser, (I), Cameron Wasson, (I)

Holt, Rita/280 Madison Ave, New York, NY   212-683-2002

Horowitz, Gary/5 E 19th St #303, New York, NY   212-473-3366
Howard Berman, (P), Steve Bronstein, (P)

Hovde, Nob/829 Park Ave, New York, NY   212-753-0462
Malcolm Kirk, (P), J Frederick Smith, (P)

Hurewitz, Gary/5 E 19th St, New York, NY   212-473-336(
Howard Berman, (P), Steve Bronstein, (P), Steve Steigman, (P)

Husak, John/568 Broadway #405, New York, NY   212-226-811(
Frank Marchese, (G), William Sloan, (I)

IJ Iglesias, Jose/1123 Broadway #714, New York, NY   212-929-796(
Stan Fellerman, (P), Sven Lindman, (I), George Ruentiz, (I)

Jacobsen, Vi/333 Park Ave S, New York, NY   212-677-377(

Jedell, Joan/370 E 76th St, New York, NY   212-861-786(

JOHNSON, BUD & EVELYNE/201 E 28TH ST, NEW YORK, NY (P 94-117)   **212-532-092(**
Kathy Allert, (I), Betty de Araujo, (I), Irene Astrahan, (I), Rowan Barnes-Murphy, (I), Cathy Beylon, (I), Carolyn Bracken, (I), Jane Chambliss-Rigie, (I), Roberta Collier, (I), Frank Daniel, (I), Ted Enik, (I), Bill Finewood, (I), Robert Gunn, (I), Yukio Kondo, (I), Mei-ku-Huang, (I), Tom LaPadula, (I), Bruce Lemerise, (I), Turi MacCombie, (I), Dee Malan, (I), Brookie Maxwell, (I), Mitch Rigie, (I), Christopher Santoro, (I), Stan Skardinski, (I), Barbara Steadman, (I), Pat Stewart, (I), Tom Tierney, (I), Tricia Zimic, (I)

K Kahn, Harvey Assoc Inc/50 E 50th St, New York, NY   212-752-849(
Alan Cober, (I), Bernard Fuchs, (I), Nicholas Gaetano, (I), Gerald Gersten, (I), Wilson McLean, (I), Bob Peak, (I), Isadore Seltzer, (I), Norman Walker, (I)

Kammler, Fred/225 E 67th St, New York, NY   212-249-444(

KANE, BARNEY & FRIENDS/18 E 16TH ST 2ND FL, NEW YORK, NY (P 45-47)   **212-206-032(**
Margaret Brown, (P), Alan Daniels, (I), Jack DeGraffenried, (I), Joe Denaro, (I), Michael Farina, (I), Nat Giorgio, (I), William Harrison, (I), Steve Hochman, (I), Steven Keyes, (I), Harvey Kurtzman, (I), Bob Lapsley, (I), Peter Lloyd, (I), Ted Lodigensky, (I), Rich Mahon, (I), Robert Melendez, (I), Sue Rother, (I), Gary Ruddell, (I), Joseph Sellars, (I), Glen Tunstull, (I), Larry Winborg, (I), Jenny Yip, (I)

Kane, Odette/119 W 23rd St, New York, NY   212-807-873(
Charles Seesselberg, (P)

Kaplan, Holly/35 W 36th St, New York, NY   212-563-273(
Bruno, (P), Cosimo, (P)

Kauss, Jean-Gabriel/122 E 42nd St #3103, New York, NY   212-370-430(
Guy Fery, (I), Jesse Gerstein, (P), Francois Halard, (P), Jacques Malignon, (P), Mike Noome, (I)

Keating, Peggy/30 Horatio St, New York, NY   212-691-465(
Bob Parker, (I), Frank Paulin, (I), Suzanne Peck, (I), Fritz Varady, (I), Carol Vennell, (I), Norma Welliver, (I)

Kenney, John Assoc/251 W 30th St 16th Fl, New York, NY   212-279-151(
James McLoughlin, (P)

Kestner, V G/427 E 77th St #4C, New York, NY   212-535-414(

Kim/209 E 25th St, New York, NY   212-679-562(

KIMCHE, TANIA/470 W 23RD ST, NEW YORK, NY (P 119-121)   **212-242-636(**
Michael Hostovich, (I), Rafal Olbinski, (I), Miriam Schottland, (I), E T Steadman, (I)

Kirchoff-Wohlberg Inc/866 UN Plaza #4014, New York, NY   212-644-202(
Angela Adams, (I), Bob Barner, (I), Esther Baron, (I), Bradley Clark, (I), Brian Cody, (I), Gwen Connelly, (I), Floyd Cooper, (I), Betsy Day, (I), Lois Ehlert, (I), Al Fiorentino, (I), Frank Fretz, (I), Jon Friedman, (I), Jeremy Guitar, (I), Konrad Hack, (I), Pamela Higgins, (I), Ron Himler, (I), Rosekrans Hoffman, (I), Gary Hoover, (I), Kathleen Howell, (I), Chris Kalle, (I), Mark Kelley, (I), Christa Kieffer, (I), Dora Leder, (I), Tom Leonard, (I), Susan Lexa, (I), Ron Logan, (I), Don Madden, (I), Jane McCreary, (I), Lyle Miller, (I), Carol Nicklaus, (I), Ed Parker, (I), Jim Pearson, (I), Charles Robinson, (I), Bronwen Ross, (I), Arvis Stewart, (I), Phero Thomas, (I), Pat Traub, (I), Lou Vaccaro, (I), Joe Veno, (I), John Wallner, (I), Alexandra Wallner, (I), Arieh Zeldich, (I)

Klein, Leslie D/130 E 37th St, New York, NY   212-683-545(
Eric Meola, (P), Digital Productions, (P)

KLIMT, BILL & MAURINE/15 W 72ND ST, NEW YORK, NY (P 122-125)   **212-799-223(**

David Fe Dland, (I), Wil Cormier, (I), Jamie DeJesus, (I),
Ted Detoy, (P), Stephen Gorman, (I), Paul Henry, (I),
Steven Huston, (I), Ken Joudrey, (I), Frank Morris, (I), Alan
Neider, (I), Bill Purdom, (I), Michael Rodericks, (I), Mark
Skolsky, (I)

Kopel, Shelly & Assoc/51 E 42nd St #716, New York, NY   212-986-3282
   Bliss Brothers, (I), Penny Carter, (I), Tom Christopher, (I),
   Marcus Hamilton, (I), Al Hering, (I), Meryl Rosner, (I)

Korman, Alison/240 E 76th St, New York, NY   212-288-6713
   David Dishop, (P), Susan Kravis, (I)

Kramer, Joan & Assoc/720 Fifth Ave, New York, NY   212-224-1758
   David Cornwell, (P), Tom DeSanto, (P), Clark Dunbar, (P),
   John Lawlor, (P), Tom Leighton, (P), James McLoughlin,
   (P), Frank Moscati, (P), Jeff Perkell, (P), John Russell, (P),
   Ken Whitmore, (P), Bill Wilkinson, (P), Edward Young, (P)

Kreis, Ursula G/63 Adrian Ave, Bronx, NY   212-562-8931
   Stephen Green-Armytage, (P), John T. Hill, (P), Bruce
   Pendleton, (P)

Lada, Joe/330 E 19th St, New York, NY   212-254-0253
   George Hausman, (P)

Lafayette-Nelson & Assoc/64 W 15th St, New York, NY   212-989-7059
Lamont, Mary/200 W 20th St, New York, NY   212-242-1087
   Jim Marchese, (P)

LANDER/OSBORN/333 E 30TH ST,
NEW YORK, NY (P 126-129)   **212-679-1358**
   Francois Cloteaux, (I), Phil Franke, (I), Mel Furukawa, (I),
   Cathy Culp Heck, (I), Saul Lambert, (I), Frank Riley, (I),
   Barron Storey, (I)

Lane Talent Inc/104 Fifth Ave, New York, NY   212-861-7225
Larkin, Mary/308 E 59th St, New York, NY   212-308-7744
   Lynn St John, (P)

LAVATY, FRANK & JEFF/50 E 50TH ST #5,
NEW YORK, NY (P 44, 130-149)   **212-355-0910**
   John Berkey, (I), Jim Butcher, (I), Don Daily, (I), Bernard
   D'Andrea, (I), Roland DesCombes, (I), Christine Duke, (I),
   Bruce Emmett, (I), Gervasio Gallardo, (I), Martin Hoffman,
   (I), Stan Hunter, (I), Chet Jezierski, (I), David McCall
   Johnston, (I), Mort Kunstler, (I), Paul Lehr, (I), Lemuel Line,
   (I), Robert LoGrippo, (I), Darrel Millsap, (I), Carlos
   Ochagavia, (I)

Lee, Alan/33 E 22nd St #5D, New York, NY   212-673-2484
   Werner Kappes, (I), Peter Vaeth, (P)

Leff, Jerry/342 Madison Ave #949, New York, NY   212-697-8525
   Franco Accornero, (I), James Barkley, (I), Ken Barr, (I),
   Tom Beecham, (I), Mike Bryan, (I), Mel Crair, (I), Ron
   DiCianni, (I), Charles Gehm, (I), Penelope Gottlieb, (I),
   Steve Gross, (I), Gary Lang, (I), Ron Lesser, (I), Dennis
   Magdich, (I), Michael Nicastre, (I), Roseann Nicotra, (I),
   John Parsons, (I), Bill Selby, (I), Jon Townley, (I), James
   Woodend, (I)

Legrand, Jean Yves & Assoc/41 W 84th St #4, New York, NY   212-724-5981
   Jim Cherry, (I), Holly Hollington, (I), Barry McKinley, (P),
   Peter Sato, (I), Jack Ward, (P)

Leone, Mindy/381 Park Ave S #710, New York, NY   212-696-5674
   Bill Kouirinis, (P)

Leonian, Edith/220 E 23rd St, New York, NY   212-989-7670
   Philip Leonian, (P)

Lerman, Gary/113 E 31st St #4D, New York, NY   212-683-5777
   Paul Barton, (P), John Bechtold, (P), Jan Cobb, (P)

Levitt, Lee/43 W 16th St #16, New York, NY   212-206-7257
Levy, Leila/4523 Broadway #7G, New York, NY   212-942-8185
   Yoav Levy, (P)

Lewin, Betsy/152 Willoughby Ave, Brooklyn, NY   718-622-3882
   Ted Lewin, (I)

Lindgren, Pat/41 Union Sq W #1228, New York, NY   212-929-5590
   Barbara Banthein, (I), Tom Bloom, (I), Regan Dunnick, (I),
   Charles White III, (I), Audrey Lavine, (I)

Locke, John Studios Inc/15 E 76th St, New York, NY   212-288-8010
   John Cayea, (I), John Clift, (I), Oscar DeMejo, (I), Jean-
   Pierre Desclozeaux, (I), Blair Drawson, (I), James Endicott,
   (I), Richard Erdoes, (I), Jean Michel Folon, (I), Michael

Foreman, (I), André François, (I), George Giusti, (I), Edward
Gorey, (I), Peter Lippman, (I), Sam Maitin, (I), Richard
Oden, (I), William Bryan Park, (I), Colette Portal, (I),
Fernando Puigrosado, (I), Hans-Georg Rauch, (I), Ronald
Searle, (I), Tim, (I), Roland Topor, (I)

Longobardi, Gerard/5 W 19th St, New York, NY   212-255-3440
Loshe, Diane/10 W 18th St, New York, NY   212-691-9920
Lott, Peter & George/60 E 42nd St #411, New York, NY   212-687-4185
   Juan Barberis, (I), Ted Chambers, (I), Tony Covo, (I), Jim
   Dickerson, (I), David Halpern, (I), Ed Kurtzman, (I), Marie
   Peppard, (I), Steen Svenson, (P)

Lynch, Alan/60 Pineapple St #26, Brooklyn, NY   718-624-7979

M

Mace, Zelda/1133 Broadway, New York, NY   212-929-7017
Madris, Stephen/445 E 77th St, New York, NY   212-744-6668
   Gary Perweiler, (P)

Manasse, Michele/1960 Broadway #2E, New York, NY   212-873-3797
Mann, Ken/20 W 46th St, New York, NY   212-944-2853
   Rebecca Blake, (P), Hashi, (P), Dicran Studio, (P)

Marchesano, Frank/35 W 36th St, New York, NY   212-563-2730
Marek & Assoc Inc/160 Fifth Ave, New York, NY   212-924-6760
Marie, Diana Rose/38 E 19th St, New York, NY   212-477-5107
Marino, Frank/35 W 36th St, New York, NY   212-563-2730
   Bruno Benvenuti, (P)

Mariucci, Marie A/32 W 39th St, New York, NY   212-944-9590
Marks, Don/50 W 17th St, New York, NY   212-807-0457
Mars, Sallie/60 E 42nd St #505, New York, NY   212-682-1490
   Don Hamerman, (P), Nobu, (P), J C Suares, (P)

Marshall, Mel/40 W 77th St, New York, NY   212-877-3921
Mason, Kathy/101 W 18th St 4th Fl, New York, NY   212-675-3809
   Don Mason, (P)

Mathias, Cindy/7 E 14th St, New York, NY   212-741-3191
   Vittorio Sartor, (I)

MATTELSON, JUDY/88 LEXINGTON AVE #12G,
NEW YORK, NY (P 160-163)   **212-684-2974**
   Guy Billout, (I), Karen Kluglein, (I), Marvin Mattelson, (I),
   Gary Viskupic, (I)

Mautner, Jane/85 Fourth Ave, New York, NY   212-777-9024
   Kozlowski, (P)

Mayo, Vicki/225 E 31st St, New York, NY   212-686-1690
   Harold Krieger, (P)

McVey, Meg/54 W 84th St # 2F, New York, NY   212-362-3739
Mendelsohn, Richard/353 W 53rd St #1W, New York, NY   212-682-2462
Mendola, Joseph/420 Lexington Ave #2911, New York, NY   212-986-5680
   Paul Alexander, (I), Robert Berrar, (I), Dan Brown, (I), Jim
   Campbell, (I), Carl Cassler, (I), Joe Csatari, (I), Jim Dye, (I),
   John Eggert, (I), Peter Fiore, (I), Antonio Gabriele, (I), Tom
   Gala, (I), Hector Garrido, (I), Mark Gerber, (I), Ted Giavis,
   (I), Dale Gustafson, (I), Chuck Hamrick, (I), Richard Harvey,
   (I), Dave Henderson, (I), John Holmes, (I), Mitchell Hooks,
   (I), Joel Iskowitz, (I), Bob Jones, (I), Stuart Kaufman, (I),
   Michael Koester, (I), Richard Leech, (I), Dennis Lyall, (I),
   Jeffery Mangiat, (I), Goeffrey McCormack, (I), Ann Meisel,
   (I), Ted Michner, (I), Mike Mikos, (I), Jonathon Milne, (I),
   Wally Neibart, (I), Tom Newsome, (I), Mike Noome, (I),
   Chris Notarile, (I), Kukalis Romas, (I), Mort Rosenfeld, (I),
   Greg Rudd, (I), Rob Sauber, (I), David Schleinkofer, (I),
   Mike Smollin, (I), Kip Soldwedel, (I), John Solie, (I), George
   Sottung, (I), Joel Spector, (I), Cliff Spohn, (I), Jeffrey
   Terreson, (I), Bill Vann, (I), Mark Watts, (I), Allen Welkis, (I),
   Ben Wohlberg, (I), Ray Yeldman, (I)

Metz, Bernard/43 E 19th St, New York, NY   212-254-4990
Michalski, Ben/118 E 28th St, New York, NY   212-683-4025
Miller, Susan/1641 Third Ave #29A, New York, NY   212-905-8400

MINTZ, LES/111 WOOSTER ST #PH C,
NEW YORK, NY (P 53)   **212-925-0491**
   Bernard Bonhomme, (I), Robert Burger, (I), Hovik Dilakian,
   (I), Amy Hill, (I), George Masi, (I), Kirsten Soderlind, (I), Kurt
   Vargo, (I), Dennis Ziemienski, (I)

Monomakhoff, Kathleen/304 E 20th St #7B, New York, NY   212-807-7703
Moretz, Eileen P/141 Wooster St, New York, NY   212-254-3766
   Charles Moretz, (P), Jeff Morgan, (P)

REPRESENTATIVES (sidebar)

MORGAN, VICKI ASSOC/194 THIRD AVE, NEW YORK, NY (P 164-175)   212-475-0440
John Alcorn, (I), Willardson + Assoc, (I), Ray Cruz, (I), Vivienne Flesher, (I), Kathy & Joe Heiner, (I), Jim Kozyra, (P), Tim Lewis, (I), Richard Mantel, (I), Wayne McLoughlin, (I), Emanuel Schongut, (I), Nancy Stahl, (I), Bruce Wolfe, (I), Wendy Wray, (I), Brian Zick, (I)

Morse, Lauren/78 Fifth Ave, New York, NY   212-807-1551
Alan Zenreich, (P)

Mosel, Sue/310 E 46th St, New York, NY   212-599-1806
Gerard Gentil, (P), Stan Shaffer, (P)

Moskowitz, Marion/342 Madison Ave #469, New York, NY   212-719-9879
Diane Teske Harris, (I), Arnie Levin, (I), Geoffrey Moss, (I), Marty Norman, (I)

MOSS, EILEEN/333 E 49TH ST #3J, NEW YORK, NY (P 295,427)   212-980-8061
Bill Cigliano, (I), Tom Curry, (I), Mike Davis, (I), Dennis Gottlieb, (I), Scott Pollack, (I)

Moss, Susan/29 W 38th St, New York, NY   212-354-8024
Louis Mervar, (P)

Mulvey Associates/1457 Broadway #1001, New York, NY   212-840-8223
Donn Albright, (I), Dick Amundsen, (I), Bill Colrus, (I), Art Cumings, (I), Ric DelRossi, (I), Bill Dula, (I), John Dyess, (I), C S Ewing, (I), Paula Goodman, (I), Les Gray, (I), Bill Hartman, (I), Phil Jones, (I), John Killgrew, (I), Peter Krempasky, (I), Edward Lee, (I), Ken Longtemps, (I), Rebecca Merrilees, (I), Larry Noble, (I), Tom Noonan, (I), Earl Norem, (I), Michael O'Reilly, (I), Tom O'Sullivan, (I), Taylor Oughton, (I), Frederick Porter, (I), Tom Powers, (I), Don Pulver, (I), Sandy Rabinowitz, (I), Herb Reed, (I), Jose Reyes, (I), John Rice, (I), Dolores Santoliquido, (I), Sally Schaedler, (I), Diane Shapiro-Cohen, (I), Gretchen Shields, (I), Bob Taylor, (I), Jim Woodend, (I), Jane Yamada, (I), Kang C Yi, (I)

NO Napaer, Michele/349 W Broadway, New York, NY   212-219-0325
Michael Abramson, (P)

National Imagemakers/31 E 17th St, New York, NY   212-475-1050

NEAIL, PAMELA R ASSOC/27-31 BLEECKER ST, NEW YORK, NY (P 176-177)   212-673-1600
Sean Daly, (I), Dennis DiVincenzo, (I), Barbara Goodrich, (I), Thea Kliros, (I), Tony Mascio, (I), Cary McKiver, (I), Ryuji Otani, (I), Brenda Pepper, (I), Janet Recchia, (I), Linda Richards, (I), Gail Severance, (I), Alex Vosk, (I), Pat Zadnik, (I)

Newborn, Milton/135 E 54th St, New York, NY   212-421-0050
Braldt Bralds, (I), Carol Gillot, (I), Robert Giusti, (I), Dick Hess, (I), Mark Hess, (I), Victor Juhasz, (I), Simms Taback, (I), David Wilcox, (I)

O'Brien, Fern/201 W 77th St #8C, New York, NY   212-873-8095

O'Rourke, Gene/200 E 62nd St, New York, NY   212-935-5027
Warren Flagler, (P), Sam Haskins, (P), Art Kane, (P), Douglas Kirkland, (P), Lincoln Potter, (P), Peter Angelo Simon, (P), Smith-Garner, (P), William Sumner, (P), John Thornton, (P), Alexis Urba, (P), Rob VanPetten, (P), John Zimmerman, (P)

Oye, Eva/307 E 44th St, New York, NY   212-286-9103

PQ Palmer-Smith, Glenn Assoc/160 Fifth Ave, New York, NY   212-807-1855
James Moore, (P), Charles Nesbitt, (P)

PENNY & STERMER GROUP/48 W 21ST ST 9TH FL, NEW YORK, NY (P 184-191)   212-243-4412
Bob Alcorn, (I), Manos Angelakis, (I), Deborah Bazzel, (I), Ron Becker, (I), Jane Clark, (I), Julian Graddon, (I), Rich Grote, (I), Michael Kanarek, (I), Andy Lackow, (I), Julia Noonan, (I), Steve Shub, (I), Gary Smith, (I), Page Wood, (I)

Peretti, Linda/420 Lexington Ave, New York, NY   212-687-7392
Ken Tannenbaum, (P)

Peters, Barbara/One Fifth Ave, New York, NY   212-777-6384
Jacques Dirand, (P), Lizzie Himmel, (P)

Petersen, Victoria/16 W 71st St, New York, NY   212-799-7021

Phyllis/38 E 19th St 8th Fl, New York, NY   212-475-3798
John Weir, (P)

Powers, Elizabeth/1414 Ave of Americas, New York, NY   212-832-2343
DiFranza Williamson, (P)

Pritchett, Tom/330 W 4th St, New York, NY   212-688-1080
Steve Durke, (I), George Parrish Jr, (I), George Kanelous, (I), Mike Robins, (I), Terry Ryan, (I)

Quercia, Mat/78 Irving Pl, New York, NY   212-477-4491

R **RAPP, GERALD & CULLEN INC/108 E 35TH ST #1, NEW YORK, NY (P 222,482)**   212-889-3337
Michael Brown, (I), Lon Busch, (I), Ken Dallison, (I), Jack Davis, (I), Bill Delvin, (I), Bob Deschamps, (I), Ray Domingo, (I), Ginnie Hoffman, (I), Lionel Kalish, (I), Sharon Knettell, (I), Lee Lorenze, (I), Allan Mardon, (I), Elwyn Mehlman, (I), Marie Michal, (I), Alex Murawski, (I), Lou Myers, (I), Gary Overacre, (I), Jerry Pinkney, (I), Charles Santori, (I), Bob Tanenbaum, (I), Michael White, (I), Barry Zaid, (I)

Ray, Marlys/350 Central Pk W, New York, NY   212-222-7680
Bill Ray, (P)

Reese, Kay Assoc/156 Fifth Ave #1107, New York, NY   212-924-515•
Jonathan Atkin, (P), Lev Borodulin, (P), Gerry Cranham, (P), Scott C Dine, (P), Claudio Edinger, (P), Ashvin Gatha, (P), Peter Gullers, (P), Arno Hammacher, (P), Jay Leviton, (P), George Long, (P), Lynn Pelham, (P), Richard Saunders, (P), Milkie Studio, (P), T Tanuma, (P)

Reid, Pamela/420 E 64th St, New York, NY   212-832-758•
Thierry des Fontaines, (P), Sandy Hill, (P), Bert Stern, (P)

RENARD, MADELINE/501 FIFTH AVE #1407, NEW YORK, NY (P 192,193)   212-490-245•
Steve Bjorkman, (I), Chas Wm Bush, (P), John Collier, (I), Etienne Delessert, (I), Bart Forbes, (I), Audra Geras, (I), Tim Girvin, (I), Lamb & Hall, (P), Miles Hardiman, (I), John Martin, (I), Al Pisano, (I), Robert Rodriguez, (I), Michael Schwab, (I), Jozef Sumichrast, (I), Kim Whitesides, (I)

Rhodes, Lela/327 West 89 St, New York, NY   212-787-388•

RIDGEWAY, KAREN/1466 BROADWAY, NEW YORK, NY (P 194,195)   212-921-191•
Scott Bricher, (I), Marilyn Jones, (I), Yemi Mardeigh, (I), Hugh McMahon, (I), Ron Morecraft, (I), David Rickerd, (I), Ron Ridgeway, (I)

Riley, Catherine/12 E 37th St, New York, NY   212-532-832•

RILEY, EDWARD T/81 GREENE ST, NEW YORK, NY (P 196)   212-925-305•
Elliot Banfield, (I), Quentin Blake, (I), Cesc, (I), Zevi Blum, (I), William Bramhall, (I), Chris DeMarest, (I), Paul Degen, (I), David Gothard, (I), Carolyn Gowdy, (I), Paul Hogarth, (I), Edward Koren, (I), Pierre Le-Tan, (I), Sara Midda, (I), Robert A Parker, (I), Cheryl Peterson, (I), Sempe, (I), Brenda Shahinian, (I), Philippe Weisbecker, (I)

Rindner, Barbara/216 E 45th St, New York, NY   212-661-085•

Rivelli, Cynthia/303 Park Ave S, New York, NY   212-254-099•

Rosenberg, Arlene/200 E 16th St, New York, NY   212-289-770•

Rudoff, Stan/271 Madison Ave, New York, NY   212-679-878•
David Hamilton, (P), Gideon Lewin, (P)

S **S I INTERNATIONAL/43 EAST 19TH ST, NEW YORK, NY (P 48-51)**   212-254-499•
Bob Bass, (I), Stephen Berger, (I), Jack Brusca, (I), Ernie Colon, (I), Richard Corben, (I), Richard Courtney, (I), Allen Davis, (I), Robert DeMichiell, (I), Walt DeRijk, (I), Robert Fine, (I), Susi Kilgore, (I), Gaetano Liberatore, (I), Sergio Martinez, (I), Vince Perez, (I), Martin Rigo, (I), Doug Rosenthal, (I), Artie Ruiz, (I), Paul Tatore, (I), Bodhi Wind, (I), Kathy Wyatt, (I)

SPAR/1123 Broadway #914, New York, NY   212-490-58•

Sacramone & Valentine/302 W 12th St, New York, NY   212-929-04•
Stephen Ladner, (P), Tohru Nakamura, (P), John Pilgreen, (P), Robin Saidman, (P), Gianni Spinazzola, (P)

Samuels, Rosemary/39 E 12th St, New York, NY   212-477-35•

Sander, Vicki/48 Gramercy Park North #3B, New York, NY   212-674-81•
Ed Gallucci, (P), George Menda, (P)

Sandlor, Cathy/470 W 24th St #5E, New York, NY | 212-242-9007
  Aaron Rapoport, (P)
Saunders, Gayle/301 E 92nd St, New York, NY | 212-722-1770
Savello, Denise/381 Park Ave S, New York, NY | 212-535-4795
Scharak, Lisa/401 E 58th St #B-4, New York, NY | 212-460-8067
Schecter Group, Ron Long/212 E 49th St, New York, NY | 212-752-4400
Schickler, Paul/135 E 50th St, New York, NY | 212-355-1044
Schochat, Kevin R/221 W 21st St #1D, New York, NY | 212-243-6229
  Chuck Carlton, (P), Douglass Grimmett, (G), Bill Kramer, (P)
Schon, Herb/1240 Lexington Ave, New York, NY | 212-737-2945
Schub, Peter & Robert Bear/37 Beekman Pl, New York, NY | 212-246-0679
  Robert Freson, (P), Alexander Lieberman, (P), Irving Penn, (P), Rico Puhlmann, (P), Snowdon, (P), Albert Watson, (P)
SEIGEL, FRAN/515 MADISON AVE 22ND FL, NEW YORK, NY (P 202,203) | **212-486-9644**
  Leslie Cabarga, (I), Cheryl Cooper, (I), Kinuko Craft, (I), Peter Cross, (I), Joe English, (I), Earl Keleny, (I)
Shamilzadeh, Sol/1155 Broadway 3rd Fl, New York, NY | 212-532-1977
  Ryszard Horowitz, (P), The Strobe Studio, (P)
Shapiro, Elaine/369 Lexington Ave, New York, NY | 212-867-8220
Sharlowe Assoc/275 Madison Ave, New York, NY | 212-683-2822
  Claus Eggers, (P), Nesti Mendoza, (P)
Sheer, Doug/29 John St, New York, NY | 212-732-4216
  Karen Kent, (P)
Shepherd, Judith/186 E 64th St, New York, NY | 212-838-3214
  Barry Seidman, (P)
SIGMAN, JOAN/336 E 54TH ST, NEW YORK, NY (P 204-206) | **212-832-7980**
  Robert Goldstrom, (I), John H Howard, (I), Daniel Kirk, (I), Jeff Seaver, (I), James Tennison, (I)
Simon, Debra/164 W 21st St, New York, NY | 212-505-5234
  Uli Rose, (P)
Simoneau, Christine/PO Box 12541, New York, NY | 212-696-2085
Sims, Jennifer/1150 Fifth Ave, New York, NY | 212-860-3005
  Clint Clemens, (P), Robert Latorre, (P)
Sjolin, Robert Nils/117 W 13th St, New York, NY | 212-242-7238
  Richard Brummett, (P)
Slocum, Linda/15 W 24th St 11th Fl, New York, NY | 212-243-0649
Slome, Nancy/121 Madison Ave, New York, NY | 212-685-8185
  Joe Berger, (P), Dennis Galante, (P)
Smith, Emily/30 E 21st St, New York, NY | 212-674-8383
Smith, Piper/194 Third Ave, New York, NY | 212-475-0440
Smith, Rita Assoc/1407 Broadway, New York, NY | 212-730-0065
SOLOMON, RICHARD/121 MADISON AVE, NEW YORK, NY (P 53-57) | **212-683-1362**
  Rick Brown, (I), Ray-Mel Cornelius, (I), Jack E. Davis, (I), Elizabeth Koda-Callan, (I), David Palladini, (I), Rodica Prato, (I), Ian Ross, (I), John Svoboda, (I), Shelley Thornton, (I)
Sonneville, Dane/130 E 63rd St #3E, New York, NY | 212-603-9530
  Leland Bobbe, (P), Jim Kinstrey, (I), John Pemberton, (P), Bob Shein, (I), Jane Sterrett, (I), Bill Truran, (P)
Spencer, Carlene/462 W 23rd St, New York, NY | 212-924-2498
  Laszlo Studio, (P), Peter Vitale, (P)
Stein, Jonathan & Assoc/353 E 77th St, New York, NY | 212-517-3648
  Mitch Epstein, (P), Burt Glinn, (P), Ernst Haas, (P), Nathaniel Lieberman, (P), Alex MacLean, (P), Gregory Murphey, (P), Kim Steele, (P), Joel Sternfeld, (P), Jeffrey Zaruba, (P)
Steiner, Susan/130 E 18th St, New York, NY | 212-673-4704
Stermer, Carol Lee/48 W 21st St 9th Fl, New York, NY | 212-243-4412
Stevens, Norma/1075 Park Ave, New York, NY | 212-427-7235
  Richard Avedon, (P)
Stockland, Bill/17 E 45th St, New York, NY | 212-972-4747
  Joel Baldwin, (P), Walter Iooss, (P), Eric Meola, (P), Michael Pruzan, (P)
Stogo, Donald/310 E 46th St, New York, NY | 212-490-1034
  Tom Grill, (P), John Lawlor, (P), Tom McCarthy, (P), Joe Morello, (P), Peter Vaeth, (P)
Stringer, Raymond/123 W 44th St #8F, New York, NY | 212-840-2891
  Ajin, (I)
Susse, Ed/56 W 22nd St 5th Fl, New York, NY | 212-243-1126
  Karl Zapp, (P)

T
Taylor, Nancy/153 E 57th St, New York, NY | 212-223-0744
Therese, Jane/6 W 20th St, New York, NY | 212-675-8067
  Nancy Brown, (P)
Thomas, Brenda & Assoc/127 W 79th St, New York, NY | 212-873-7236
TISE, KATHERINE/200 E 78TH ST, NEW YORK, NY (P 58-61) | **212-570-9069**
  Raphael Boguslav, (I), John Burgoyne, (I), Bunny Carter, (I), Cheryl Roberts, (I), Cathleen Toelke, (I)
Townsend, Kris/18 E 18th St, New York, NY | 212-243-2484
  David W Hamilton, (P)
Tralongo, Katrin/144 W 27th St, New York, NY | 212-255-1976
  Mickey Kaufman, (P)

UV
Umlas, Barbara/131 E 93rd St, New York, NY | 212-534-4008
  Hunter Freeman, (P)
Uzarski, John/80 Varick St #4B, New York, NY | 212-966-6782
  Richard Apple, (P)
Van Arnam, Lewis/154 W 57th St, New York, NY | 212-541-4787
  Paul Amato, (P), Mike Reinhardt, (P)
Van Orden, Yvonne/119 W 57th St, New York, NY | 212-265-1223
  Joe Schneider, (P)
Vance, Joy/515 Broadway #2B, New York, NY | 212-219-0808
  Al Satterwhite, (P)
VisualWorks Inc/545 W 45th St, New York, NY | 212-489-1717
Vollbracht, Michelle/225 E 11th St, New York, NY | 212-475-8718
  Walter Wick, (P)
Von Schreiber, Barbara/315 Central Pk West, New York, NY | 212-873-6594
  Jean Pagliuso, (P), Hiro, (P), Neal Slavin, (P)

W
Ward, Wendy/200 Madison Ave #2402, New York, NY | 212-684-0590
Wasserman, Ted/331 Madison Ave #1007, New York, NY | 212-867-5360
Watterson, Libby/350 E 30th St, New York, NY | 212-696-1461
  Karen Leeds, (P)
Wayne, Philip/66 Madison Ave #9C, New York, NY | 212-889-2836
  Roberto Brosan, (P)
Weissberg, Elyse/299 Pearl St #5E, New York, NY | 212-406-2566
  Jack Reznicki, (P), Bill Smith, (P)
Wheeler, Paul/50 W 29th St #11W, New York, NY | 212-696-9832
  John Dominis, (P), Greg Edwards, (P), Foto Shuttle Japan, (P), Seth Joel, (P), John McGrail, (P), Joe McNally, (P), Michael Melford, (P), Aaron Rapoport, (P), Steven Smith, (P), Peter Tenzer, (P), Leroy Woodson, (P)
Williamson, Jack/1414 Ave of the Americas, New York, NY | 212-832-2343
  DiFranza Williamson, (P)

YZ
Yellen, Bert & Assoc/838 Ave of Americas, New York, NY | 212-605-0555
  Bill Connors, (P), Joe Francki, (P), Gordon Munro, (P)
Youngs, Maralee/318 E 39th St, New York, NY | 212-679-8124
Zanetti, Lucy/139 Fifth Ave, New York, NY | 212-473-4999

NORTHEAST

AB
Ackermann, Marjorie/2112 Goodwin Lane, North Wales, PA | 215-646-1745
  H Mark Weidman, (P)
Andrews, Carolyn/109 Somerstown Rd, Ossining, NY | 914-762-5335
  Whitney Lane, (P)
Art Source/444 Bedford Rd, Pleasantville, NY | 914-747-2220
Bancroft, Carol & Friends/185 Goodhill Rd, Weston, CT | 203-226-7674
  Bill & Judy Anderson, (I), Cal & Mary Bausman, (I), Wendy Biggins, (I), Jim Cummins, (I), Susan Dodge, (I), Andrea Eberbach, (I), Marla Frazee, (I), Bob Giuliani, (I), Fred Harsh, (I), Ann Iosa, (I), Laurie Jordan, (I), Bryan Jowers, (I), Barbara Lanza, (I), Mila Lazarevich, (I), Karen Loccisano, (I), Jimmy Longacre, (I), Al Lorenz, (I), Laura Lydecker, (I), Stephen Marchesi, (I), Bob Masheris, (I), Elizabeth Miles, (I), Yoshi Miyake, (I), Nancy Munger, (I), Rodney Pate, (I), Jackie Rogers, (I), Gail Roth, (I), Miriam Schottland, (I), Blanche Sims, (I), Charles Varner, (I), John Weecks, (I), Linda Boehm Weller, (I), Ann Wilson, (I), Chuck Wimmer, (I), Debby Young, (I)

Please send us your additions and updates.

Bauchner, Susan/774 Lincoln Ave, Bridgeport, CT — 203-335-5859
  Jacques Charlas, (P)
Beckelman, Barbara/251 Greenwood Ave, Bethel, CT — 203-797-8188
Berezansky, Catherine/35 S Van Brunt St, Englewood, NJ — 201-894-5120
  Frank Aiello, (P), Rule-Master, (GD)
Birenbaum, Molly/7 Williamsburg Dr, Cheshire, CT — 203-272-9253
  Alice Coxe, (I), W E Duke, (I), Sean Kernan, (P), Joanne Schmaltz, (P), Paul Selwyn, (I)
Bloch, Peggy J/464 George Rd #5A, Cliffside Park, NJ — 201-943-9435
Brown, Jill/911 State St, Lancaster, PA — 717-393-0918
  brt Photo Illustration, (P)

CD
Camp, Woodfin Inc/925 1/2 F St NW, Washington, DC — 202-638-5705
Chandoha, Sam/RD 1 PO Box 287, Annandale, NJ — 201-782-3666
Correia, Joseph/11 Cabot Rd, Woburn, MA — 617-933-3267
  Gorchev & Gorchev, (P)
DeBren, Alan/355 Pearl St, Burlington, VT — 802-864-5916
  John Goodman, (P)
Donaldson, Selina/37 Hemlock, Arlington, MA — 617-646-1687

EF
ELLA/229 BERKELEY #52, BOSTON, MA (P 74-78) — 617-266-3858
  Norman Adams, (P), Bente Adler, (I), Wilbur Bullock, (I), Rob Cline, (I), Jack Crompton, (I), Anna Davidian, (I), Susan Dodge, (I), Sharon Drinkwine, (I), Anatoly Dverin, (I), Scott Gordley, (I), Eaton & Iwen, (I), Roger Leyonmark, (I), Janet Mager, (I), Bruce Sanders, (I), Ron Toelke, (I)
Franco, Evelyn/1072 Greendale Ave, Needham, MA — 617-444-4190

GH
Geng, Maud/13 Gloucester St, Boston, MA — 617-236-1920
Giandomenico, Terry/13 Fern Ave, Collingswood, NJ — 609-854-2222
  Bob Giandomenico, (P)
Gibbons, Mary/77 Taff Ave, Stamford, CT — 203-357-1777
  Jonathon Sloane, (P), Martin Tornallyay, (P)
Gidley, Fenton/43 Tokeneke Rd, Darien, CT — 212-772-0846
Goldstein, Gwen/91 Hundred Rd, Wellesley Hills, MA — 617-235-8658
  Michael Blaser, (I), Don Demers, (I), Lane Gregory, (I), Gary Torrisi, (I), Joe Veno, (I)
Gruder, Jean/1148 Parsippany Blvd, Parsippany, NJ — 201-334-0353
Gunn Associates/275 Newbury St, Boston, MA — 617-267-0618
Haas, Ken/PO Box 86, Oley, PA — 215-987-3711
  Peter Leach, (P), Ken Ravel, (I), Michael Schroeder, (I), Emilie Snyder, (I), Peter Treiber, (P)
Hone, Claire/2130 Arch Street, Philadelphia, PA — 215-568-5434
Hopkins, Nanette/18 North New St, West Chester, PA — 215-431-3240
  Rick Davis, (P)
Hubbell, Marian/99 East Elm St, Greenwich, CT — 203-629-9629

KL
Kaltenbach, Faith/PO Box 317, Lititz, PA — 717-626-0296
  Grant Heilman, (P)
Kanefield, Andrew/14 North Gate, West Newton, MA — 617-965-3557
  Christopher Cunningham, (P), Peter Jones, (P), Bob O'Shaughnessy, (P), Lewis Portnoy, (P)
Krongard, Paula/1 Riverview Dr W, Upper Montclair, NJ — 201-783-6155
  Skip Hine, (P), Bill White, (P)
Kurlansky, Sharon/192 Southville Rd, Southborough, MA — 617-872-4549
  Steve Alexander, (I), Charles Freeman, (I), Judy Gailen, (I), John Gamache, (I), Susan Hanson, (I), Peter Harris, (I), Terry Van Heusen, (I), Geoffrey Hodgkinson, (I), Mark Kelly, (I), Dorthea Sierra, (I), Colleen, (I)
Labonty, Deborah/PO Box 7446, Lancaster, PA — 717-872-8198
  Tim Schoon, (I)
Lipman, Deborah/506 Windsor Dr, Framingham, MA — 617-451-6528
  Mark Fisher, (I), Richard A. Goldberg, (I), James Hanlon, (I), Richard M. Joachim, (I), Armen Kojoyian, (I), Carol LaCourse, (I), Katherine Mahoney, (I)

MO
McNamara, Paula B/182 Broad St, Wethersfield, CT — 203-563-6159
  Jack McConnell, (P)
Metzger, Rick/186 South St, Boston, MA — 617-426-2290
  Steve Grohe, (P)
Morgan, Wendy/5 Logan Hill Rd, Northport, NY — 516-757-5609
  Susan Aldrich, (I), Jeff Bravata, (I), Chris Dabrowski, (I),

Scott Gordley, (I), Jan LaRoche, (P), Don Landwehrle, (P), Preston Lyon, (P), Al Margolis, (I), David Rankin, (I), Fred Schrier, (I), Art Szabo, (P), Wozniaks, (I), J. David Wilder, (P)
Oreman, Linda/15 Atkinson St, Rochester, NY — 716-232-1585
  Nick Angello, (I), Roger DeMuth, (I), Bill Finewood, (I), Doug Gray, (I), Stephen Moscowitz, (I)

PR
PALULIAN, JOANNE/18 MCKINLEY ST, ROWAYTON, CT (P 182,183) — 203-866-3734
  Scott Barrows, (I), David Lesh, (I), Kirk Moldoff, (I), Dickran Palulian, (I), Walt Spitzmiller, (I)
Photo-Graphic Agency/58 Pine St, Malden, MA — 617-944-3166
Publishers Graphics/251 Greenwood Ave, Bethel, CT — 203-797-8188
Putscher, Tony/2303 Green St, Philadelphia, PA — 215-569-8890
Radxevich Standke/15 Intervale Terr, Reading, MA — 617-944-3166
  Christian Delbert, (P)
Reese-Gibson, Jean/4 Puritan Rd, N Beverly, MA — 617-927-5006
Robbins, David Group/256 Arch Rd, Avon, CT — 203-673-6530
  Mike Eagle, (I)
Rubenstein, Len/One Winthrop Sq, Boston, MA — 617-482-0666
  Jim Conaty, (P)

ST
Satterthwaite, Victoria/115 Arch St, Philadelphia, PA — 215-925-4233
  Michael Furman, (P)
Schooley & Associates/21 Roseld Ave, Deal, NJ — 201-531-3412
  Lorraine Dey, (I), Kevin Dougherty, (I), Geoffrey Gove, (I), William Laird, (I), Gary Smith, (I)
Shea, Sandra/118 Old Boston Post Rd, Old Saybrook, CT — 203-388-1755
Smith, Wayne R/145 South St Penthouse, Boston, MA — 617-426-726
  Robert Brooks, (I), John Holt, (I), Ben Luce, (I), Ed Porzio, (I)
Snyder, Diane/3 Underwood Rd, Wyncote, PA — 215-572-119
  Craig Bakley, (I), David Christiana, (I), Michael McNelly, (I), Verlin Miller, (I), Roseman, Shelly, (P), Lee Wojner, (P)
Spencer, Sandy/700 S 10th St, Philadelphia, PA — 215-238-120
  Anthony Ward, (P)
Spiak, Al/35 Monroe Ave, Dumont, NJ — 201-387-939
Stevens, Rick/925 Penn Ave #404, Pittsburgh, PA — 412-765-356
Ternay, Louise/119 Birch Ave, Bala Cynwyd, PA — 215-667-862
  Bruce Blank, (P), Len Epstein, (I), Don Everhart, (I), Geri Grienke, (I), Peter Sasten, (G), Bill Ternay, (I), Kate Ziegler, (I)

UV
Unicorn/1148 Parsippany Blvd, Parsippany, NJ — 201-334-035
  Greg Hildebrandt, (I)
Valen Assocs/PO Box 8, Westport, CT — 203-227-780
  George Booth, (C), Whitney Darrow, (C), Joe Farris, (C), William Hamilton, (C), Stan Hunt, (C), Anatol Kovarsky, (C), Henry Martin, (C), Frank Modell, (C), Mischa Richter, (C), Charles Saxon, (C), Jim Stevenson, (C), Henry Syverson, (C), Bob Weber, (C), Rowland Wilson, (I), Bill Ziegler, (I)

W
Waterman, Laurie/130 South 17th St, Philadelphia, PA — 215-988-039
Wayne, Lynn/99 Wilson Ave, Windsor, CT — 203-522-314
Wigon, Leslie/191 Plymouth Dr, Scarsdale, NY — 914-472-945
WOLFE, DEBORAH LTD/731 NORTH 24TH ST, PHILADELPHIA, PA (P 211) — 215-232-666
  Steve Cusano, (I), Harry Davis, (I), Robert Hakalski, (P), Robin Hodgkiss, (I), Ron Lehew, (I), Bill Margerin, (I), Bruce McAllister, (P), Scott Petters, (I), Bob Schenker, (I), Jim Sharpe, (I), Charles Weckler, (P), Allan Weitz, (P), Alan White, (P), Frank Williams, (I), Liz Wuillerman, (P)
Worrall, Dave/125 S 18th St, Philadelphia, PA — 215-567-288
  Weaver Lilley, (P)

SOUTHEAST

BC
Babcock, Nancy/1496 N Morningside Dr NE, Atlanta, GA — 404-876-01
Beck, Susanne/2721 Cherokee Rd, Birmingham, AL — 205-871-66
  Charles Beck, (P)

REPRESENTATIVES CONT'D.

Please send us your additions and updates.

Burnett, Yolanda/559 Dutch Vall Rd, Atlanta, GA   404-079-5050
   Jim Copland, (P), Charlie Lathem, (P)

Centini, Gail/333 Adams St, Decatur, GA   404-377-8383
   Eric Henderson, (P), Kenny Higdon, (I), Trevor Irvin, (I), Arthur Tilly, (P)

Couch, Tom/1164 Briarcliff Rd NE #2, Atlanta, GA   404-872-5774
   Granberry/Anderson Studio, (P)

FHJ
Fink, Duncan/437 S Tryon St, Charlotte, NC   704-377-4217
   Ron Chapple, (P), Mitchell Kearney, (P)

Forbes, Pat/11459 Waterview Cluster, Reston, VA   703-437-7042
   Kay Chenush, (P)

Hathcox, Julia/5730 Arlington Blvd, Arlington, VA   703-845-5831
   David Hathcox, (P)

Jett & Agson/1340 S 6th St, Louisville, KY   502-634-4911

Jourdan, Carolyn/520 Brickell Key Dr #1417, Miami, FL   305-372-9425

Judge, Marie/9452 SW 77th Ave, Miami, Fl   305-595-1700

M
LINDEN, TAMARA/3500 PIEDMONT RD #430, ATLANTA, GA (P 151)   **404-262-1209**
   Tom Fleck, (I), Joe Ovies, (I), Charles Passarelli, (I), Larry Tople, (I)

McGee, Linda/1816 Briarwood Ind Ct, Atlanta, GA   404-633-1286

McLean Represents/401 W Peachtree St NW #1720, Atlanta, GA   404-221-0798
   Joe Isom, (I), Jack Jones, (I), Martin Pate, (I), Steve Spetseris, (I), Warren Weber, (I)

S
Phelps, Katie/3210 Peachtree Rd NW #14, Atlanta, GA   404-233-0022

Pollard, Kiki/848 Greenwood Ave NE, Atlanta, GA   404-875-1363
   Betsy Alexander, (G), John Findley, (I), Dennis Guthrie, (I), James Soukup, (I), Mark Stanton, (I)

Prentice, Nancy/315-A Pharr Rd, Atlanta, GA   404-366-1080

PROPST, SHERYLE/PO BOX 1583, NORCROSS, GA (P 315)   **404-263-9296**
   Michael Davis, (I), Fred Gerlich, (P), Herring & Klem, (I), Reggie Stanton, (I)

Silva, Naomi/100 Bldg Colony Sq #200, Atlanta, GA   404-892-8314
   Joe DiNicola, (I), Rob Horn, (G), Christy Sheets Mull, (I), Alan Patton, (A), Gary Penca, (I), Don Sparks, (P)

Sumpter, Will/1106 W Peachtree St #106, Atlanta, GA   404-874-2014

TW
Torres, Martha/927 Third St, New Orleans, LA   504-895-6570

Wells, Susan/51434 Timber Trails, Atlanta, GA   404-255-1430
   Paul Blakey, (I), Jim Caraway, (I), Don Loehle, (I), Richard Loehle, (I), Randall McKissick, (I), Monte Varah, (I), Beth White, (I)

West, Mike/1157 W Peachtree NW, Atlanta, GA   404-292-2704

Wexler, Marsha Brown/6108 Franklin Pk Rd, McLean, VA   703-241-1776

Williams, Phillip/1106 W Peachtree St #201, Atlanta, GA   404-873-2287
   Jamie Cook, (P), Chipp Jamison, (P), Rick Lovell, (I), Kenvin Lyman, (G), Bill Mayer, (I), David McKelvey, (I), John Robinette, (I)

WOODEN REPS/1151 W PEACHTREE ST NW, ATLANTA, GA (P 213-221)   **404-892-6303**
   Bob August, (I), Image Electronic, (I), Stefan Findal, (P), Mike Hodges, (I), Johanna Hogenkamp, (I), Kevin Hulsey, (I), Chris Lewis, (I), David Marks, (I), Theo Rudnak, (I), Joe Saffold, (I), Michael West, (P), Bruce Young, (I)

MIDWEST

AB
Andoniadis, Nina/900 Mark Ln #302, Wheeling, IL   312-253-7488

Appleman, Norm/679 E Mandoline, Madison Hts, MI   313-589-0066
   Art Hansen, (P), Jerry Kolesar, (P), Larry Melkus, (P), Glenn Schoenbach, (P)

ART STAFF INC/1200 PENOBSCOT BLDG, DETROIT, MI (P 62,63)   **313-963-8240**

Ball, John/203 N Wabash, Chicago, IL   312-332-6041

BARTELS, CECI ASSOC/111 JEFFERSON RD, ST LOUIS, MO (P 371,386)   **314-961-1670**

   Eric Dinyer, (I), Shannon Kriegshauser, (I), Don Kueker, (I), Greg MacNair, (I), Jean Probert, (I), Terry Sirrell, (I), Terry Speer, (I)

Berk, Ida/1350 N La Salle, Chicago, IL   312-944-1339

Birdwell, Steven/208 W Kinzie St, Chicago, IL   312-467-1430
   Robert Meyer, (P)

Brenna, Allen/Southgate Plaza #515, Minneapolis, MN   612-835-1831

Brenner, Harriet/660 W Grand Ave, Chicago, IL   312-243-2730

Brooks, Douglas/1230 W Washington Blvd, Chicago, Il   312-226-4060
   VanKirk Photo, (P)

Buermann, Jeri/321 N 22nd St, St Louis, MO   314-231-8690

CD
Chauncey, Michelle/1029 N Wichita #13, Wichita, KS   316-262-6733

Christell, Jim & Assoc/307 N Michigan Ave #1008, Chicago, IL   312-236-2396
   Michel Ditlove, (P), Ron Harris, (P)

Cohen, Janice/117 North Jefferson, Chicago, IL   312-454-0680

Coleman, Woody/1295 Old River Rd, Cleveland, OH   216-621-1771
   Stuart Daniels, (I), Vladimir Kordic, (I), Ernest Norcia, (I), Bob Novack, (I), Ezra Tucker, (I)

Creative Source/360 N Michigan, Chicago, IL   312-649-9777
   Ron Mahoney, (I), Tom McCaffrey, (I), Hugo Prado, (I), Harley Shelton, (I), Don Tate, (I), Clark Tate, (I)

DeWalt & Assoc/3447 N 79th St, Milwaukee, WI   414-449-2263
   Tom Fritz, (P)

Dix, Barbara/4715 N Ronald St, Harwood Heights, IL   312-867-5445

Dodge, Tim/2412 E Stratford Ct, Milwaukee, WI   414-964-9558
   Barbara Ericksen, (I), Jeff Hangartner, (I), Ken Hanson, (G), Paul Henning, (P), Tom Kwas, (P), Dave Vander Veen, (P)

Dolby, Karen/215 W Ohio, Chicago, IL   312-321-1770

EF
Emerich Studios/300 W 19th Terrace, Kansas City, MO   816-474-8888

Erdos, Kitty/210 W Chicago, Chicago, IL   312-787-4976

Feldman, Kenneth/30 E Huron, Chicago, IL   312-337-0447

Fiat, Randi/208 W Kinzie, Chicago, IL   312-784-2343

Fleming, Laird Tyler/1 Memorial Dr, St Louis, MO   314-982-1700
   John Bilecky, (P), Willardson & White, (P)

Frayer, Pam & Assoc/435 N Michigan Ave #1832, Chicago, IL   312-644-5558

Fried, Monica/1546 N Orleans, Chicago, IL   312-642-8715

Frost, Brent & Laumer, Dick/4037 Queen Ave S, Minneapolis, MN   612-922-3440

GH
Green Gotfried & Assoc/29 E Ohio, Chicago, IL   312-661-0024

Hanson, Jim/540 N Lake Shore Dr, Chicago, IL   312-527-1114
   Bob Bender, (P), Richard Fegley, (P), Bob Gelberg, (P), Rob Johns, (P), Rick Mitchell, (P), Barry O'Rourke, (P), John Payne, (P), Al Satterwhite, (P)

Harlib, Joel/405 N Wabash #3203, Chicago, IL   312-329-1370
   Bob August, (I), John Casado, (I), Lawrence Duke, (P), Peter Elliott, (P), Marty Evans, (P), Ignacio Gomez, (I), Barbara Higgins-Bond, (I), DeWitt Jones, (P), Richard Leech, (I), Tim Lewis, (I), Peter Lloyd, (I), Bret Lopez, (P), David McMacken, (I), Dennis Mukai, (I), Joe Ovies, (I), Matthew Rolston, (P), Todd Shorr, (I), Jay Silverman, (P), Bill Vann, (I), Allan Weitz, (P), Kim Whitesides, (I), Bruce Wolfe, (I), Bob Ziering, (I)

Hartig, Michael/3620 Pacific, Omaha, NB   402-345-2164

Heinen, Sandy/219 N 2nd St #409, Minneapolis, MN   612-332-3671

Higgens Hegner Genovese Inc/510 N Dearborn St, Chicago, IL   312-644-1882

Hogan, Myrna & Assoc/333 N Michigan, Chicago, IL   312-372-1616
   Terry Heffernan, (P)

Hoke, Wayne & Assoc/17 N Elizabeth St, Chicago, IL   312-666-0175

Horton, Nancy/939 Sanborn, Palatine, IL   312-934-8966

Hull, Scott/7026 Corporate Way #211, Dayton, OH   513-433-8383
   Tracy Britt, (I), Andy Buttram, (I), David Groff, (I), David Lesh, (I), John Maggard, (I), Larry Martin, (I), Ernest Norcia, (I), Mark Riedy, (I), Don Vanderbeck, (I)

JK
Jenkins, John/1147 W Ohio #403, Chicago, IL   312-243-6580

Jeske, Kurt/612 S Clinton, Chicago, IL   312-922-9200

Kamin, Vince & Assoc/111 E Chestnut, Chicago, IL   312-787-8834
   Ron Lieberman, (I), Mary Anne Shea, (I), Roy Volkman, (P)

REPRESENTATIVES CONT'D.

Please send us your additions and updates.

Kapes, Jack/233 E Wacker Dr #1412, Chicago, IL   312-565-0566
    Stuart Block, (P), John Cahoon, (P), Jerry Friedman, (P),
    Carl Furuta, (P), Klaus Lucka, (P), Dan Romano, (I), Nicolas
    Sidjakov, (G)
Karabatsos, Trish/730 N Franklin, Chicago, IL   312-243-8578
Kezelis, Elena/215 W Illinois, Chicago, IL   312-644-7108
Kleber, Gordon/125 W Hubbard, Chicago, IL   312-661-1362
Koralik, Connie/26 E Huron, Chicago, IL   312-944-5680
    Robert Keeling, (P), Kazu, (P)
Krisher, Deborah/900 N Franklin, Chicago, IL   312-642-2724
    Richard Mack, (P)

L
Lakehomer & Assoc/405 N Wabash #1402, Chicago, IL   312-644-1766
    Tim Schultz, (P)
Lasko, Pat/452 N Halsted, Chicago, IL   312-243-6696
    Ralph King, (P)
Levey, Rebecca/15 W Delaware PL, Chicago, IL   312-329-9040
Linzer, Jeff/4001 Forest Rd, Minneapolis, MN   612-926-4390
Lonier, Terry/215 W Ohio #5W, Chicago, IL   312-527-1880
Lukmann, Geri/314 W Institute Pl, Chicago, IL   312-787-1774
    Brent Carpenter, (PH), Steve Nozicka, (P)

M
McManus, Mike/3423 Devon Rd, Royal Oak, MI   313-549-8196
McMasters, Deborah/157 W Ontario, Chicago, IL   312-943-9007
    Richard Foster, (P)
McNamara Associates/1250 Stephenson Hwy, Troy, MI   313-583-9200
    Max Alterruse, (I), Gary Ciccarelli, (I), Garry Colby, (I),
    Hank Kolodziej, (I), Chuck Passarelli, (I), Tony Randazzo,
    (I), Gary Richardson, (I), Dick Scullin, (I), Don Wieland, (I)
McNaughton, Toni/233 E Wacker #2904, Chicago, IL   312-938-2148
    Pam Haller, (P), Rodica Prato, (I), James B. Wood, (P)
Melkus, Larry/679 Mandoline, Madison Hts, MI   313-589-0066
Miller, Richard/743 N Dearborn, Chicago, IL   312-280-2288
    Paul Barton, (P), Morton Beebe, (P), Rebecca Blake, (P),
    Chris Butler, (I), Geoffrey Clifford, (P), Marc Hauser, (P),
    Richard High, (C), Bob Krogle, (I), Jim Krogle, (I), Robert
    Sacco, (P)
Mohlman, Jeanette/114 W Illinois, Chicago, IL   312-321-1570
Mohlo, David/ Werremeyer Inc/12837 Flushing Meadow Dr,
    St Louis, MO   314-966-3770
Moore, Amanda/1752 N Mohawk, Chicago, IL   312-337-0880
    Peter Sagara, (P)
Moore, Connie/1540 N North Park, Chicago, IL   312-787-4422
    Richard Shirley, (I)
Moshier & Maloney/535 N Michigan, Chicago, IL   312-943-1668
    Nicolette Anastas, (I), Dave Wilson & Assoc, (I), Steve
    Carr, (P), Dan Clyne, (I), Ron DiCianni, (I), David Gaadt, (I),
    John Hamagami, (I), Rick Johnson, (I), Bill Kastan, (I), Ed
    Lindlof, (I), Dennis Luzak, (I), Colleen Quinn, (I), Paul
    Ristau, (I), Stephen Rybka, (I), Skidmore-Sahratian, (I), Al
    Stine, (I), Jim Trusilo, (I), John Youssi, (I)
Moy, Charlene/30 E Huron, Chicago, IL   312-337-0447
Murphy, Sally/70 W Hubbard, Chicago, IL   312-346-0720

NO
Nagan, Rita/1514 NE Jefferson St, Minneapolis, MN   612-788-7923
Nelson, Sandy/315 W Walton, Chicago, IL   312-266-8029
Newman, Richard/1866 N Burling, Chicago, IL   312-266-2513
Nicholson, Richard B/2310 Denison Ave, Cleveland, OH   216-398-1494
    Martin Reuben, (P), Mike Steinberg, (P), Al Teufer, (P), J
    David Wilder, (P)
Nicolini, Sandra/230 N Michigan #523, Chicago, IL   312-346-1648
    Elizabeth Ernst, (P), Tom Petroff, (P)
O'Brien-Stieber/203 N wabash #1600, Chicago, IL   312-726-9690
O'Farrel, Eileen/311 Good Ave, Des Plaines, IL   312-297-5447
O'Grady Advertising Arts/333 North Michigan Ave #2200,
    Chicago, IL   312-726-9833
O'Neill, Mary/17006 Woodbury Ave, Cleveland, OH   216-252-6238
Osler, Spike/2616 Industrial Row, Troy, MI   313-280-0640
    Mark Coppos, (P), Madison Ford, (P), Rob Gage, (P), Rick
    Kasmier, (P), Jim Secreto, (P)

P
Parker, Tom/1750 N Clark, Chicago, IL   312-266-2891

Peterson, Vicki/535 N Michigan Ave #2802, Chicago, IL   312-467-0780
    Charlie Gold, (P), Elyse Lewin, (P), Howard Menken, (P),
    Robert Stovons, (P), Charlie Westerman, (P)
Phase II/155 N Michigan Ave, Chicago, IL   312-565-0030
    Bill Cigliano, (I), Michael Elins, (I), David Krainik, (I), Kathy
    Petrauskas, (I), Mark Sauck, (I), Richard Taylor, (I)
Photo Services Owens-Corning/Fiberglass Towers, Toledo, OH   419-248-8041
    Jay Langlois, (P), Joe Sharp, (P)
Platzer, Karen & Assoc/535 N Michigan Ave, Chicago, IL   312-467-1981
    Larry Banner, (P), Michael Caporale, (P), Ray Cioni, (I)
Pool, Linda/6905 E 102nd St, Kansas City, MO   816-761-7314
Potts, Carolyn/1872 N Clybourn, Chicago, IL   312-664-9336
    Barbara Bersell, (P), John Craig, (I), Alan Dolgins, (P),
    Gregory Murphey, (P), Fred Nelson, (I), Joe Ovies, (I), Kulp
    Productions, (P), Leslie Wolf, (I)
Potts, Vicki/139 N Wabash, Chicago, IL   312-726-5678
    Mitchell Einhorn, (P), Mercer Engelhard, (P), David
    Gerhardt, (P), Kathy Sanders, (P)
Pride, Max/401 W Superior, Chicago, IL   312-664-5392

R
Rabin, Bill & Assoc/666 N Lake Shore Dr, Chicago, IL   312-944-6655
    John Alcorn, (I), Joel Baldwin, (P), Joe Baraban, (P), Roger
    Beerworth, (I), Guy Billout, (I), Howard Bjornson, (P),
    Thomas Blackshear, (I), R O Blechman, (I), Charles William
    Bush, (P), JoAnn Carney, (P), John Collier, (I), Jackie
    Geyer, (I), Paul Giovanopoulos, (I), Tim Girvin, (G), Robert
    Giusti, (I), Kunio Hagio, (I), Lamb & Hall, (P), Mark Hess, (I),
    Richard Hess, (I), Walter Ioss, (I), Art Kane, (P), Rudi
    Legname, (P), Daniel Maffia, (I), Jay Maisel, (P), Dan
    Malinowski, (P), Jim Matusik, (P), Eric Meola, (P), Eugene
    Mihaesco, (I), Richard Noble, (P), Robert Rodriguez, (I),
    Reynold Ruffins, (I), Michael Shwab, (I), Ed Sorel, (I),
    George Stavrinos, (I), Simms Taback, (I), Ezra Tucker, (I),
    Pete Turner, (P), David Wilcox, (I)
Ray, Rodney/405 N Wabash #3106, Chicago, IL   312-472-6550

S
Scarff, Signe/22 W Erie, Chicago, IL   312-266-8353
    Larry Kolze, (P)
Sell, Dan/233 E Wacker, Chicago, IL   312-565-2701
    Alvin Blick, (I), Paul Bond, (I), Wayne Carey, (I), Justin
    Carroll, (I), Bobbye Cochran, (I), Wil Cormier, (I), Bill
    Ersland, (I), Rick Farrell, (I), Dick Flood, (I), Bill Harrison, (I),
    Dave LaFleur, (I), Gregory Manchess, (I), Bill Mayer, (I),
    Frank Morris, (I), Tim Raglin, (I), Ian Ross, (I), Mark
    Schuler, (I), R J Shay, (I), Jay Songero, (I), Dale Verzaal,
    (I), Jay, (I), Fran Vuksanovich, (I), Phil Wendy, (I), John
    Zielinski, (I)
Shulman, Salo/215 W Ohio, Chicago, IL   312-337-3241
    Stan Stansfield, (P)
Siegel, Gerald & Assoc/506 N Clark, Chicago, IL   312-661-1818
    Ralph Cowan, (P), Mike Fisher, (I), George Hamblin, (I),
    Kevin Hulsey, (I), Jan Jones, (I), Steve Mayse, (I), Paul
    Ristau, (I), Elwood Smith, (I)
Sims, Mel/441 N LaSalle, Chicago, IL   312-644-746
Skillicorn, Roy/233 E Wacker #29031, Chicago, IL   312-856-162
    Wickart Brothers, (I), Tom Curry, (I), David Scanlon, (I)
Snowberger, Ann/405 N Wabash #4705, Chicago, IL   312-661-166

TV
Timon, Clay & Assoc Inc/540 N Lake Shore Dr, Chicago, IL   312-527-111
    Bob Bender, (P), Michael Fletcher, (P), Larry Dale Gordon,
    (P), Don Klumpp, (P), Chuck Kuhn, (P), Barry O'Rourke,
    (P), Al Satterwhite, (P), Michael Slaughter, (P)
Trembeth, Rich/30 E Huron #4904, Chicago, IL   312-727-109
Trinko, Genny/126 W Kinzie St, Chicago, IL   312-222-924
    Cam Chapman, (P)
Trott, David/32588 Dequiendre, Warren, MI   313-978-893
Tuke, Joni/368 W Huron, Chicago, IL   312-787-682
    Jay Ahrend, (P), David Beck, (I), Dan Blanchette, (I), Ken
    Goldammer, (I), Chris Hopkins, (I), Susan Kindst, (P), Brian
    Otto, (I), John Welzenbach, (P), Ken Westphal, (I)
Virnig, Janet/3308 Girard Ave S, Minneapolis, MN   612-822-644

REPRESENTATIVES CONT'D.

Please send us your additions and updates.

WYZ

Wainman, Rick & Assoc/166 E Superior #212, Chicago, IL	312-337-3960
Warner, Rebecca/230 W Huron, Chicago, IL	312-951-0880
Wilson, Mike/6959 N Hamilton, Chicago, IL	312-338-4344
Yunker, Kit/ Allchin, Scott/505 N Lakeshore Dr #3501, Chicago, IL	312-321-0655
Zann, Sheila/502 N Grove, Oak Park, IL	312-386-2864

Arnold Zann, (P)

SOUTHWEST

AB

Art Rep Inc/3511 Cedar Springs #4A, Dallas, TX	214-521-5156

Tom Bailey, (I), Lee Lee Brazeal, (I), Ellis Chappell, (I),
Dean St Clair, (I), Tom Curry, (I), Tom Curry, (I), M John
English, (I), Tom Evans, (I), Tim Girvin, (I), Bill Harrison, (I),
Jim Jacobs, (I), Kent Kirkley, (P), Gary McCoy, (P),
Genevieve Meek, (I), Frank Morris, (I), Michael Schwab, (I),
Andrew Vracin, (P), Kim Whitesides, (I), Terry Widener, (I)

Assid, Carol/122 Parkhouse, Dallas, TX	214-748-3765
Booster, Barbara/4001 Bryn Mawr, Dallas, TX	214-373-4284

CD

Callahan, Joe/330 E Mitchell, Phoenix, AZ	602-248-0777

Tom Gerczynski, (P), Mike Gushock, (I), Jon Kleber, (I),
Howard Post, (I), Dan Ruiz, (I), Mark Sharpls, (I), Dan
Vermillion, (P), Balfour Walker, (P)

Campbell, Patty/2610 Catherine, Dallas, TX	214-946-6597

Douglas Doering, (P)

Cobb, Lisa & Assoc/2200 N Lamar #202, Dallas, TX	214-939-0032
Crowder, Bob/3603 Parry Ave, Dallas, TX	214-823-9000

Barry Kaplan, (P), Moses Olmoz, (P), Al Rubin, (P)

Devereux, Julien/2707 Stemmons Frwy #160, Dallas, TX	214-634-0222

Faustino, (P)

DiOrio, Diana/1819 Augusta Ct #148, Houston, TX	713-266-9390

John Collier, (I), Ray Mel Cornelius, (I), Regan Dunnick, (I),
Larry Keith, (I), Bahid Marinfar, (I), Dennis Mukai, (I), Thom
Ricks, (I)

EFH

Edwards, Nancy/2121 Regency Dr, Irving, TX	214-438-4114
Freeman, Sandra/3333 Elm, Dallas, TX	214-742-4302
Fuller, Alyson/5610 Maple Ave, Dallas, TX	214-688-1855
Hamilton, Chris/3900 Lemmon, Dallas, TX	214-526-2050
Hooper, Don/PO Box 815443, Dallas, TX	214-492-1086

Tim Bowers, (I), Steve Chenn, (P), Bill Craft, (P), Terrell
Mashaw, (I)

MN

Lynch, Larry/3527 Oak Lawn Ave #145, Dallas, TX	214-521-6169

Morton Beebe, (P), Robert Latorre, (P), Richard Wahlstrom,
(P)

McCann, Liz/3000 Carlisle #206, Dallas, TX	214-630-7756

Bill Crumpt, (P), Michael Doret, (I), Ben James, (I), Phil
Kretchmar, (P), James B. Wood, (P)

Noble, Peter/8344 East RL Thornton #300, Dallas, TX	214-328-6676

SW

Photocom Inc/1707 S Ervay, Dallas, TX	214-428-8781

Louis Reens, (P)

Production Services/1711 Hazard, Houston, TX	713-529-7916

George Craig, (P), C Bryan Jones, (P), Thaine Manske, (P)

Smith, Linda/3511 Cedar Springs #4A, Dallas, TX	214-521-5156
Washington, Dick/914 Westmoreland, San Antonio, TX	512-342-2009
Willard, Paul Assoc/313 E Thomas Rd #205, Phoenix, AZ	602-279-0119

Kevin Cruff, (P), Kateri, (I), Matthew Foster, (I), Rick Gayle,
(P), Rick Kirkman, (I), Kevin MacPherson, (I), Curtis Parker,
(I), Nancy Pendleton, (I), Bob Peters, (I), Wayne Watford, (I)

ROCKY MOUNTAIN

F

Cornell, Kathleen/90 Corona #508, Denver, CO	303-778-6016

Nancy Duell, (I), Miles Hardiman, (I), Masami, (I), Daniel

McGowan, (I), Jan Oswald, (P), David Spira, (I), Bonnie
Timmons, (I)

Foremark Studios/PO Box 10346, Reno, NV	702-786-3150

KN

Kelly, Rob/2215 E Mississippi, Denver, CO	303-698-0073

Pat Fujisaki, (I), Ron Sauter, (I)

NO COAST GRAPHICS/2544 15TH ST, DENVER, CO (P 179-181)	**303-458-7086**

John Cuneo, (I), Cindy Enright, (I), Tom Nikosey, (I), Chris
Payne, (I), Mike Steirnagle, (I)

Nosti, Gary/216 Racquette Dr, Fort Collins, CO	303-221-4546

RS

Roberts, Hallie/16 W 13th Ave, Denver, CO	303-534-7267
Ryan, Patti/550 E 12th Ave #910, Denver, CO	303-832-9214

Bob Fader, (P)

Sperling, Alice/1050 Corona #307, Denver, CO	303-832-4686
Synchrony/655 Broadway #800, Denver, CO	303-825-7513

WEST

AB

Albertine, Dotti/202 Westminister Ave #A, Venice, CA	213-392-4877
Aline, France/145 N Orange, Los Angeles, CA	213-933-2500

Guy Billout, (I), Thomas Blackshear, (I), Steve Hulen, (P),
Michael Lamotte, (P), Bret Lopez, (P), Manuel Nunez, (I),
Dave Scanlon, (I), Michael Schwab, (I), Peggy Sirota, (P),
Bob Stevens, (P), Ezra Tucker, (I), Kim Whitesides, (I),
Bruce Wolfe, (I), Bob Zoell, (I)

Annika/8301 W Third St, Los Angeles, CA	213-460-2988
Braun, Kathy/75 Water St, San Francisco, CA	415-543-7377

Arnold & Assoc, (F), Sandra Belce, (L), Tandy Belew, (G),
Michael Bull, (I), Anka, (I), Eldon Doty, (I), Boyington Film,
(F), Jim Fulp, (I), Stephen Osborn, (I), Jim Parkinson, (L),
Allan Rosenberg, (P), Diane Tyler, (MU)

Broadhurst, Cynde/9 Dove Pl, Novato, CA	415-382-1301

Christopher Hopkins, (P), John F Martin, (P)

Brooks/6628 Santa Monica Blvd, Los Angeles, CA	213-463-5678

Mike Chesser, (P)

Brown, Dianne/732 N Highland, Los Angeles, CA	213-464-2775

David LeBon, (P), Bill Werts, (P)

Burlingham, Tricia/10355 Ashton Ave, Los Angeles, CA	213-271-3982

C

Caplan, Deborah/654 Cloverdale Ave #204, Los Angeles, CA	213-935-8248
Carroll, J J/PO Box 3881, Manhattan Beach, CA	213-318-1066

Fred Nelson, (I)

Church, Spencer/515 Lake Washington Blvd, Seattle, WA	206-324-1199

John Fretz, (I), Terry Heffernan, (P), Mits Katayama, (I),
Ann Marra, (G), Scott McDougall, (I), Dale Nordell, (I),
Marilyn Nordell, (I), Ted Rand, (I), Diane
Solvang-Angell, (I), Dugald Stermer, (I), West Stock, (S),
Craig Walden, (I), Dale Windham, (P)

Collier, Jan/166 South Park, San Francisco, CA	415-552-4252

Barbara Banthien, (I), Bunny Carter, (I), Chuck Eckart, (I),
Cris Hammond, (I), Robert Hunt, (I), Kathy O'Brien, (I),
Bernard Phillips, (P), Gretchen Schields, (I), Robert Steele,
(I)

Cook, Warren/PO Box 2159, Laguna Hills, CA	714-770-4619

Kathleen Norris Cook, (P)

Cormany, Paul/11607 Clover Ave, Los Angeles, CA	213-828-9653

Mark Busacca, (I), Bryant Eastman, (I), Dave Eichenberger,
(I), Bob Gleason, (I), Lamb & Hall, (P), Jim Heimann, (I),
Bob Krogle, (I), Gary Norman, (I), Ed Scarisbrick, (I), Stan
Watts, (I), Dick Wilson, (I), Andy Zito, (I)

Courtney, Mary Ellen/1808 Diamond, S Pasadena, CA	213-202-0344

Douglas Bevans, (I), Bart Doe, (I), Matt Mahurin, (I), Paul
Maxon, (P), Linda Medina, (I), Judy Reed, (I), Jeff Scales,
(P), Chuck Schmidt, (I), Diane Teske-Harris, (I)

Crosse, Annie/10642 Vanora Dr, Sunland, CA	818-352-5173

Wendy Lagerstrom, (I), Mike Nelson, (I), Henri Parmentier,
(I), Ted Sizemore, (I), Terry Smith, (I)

DE

Diskin, Donnell/143 Edgemont, Los Angeles, CA	213-383-9157

REPRESENTATIVES CONT'D.

Please send us your additions and updates.

Drayton, Sheryl/5018 Dumont Pl, Woodland Hills, CA	818-347-2227
Dubow & Hutkin/7461 Beverly Blvd #405, Los Angeles, CA	213-938-5177
Terry Anderson, (I), Dick Ellescas, (I), Marc Ericksen, (I), Ignacio Gomez, (I), Roger Hubbard, (I), Richard Ikkanda, (I), Paul Kratter, (I), Mike Rogers, (I), Larry Salk, (I)	
Epps, Susan/1226 Alameda Padre Serra, Santa Barbara, CA	805-962-2074
Epstein, Rhoni & Assoc/3814 Franklin Ave, Los Angeles, CA	213-663-2388

FG

Feliciano, Terrianne/16782 Red Hill #B, Irvine, CA	714-250-4357
Fleming, Laird Tyler/407 1/2 Shirley Pl, Beverly Hills, CA	213-552-4626
John Bilecky, (P), Willardson & White, (P)	
Fletcher, Lois/28956 West Lake Vista Dr, Agoura, CA	818-707-1010
Earl Miller, (P)	
George, Nancy/360 1/2 N Mansfield Ave, Los Angeles, CA	213-935-4696
Brent Bear, (P), Sid Bingham, (I), Justin Carroll, (I), Randy Chewning, (I), Bruce Dean, (I), Steve Hendricks, (I), Hank Hinton, (I), Gary Hoover, (I), Richard Kriegler, (I), Larry Lake, (I), Gary Lund, (I), Rob Sprattler, (I), Bruce Wilson, (P)	
Gilbert, Sam/410 Sheridan, Palo Alto, CA	415-325-2102
Gray, Connie/248 Alhambra, San Francisco, CA	415-331-9111
Steven Fucuda, (P), Max Gisko, (I), Bob Gleason, (I), John Lund, (I), Mark McLandish, (I), Joel Nakamura, (I), Fred Nelson, (I), Gary Norman, (I), David Oshiro, (G), Suzanne Phister, (I), Michael Utterbock, (P), Will Westin, (I), Barry Wetmore, (I)	
Gray, Pam/1912 Hermosa Ave #F, Hermosa Beach, CA	213-374-3606
Group West Inc/5455 Wilshire Blvd #1212, Los Angeles, CA	213-937-4472
Neil Boyle, (I), Nixon Galloway, (I), Frank Germain, (I), Roger Hammond, (I), Fred Hatzer, (I), Ron McKee, (I), Norman Merritt, (I), Bill Robles, (I), Ren Wicks, (I)	

H

Hackett, Pat/2030 First Ave #201, Seattle, WA	206-623-9459
Bill Cannon, (P), Steve Coppin, (I), Larry Duke, (I), Bill Evans, (I), Norman Hathaway, (I), Ed Hauser, (I), Larry Lubeck, (I), Bill Mayer, (I), Mike Schumacher, (I), John C Smith, (I), John Terence Turner, (P)	
Haigh, Nancy/90 Natoma St, San Francisco, CA	415-391-1646
Halcomb, Mark/1259-A Folsom, San Francisco, CA	415-861-8877
Hallowell, Wayne/11046 McCormick, North Hollywood, CA	818-769-5694
Dick Birkey, (I), Alden Butcher, (AV), Emerson/Johnson/ MacKay, (I), Dimensional Design, (G), Terry Hambright, (I), Ray Howlett, (I), Bill McCormick, (G), Louis McMurray, (I), Pro/Stock, (P), Lollie Ortiz, (I), Diana Robbins, (I), Larry Schenkar, (P), Greg Smith, (P), Ed Vartanian, (I)	
Hart, Vikki/409 Bryant St, San Francisco, CA	415-495-4278
Jim Blakely, (P), Robert Evans, (I), G K Hart, (P), Kevin Hulsey, (I), Aleta Jenks, (I), Tom Kamifuji, (I), Heather King, (I), Julie Tsuchiya, (I), Jonathan Wright, (I)	
Hauser, Barbara/7041 Hemlock St, Oakland, CA	415-339-1885
Hedge, Joanne/1838 El Cerrito Pl #3, Hollywood, CA	213-874-1661
Rebecca Archey, (I), Keith Batcheller, (I), Delana Bettoli, (I), Chris Dellorco, (I), Bo Hylen, (P), Jeff Leedy, (I), Bette Levine, (I), Kenvin Lyman, (I), David McMacken, (I), Dennis Mukai, (I), Vida Pavesich, (I), William Rieser, (I)	
Hillman, Betsy/2230 Francisco #106, San Francisco, CA	415-563-2243
Chuck Bowden, (I), Tim Boxell, (I), Hiro Kimura, (I), John Marriott, (P), HKM Productions, (P), Greg Spalenka, (I), Joe Spencer, (I), Jeremy Thornton, (I), Jackson Vereen, (P)	
Hodges, Jeanette/12401 Bellwood, Los Alamitos, CA	213-431-4343
Ken Hodges, (I)	
Hughes, April/1350 California #302, San Francisco, CA	415-441-4602
Sam Errico, (P), Sharon Harker, (I), Steve Hofheimer, (I), Dave Jensen, (I), Eric Joyner, (I), Paul Matsuda, (P), Jim Spence, (I), Barton Stabler, (I), Diana Thewlis, (I), Javier Tsang, (GD), Glenn Tunstull, (I), Mike Yeung, (L)	
Hyatt, Nadine/PO Box 2455, San Francisco, CA	415-543-8944
Jeanette Adams, (I), Rebecca Archey, (I), Charles Bush, (P), Frank Cowan, (P), Marty Evans, (P), Gerry Gersten, (I), John Hyatt, (I), Bret Lopez, (P), Tom McClure, (I), Jan Schockner, (L), Victor Stabin, (I), Liz Wheaton, (I)	

JK

Jorgensen, Donna/609 East Summit Ave, Seattle, WA	206-284-5080
Alice Brickner, (I), Frank Denman, (P), Fred Hilliard, (I), Richard Kehl, (I), Doug Keith, (I), David Lund, (I), Robert Peckham, (I), Tim Stevenson, (I)	
Kelly, Jim/1350 Wilshire, Santa Ana, CA	714-835-8449
Kirsch, Melanie/2643 S Fairfax Ave, Culver City, CA	213-651-3706
Knable, Ellen/PO Box 67725, Los Angeles, CA	213-855-8855
Charles Bush, (P), Stan Caplan, (P), Mark Coppos, (P), David Erramouspe, (I), Joe Heiner, (I), Kathy Heiner, (I), John Hyatt, (I), Rudi Legname, (P), Vigon/Nahas/Vigon, (I), Robert Rodriguez, (I), Jonathan Wright, (I), Brian Zick, (I)	
Koeffler, Ann/1555 Greenwich #9, San Francisco, CA	415-885-271
Randy Berrett, (I), Karl Edwards, (I), Bob Hickson, (I), Paul Kratter, (I), Kevin O'Shea, (I), Michael Pearce, (I), Stephen Peringer, (I), Ken Rosenberg, (I), Chris Shorten, (P), Sarn Suvityasiri, (I)	

L

Laycock, Louise/Storyboards/8800 Venice Blvd, Los Angeles, CA	213-870-6565
Lee & Lou/618 S Western Ave #202, Los Angeles, CA	213-388-9465
Rob Gage, (P), Bob Grigg, (P), Richard Leech, (I)	
Lilie, Jim/1801 Franklin St #404, San Francisco, CA	415-441-438
Lou Beach, (I), Alan Dolgins, (P), David Fischer, (P), Patricia Mahoney, (I), Masami Miyamoto, (I), Larry Noble, (I), Robert Rodriguez, (I), Dugald Stermer, (I), Ezra Tucker, (I), Stan Watts, (I), Dennis Ziemienski, (I)	
Lippert, Tom/West End Studios/1100 Glendon #732, Los Angeles, CA	213-279-153
Littles, Dolores/1086 Sycamore Ave, Los Angeles, CA	213-937-663

MO

Magestic, Michael/23316 Burbank Blvd, Woodland Hills, CA	818-703-834
MARIE, RITA & FRIENDS/6376 W 5TH ST, LOS ANGELES, CA (P 152-159)	**213-934-339**
Gene Allison, (I), Chris Consani, (I), Jim Endicott, (I), Marla Frazee, (I), Aleta Jencks, (I), Hiro Kimura, (I), Gary Pierazzi, (I), Robert Pryor, (I), Paul Rogers, (I), Greg Rowe, (I), Gary Ruddell, (I), Dick Sakahara, (I)	
Martha Productions/1830 S Robertson Blvd #203, Los Angeles, CA	213-204-177
Bob Brugger, (I), Jacques Devaud, (I), Stan Evenson, (I), Tracy Garner, (I), John Hamagami, (I), William Harrison, (I), Arthur Hill, (I), Catherine Leary, (I), Ed Lindlof, (I), Rudy Obrero, (I), Cathy Pavia, (I), Wayne Watford, (I)	
McBride, Elizabeth/70 Broadway, San Francisco, CA	415-421-632
Keith Criss, (I), Robert Holmes, (P), Patricia Pearson, (I), Bill Sanchez, (I), Earl Thollander, (I), Tom Vano, (P)	
McCullough, Gavin/638 S Van Ness, Los Angeles, CA	213-382-628
McKenzie, Dianne/839 Emerson St, Palo Alto, CA	415-322-803
Victor Budnik, (P)	
Media Services/Gloria Peterson/10 Aladdin Terr, San Francisco, CA	415-928-303
Melrose, Penny/1333 Lawrence Expwy #150, Santa Clara, CA	408-737-949
Michaels, Martha/3279 Kifer Rd, Santa Clara, CA	408-735-844
Mix, Eva/PO Box 475, Cotati, CA	707-584-160
Morris, Leslie/1062 Rengstorff Ave, Mountain View, CA	415-966-830
Paul Olsen, (I)	
Ogden, Robin/412 N Doheny Dr, Los Angeles, CA	213-858-094
Karen Bell, (I), Joe Crabtree, (I), Steve Gray, (I), Gerry Hampton, (I), Lou LaRose, (I), Jim Miller, (P), Julie Perron, (I), Ken Rosenberg, (I), Jeannie Winston, (I), Corey Wolfe, (I), Jane vanTamelan, (I)	

PQ

Parrish, Dave/Photopia/PO Box 2309, San Francisco, CA	415-441-561
Parsons, Ralph/1232 Folsom St, San Francisco, CA	415-339-188
Pate, Randy/The Source/PO Box 687, North Hollywood, CA	818-985-818
Pierceall, Kelly/25260 Piuma Rd, Malibu, CA	213-559-432
Piscopo, Maria/2038 Calvert Ave, Costa Mesa, CA	714-556-613
Adrienne Warren, (P)	
Quon, Milton/3900 Somerset Dr, Los Angeles, CA	213-293-070
Mike Quon, (P)	

R

Robbins, Leslie/68 Cumberland St, San Francisco, CA — 415-826-8741
  Jim Korte, (I), James LaMarche, (I), Scott Miller, (I), Vida Pavesich, (I), Julie Peterson, (I), David Tise, (P), Tom Wyatt, (P)

Rosenthal, Elise/3443 Wade St, Los Angeles, CA — 213-306-6878
  Saul Bernstein, (I), Chris Butler, (I), Alan Daniels, (I), Jim Deneen, (I), Myron Grossman, (I), Alan Hashimoto, (I), James Henry, (I), Tim Huhn, (I), Jim McKiernan, (I), Kenton Nelson, (I), Peter Palombi, (I), Tom Pansini, (I), Kim Passey, (I), Bill Robles, (I), Tom Tomita, (I), Will Weston, (I), Larry Winborg, (I)

S

Salisbury, Sharon/116 W Blithedale, Mill Valley, CA — 415-495-4665
  Keith Batcheller, (I), Craig Calsbeck, (I), Jim Endicott, (I), Bob Graham, (I), Bo Hylen, (P), Larry Keenan, (P), Bette Levine, (I), Dave McMacken, (I), Robert Mizono, (P), Vida Pavesich, (I)

SALZMAN, RICHARD W/1352 HORNBLEND ST, SAN DIEGO, CA (P 197-201) — 619-272-8147
  Tony Baker, (I), Ruben DeAnda, (I), Manuel Garcia, (I), Jason Harlem, (P), Denise Hilton-Putnam, (I), Joyce Kitchell, (I), Bernie Lansky, (C), Gordon Menzie, (P), Dave Mollering, (I), Imagery That Moves, (G), Dianne O'Quinn-Burke, (I), Everett Peck, (I), Nono Remos, (R), Terry Smith, (I), Walter Stuart, (I), Jonathan Wright, (I), Daniels, (I)

Sandler, Neil/3443 Wade St, Los Angeles, CA — 213-306-6878

Scott, Freda/244 Ninth St, San Francisco, CA — 415-775-6564
  Sherry Bringham, (L), David Campbell, (P), Abe Gurvin, (I), Gayle Kabaker, (I), Jeff Leedy, (F), Francis Livingston, (I), Diane Padys, (P), Susan Schelling, (P)

Scroggy, David/2124 Froude St, San Diego, CA — 619-222-2476
  Ed Abrams, (I), Jodell D Abrams, (I), Joe Chiado, (I), Rick Geary, (I), John Pound, (I), Hal Scroggy, (I), Debbie Tilley, (I)

Sindell, Richard/811 20th St #107, Santa Monica, CA — 213-453-4033

Slobodian, Barbara/745 N Alta Vista Blvd, Hollywood, CA — 213-935-6668
  Bob Greisen, (I), David Kaiser, (I), Tom O'Brien, (P), Forest Sigwart, (I), Scott Slobodian, (P)

Sobol, Lynne/4302 Melrose Ave, Los Angeles, CA — 213-665-5141
  Frank Marquez, (I), Arthur Montes de Oca, (P)

Steinberg, John/10434 Corfu Lane, Los Angeles, CA — 213-279-1775
  Jay Ahrent, (P), John Alvin, (I), Bo Gehring & Associates, (I), Beau Daniels, (I), Alan Daniels, (I), Precision Illustration, (I), David Kimble, (I), Reid Miles, (P), Richard Moore, (P), Larry Noble, (I), Frank Page, (I), Mark Stehrenberger, (I), Ed Wexler, (I)

Studio Artists Inc/630 S Van Ness Ave, Los Angeles, CA — 213-382-6281
  Chuck Coppock, (I), George Francuch, (I), Bill Franks, (I), Duane Gordon, (I)

Sullivan, Diane/3727 Buchanan, San Francisco, CA — 415-563-8884
  Lawrence Duke, (P)

Sweet, Ron/716 Montgomery St, San Francisco, CA — 415-433-1222
  Charles East, (D), John Hamagami, (I), Bob Haydock, (I), Gregg Keeling, (I), Richard Leech, (I), Walter Swarthout, (P), Don Weller, (I), Bruce Wolfe, (I), James B Wood, (P)

T

Tabke, Tim/35-23 Ryder St, Santa Clara, CA — 408-733-5855

Taggard, Jim/PO 4064 Pioneer Square Station, Seattle, WA — 206-938-1898
  Sjef's-Photographie, (P)

Tanner, Lisa/11649 Mayfield Ave, Los Angeles, CA — 213-207-1668

Todd, Deborah/259 Clara St, San Francisco, CA — 415-495-3556

TRIMPE, SUSAN/2717 WESTERN AVE, SEATTLE, WA (P 208-210) — 206-728-1300
  Don Baker, (I), Wendy Edelson, (I), Stephen Peringer, (I)

V

Vandamme, Mary/1165 Francisco #5, San Francisco, CA — 415-433-1292
  John Blaustein, (P), John Collier, (I), Robert Giusti, (I), Joe and Kathy Heiner, (I), Alan Krosnick, (P), Kenvin Lyman, (I), Dennis Mukai, (I), Bill Rieser, (I), Ed Scarisbrick, (I), Michael Schwab, (I), Charles Shields, (I), Rick Strauss, (P), Carol Wald, (I), Kim Whitesides, (I)

Visages/8228 Sunset Blvd #230, Los Angeles, CA — 213-650-8880

W

Wagoner, Jae/200 Westminster Ave #A, Venice, CA — 213-392-4877
  Tim Alt, (I), Michael Backus, (I), Roger Beerworth, (I), Stephen Durke, (I), Steve Jones, (I), Lee MacLeod, (I), Craig Nelson, (I), Robert Tanenbaum, (I), Don Weller, (I)

Wiegand, Chris/7106 Waring Ave, Los Angeles, CA — 213-931-5942

YZ

Youmans, Jill/1021 1/2 N La Brea, Los Angeles, CA — 213-469-8624
  Dan Cooper, (I), Jeff George, (I), Brian Leng, (P), Jeff Leung, (I), Christine Nasser, (I), Joyce Patti, (I), Bill Salada, (I)

Young, Jill/Compendium Inc/945 Front St #201, San Francisco, CA — 415-392-0542
  Judy Clifford, (I), Armondo Diaz, (P), Celeste Ericsson, (I), Marilee Heyer, (I), Rae Huestis, (G), Mary Jew, (G), Bonnie Matza, (G), Barbara Muhlhauser, (G), Martin Schweitzer, (G), Donna Mae Shaver, (P), Cecily Starin, (I), Sarn Suvityasiri, (I), Ed Taber, (I), Carlotta Tormey, (I)

Zank, Elen/262 Donahue St, Sausalito, CA — 415-332-3739
  Chip Carroon, (P)

Zimmerman, Delores H/9135 Hazen Dr, Beverly Hills, CA — 213-273-2642

NOTES:

ILLUSTRATORS

NEW YORK CITY

A

Abraham, Daniel E/425 Fifth Ave	718-499-4006
ABRAMS, KATHIE/41 UNION SQUARE W #1001 (P 256)	**212-741-1333**
Accornero, Franco/620 Broadway	212-674-0068
Acuna, Ed/353 W 53rd St #1W	212-682-2462
Adams, Angela/866 UN Plaza #4014	212-644-2020
ADAMS, JEANETTE/261 BROADWAY (P 257)	**212-732-3878**
ADAMS, JEFFREY/95 HORATIO ST (P 79)	**212-807-0840**
Aiese, Bob/925 E 14th St	718-253-2367
AIRSTREAM/ PAT BAILEY/60 E 42ND ST #505 (P 10)	**212-682-1490**
AIRSTREAM/ PAM WALL/60 E 42ND ST #505 (P 11)	**212-682-1490**
AJHAR, BRIAN/321 E 12TH ST #30 (P 258)	**212-254-0694**
Albahae, Andrea/2721 Batchelder St	718-934-7004
ALCORN, BOB/48 W 21ST ST 9TH FL (P 188)	**212-243-4412**
Alcorn, Stephen/194 Third Ave	212-475-0440
Allaux, Jean Francois/21 W 86th St	212-873-8404
Alleman, Annie/38 E 21st St	212-496-1353
Allen, Julian/31 Walker St	212-925-6550
Allen, Terry/291 Carroll St	718-624-1210
ALLERT, KATHY/201 E 28TH ST (P 108)	**212-532-0928**
Alpert, Alan/405 E 54th St	212-741-1631
Alpert, Olive/9511 Shore Rd	718-833-3092
Alves, Harold/381 Park Ave S 11th Fl	212-684-6984
Amity, Elena/339 E 77th St	212-879-4690
Amsel, Richard/353 E 83rd St	212-744-5599
Anderson, Mark/301 W 37th St 5th Fl	212-455-7441
ANDERSON, RICHARD/60 E 42ND ST #505 (P 12)	**212-682-1490**
Angelakis, Manos/48 W 21st St 9th Fl	212-243-4412
Angerame, Diane/1531 149th St	718-353-0502
ANTONIOS, TONY/60 E 42ND ST #505 (P 13)	**212-682-1490**
Appel, Albert/119 W 23rd St	212-989-6585
Arcelle, Joan/430 W 24th St	212-924-1865
Aristovulos, Nick/16 E 30th St	212-725-2454
Arnold, Robert/149 W 14th St	212-989-7049
ARNOLDI, PER/60 E 42ND ST #505 (P 14)	**212-682-1490**
The Art Farm/420 Lexington Ave	212-688-4555
Assel, Steven/472 Myrtle Ave	718-789-1725
ASTRAHAN, IRENE/201 E 28TH ST (P 94)	**212-532-0928**
Azzopardi, Frank/1039 Victory Blvd	718-273-4343

B

Bacall, Aaron/204 Arlene St	718-494-0711
Backhaus, R B/280 West End Ave	212-877-4792
BAKER, GARIN/35 W 92ND ST #7A (P 15)	**212-865-1975**
Baker, Nancy/423 Atlantic Ave #3L	718-330-0349
Baldus, Fred/29 Jones St	212-620-0423
Balin, Racquel/334 W 87th St #PH B	212-496-8358
Ballantyne, Joyce/353 W 53rd St #1W	212-682-2462
Balsutta, Mary Lynn/41 E 22nd St #4A	212-777-2944
BANFIELD, ELLIOT/81 GREENE ST (P 196)	**212-925-3053**
Barancik, Cathy/140 Grand St	212-226-2329
Barberis, Juan C/60 E 42nd St	212-687-4185
Barner, Bob/866 UN Plaza #4014	212-644-2020
Barnes, Michele/111 Sullivan St #3B	212-219-9269
BARNES-MURPHY, ROWAN/201 E 28TH ST (P 113)	**212-532-0928**
Baron, Esther/866 UN Plaza #4014	212-644-2020
Barr, Ken/342 Madison Ave	212-697-8525
BARRETT, RON/2112 BROADWAY #402A (P 265)	**212-874-1370**
Barry, Rick/159 W 23rd St	718-232-2484
BARRY, RON/165 E 32ND ST (P 81)	**212-686-3514**
BARTALOS, MICHAEL/81 SECOND AVE #3 (P 266)	**212-254-5858**
BARUFFI, ANDREA/72 BARROW ST #6G (P 267)	**212-989-8357**
Bass, Bob/43 E 19th St	212-254-4996
Bauer, Carla Studio/156 Fifth Ave #1100	212-807-8305
Bauman, Jill/PO Box 152	718-631-3160
BAZZEL, DEBORAH/48 W 21ST ST 9TH FL (P 189)	**212-243-4412**
Becker, Ron/265 E 78th St	212-535-8052
Beecham, Tom/342 Madison Ave #949	212-697-8525
Bego, Dolores/155 E 38th St	212-697-6170
Bellows, Amelia/118 E 25th St 6th Fl	212-777-7012
BENDELL, NORM/18 E 17TH ST 3RD FL (P 268)	**212-807-6627**
BERGER, STEPHEN/43 E 19TH ST (P 48)	**212-254-4996**
BERKEY, JOHN/50 E 50TH ST (P 133)	**212-355-0910**
Berran, Robert/420 Lexington Ave #2911	212-986-5680
BERRY, FANNY MELLET/155 E 38TH ST (P 83)	**212-697-6170**
BEYLON, CATHY/201 E 28TH ST (P 111)	**212-532-0928**
Billout, Guy/88 Lexington Ave #12G	212-684-2974
BILMES, SEMYON/15-69 OCEAN AVE #3J (P 271)	**718-338-4268**
Blackwell, Garie/60 E 42nd St #505	212-682-1490
Blake, Quentin/81 Greene St	212-925-3053
BLAKEY, PAUL/226 E 53RD ST (P 72)	**212-755-4945**
BLOOM, TOM/235 E 84TH ST #17 (P 274,275)	**212-628-6861**
Blubaugh, Susan/101 W 75th St #1A	212-874-2945
Blum, Zevi/81 Greene St	212-925-3053
BLUME, GEORGE/350 E 89TH ST (P 465)	**212-502-3976**
Blumrich, Christopher/67 Irving Place	212-674-8080
Bodner, Alan/111-10 76th Rd #2E	718-544-2584
Boguslav, Raphael/200 E 78th St	212-570-9069
BONHOMME, BERNARD/111 WOOSTER ST #PH C (P 52)	**212-925-0491**
Bordelon, Melinda/60 E 42nd St #505	212-682-1490
Boyd, Harvey/24 Fifth Ave	212-475-5235
Boyd, Kris/318 E 89th St #1D	212-876-4361
Bozzo, Frank/400 E 85th St #5J	212-535-9182
BRACKEN, CAROLYN/201 E 28TH ST (P 110)	**212-532-0928**
Bralds, Braldt/135 E 54th St	212-421-0050
BRAMHALL, WILLIAM/81 GREENE ST (P 196)	**212-925-3053**
Brandt, Joan/15 Gramercy Park S	212-473-7874
Brautigan, Doris/350 W 30th St	212-736-7698
Brayman, Kari/333 W 55th St	212-582-6137
Breinberg, Aaron/1123 Broadway	212-243-4929
BRICHER, SCOTT/1466 BROADWAY (P 195)	**212-921-1919**
BRICKNER, ALICE/4720 GROSVENOR AVE (P 279)	**212-549-5909**
BRILLHART, RALPH/310 MADISON AVE (P 40,42)	**212-867-8092**
Broderson, Charles/873 Broadway #612	212-925-9392
Brofsky, Miriam/186 Riverside Dr	212-595-8094
BROOKS, ANDREA/99 BANK ST #3G (P 235)	**212-924-3085**
Brooks, Clare Vanacore/415 W 55th St	212-245-3632
BROOKS, HAL/20 W 87TH ST (P 66)	**212-595-5980**
BROOKS, LOU/415 W 55TH ST (P 280,281)	**212-245-3632**
Brothers, Barry/1922 E 18th St	718-336-7540
Brown, Bob/267 Fifth Ave #706	212-686-5576
Brown, Bradford/151 E 20th St #3A	212-231-8223
Brown, Dan/420 Lexington Ave	212-986-5680
BROWN, DONALD/129 E 29TH ST (P 282)	**212-532-1705**
Brown, Judith Gwyn/522 E 85th St	212-288-1599
Brown, Kirk Q/1092 Blake Ave	718-342-4569
BRUSCA, JACK/43 E 19TH ST (P 48)	**212-254-4996**
BRYAN, DIANA/200 E 16TH ST #1D (P 284)	**212-475-7927**
Bryan, Mike/420 Lexington Ave	212-697-8525
Bryant, Rick J/18 W 37th St #301	212-594-6718
BUCHANAN, YVONNE/411 14TH ST (P 285)	**718-965-3021**
BURGER, ROBERT/111 WOOSTER ST #PH C (P 52)	**212-925-0491**
BURGOYNE, JOHN/200 E 78TH ST (P 58,59)	**212-570-9069**
Byrd, Bob/353 W 53rd St #1W	212-682-2462

C

CAIN, DAVID/200 W 20TH ST #607 (P 236)	**212-691-5783**
Campbell, Jim/420 Lexington Ave #2911	212-986-5680
Cantarella, Virginia Hoyt/107 Sterling Pl	718-622-2061
Caras, Peter/157 W 57th St	212-247-1130
CARBONE, KYE/241 UNION ST (P 289)	**718-802-9143**
Carr, Noell/30 E 14th St	212-675-1015
CARTER, BUNNY/200 E 78TH ST (P 60)	**212-570-9069**
Carter, Penny/342 Madison Ave #261	212-986-3282
Casale, Paul/5304 11th Ave	718-633-7909
CASCIO, PETER/317 E 18TH ST #5C (P 290)	**212-228-6876**
Cassler, Carl/420 Lexington Ave #2911	212-986-5680
Cavanagh, Dorothe/752 West End Ave #23J	212-662-1490
Cellini, Eva/157 W 57th St	212-247-1130
Cellini, Joseph/157 W 57th St	212-247-1130
Ceribello, Jim/35 Holcomb Ave	718-317-5972
Cesc/81 Greene St	212-925-3053
CETLIN, MARSHALL/62 LEROY ST (P 69)	**212-243-7869**
CHAMBLISS-RIGIE, JANE/201 E 28TH ST (P 114)	**212-532-0928**

Charmatz, Bill/25 W 68th St	212-595-3907
Chen, Tony/53-31 96th St	718-699-4813
Chermayeff, Ivan/58 W 15th St	212-741-2539
CHERNISHOV, ANATOLY/3967 SEDGWICK AVE	
#20F (P 292)	**212-884-8122**
Chester, Harry/501 Madison Ave	212-752-0570
Chironna, Ronald/135 Sturges St	718-720-6142
Chorao, Kay/290 Riverside Dr	212-749-8256
Chow, Ted/179 Bay 35th St	212-594-8802
Christopher, Tom/342 Madison Ave #261	212-986-3282
Chwast, Seymour/67 Irving Place	212-677-3506
CIARDIELLO, JOE/203 CENTER ST (P 293)	**718-351-2289**
Ciccarielli, Gary/353 W 53rd St #1W	212-682-2462
CIESIEL, CHRISTINE G/101 MACDOUGAL ST (P 65)	**212-982-9461**
Cieslawski, Steven/321 86th St #H-1	718-748-8746
CLARK, JANE/48 W 21ST ST 9TH FL (P 190)	**212-243-4412**
Clarke, Robert/159 W 53rd St	212-581-4045
Cloteaux, Francois/333 E 30th St	212-679-1358
Cody, Brian/866 UN Plaza #4014	212-644-2020
COLLIER, JOHN/501 FIFTH AVE #1407 (P 192)	**212-490-2450**
COLLIER, ROBERTA/201 E 28TH ST (P 109)	**212-532-0928**
COLON, ERNIE/43 E 19TH ST (P 50)	**212-254-4996**
Colton, Keita/165 E 32nd St	212-686-3514
Comito, John/400 E 55th St	212-832-6728
Conley, Frank P/14 E 52nd St	212-759-6791
Connelly, Gwen/866 UN Plaza #4014	212-644-2020
Conner, Mona/1 Montgomery Pl #8	718-636-1527
Continuity Graphics Assoc'd Inc/62 W 45th St	212-869-4170
CONWAY, MICHAEL/316 E 93RD ST #23 (P 300)	**212-369-0019**
Cook, David/60 E 42nd St #428	212-867-8092
Cooley, Gary/23 W 35th St	212-695-2426
Cooper, Cheryl/515 Madison Ave	212-486-9644
Cooper, Floyd/866 UN Plaza #4014	212-644-2020
Cooper, Robert/420 Madison Ave #401	212-980-3510
Cooperstein, Sam/677 West End Ave	212-864-4064
CORBEN, RICHARD/43 E 19TH ST (P 49)	**212-254-4996**
CORNELIUS, RAY-MEL/121 MADISON AVE (P 57)	**212-683-1362**
CORNELL, LAURA/118 E 93RD ST #1A (P 301)	**212-534-0596**
Corvi, Donna/568 Broadway	212-925-9622
COUCH, GREG/112 WILLOW ST #5A (P 303)	**718-625-1298**
Coulson, David/32 Thompson St #1	212-431-5468
COURTNEY, RICHARD/43 E 19TH ST (P 49)	**212-254-4996**
Cove, Tony/60 E 42nd St	212-687-4185
Crair, Mel/342 Madison Ave #949	212-697-8525
Crawford, Margery/237 E 31st St	212-686-6883
Crawford, Robert/340 E 93rd St #9I	212-722-4964
Crews, Donald/653 Carroll St	718-636-5773
Cross, Peter/515 Madison Ave 22nd Fl	212-486-9644
Crosthwaite, Royd/50 E 50th St #5	212-355-0910
CRUSE, HOWARD/88-11 34TH AVE #5D (P 310)	**718-639-4951**
CRUZ, RAY/162 W 13TH ST (P 170)	**212-243-1199**
Csatari, Joe/420 Lexington Ave #2911	212-986-5680
Cuevos, Stillerman, Plotkin/230 E 44th St	212-661-7149
Cummings, Pat/28 Tiffany Pl	718-834-8584
Cunningham, Jean/177 Waverly Pl #4F	212-675-1731
Cunningham, Robert M/177 Waverly Pl #4F	212-675-1731
CUSACK, MARGARET/124 HOYT ST (P 312)	**718-237-0145**
CUSHWA, TOM/303 PARK AVE S #511 (P 313)	**212-228-2615**
D Dacey, Bob/157 W 57th St	212-247-1130
Dalaney, Jack/184 Thompson St	211-777-7713
Dale, Robert/1573 York Ave	212-535-2505
Dallison, Ken/108 E 35th St #1	212-889-3337
DALY, SEAN/85 SOUTH ST (P 176)	**212-668-0031**
D'ANDREA, BERNARD/50 E 50TH ST #5 (P 146)	**212-355-0910**
D'Andrea, Domenick/50 E 50th St #5	212-355-0910
DANIEL, FRANK/201 E 28TH ST (P 104)	**212-532-0928**
Daniels, Alan/18 E 16th St 2nd Fl	212-206-0322
DANIELS, SID/12 E 22ND ST #11B (P 314)	**212-673-6520**
DARDEN, HOWARD/22 W 45TH ST (P 67)	**212-398-9540**
Darrer, Tony/515 E 79th St	212-628-0708
Davidson, Everett/60 E 42nd St #505	212-682-1490

DAVIS, ALLEN/141-10 25TH RD #3A (P 49)	**718-463-096●**
Davis, Nelle/20 E 17th St 4th Fl	212-807-773
Davis, Paul/14 E 4th St	212-460-964●
DAWSON, JOHN/310 MADISON AVE (P 40,41)	**212-867-809●**
Day, Betsy/866 UN Plaza #4014	212-644-202●
DEARAUJO, BETTY/201 E 28TH ST (P 117)	**212-532-092●**
Deas, Michael/39 Sidney Pl	718-852-563●
Deel, Guy/60 E 42nd St #428	212-867-809●
DEETER, CATHERINE/60 E 42ND ST #505 (P 16)	**212-682-149●**
Degen, Paul/81 Greene St	212-925-305●
DeGraffenried, Jack/18 E 16th St	212-206-032●
DEJESUS, JAMIE/15 W 72ND ST (P 122)	**212-799-223●**
Del Rosso, Richard/33 W 89th St #1A	212-580-838●
DeLattre, Georgette/100 Central Park South	212-247-685●
DEMAREST, CHRIS/81 GREENE ST (P 196)	**212-925-305●**
DeMichiell, Robert/43 E 19th St	212-254-499●
Denaro, Joseph/18 E 16th St	212-206-032●
DERIJK, WALT/43 E 19TH ST (P 50)	**212-254-499●**
DESCOMBES, ROLAND/50 E 50TH ST #5 (P 140)	**212-355-091●**
Deschamps, Bob/108 E 35th St #1	212-889-333●
Devlin, Bill/108 E 35th St #1	212-889-333●
Dewey, Kenneth F/226 E 53rd St	212-755-494●
Diamond Art Studio/11 E 36th St	212-685-662●
DiCione, Ron/342 Madison Ave #949	212-697-852●
DICKENS, HOLLY/60 EAST 42ND ST. (P 17)	**212-682-149●**
DiComo Comp Art/12 W 27th St	212-689-867●
DIETZ, JIM/165 E 32ND ST (P 80,81)	**212-686-351●**
DILAKIAN, HOVIK/111 WOOSTER ST #PH C (P 52)	**212-925-049●**
Dittrich, Dennis/42 W 72nd St #12B	212-595-977●
DiVincenzo, Dennis/233 E 82nd St	212-772-844●
DODDS, GLENN/392 CENTRAL PARK WEST	
#9M (P 320,321)	**212-679-363●**
Domingo, Ray/108 E 35th St #1	212-889-333●
Domino, Bob/60 Sutton Pl South	212-935-013●
D'Onofrio, Alice/866 UN Plaza #4014	212-644-202●
DORET, MICHAEL/12 E 14TH ST (P 322)	**212-929-168●**
DORET/ SMITH STUDIOS/12 E 14TH ST (P 322,323)	**212-929-168●**
D'Ortenzio, Alfred/353 W 53rd St #1W	212-682-246●
Drovetto, Richard/355 E 72nd St	212-861-092●
DRUCKER, MORT/226 E 53RD ST (P 70)	**212-755-494●**
Duarte, Mary/350 First Ave #9E	212-674-451●
Dubanevich, Arlene/866 UN Plaza #4014	212-644-202●
Dudash, Michael/157 W 57th St	212-247-113●
Dudzinski, Andrzej/52 E 81st St	212-628-698●
Duke, Randy/235 E 149th St	212-292-122●
Dupont, Lane/353 W 53rd St #1W	212-682-246●
Dyess, John/157 W 57th St	212-247-113●
E Eagle, Cameron/170 E 3rd St #4J	212-777-60●
Eggert, John/420 Lexington Ave #2911	212-986-568●
Egielski, Richard/463 West St	212-255-93●
Ehlert, Lois/866 UN Plaza #4014	212-644-202●
Ehrenfeld, Jane/330 E 90th St #4B	212-534-52●
EISNER, GIL/310 W 86TH ST #11A (P 328)	**212-595-20●**
Ellis, Dean/30 E 20th St	212-254-755●
Elmer, Richard/504 E 11th St	212-598-40●
Ely, Richard/207 W 86th St	212-874-48●
EMERSON, CARMELA/110-20 71ST AVE #519 (P 329)	**718-793-21●**
Emerson, Matt (Emerson-Wajdowicz)/1123 Broadway	212-807-81●
EMMETT, BRUCE/285 PARK PL (P 147)	**718-636-52●**
Endewelt, Jack/50 Riverside Dr	212-877-05●
ENIK, TED/82 JANE ST #4A (P 103)	**212-620-59●**
Ennis, John/60 E 42nd St #428	212-867-80●
Epstein, Aaron/301 E 90th St #4B	212-410-71●
Ettlinger, Doris/73 Leonard St	212-226-03●
Eutemy, Loring/51 Fifth Ave	212-741-01●
Evcimen, Al/305 Lexington Ave	212-889-29●
F Familton, Herb/59 W 10th St #1D	212-254-29●
Faria, Jeff/27 W 20th St 10th Fl	212-989-29●
Farina, Michael/18 E 16th St 2nd Fl	212-206-03●
Farmakis, Andreas/835 Third Ave	212-758-52●

FARRELL, MARYBETH/320 W 76TH ST #2G (P 331)	**212-799-7486**
Fasolino, Teresa/58 W 15th St	212-741-2539
FAULKNER, MATT/435 CLINTON ST #4 (P 332)	**718-858-1724**
FeBland, David/670 West End Ave	212-580-9299
Feigeles, Neil/920 E 17th St	718-377-4418
FERNANDES, STANISLAW/35 E 12TH ST (P 334,335)	**212-533-2648**
Fichera, Maryanne/12 W 27th St	212-689-8670
FILIPPUCCI, SANDRA/270 PARK AVE S #9B (P 237)	**212-477-8732**
FINE, ROBERT/43 E 19TH ST (P 51)	**212-254-4996**
FINEWOOD, BILL/201 E 28TH ST (P 100)	**212-532-0928**
Fiore, Peter/420 Lexington Ave #2911	212-986-5680
Fiorentino, Al/866 UN Plaza #4014	212-644-2020
Fitzgerald, Frank/212 E 89th St	212-722-6793
FLAHERTY, DAVID/534 W 50TH ST (P 337)	**212-765-7201**
FLESHER, VIVIENNE/194 THIRD AVE (P 171)	**212-475-0440**
Foster, B Lynne/540 Ft Washington Ave #3D	212-781-1055
Fox, Barbara/301 W 53rd St	212-245-7564
FRANCIS, JUDY/110 W 96TH ST (P 338)	**212-866-7204**
Fraser, Betty/240 Central Park South	212-247-1937
Freas, John/353 W 53rd St #1W	212-682-2462
FREEMAN, IRVING/145 FOURTH AVE #9K (P 339)	**212-674-6705**
Freeman, Tom/157 W 57th St	212-247-1130
Fretz, Frank/866 UN Plaza #4014	212-644-2020
Fricke, Warren/15 W 72nd St	212-799-2231
Fried, Janice/51 W 46th St #3B	212-398-0067
Friedman, Jon/866 UN Plaza #4014	212-644-2020
Froom, Georgia/62 W 39th St #803	212-944-0330
FUNTASTIC STUDIOS/506 W 42ND ST (P 340)	**212-239-8245**
FURUKAWA, MEL/116 DUANE ST (P 128)	**212-349-3225**
G Gabriele, Antonio J/420 Lexington Ave #2911	212-986-5680
GADINO, VICTOR/1601 THIRD AVE (P 18)	**212-534-7206**
Gaetano, Nicholas/821 Broadway 6th Fl	212-674-5749
Gala, Tom/420 Lexington Ave #2911	212-986-5680
GALE, CYNTHIA/229 E 88TH ST (P 341)	**212-860-5429**
GALLARDO, GERVASIO/50 E 50TH ST (P 145)	**212-355-0910**
Galub, Meg/405 W 57th St	212-757-3506
GAMBALE, DAVID/200 W 15TH ST (P 38, 39)	**212-243-4209**
Garrido, Hector/420 Lexington Ave #2911	212-986-5680
Garrison, Barbara/12 E 87th St	212-348-6382
Gaster, Joanne/201 E 30th St #43	212-686-0860
Gayler, Anne/320 E 86th St	212-734-7060
Gehm, Charles/342 Madison Ave #949	212-697-8525
Gem Studio/420 Lexington Ave #220	212-687-3460
GENOVA, JOE/60 E 42ND ST #505 (P 19)	**212-682-1490**
Gentile, John & Anthony/850 Seventh Ave #1006	212-757-1966
GERAS, AUDRA/501 FIFTH AVE #1407 (P 192)	**212-490-2450**
Gerber, Mark & Stephanie/159 Madison Ave	212-684-7137
Gershinowitz, George/PO Box 204 Chelsea Sta	212-691-1376
Gersten, Gerry/1380 Riverside Dr	212-928-7957
Giavis, Ted/420 Lexington Ave #2911	212-986-5680
Giglio, Richard/299 W 12th St	212-675-7642
Gignilliat, Elaine/150 E 56th St	212-935-1943
GILLOT, CAROL/162 W 13TH ST (P 343)	**212-243-6448**
Giorgio, Nate/18 E 16th St	212-206-0322
Giovanopoulos, Paul/216 E 45th St	212-661-0850
Giusti, Robert/350 E 52nd St #80	212-752-0179
Gold, Marcy/200 E 28th St #2C	212-685-4974
Goldman, Richard/36 W 20th St	212-675-3021
GOLDSTROM, ROBERT/471 FIFTH ST (P 205)	**718-768-7367**
Good Guys/596 Broadway #1216	212-226-8018
Goodell, Jon/866 UN Plaza #4014	212-644-2020
Goodrich, Carter/140 W 22nd St 7th Fl	212-243-3954
Gordon, Rebecca/201 W 16th St	212-989-5762
Gorman, Stephen/15 W 72nd St	212-799-2231
GOTHARD, DAVID/81 GREENE ST (P 196)	**212-925-3053**
Gottfried, Max/82-60 116th St #CC3	718-441-9868
Gottlieb, Penelope/342 Madison Ave #949	212-679-8525
GOWDY, CAROLYN/81 GREENE ST (P 196)	**212-925-3053**
Graboff, Abner/310 Madison Ave	212-687-2034
Grace, Alexa/70 University Pl	212-254-4424
GRADDON, JULIAN/48 W 21ST ST 9TH FL (P 187)	**212-243-4412**

Graham, Mariah/670 West End Ave	212-580-8001
Grammer, June/126 E 24th St #3B	212-475-4745
GRAPHIC ASSOC/ RON FLEMING/60 E 42ND ST #505 (P 20)	**212-682-1490**
GRAPHIC ASSOC/ CLAY TURNER/60 E 42ND ST #505 (P 21)	**212-682-1490**
Grashow, David/215 E 31st St	212-684-3448
Gray, John/264 Van Duzer St	718-447-6466
GRAY, SUSAN/42 W 12TH ST #5 (P 344)	**212-675-2243**
Greifinger, Mel/200 W 15th St	212-243-4209
Greis, Gene/215 W 10th St	212-206-6392
GRIESBACH/MARTUCCI/35 STERLING PL (P 22,23)	**718-622-1831**
Griffel, Barbara/8006 47th Ave	718-446-0285
GRIFFIN, JAMES/310 MADISON AVE (P 41)	**212-867-8092**
Grinko, Andy/125 Cedar St	212-732-5308
Gross, Mort/2 Park Ave #1804	212-686-4788
Gross, Steve/342 Madison Ave	212-697-8525
Grossman, Robert/19 Crosby St	212-925-1965
GROTE, RICH/48 W 21ST ST 9TH FL (P 185)	**212-243-4412**
Guarnaccia, Steven/89 Bleecker St #6B	212-420-0108
Guitar, Jeremy/866 UN Plaza #4014	212-644-2020
Gumen, Murad/33-25 90th St #6K	718-478-7267
GUNN, ROBERT/201 E 28TH ST (P 96)	**212-532-0928**
GURBO, WALTER/55 HUDSON ST #3A (P 91)	**212-775-1810**
Gusson, Steven/105 Bergen St	718-852-7791
H Haas, Arie/62 W 45th St	212-382-1677
Hack, Konrad/866 UN Plaza #4014	212-644-2020
HAHN, MARIKA/11 RIVERSIDE DR (P 346)	**212-580-7896**
HALL, DEBORAH ANN/105-28 65TH AVE #6B (P 347)	**718-896-3152**
HALL, JOAN/155 BANK ST #H954 (P 348)	**212-243-6059**
Hallgren, Gary/6 W 37th St #5	212-947-1054
Hamrick, Chuck/420 Lexington Ave #2911	212-986-5680
HARRINGTON, GLENN/165 E 32ND ST (P 350)	**212-686-3514**
Harris, Diane Teske/342 Madison Ave #469	212-719-9879
Harrison, Sean/1349 Lexington Ave	212-369-3831
HARRISON, WILLIAM/18 E 16TH ST (P 45)	**212-206-0322**
Hart, Veronika/60 E 42nd St #505	212-682-1490
Harvey, Richard/420 Lexington Ave #2911	212-986-5680
HARWOOD, LAUREL/90 LEXINGTON AVE #3A (P 351)	**212-532-0248**
Hays, Michael/43 Cheever Pl	718-852-2731
HECK, CATHY/333 E 30TH ST (P 129)	**915-686-9343**
Hedin, Donald/157 W 57th St	212-247-1130
Heindel, Robert/211 E 51st St	212-755-1365
Heller, Karen/300 W 108th St	212-866-5879
HENDERSON, ALAN/31 JANE ST (P 69)	**212-243-0693**
HENRY, PAUL/15 W 72ND ST (P 123)	**212-799-2231**
Herbick, David/5 Montague Terrace	718-852-6450
HERDER, EDWIN/310 MADISON AVE (P 40,42-3)	**212-867-8092**
Hering, Al/342 Madison Ave #261	212-986-3282
Herman, Tim/420 Madison Ave #401	212-980-3510
Hernandez, Richard/144 Chambers St	212-732-3474
Herrmann, Hal/50 E 50th St	212-752-8490
Hess, Mark/135 E 54th St	212-421-0050
Hewitt, Margaret/31 Ocean Pkwy #3N	718-436-0386
Higgins, Pamela/866 UN Plaza #4014	212-644-2020
HILL, AMY/111 WOOSTER ST #PH C (P 52)	**212-925-0491**
Himler, Ron/866 UN Plaza #4014	212-644-2020
Hochman, Steve/18 E 16th St 2nd Fl	212-206-0322
Hoffman, Ginnie/108 E 35th St #1	212-889-3337
Hoffman, Rosekrans/866 UN Plaza #4014	212-644-2020
Hogarth, Paul/81 Greene St	212-925-3053
Holland, Brad/96 Greene St	212-226-3675
Holmes, John/420 Lexington Ave #2911	212-986-5680
Holst, Joni/1519 81st St	212-661-9700
Hooks, Mitchell/321 E 83rd St	212-737-1853
Hoover, Gary/866 UN Plaza #4014	212-644-2020
Hortens, Walter/154 E 64th St	212-838-0014
Hosner, William/420 Madison Ave #401	212-980-3510
HOSTOVICH, MICHAEL/127 W 82ND ST #9A (P 119)	**212-580-2175**
HOWARD, JOHN/336 E 54TH ST (P 204)	**212-832-7980**
Howell, Kathleen/866 UN Plaza #4014	212-644-2020

HUANG, MEI-KU/201 E 28TH ST (P 99)	**212-532-0928**
The Hub/16 E 16th St 4th Fl	212-675-8500
Hubert, Laurent/216 E 45th St	212-661-0850
HUERTA, CATHERINE/60 E 42ND ST #505 (P 24)	**212-682-1490**
Huffman, Tom/130 W 47th St #6A	212-819-0211
Hughes, Mary Ellen/403 E 70th St	212-288-8375
Hull, Cathy/236 E 36th St	212-683-8559
HUNT, JIM/420 MADISON AVE #401 (P 36)	**212-980-3510**
HUNTER, STAN/50 E 50TH ST (P 138)	**212-355-0910**
HUSTON, STEVEN/15 W 72ND ST (P 123)	**212-799-2231**
HUTTNER & HILLMAN/137 E 25TH ST (P 357)	**212-532-6062**
Idelson, Joyce/11 Riverside Dr	212-877-6161
Image Network Inc/645 West End Ave	212-877-1734
Incandescent Ink Inc/111 Wooster St #PH C	212-925-0491
Incisa, Monica/141 E 56th St	212-752-1554
INOUE, IZUMI/311 E 12TH ST (P 359)	**212-473-1614**
Iskowitz, Joel/420 Lexington Ave #2911	212-986-5680
Ivenbaum, Elliott/267 W 90th St	212-664-5656
JABEN, SETH/47 E 3RD ST #3 (P 360)	**212-260-7859**
Jamieson, Doug/42-20 69th St	718-565-6034
Jampel, Judith/148 Columbus Ave	212-873-5234
JASPER, JACKIE/165 E 32ND ST (P 80,81)	**212-686-3514**
Jeffers, Kathy/106 E 19th St 12th Fl	212-475-1756
Jetter, Frances/390 West End Ave	212-580-3720
JEZIERSKI, CHET/50 E 50TH ST (P 149)	**212-355-0910**
Jobe, Jody/875 W 181st St	212-795-4941
Johnson, Doug/45 E 19th St	212-260-1880
Johnson, Kristin/902 Broadway #1609	212-477-4033
Jones, Bob/420 Lexington Ave #2911	212-986-5680
JONES, MARILYN/1466 BROADWAY (P 194)	**212-921-1919**
JONES, RANDY/323 E 10TH ST (P 364)	**212-677-5387**
Jorg, Liz/121 Brompton Rd	516-248-7036
JOSEPH, PAULA/147 W 13TH ST #2F (P 365)	**212-242-6137**
JOUDREY, KEN/15 W 72ND ST (P 125)	**212-799-2231**
JUST, HAL/155 E 38TH ST (P 82)	**212-697-6170**
Kahn, Sandra/344 E 49th St #7A	212-759-0630
Kallan, Elizabeth Kada/67 Irving Place	212-674-8080
Kalle, Chris/866 UN Plaza #4014	212-644-2020
KANAREK, MICHAEL/48 W 21ST ST 9TH FL (P 184)	**212-243-4412**
Kane, Harry/310 E 49th St	212-486-0180
KANE, KID/60 E 42ND ST #505 (P 25)	**212-682-1490**
Kappes, Werner/33 E 22nd St #5D	212-673-2484
Karlin, Bernie/41 E 42nd St	212-687-7636
Katsin, Nancy/417 E 72nd St #3B	212-535-7786
KATZ, LES/451 WESTMINSTER (P 241)	**718-284-4779**
Kaufman, Curt/215 W 88th St	212-873-9841
Kaufman, Stuart/420 Lexington Ave #2911	212-986-5680
KELENY, EARL/515 MADISON AVE 22ND FL (P 203)	**212-486-9644**
KELLEY, BARBARA/555 10TH ST (P 366)	**718-788-2465**
Kelley, Mark/866 UN Plaza #4014	212-644-2020
Kelly, Susannah/77 Perry St	212-206-8960
Kendrick, Dennis/99 Bank St	212-924-3085
Keyes, Steven/18 E 16th St	212-206-0322
Kibbee, Gordon/6 Jane St	212-989-7074
Kidd, Tom/19 Broadway Terrace	212-569-1421
Kieffer, Christa/866 UN Plaza #4014	212-644-2020
King, Jean/315 Riverside Dr	212-866-8488
Kingston, James/31 E 31st St	212-685-2520
KIRK, DANIEL/85 SOUTH ST #6N (P 206)	**212-825-0190**
KLAVINS, ULDIS/310 MADISON AVE (P 41,43)	**212-867-8092**
Klein, David G/257 Winsdor Pl	718-788-1818
Klein, Renee/291 Carroll St	718-841-4464
KLUGLEIN, KAREN/88 LEXINGTON AVE #12G (P 161)	**212-684-2974**
Knettell, Sharon/108 E 35th St #1	212-889-3337
Knight, Jacob/216 E 45th St	212-661-0850
Koester, Michael/420 Lexington Ave #2911	212-986-5680
KONDO, YUKIO/201 E 28TH ST (P 98)	**212-532-0928**
Koren, Edward/81 Greene St	212-925-3053
Kosarin, Linda/21 W 38th St	212-840-7676

Kotzky, Brian/132-42 Booth Memorial Ave	718-353-548
KOVALCIK, TERRY/48 W 20TH ST (P 369)	**212-620-777**
Krakovitz, Harlan/300 E 33rd St #5P	212-679-405
Kramer, Carveth/216 E 45th St	212-661-085
KRETSCHMANN, KARIN/323 W 75TH ST #1A (P 370)	**212-724-500**
KUBINYI, LASZLO/226 E 53RD ST (P 73)	**201-833-442**
Kuester, Bob/353 W 53rd St #1W	212-682-246
Kukalis, Romas/420 Lexington Ave #2911	212-986-568
KUNSTLER, MORT/50 E 50TH ST (P 137)	**212-355-09**
KUPER, PETER/250 W 99TH ST #9C (P 372)	**212-864-572**
Kursar, Ray/1 Lincoln Plaza #43R	212-873-560
Kurtzman, Edward/60 E 42nd St	212-687-418
KURTZMAN, HARVEY/18 E 16TH ST (P 47)	**212-206-032**
Lacey, Lucille/77-07 Jamaica Ave	718-296-181
LACKOW, ANDY/1325 THIRD AVE (P 243)	**212-472-88**
Ladas, George/157 Prince St	212-673-220
Lakeman, Steven/115 W 85th St	212-877-888
Lambert, Saul/138 E 13th St	212-260-368
LAMUT,SONJA & JAKESEVIC, NENAD/165 E 32ND ST (P 80)	**212-686-351**
LANDIS, JOAN/6 JANE ST (P 373)	**212-989-707**
Lang, Cecily/19 Jones St #21	212-206-125
Lang, Gary/342 Madison Ave	212-697-852
LAPADULA, TOM/201 E 28TH ST (P 101)	**212-532-09**
LAPINSKI, JOE/420 MADISON AVE #401 (P 37)	**212-980-35**
Laporte, Michelle/216 E 45th St	212-661-08
LASHER, MARY ANN/60 E 42ND ST #505 (P 26)	**212-682-14**
Laslo, Larry/179 E 71st St	212-737-23
Laurence, Karen/216 E 45th St	212-661-08
LAUTER, RICHARD/310 MADISON AVE (P 42)	**212-867-80**
Lawton, Nancy/601 W 113 St #9B	212-222-02
LE-TAN, PIERRE/81 GREENE ST (P 196)	**212-925-30**
Leach, Richard/62 W 39th St #803	212-869-097
LEBBAD, JAMES A/220 FIFTH AVE #1707 (P 375)	**212-679-22**
Leder, Dora/866 UN Plaza #4014	212-644-20
LEHR, PAUL/50 E 50TH ST #5 (P 148)	**212-355-09**
LEMERISE, BRUCE/201 E 28TH ST (P 115)	**212-532-09**
Leonard, Richard/212 W 17th St #2B	212-243-66
Leonard, Tom/866 UN Plaza #4014	212-644-20
Lesser, Ron/342 Madison Ave #949	212-697-85
Lettick, Birney/121 E 35th St	212-532-05
Levin, Arnie/342 Madison Ave #469	212-719-98
LEVINE, BETTE/60 E 42ND ST #505 (P 27)	**212-682-14**
Levine, Rena/200 Bethel Loop #12G	718-642-73
Levine, Ron/1 W 85th St #4D	212-787-74
Levirne, Joel/151 W 46th St	212-869-83
Levy, Frank/305 E 40th St #5Y	212-557-82
LEVY, ROBERT S/835 THIRD AVE 4TH FL (P 378)	**212-986-88**
Lewin, Ted/152 Willoughby Ave	718-622-38
LEWIS, HOWARD B/140 W 22ND ST 7TH FL (P 379)	**212-243-39**
LEWIS, TIM/194 THIRD AVE (P 169)	**212-475-04**
Lexa, Susan/866 UN Plaza #4014	212-644-20
Liberatore, Gaetano/43 E 19th St	212-254-49
Lieberman, Ron/109 W 28th St	212-947-06
Lilly, Charles/56 W 82nd St #15	212-873-36
Lindberg, Jeffery K/449 50th St	718-492-11
Lindlof, Ed/353 W 53rd St #1W	212-682-24
LINE, LEMUEL/50 E 50TH ST (P 141)	**212-355-09**
LITTLE APPLE ART/409 SIXTH AVE (P 380)	**718-499-70**
LLOYD, PETER/18 E 16TH ST (P 47)	**212-206-03**
LOGRIPPO, ROBERT/50 E 50TH ST #5 (P 142)	**212-355-09**
LODIGENSKY, TED/18 E 16TH ST (P 46)	**212-206-03**
Lopez, Antonio/31 Union Square W #10A	212-924-20
Lovitt, Anita/308 E 78th St	212-628-81
Low, William/31 Ocean Pkwy #2C	718-436-20
Lozner, Ruth/62 W 71st St	212-362-74
LUCE, BEN/5 E 17TH ST, (P 242)	**212-230-33**
Lulevitch, Tom/101 W 69th St #4D	212-362-33
Lustig, Loretta/99 Madison Ave	212-679-86
Lutterbeck, KAren/333 W 20th St #4	212-924-25
Lyall, Dennis/420 Lexington Ave #2911	212-986-56

CONT'D.

Please send us your additions and updates.

M

MACCOMBIE, TURI/201 E 28TH ST (P 107)	**212-532-0928**
Mack, Stan/226 E 53rd St	212-755-4945
Maddalone, John/1123 Broadway #310	212-807-6087
Madden, Don/866 U N Plaza #4014	212-644-2020
Magagna, Anna Marie/2 Tudor City Pl	212-840-1234
Mahon, Rich/18 E 16th St	212-206-0322
Mahoney, Ron/353 W 53rd St #1W	212-682-2462
Maitz, Don/50 E 50th St #5	212-355-0910
MALAN, DEE/201 E 28TH ST (P 117)	**212-532-0928**
Malonis, Tina/246 W 20th St #2C	212-675-6280
Mambach, Alex/102-35 64th Rd	718-275-4269
Manders, John/98 Bergen St	718-596-5468
Mangiat, Jeffrey/420 Lexington Ave #2911	212-986-5680
Manos, Jim/342 Madison Ave #261	212-986-3282
MANTEL, RICHARD/194 THIRD AVE (P 166)	**212-475-0440**
Manyum, Wallop/37-40 60th St	718-476-1478
Marcellino, Fred Studio/432 Park Ave S #601	212-532-0150
Mardon, Allan/108 E 35th St #1	212-889-3337
Marich, Felix/420 Madison Ave #401	212-980-3510
Marinelli, Robert/165 Bryant Ave	718-979-4018
Martin, Bruce Rough Riders/389 Ave of Americas	212-620-0539
MARTIN, JOHN/501 FIFTH AVE #1407 (P 193)	**212-490-2450**
MARTINEZ, JOHN/55 HUDSON ST #3A (P 86)	**212-775-1810**
MARTINEZ, SERGIO/43 E 19TH ST (P 51)	**212-254-4996**
MARTINOT, CLAUDE/145 SECOND AVE #20 (P 390)	**212-473-3137**
MASI, GEORGE/111 WOOSTER ST #PH C (P 52)	**212-925-0491**
MASLEN, BARBARA/45 W 18TH ST (P 391)	**212-686-6559**
Mason, Brick/349 E 14th St #3R	212-777-4297
Mathewuse, James/157 W 57th St	212-247-1130
Mathieu, Joseph/215 E 31st St	212-684-3448
MATSUYOSHI, AKIO/165 PERRY ST #1B (P 392)	**212-242-7043**
MATTELSON, MARVIN/88 LEXINGTON AVE #12G (P 162,163)	**212-684-2974**
MAXWELL, BROOKIE/53 IRVING PL (P 116)	**212-475-6909**
McAllister, Kevin/163-19 26th Ave	718-746-3998
McCormack, Geoffrey/420 Lexington Ave #2911	212-986-5680
McCoy, Steve/260 Riverside Dr	212-866-9536
McCreary, Jane/866 UN Plaza #4014	212-644-2020
MCDANIEL, JERRY/155 E 38TH ST (P 85)	**212-697-6170**
McKie, Roy/75 Perry	212-989-5186
McLean, Wilson/50 E 50th St	212-752-8490
McLoughlin, Wayne/194 Third Ave	212-475-0440
MCPHEETERS, NEAL/16 W 71ST ST (P 396)	**212-799-7021**
Mead, Kimble Pendleton/125 Prospect Park West	718-768-3632
Mehlman, Elwyn/108 E 35th St #1	212-889-3337
Meisel, Ann/420 Lexington Ave #2911	212-986-5680
MEISEL, PAUL/90 HUDSON ST #5E (P 397)	**212-226-5463**
Meisler, Meryl/553 8th St	718-499-9836
Melendez, Robert/18 E 16th St 2nd Fl	212-206-0322
MERRELL, PATRICK/48 W 20TH ST (P 398)	**212-620-7777**
MEYEROWITZ, RICK/68 JANE ST (P 400,401)	**212-989-2446**
Michaels, Bob/304 E 49 St	212-752-1185
Michal, Marie/108 E 35th St #1	212-889-3337
Michner, Ted/420 Lexington Ave #2911	212-986-5680
Midda, Sara/81 Greene St	212-925-3053
Mikos, Mike/420 Lexington Ave #2911	212-986-5680
Milicic, Michael/587 Ft Washington Ave #10E	212-878-3849
MILLER, CLIFF/310 MADISON AVE (P 40)	**212-867-8092**
Miller, Lyle/866 UN Plaza #4014	212-644-2020
Milne, Jonathon/420 Lexington Ave	212-986-5680
MINOR, WENDELL/277 W 4TH ST (P 41)	**212-691-6925**
MITCHELL, CELIA/361 WASHINGTON AVE #3A (P 402)	**718-783-0847**
Mitchell, Maceo/446 Central Park West #4E	212-865-1059
Mitsuhashi, Yoko/43 E 29th St	212-683-7312
Miyamoto, Linda/PO Box 2310	718-596-4787
Montague, Andrea/19 Broadway Terrace	212-569-1421
MONTIEL, DAVID/115 W 16TH ST #211 (P 403)	**212-989-7426**
Moraes, Greg/60 E 42nd St #428	212-867-8092
MORGAN, JACQUI/315 E 58TH ST (P 408)	**212-421-0766**
Morgen, Barry/337 W 87th St #G	212-595-6835
MORRIS, FRANK/15 W 72ND ST (P 122)	**212-799-2231**

MORRISON, DON/155 E 38TH ST (P 85)	**212-697-6170**
MORSE, BILL/60 E 42ND ST #505 (P 28)	**212-682-1490**
Moseley, Marshall/409 Sixth Ave	718-499-7045
Moseley, Richie/409 Sixth Ave	718-499-7045
Moss, Geoffrey/315 E 68th St	212-472-9474
Murawski, Alex/108 E 35th St #1	212-889-3337
MYERS, DAVID L/228 BLEECKER ST #8 (P 409)	**212-989-5260**
Myers, Lou/108 E 35th St #1	212-889-3337

N

Najaka, Marlles/241 Central Park West	212-580-0058
Nakai Sacco & Crowell/466 Lexington Ave 4th Fl	212-210-6905
NAKAMURA, JOEL/95 HORATIO ST (P 79)	**212-807-0840**
NAZZ, JAMES/159 SECOND AVE (P 410)	**212-228-9713**
Neff, Leland/506 Amsterdam Ave #61	212-724-1884
NELSON, CRAIG/60 E 42ND ST #505 (P 29)	**212-682-1490**
NEMIROV, MEREDITH/110 KENT ST (P 412)	**718-389-5972**
Nessim, Barbara/240 E 15th St	212-677-8888
NEUBECKER, ROBERT/395 BROADWAY #14C (P 413)	**212-219-8435**
Neumann, Ann/444 Broome St	212-431-7141
Newsome, Tom/420 Lexington Ave #2911	212-986-5680
Newton, Richard/157 W 57th St	212-247-1130
NEYMAN-LEVIKOVA, MARINA/155 E 38TH ST (P 84)	**212-697-6170**
NG, MICHAEL/58-35 155TH ST (P 414)	**718-461-8264**
Nicastre, Michael/342 Madison Ave #949	212-697-8525
Nicholas, Jess/18 E 16th St	212-206-0322
Nicklaus, Carol/866 UN Plaza #4014	212-644-2020
Nicotra, Roseann/342 Madison Ave #949	212-697-8525
NITZBURG, ANDREW/165 E 32ND ST (P 80)	**212-686-3514**
NOFTSINGER, PAMELA/7 CORNELIA ST #2E (P 416)	**212-316-4241**
NOONAN, JULIA/873 PRESIDENT ST (P 186)	**718-622-9268**
Notarile, Chris/420 Lexington Ave #2911	212-986-5680

O

Oberheide, Heide/295 Washington Ave #5B	718-622-7056
OCHAGAVIA, CARLOS/50 E 50TH ST (P 139)	**212-355-0910**
Odom, Mel/252 W 76th St #B1	212-724-9320
Oelbaum, Fran/200 W 15th St	212-243-4209
Olanoff, Greg/60 E 42nd St #428	212-867-8092
OLBINSKI, RAFAL/470 W 23RD ST (P 121)	**212-242-6367**
Olitsky, Eve/235 W 102nd St #12K	212-678-1045
Olsen, Mimi Vang/545 Hudson St	212-675-5410
Olson, Richard A/85 Grand St	212-925-1820
Orlin, Richard/2550 Olinville Ave	212-882-6177
ORLOFF, DENNIS/682 CARROLL ST #1 (P 417)	**718-965-0385**
Osaka, Rick/14-22 30th Dr	718-956-0015

PQ

PANTUSO, MIKE/350 E 89TH ST (P 465)	**212-534-3511**
PARKER, ROBERT ANDREW/81 GREENE ST (P 196)	**212-925-3053**
Parle Portraits/100 LaSalle St	212-663-7361
Parsons, John/342 Madison Ave #949	212-697-8525
Paslavsky, Evan/510-7 Main St N	212-759-3985
Passons, John/342 Madison Ave	212-697-8525
Pasternak, Robert/114 W 27th St	212-675-0002
Paul, Tony/235 E 49th St	212-307-6188
Peak, Bob/50 E 50th St	212-752-8490
Pearson, Jim/866 UN Plaza #4014	212-644-2020
Peele, Lynwood/344 W 88th St	212-799-3305
PELAVIN, DANIEL/46 COMMERCE ST (P 421)	**212-929-2706**
PERCIVALLE, ROSANNE/240 W 15TH ST #11 (P 423)	**212-243-6589**
PEREZ, VINCE/43 E 19TH ST (P 51)	**212-254-4996**
Perini, Benny/88 Richmond St	718-235-4979
PETERSON, CHERYL/81 GREENE ST (P 196)	**212-925-3053**
Peterson, Robin/411 West End Ave	212-724-3479
Petragnani, Vincent/420 Madison Ave #401	212-980-3510
Pettingill, Ondre/245 Bennett Ave #7B	212-942-1993
Pierson, Mary Louise/310 W 56th St	212-315-3516
PINKNEY, DEBBIE/55 HUDSON ST #3A (P 90)	**212-775-1810**
Piscopia, Joe/114 Beadel St	718-384-2206
Plastic Triangle/146 W 16th St #4B	718-875-9345
Podwill, Jerry/108 W 14th St	212-255-9464
POLADIAN, GIRAIR/130 GALE PL (P 426)	**212-601-2520**
Powell, Ivan/58 W 15th St	212-741-2539
Powers, Christine/198 Berkeley Pl	718-783-1266

ILLUSTRATORS CONT'D.

Please send us your additions and updates.

ILLUSTRATORS

PRATO, RODIKA/121 MADISON AVE (P 56)	**212-683-1362**
PURDOM, BILL/780 MADISON AVE #7A (P 124)	**212-988-4566**
Quartuccio, Dom/5 Tudor City Pl #2201	212-661-1173
QUON, MIKE DESIGN OFFICE/568 BROADWAY	
#703 (P 428)	**212-226-6024**
R Racz, Michael/224 Ave B #23	212-477-0401
RADIGAN, BOB/55 HUDSON ST #3A (P 93)	**212-775-1810**
RAGLAND, GREG/95 HORATIO ST (P 79)	**212-807-0840**
Raglin, Tim/138 W 74th St	212-873-0538
Rainbow Grinder/55 Hudson St #3A	212-775-1810
RANE, WALTER/310 MADISON AVE (P 41)	**212-867-8092**
RAPP, GERALD & CULLEN/108 E 35TH ST #1 (P 482)	**212-889-3337**
Realo, Perry A/155 E 2nd St #4B	212-254-5635
Reay, Richard/515 W 236th St	212-884-2317
Reddin, Paul/120 Windsor Pl	718-965-0647
Reed, Chris/14 E 4th St #817	212-677-7198
REINGOLD, ALAN/155 E 38TH ST (P 82)	**212-697-6170**
Renfro, Ed/250 E 83rd St	212-879-3823
Reott, Paul/51-10 Van Horn St	718-426-1928
REYNOLDS, SCOTT/308 W 30TH ST #9B (P 430)	**212-239-0009**
RICH, ANNA M/777 ST MARKS AVE (P 431)	**718-604-0121**
RICHARDS, LINDA/128 E 91ST ST (P 177)	**212-772-8444**
RIDGEWAY, RON/1466 BROADWAY (P 195)	**212-921-1919**
RIGIE, MITCH/201 E 28TH ST (P 102)	**212-532-0928**
RIGO, MARTIN/43 E 19TH ST (P 49)	**212-254-4996**
Risko, Robert/201 W 11th St	212-989-6987
RIXFORD, ELLEN/308 W 97TH ST (P 83)	**212-865-5686**
Roberts, Cheryl/200 E 78th St	212-570-9069
Robinson, Charles/866 UN Plaza #4014	212-644-2020
ROGERS, LILLA/255 CLINTON ST (P 433)	**718-624-6862**
ROMAN, BARBARA/48-53 205TH ST (P 434)	**718-229-6393**
Romer, Dan/125 Prospect Park W	718-768-3632
ROMERO, JAVIER/327 W 21ST ST #2E (P 435)	**212-206-9175**
Root, Barry/265 Riverside Dr #4F	212-662-2290
Rosen, Terry/101 W 81st St #508	212-580-4784
Rosenblum, Richard/392 Fifth Ave	212-279-2068
Rosenfeld, Mort/420 Lexington Ave #2911	212-986-5680
ROSENTHAL, DOUG/24 FIFTH AVE (P 50)	**212-475-9422**
Rosenthal, Marc/230 Clinton St	718-855-3071
Rosenzweiz, Myra/310 W 90th St	212-362-9871
Rosner, Meryl/342 Madison Ave #261	212-986-3282
Ross Design Assoc Inc/27 W 20th St	212-206-0044
Ross, Barry/211 W 102nd St #5A	212-663-7386
Ross, Bronwen/866 UN Plaza #4014	212-644-2020
ROSS, RICHARD/204 W 20TH ST (P 437)	**212-675-8800**
Roy, Frederick/205 W 14th St	212-206-8789
Rubel, Nicole/349 W 85th St #61	212-799-5855
Rudd, Greg/420 Lexington Ave #2911	212-986-5680
RUDDELL, GARY/18 E 16TH ST (P 47)	**212-206-0322**
Rudenjack, Phyllis/245 E 72nd St	212-772-2813
RUFF, DONNA/595 WEST END AVE (P 438)	**212-255-1635**
Ruffins, Reynold/38 E 21st St	212-674-8150
RUIZ, ARTIE/43 E 19TH ST (P 50)	**212-254-4996**
Russell, Billy D/152 W 58th St #6D	212-873-7975
RUSSELL, MELISSA/350 E 89TH ST (P 465)	**212-502-3976**
S Sabanosh, Michael/433 W 34th St #18B	212-947-8161
Sabin, Robert/60 E 42nd St #428	212-867-8092
Salaverry, Philip/20 W 20th St	212-929-6228
Saldutti, Denise/463 West St #354H	212-255-9328
Salerno, Steve/75 E 7th St	212-673-2298
SALINA, JOE/60 E 42ND ST #505 (P 30)	**212-682-1490**
SAMUELS, MARK/163 CORSON AVE (P 247)	**718-447-8536**
Sandler, Barbara/221 W 20th St	212-691-2052
SANTORO, CHRISTOPHER/201 E 28TH ST (P 112)	**212-532-0928**
Sargent, Claudia K/15-38 126th St	718-461-8280
Saris, Anthony/103 E 86th St	212-831-6353
Saska, Kathy/41 Union Sq W #1001	212-255-5539
Sauber, Rob/420 Lexington #2911	212-986-5680
Sawka, Jan/353 W 53rd St #1W	212-682-2462
Schaare, Harry/60 E 42nd St #428	212-867-8092

SCHALLER, TOM/2255 BROADWAY #303 (P 439)	**212-362-5524**
Schimoler, Thomas/181 Baltic St #1	718-237-1586
Schleinkofer, David/420 Lexington Ave #2911	212-986-5680
Schmidt, Bill/60 E 42nd St #428	212-867-8092
SCHMIDT, CHUCK/420 MADISON AVE #401 (P 37)	**212-980-3510**
Schneegass, Martin/35 Carmine #9	212-759-6300
SCHONGUT, EMANUEL/194 THIRD AVE (P 167)	**212-475-0440**
SCHOTTLAND, MIRIAM/470 W 23RD ST (P 442)	**212-242-6367**
SCHREIER, JOSHUA/466 WASHINGTON ST (P 444)	**212-925-0472**
SCHWARZ, JILL KARLA/80 N MOORE ST (P 445)	**212-227-2444**
Scrofani, Joe/353 W 53rd St #1W	212-682-2462
SEAVER, JEFFREY/130 W 24TH ST #4B (P 447)	**212-741-2279**
Selby, Bill/342 Madison Ave #949	212-697-8525
Seltzer, Isadore/336 Central Park West	212-666-1561
SEMPE/81 GREENE ST (P 196)	**212-925-3053**
Shafer, Ginger/113 Washington Pl	212-989-7697
Shahinian, Brenda/81 Greene St	212-925-3053
SHAP, SANDRA/420 MADISON AVE #401 (P 36)	**212-980-3510**
Shea, Mary Anne/224 W 29th St	212-239-1076
Shefts, Joelle/24 Bond St	212-228-7640
Shega, Marla/60 E 42nd St #505	212-682-1490
Shenefield, Barbara/22 W 25th St	212-677-0740
Sherman, Mary/165 E 32nd St	212-686-3514
Shields, Charles/226 E 53rd St	212-755-4945
Shub, Steve/48 W 21st St 9th Fl	212-243-4412
Siegel, Norm/333 E 49th St	212-980-8061
Silverman, Burt/324 W 71st St	212-799-3399
Singer, Alan D/70 Prospect Park W	718-768-6664
Singer, Paul Design/494 14th St	718-499-8172
SKARDINSKI, STAN/201 E 28TH ST (P 106)	**212-532-0928**
SKOLSKY, MARK/15 W 72ND ST (P 123)	**212-799-2231**
SLACK, CHUCK/60 E 42ND ST #505 (P 31)	**212-682-1490**
Slackman, Charles B/320 E 57th St	212-758-8233
Slavin, Fran/452 Myrtle Ave	718-403-9643
SLOAN, WILLIAM/568 BROADWAY #405 (P 450)	**212-226-8110**
SMALLEY, GUY/40 E 34TH ST #203 (P 451)	**212-683-0335**
Smith, Brett/353 W 53rd St #1W	212-682-2462
SMITH, GARY/48 W 21ST ST 9TH FL (P 191)	**212-243-4412**
SMITH, JEFFREY/226 E 53RD ST (P 70)	**212-755-4945**
Smith, Joseph/159 John St #6	212-825-1479
SMITH, LAURA/12 E 14TH ST #4D (P 323)	**212-206-9162**
Smith, Trudi/866 UN Plaza #4014	212-644-2020
Smith, Vicki/504 E 5th St #6C	212-475-1679
Smollin, Mike/420 Lexington Ave #2911	212-986-5680
Smythe, Danny/420 Madison Ave #401	212-980-3510
SNEBERGER, DAN/310 MADISON AVE (P 42)	**212-867-8092**
SODERLIND, KIRSTEN/111 WOOSTER ST # PH C (P 52)	**212-925-0491**
Soldwedel, Kip/420 Lexington Ave #2911	212-986-5680
Solie, John/420 Lexington Ave #2911	212-986-5680
Solomon, Debra/536 W 111th St #55	212-662-5619
Soloski, Tommy/106 E 19th St	212-674-1460
Sottung, George/420 Lexington Ave #2911	212-986-5680
Spector, Joel/420 Lexington Ave #2911	212-986-5680
SPOLLEN, CHRIS/203 CENTER ST (P 457)	**718-979-9695**
SPOSATO, JOHN/43 E 22ND ST (P 458)	**212-477-3909**
STABIN, VICTOR/100 W 15TH ST #4I (P 248)	**212-243-7685**
STAHL, NANCY/194 THIRD AVE (P 168)	**212-475-0440**
STALLARD, PETER/60 E 42ND ST #505 (P 32)	**212-682-1490**
Stamaty, Mark Alan/118 MacDougal St	212-475-1620
Staples, Matthew/141 W 36th St 14th Fl	212-279-7932
Stavrinos, George/76 W 86th St #6D	212-724-1550
STEADMAN, BARBARA/330 E 33RD ST #10A (P 105)	**212-684-6326**
STEADMAN, E T/470 W 23RD ST (P 120)	**212-242-6367**
STEINER, FRANK/310 MADISON AVE (P 42,43)	**212-867-8092**
Stephens, Lynn/52 W 87th St #4A	212-787-6192
Sternglass, Arno/622 Greenwich St	212-675-5667
STERRETT, JANE/160 FIFTH AVE #700 (P 461)	**212-929-2566**
Stewart, Arvis/866 UN Plaza #4014	212-644-2020
STEWART, PAT/201 E 28TH ST (P 108)	**212-352-0920**
Stillerman, Robbie/230 E 44th St #2F	212-661-7140
STILLMAN, SUSAN/126 W 71ST ST #5A (P 462)	**212-724-5632**
Stone, Gilbert/58 W 15th St	212-741-2539

Please send us your additions and updates.

Strachan, Bruno/224 E 11th St #24	212-228-3419
Streeter, Sabina/141 Wooster St	212-254-7436
Strimban, Robert/349 W 20th St	212-243-6965
SUARES, J C/60 E 42ND ST #505 (P 33)	**212-682-1490**
Sullivan, Suzanne Hughes/1960 Broadway #2E	212-873-3797
SWENY, STEPHEN/217 E 29TH ST #52 (P 463)	**212-532-4072**
Szabo, Gustav/440 West End Ave	212-362-7376
Szilagyi, Mary/410 Central Park West	212-666-7578
Szygiel, Jas/165 E 32nd St	212-686-3514

T
Taba, Eugene/1185 Sixth Ave 8th Fl	212-730-0101
Taback, Simms/38 E 21st St	212-674-8150
Taleporos, Plato/400 Second Ave	212-689-3138
Tankersley, Paul/29 Bethune St	212-924-0015
Taylor, Curtise/29 E 22nd St	212-473-6886
TAYLOR, DOUG/106 LEXINGTON AVE (P 232,233)	**212-674-6346**
Taylor, Katrina/216 E 45th St	212-661-0850
Tedesco, Michael/47 Joralemon St	718-596-4179
Ten, Arnie/446 62nd St	718-745-8477
Terreson, Jeffrey/420 Lexington Ave #2911	212-986-5680
Theakston, Greg/15 W 72nd St	212-799-2231
Thomas, Phero/866 UN Plaza #4014	212-644-2020
THORNTON, SHELLEY/121 MADISON AVENUE (P 55)	**212-683-1362**
TIERNEY, TOM/201 E 28TH ST (P 95)	**212-532-0928**
Tobre, Marie/342 Madison Ave #949	212-697-8525
Tocchet, Mark/1071 Arnow Ave	212-654-4667
Tod-Kat Studios/353 W 53rd St #1W	212-682-2462
TORPEDO STUDIOS/350 E 89TH ST (P 465)	**212-502-3976**
TRAVERS, ROBERT/310 MADISON AVE (P 43)	**212-867-8092**
TRONDSEN, BOB/310 MADISON AVE (P 43)	**212-867-8092**
TROSSMAN, MICHAEL/411 WEST END AVE #16D (P 250)	**212-799-6852**
Trull, John/1573 York Ave	212-535-5383
Tunstull, Glenn/47 State St	718-875-9356

UV
Uhler, Ms Kimane/47-25 40th St	718-729-0635
URAM, LAUREN/251 WASHINGTON AVE (P 467)	**718-789-7717**
Vaccaro, Lou/866 UN Plaza #4014	212-644-2020
VALLA, VICTOR/310 MADISON AVE (P 40,43)	**212-867-8092**
Van Horn, Michael/49 Crosby St	212-226-8341
Varlet-Martinelli/200 W 15th St	212-243-4209
VAUX, JACQUIE MARIE/165 E 32ND ST (P 81)	**212-686-3514**
Vebell, Victoria/157 W 57th St	212-247-1130
Vecchio, Carmine/200 E 27th St	212-683-2679
Velasquez, Eric/226 W 113th St	212-866-2209
VENTURA, DANA/134 W 32ND ST #602 (P 468)	**212-244-4270**
VERMONT, HILLARY/218 EAST 17TH ST (P 469)	**212-674-3845**
Victor, Joan B/863 Park Ave #11E	212-988-2773
Vitsky, Sally/157 W 57th St	212-247-1130
VIVIANO, SAM/25 W 13TH ST (P 470,471)	**212-242-1471**
Vizbar, Milda/529 E 84th St	212-714-9770
Voth, Gregory/231 W 20th St	212-807-9766

W
Wajdowicz, Jurek/1123 Broadway	212-807-8144
WALD, CAROL/57 E 78TH ST (P 473)	**212-737-4559**
WALDMAN, MICHAEL/506 W 42ND ST (P 340)	**212-239-8245**
WALKER, JEFF/310 MADISON AVE (P 41,42)	**212-867-8092**
Walker, John S/47 Jane St	212-242-3435
WALLER, CHARLES/35 BETHUNE ST PH C (P 474)	**212-752-4392**
Wallner, Alexandra & John/866 UN Plaza #4014	212-644-2020
WANAMAKER, JO ANN/225 W 86TH ST (P 475)	**212-724-1786**
Warhola, James/23-11 40th Ave	718-937-6467
Wasserman, Randi/28 W 11th St	212-254-0468
WASSON, CAMERON/4 S PORTLAND AVE #3 (P 88)	**718-875-8277**
Weaver, Robert/42 E 12th St	212-254-4289
Weiman, Jon/147 W 85th St #3F	212-787-3184
Weinstein, Maury/40 W 27th St 5th Fl	212-684-6700
WEISBECKER, PHILIPPE/81 GREENE ST (P 196)	**212-925-3053**
WEISSER, CARL/38 LIVINGSTON ST #33 (P 477)	**718-834-0952**
Weissman, S Q/2510 Fenton Ave	212-654-5381
Wells, Skip/244 W 10th St	212-242-5563
Westlake, Laura/225 Lafayette St	212-334-9310
Whistl'n Dixie/200 E 58th St	212-935-9522

White, Richard A/250 Washington Ave	718-783-3244
Whitehead, Samuel B/206 Eighth Ave	718-965-2047
Whitehouse, Debora/55 Bethune St	212-242-1407
WILKINSON, BILL/155 E 38TH ST (P 84)	**212-697-6170**
WILKINSON, CHUCK/60 E 42ND ST #505 (P 34)	**212-682-1490**
WILLARDSON + ASSOC/194 THIRD AVE (P 173)	**212-475-0440**
Williams, Richard/58 W 15th St	212-741-2539
Wilson, Deborah C/339 E 33rd St #1R	212-532-5205
WIND, BODHI/43 E 19TH ST (P 48)	**212-254-4996**
Winkowski, Fred/48 W 71st St	212-724-3136
Winters, Nina/20 W 77th St	212-877-3089
Wohlberg, Ben/43 Great Jones St	212-254-9663
WOLFF, PUNZ/151 E 20TH ST #5G (P 255)	**212-254-5705**
Wood, Page/48 W 21st St 9th Fl	212-243-4412
Woodend, James/342 Madison Ave #949	212-697-8525
Word-Wise/325 W 45th St	212-246-0430
WRAY, WENDY/194 THIRD AVE (P 172)	**212-475-0440**
WYATT, KATHY/43 E 19TH ST (P 48)	**212-254-4996**
Wynne, Patricia/446 Central Pk West	212-865-1059

YZ
Yankus, Marc/179 Prince St	212-228-6539
Yeldham, Ray/420 Lexington Ave #2911	212-986-5680
YEMI/605 E 11TH ST (P 195)	**212-477-2007**
YIANNIAS, VICKI/200 W 15TH ST (P 38, 39)	**212-243-4209**
Yip, Jenny/6103 Twentieth Ave	718-236-0349
York, Judy/165 E 32nd St	212-686-3514
YULE, SUSAN HUNT/176 ELIZABETH ST (P 38, 39)	**212-226-0439**
Zagorski, Stanislaw/142 E 35th St	212-532-2348
Zaid, Barry/108 E 35th St #1	212-889-3337
Zann, Nicky/155 W 68th St	212-724-5027
Zeldich, Arieh/866 UN Plaza #4014	212-644-2020
ZIEMIENSKI, DENNIS/55 CHEEVER PL (P 52)	**718-643-7055**
Ziering, Bob/151 W 74th St	212-873-0034
ZIMIC, TRICIA/201 E 28TH ST (P 97)	**212-532-0928**
Zimmerman, Jerry/48 W 20th St 2nd Fl	212-620-7777
Zitting, Joel/333 E 49th St #3J	212-980-8061
Zwarenstein, Alex/15 W 72nd St	212-799-2231

NORTHEAST

A
Abel, Ray/18 Vassar Pl, Scarsdale, NY	914-725-1899
Adam Filippo & Moran/1206 Fifth Ave, Pittsburgh, PA	412-261-3720
Adams, Norman/229 Berkeley #52, Boston, MA	617-266-3858
Addams, Charles/PO Box 8, Westport, CT	203-227-7806
Adler, Bente/103 Broad St, Boston, MA	617-266-3858
Ahmed, Ghulan Hassan/5738 Edgepark Rd, Baltimore, MD	301-444-8246
ALCORN, JOHN/RFD #2 BOX 179, LYME, CT (P 165)	**203-434-8533**
ALDRICH, SUSAN/PO BOX 114, NORTHPORT, NY (P 259)	**516-261-6220**
ALEXANDER, PAUL R/37 PINE MOUNTAIN RD, REDDING, CT (P 260)	**203-544-9293**
ALSOP, MARK/324 AUBURNDALE AVE, AUBURNDALE, MA (P 262)	**617-527-7862**
AMICOSANTE, VINCENT/33 ROUTE 5, EDGEWATER, NJ (P 92)	**201-886-9354**
Ancas, Karen/7 Perkins Sq #11, Jamaica Plain, MA	617-522-2958
Archambault, David/56 Arbor St, Hartford, CT	203-523-9876
The Art Source/201 King St, Chappaqua, NY	914-238-4221
Ashmead, Hal/39 Club House Dr, Woodbury, CT	203-263-3466
Avati, Jim/10 Highland Ave, Rumson, NJ	201-530-1480

B
Baker, Laurie/33 Richdale Ave, Cambridge, MA	617-492-5689
Bakley, Craig/68 Madison Ave, Cherry Hill, NJ	609-428-6310
Ball, Harvey/340 Main St, Wooster, MA	617-752-9154
Bang, Molly Garrett/43 Drumlin Rd, Falmouth, MA	617-540-5174
Bangham, Richard/2006 Cascade Rd, Silver Spring, MD	301-649-1919
Banta, Susan/72 Newbern Ave, Medford, MA	617-396-1792
Barkley, James/25 Brook Manor, Pleasantville, NY	914-769-5207
Barrett, Tom/90 Myrtle St #4, Boston, MA	617-742-5143
Baxter, Robert/Conte Pl #2, Westport, CT	203-226-3011
The Becherman Group/35 Mill St, Bernardsville, NJ	201-766-9238
Bedard, Rob (Ms)/6110 Executive Blvd #610, Rockville, MD	301-231-5110

Belser, Burkey/1636 R St NW, Washington, DC	202-462-1482
Benson, John D/2113 Townhill Rd #C, Baltimore, MD	301-665-3395
Berlin, Rick/220 Ferris Ave, White Plains, NY	914-946-1950
Berry, Sheila & Richard/803 E 5th St, South Boston, MA	617-269-1338
Biggins, Wendy/185 Goodhill Rd, Weston, CT	203-226-7674
Birmingham, Lloyd P/Peekskill Hollow Rd, Putnam Valley, NY	914-528-3207
Bomzer Design Inc/66 Canal St, Boston, MA	617-227-5151
BONO, PETER/59 VAN HOUTEN, PASSAIC, NJ (P 276)	**201-778-5489**
Booth, Brenda/PO Box 596, Chappaqua, NY	914-238-5325
Booth, George/PO Box 8, Westport, CT	203-227-7806
Boynton, Lee A/7 Gladden Rd, Annapolis, MD	301-263-6336
Brautigan, Don/29 Cona Ct, Haledon, NJ	201-956-7710
Breeden, Paul M/Sullivan Harbor Farm, Sullivan Harbor, ME	207-422-3007
Breiner, Joanne/11 Webster St, Medford, MA	617-354-8378
Brickman, Robin/32 Fort Hoosac Pl, Williamstown, MA	201-872-2496
Bridy, Dan Visuals Inc/119 First Ave, Pittsburgh, PA	412-288-9362
Brown, Michael D/416 Hungerford Dr, Rockville, MD	301-762-4474
Bucella, Martin/72 Martinique Dr, Cheektowaga, NY	716-668-0040
Bullock, Wilbur/229 Berkeley #52, Boston, MA	617-266-3858
Burroughs, Miggs/PO Box 6, Westport, CT	203-227-9667
Burrows, Bill & Assoc/103 E Read St, Baltimore, MD	301-752-4615
Buschini, Maryanne/602 N 16th St #O, Philadelphia, PA	215-235-7838
BUTCHER, JIM/1357 E MACPHAIL RD, BEL AIR, MD (P 135)	**301-879-6380**

C

CABARGA, LESLIE/258 W TULPEHOCKEN, PHILADELPHIA, PA (P 286)	**215-438-9954**
Cable, Jerry/29 Station Rd, Madison, NJ	201-966-0124
CAGLE, DARYL/17 FOREST LAWN AVE, STAMFORD, CT (P 287)	**203-359-3780**
Callahan, Kevin/26 France St, Norwalk, CT	203-847-2046
Calver, Dave/271 Mulberry St, Rochester, NY	716-271-6208
CAPORALE, WENDE L/STUDIO HILL FARM RTE 116, N SALEM, NY (P 288)	**914-669-5653**
Cardella, Elaine/215 Clinton St, Hoboken, NJ	201-656-3244
Carlson, Frederick H/2335 Meadow Dr, Pittsburgh, PA	412-371-8951
Carson, Jim/18 Orchard St, Cambridge, MA	617-661-3321
Casilla, Robert/36 Hamilton Ave, Yonkers, NY	914-963-8165
Catalano, Sal/114 Boyce Pl, Ridgewood, NJ	201-447-5318
Chandler, Jean/385 Oakwood Dr, Wyckoff, NJ	201-891-2381
Cheng, Judith/88-57 195th St, Hollis, NY	718-465-5598
Cincotti, Gerald/371 Beacon St, Boston, MA	617-236-0456
Clark, Bradley/99 Mill St, Rhinebeck, NY	914-876-2615
Clark, Cynthia Watts/99 Mill St, Rhinebeck, NY	914-876-2615
Clark, Patricia C/6201 Benalder Dr, Bethesda, MD	301-229-2986
CLARKE, BOB/46 WASHBURN PARK, ROCHESTER, NY (P 296,297)	**716-442-8686**
CLINE, ROB/229 BERKELEY #52, BOSTON, MA (P 76)	**617-266-3858**
Cober, Alan E/95 Croton Dam Rd, Ossining, NY	914-941-8696
Codd, Mary/1 Richmond Square, Providence, RI	401-273-9898
Cohen, A R/2249 Rogene Dr, Baltimore, MD	301-358-3065
Cohen, Dee/2930 McKinley St NW, Washington, DC	202-364-1118
Cohen, Susan D/208 Park Ave #3R, Hoboken, NJ	201-659-5472
Collyer, Frank/RR 1 Box 266, Stony Point, NY	914-947-3050
Concept One/Gizmo/366 Oxford St, Rochester, NY	716-461-4240
Condon, Ken/42 Jefferson St, Cambridge, MA	617-492-4301
CONGE, BOB/28 HARPER ST, ROCHESTER, NY (P 298,299)	**716-473-0291**
Console, Carmen/8 Gettysburg St, Voorhees, NJ	215-463-6110
Cook, Susan Anderson/675 Leone St, Woodbridge, NJ	201-750-0977
Cooper, Bob/311 Fern Dr, Atco Post Office, NJ	609-767-0967
Cornell, Jeff/58 Noyes Rd, Fairfield, CT	203-259-7715
Cosatt, Paulette/60 South St, Cresskill, NJ	201-568-1436
Costas, Laura/1816 Kilbourne Pl NW, Washington, DC	202-265-4499
CRAFT, KINUKO/RFD #1 PO BOX 167, NORFOLK, CT (P 202)	**203-542-5018**
CRAMER, D L/10 BEECHWOOD DR, WAYNE, NJ (P 305)	**201-628-8793**
CROFUT, BOB/225 PEACEABLE ST, RIDGEFIELD, CT (P 308,309)	**203-431-4304**
CROMPTON, JACK/229 BERKELEY #52, BOSTON, MA (P 74)	**617-266-3858**
CUSANO, STEVE/731 N 24TH ST, PHILADELPHIA, PA (P 211)	**215-232-6666**

D

DAILY, DON/57 ACADEMY RD, BALA CYNWYD, PA (P 136)	**215-664-5729**
Dally, Lyman M/166 Beachwood Rd, Parsippany, NJ	201-887-1338
Daly, Tom/47 E Edsel Ave, Palisades Park, NJ	201-943-1837
Darrow, Whitney/PO Box 8, Westport, CT	203-227-7806
DAVIDIAN, ANNA/229 BERKELEY #52, BOSTON, MA (P 76)	**617-266-3858**
Davidson, Peter/144 Moody St, Waltham, MA	617-899-3239
Davis, Gary/16 Yale Ave, Wakefield, MA	617-245-2628
DAVIS, HARRY/731 N 24TH ST, PHILADELPHIA, PA (P 211)	**215-232-6666**
Dawes, Joseph/20 Church Ct, Closter, NJ	201-767-8127
Dedini, Eldon/PO Box 8, Westport, CT	203-227-7806
Deigen, Jim and Assoc/625 Stanwick St, Pittsburgh, PA	412-391-1698
DeKiefte, Kees/185 Goodhill Rd, Weston, CT	203-226-7674
Demarest, Robert/87 Highview Terr, Hawthorne, NJ	201-427-9639
Demers, Donald/15 Liberty St, Waltham, MA	207-439-1463
DEMUTH, ROGER TAZE/2627 DEGROFF RD, NUNDA, NY (P 319)	**716-468-2685**
Dey, Lorraine/10 Highland Ave, Rumson, NJ	201-530-1480
Dior, Jerry/9 Old Hickory Ln, Edison, NJ	201-561-6536
Dodge, Paul/731 N 24th St, Philadelphia, PA	215-232-6666
DODGE, SUSAN/229 BERKELEY #52, BOSTON, MA (P 74)	**617-266-3858**
Dougherty, Kevin/10 Highland Ave, Rumson, NJ	201-530-1480
Drescher, Joan/23 Cedar, Hingham, MA	617-749-5179
DRINKWINE, SHARON/229 BERKELEY #52, BOSTON, MA (P 75)	**617-266-3858**
Driver, Ray/5725-B Harpers Farm, Columbia, MD	301-596-6955
DUKE, CHRISTINE/MAPLE AVE BOX 471, MILLBROOK, NY (P 132)	**914-677-9510**
Duke, W E Illustration/216 Walnut St, Holyoke, MA	413-536-8269
Dunne, Tom/16 Cherry St, Locust Valley, NY	516-676-3641
DVERIN, ANATOLY/229 BERKELEY #52, BOSTON, MA (P 75)	**617-266-3858**

E

Eagle, Mike/7 Captains Ln, Old Saybrook, CT	203-388-5654
Ebel, Alex/30 Newport Rd, Yonkers, NY	914-961-4058
Echevarria, Abe/Box 98 Anderson Rd, Sherman, CT	203-355-1254
Eckstein, Bob/107 Cherry Lane, Medford, NY	516-654-0291
Einsel, Naiad/26 S Morningside Dr, Westport, CT	203-226-0709
Einsel, Walter/26 S Morningside Dr, Westport, CT	203-226-0709
Enos, Randall/11 Court of Oaks, Westport, CT	203-227-4785
Epstein, Dave/Dows Ln, Irvington-on-Hudson, NY	914-591-7470
Epstein, Len/720 Montgomery Ave, Narbeth, PA	215-664-4700
Estey, Peg/7 Garden Ct, Cambridge, MA	617-876-1142
Eucalyptus Tree Studio/2220 N Charles St, Baltimore, MD	301-243-0211

F

FARNSWORTH, BILL/PO BOX 653, NEW MILFORD, CT (P 330)	**203-355-1649**
Farris, Joe/PO Box 8, Westport, CT	203-227-7806
FEINEN, JEFF/4702 SAWMILL RD, CLARENCE, NY (P 333)	**716-759-8406**
Fiedler, Joseph D/500 Sampsonia Way, Pittsburgh, PA	412-322-7245
Fisher, Mark/506 Windsor Dr, Framingham, MA	617-451-6528
Ford, Pam/251 Greenwood Ave, Bethel, CT	203-797-8181
Foster, Susan/3903 Rosemary St, Chevy Chase, MD	301-652-3849
FRANKE, PHIL/10 NEHRING AVE, BABYLON VILLAGE, NY (P 126)	**516-661-5775**
Friebel, Dave/1015 Chestnut St, Philadelphia, PA	215-238-9888
Frinta, Dagmar/87 Hope St, Providence, RI	401-273-6125
Fuchs, Bernard/3 Tanglewood Ln, Westport, CT	203-227-464
Fuller, Steve/7 Winding Brook Dr, Guilderland, NY	518-456-7496

G

Gaadt, George/888 Thorn, Sewickley, PA	412-741-516
Gallon, Dale B/1180 Knoxlyn Rd, Gettysburg, PA	717-334-101
GARLAND, MICHAEL/78 COLUMBIA AVE, HARTSDALE, NY (P 342)	**914-946-453**
Gerlach, Cameron/2644 N Calvert St, Baltimore, MD	301-889-309
Geyer, Jackie/107 6th St #207 Fulton Bldg, Pittsburgh, PA	412-261-111
Gist, Linda E/224 Madison Ave, Fort Washington, PA	215-643-375
Giuliani, Alfred/10 Woodland Terrace, Lincroft, NJ	201-741-875
Glanzman, Louis S/154 Handsome Ave, Sayville, NY	516-589-261
Glasbergen, Randy J/4 Chapel St, Sherburne, NY	607-674-949
Glazer, Ted/28 West View Rd, Spring Valley, NY	914-354-152
Glessner, Marc/24 Evergreen Rd, Somerset, NJ	201-249-503

**GOLDBERG, RICHARD/360 CONGRESS ST 5TH FL,
   BOSTON, MA (P 238)**   **617-338-6369**
Goldinger, Andras/215 C St SE #310, Washington, DC   202-543-9029
Goldman, Marvin/RD 3 Gypsy Trail Rd, Carmel, NY   914-225-8611
GORDLEY, SCOTT/229 BERKELEY #52, BOSTON, MA (P 75)   **617-266-3858**
Gordon, Barry/12700 Chilton Cir, Silver Spring, MD   301-384-2445
Grashow, James/14 Diamond Hill Rd, W Redding, CT   203-938-9195
Green, Norman/11 Seventy Acres Rd, W Redding, CT   203-438-9909
Gustafson, Dale/56 Fourbrooks Rd, Stamford, CT   203-322-5667
Gyson, Mitch/4412 Colmar Gardens Dr E, Baltimore, MD   301-243-3430

H Haas, Gordon/1-B Walden Pl, Montclair, NJ   201-746-0539
Haefele, Steve/2101 Crompond Rd, Peekskill, NY   914-736-0785
Haffner, Marilyn/185 Holworthy St, Cambridge, MA   617-354-0696
HALLMAN, TOM/38 S 17TH ST, ALLENTOWN, PA (P 349)   **215-776-1144**
Hamilton, William/PO Box 8, Westport, CT   203-227-7806
Handelsman, Bud/PO Box 8, Westport, CT   203-227-7806
Handville, Robert T/99 Woodland Dr, Pleasantville, NY   914-769-3582
Haney, William/16 River Road RD #3, Neshanic Station, NJ   201-369-3848
Harden, Laurie/20 Overlook Rd, Boonton Township, NJ   201-335-4578
Hardy, Neil O/2 Woods Grove, Westport, CT   203-226-4446
Harris, Ellen/125 Pleasant St #602, Brookline, MA   617-739-1867
Harris, Peter/37 Beech St, Wrentham, MA   617-384-2470
Harsh, Fred/185 Goodhill Rd, Weston, CT   203-226-7674
Harsh, William/8 Euliata Terr, Brighton, MA   617-427-5182
Harvey, Paul/45 Fern Valley Rd, Weston, CT   203-226-5234
Hazelton, Betsey/106 Robbins Dr, Carlisle, MA   617-369-5309
Healy, Deborah/72 Watchung Ave, Upper Montclair, NJ   201-746-2549
Hearn, Diane Dawson/22 Spring St, Pauling, NY   914-855-1152
Hearn, Walter/22 Spring St, Pauling, NY   914-855-1152
Heath, R Mark/4338 Roland Springs Dr, Baltimore, MD   301-366-4633
HEIMANN, STEVE/PO BOX 406, ORADELL, NJ (P 353)   **201-345-9132**
Hejja, Attila/300 Edward St, Roslyn Heights, NY   516-621-8054
Henderson, Dave/7 Clover Ln, Verona, NJ   201-783-5791
Herrick, George W/384 Farmington, Hartford, CT   203-527-1940
Herring, Michael/5 Overlook Rd, Ossining, NY   914-762-5045
Hess, Richard/Southover Farms RT 67, Roxbury, CT   203-354-2921
Heyck, Edith/92 Water St, Newburyport, MA   617-462-9027
Hildebrandt, Greg/1148 Parsippany Blvd, Parsippany, NJ   201-334-0353
Hildebrandt, Tim/10 Jackson Ave, Gladstone, NJ   201-234-2149
HOFFMAN, MARTIN/RD 2 BOX 50, WORCESTER, MA (P 143)   **607-638-5472**
Hogan, Jamie/36 Green St, Jamaica Plain, MA   617-522-5503
Howard, Bill/5301 New Hampshire Ave NW, Washington, DC   202-882-6253
Huehnergarth, John/196 Snowden Ln, Princeton, NJ   609-921-3211
Huelsman, Amy/24 S Calumet Ave, Hastings on Hudson, NY   914-478-0596
HUERTA, GERARD/45 CORBIN DR, DARIEN, CT (P 239)   **203-656-0505**
Huffaker, Sandy/375 Snowden Lane, Princeton, NJ   609-924-2883
Hulsey, John/Rte 9D, Garrison, NY   914-424-3544
Hunt, Stan/PO Box 8, Westport, CT   203-227-7806
Hurwitz, Joyce/7314 Burdette Ct, Bethesda, MD   301-365-0340
HUYSSEN, ROGER/45 CORBIN DR, DARIEN, CT (P 240)   **203-656-0200**

JK Ilosa, Ann/185 Goodhill Rd, Weston, CT   203-226-7674
Ish, Gary/45 Newbury St, Boston, MA   617-247-4168
Irwin, Virginia/174 Chestnut Ave #2, Jamaica Plain, MA   617-522-0580
Jaeger Design Studio/2025 I St NW #622, Washington, DC   202-785-8434
Jean, Carole/45 Oriole Dr, Roslyn, NY   516-742-3322
**JOHNSON, B E/366 OXFORD ST,
   ROCHESTER, NY (P 362,363)**   **716-461-4240**
Johnson, David A/299 South Ave, New Canaan, CT   203-966-3269
Jones, George/52 Old Highway, Wilton, CT   203-762-7242
Jones, John R/335 Town St, East Haddam, CT   203-873-9950
Jones, Robert/47 W Stewart, Lansdowne, PA   215-626-1245
Jones, Roger/15 Waldo Ave, Somerville, MA   617-628-1487
Jordan, Laurie/185 Goodhill Rd, Weston, CT   203-226-7674
Jordan, Polly/29 Warren Ave, Somerville, MA   617-776-0329
Kalish, Lionel/PO Box 882, Woodstock, NY   914-679-8156
Kane, Michael/113 Monroe St, Rahway, NJ   201-381-0127
Kanelous, George/2466 Kerry Ln, Bellmore, NY   516-221-8523
Kilroy, John/28 Fairmount Way, Nantasket, MA   617-925-0582
Kingham, Dave/42 Blue Spruce Circle, Weston, CT   203-226-3106
Kingsbury, Guy/305 High St, Milford, CT   914-225-3855

Kinstrey, Jim/35 Bryant Pl, Lodi, NJ   201-772-1781
Kline, Rob/39 Newbury St 2nd Fl, Boston, MA   617-536-2132
**KNABEL, LONNIE/20 BERKELEY CT,
   BROOKLINE, MA (P 367)**   **617-232-1291**
Koeppel, Gary/368 Congress, Boston, MA   617-426-8887
Kossin, Sanford/143 Cowneck Rd, Port Washington, NY   516-883-3038
Kovarsky, Anatol/PO Box 8, Westport, CT   203-227-7806
Kyriacos, Betty/2221 Penfield Ln, Bowie, MD   703-527-7696

L LaCaourse, Carol/506 Windsor Dr, Framingham, MA   617-451-6528
LaGrone, Roy/25 Indiana Rd, Somerset, NJ   201-463-4515
Laird, William/10 Highland Ave, Rumson, NJ   201-530-1480
Langdon, John/106 S Marion Ave, Wenonah, NJ   609-468-7868
Lanza, Barbara/PO Box 118, Pine Island, NY   914-258-4601
Lasasso, Gary/49 Foxhall Ave, Kingston, NY   914-331-3333
Lawton, April/31 Hampshire Dr, Farmingdale, NY   516-454-0868
Layman, Linda J/Hill Rd, South Hamilton, MA   617-468-4297
Lazarevich, Mila/185 Goodhill Rd, Weston, CT   203-226-7674
Leamon, Tom/18 Main St, Amherst, MA   413-256-8423
Lehew, Ron/17 Chestnut St, Salem, NJ   609-935-1422
Leibow, Paul/369 Lantana Ave, Englewood, NJ   201-567-2561
Levine, Ned/301 Frankel Blvd, Merrick, NY   516-378-8122
Lewczak, Scott/95 Kimberly Rd, Colonia, NJ   201-388-5262
Lewis, Alex (Ms)/2200 20th St NW, Washington, DC   202-462-5326
**LEYONMARK, ROGER/229 BERKELEY #52,
   BOSTON, MA (P 77)**   **617-266-3858**
Lidbeck, Karin/185 Goodhill Rd, Weston, CT   203-226-7674
Loccisano, Karen/185 Goodhill Rd, Weston, CT   203-226-7674
Logan, Ron/PO Box 306, Brentwood, NY   516-273-4693
Longacre, Jimmy/185 Goodhill Rd, Weston, CT   203-226-7674
LORENZ, AL/185 GOODHILL RD, WESTON, CT (P 381)   **203-226-7674**
Lorenz, Lee/PO Box 8, Westport, CT   203-227-7806
LOSE, HAL/533 W HORTTER ST, PHILADELPHIA, PA (P 382)   **215-849-7635**
Lowes, Tom/41 Hartsen St, Rochester, NY   716-442-8325
LUBEY, DICK/726 HARVARD, ROCHESTER, NY (P 384)   **716-442-6075**
LUZAK, DENNIS/PO BOX 342, REDDING RIDGE, CT (P 385)   **203-938-3158**
Lynn, Kathy/1741 Bainbridge, Philadelphia, PA   215-545-5039

M MDB Communications/932 Hungerford Dr #23, Rockville, MD   301-279-9093
MacArthur, Dave/147 E Bradford Ave #B, Cedar Grove, NJ   201-857-1046
MacFarland, Jean/Laurel Lake Rd, Lenox, MA   413-637-3647
Maffia, Daniel/236 S Dwight Pl, Englewood, NJ   201-871-0435
MAGER, JANET/229 BERKELEY #52, BOSTON, MA (P 74)   **617-266-3858**
Mahoney, Katherine/60 Hurd Rd, Belmont, MA   617-489-0406
Mandel, Saul/163 Maytime Dr, Jericho, NY   516-681-3530
Mariuzza, Pete/146 Hardscrabble Rd, Briarcliff Manor, NY   914-769-3310
Marmo, Brent/4 Davis Ct, Brookline, MA   617-395-8977
Martin, Henry/PO Box 8, Westport, CT   203-227-7806
MARTIN, RICHARD/485 HILDA ST (P 389)   **516-221-3630**
MASCIO, TONY/4 TETON CT, VOORHEES, NJ (P 244)   **215-567-1585**
Mattingly, David/1112 Bloomfield St, Hoboken, NJ   201-659-7404
Mattiucci, Jim/247 N Goodman St, Rochester, NY   716-271-2280
Mayforth, Hal/19 Irma Ave, Watertown, MA   617-923-4668
Mayo, Frank/265 Briar Brae, Stamford, CT   203-322-3650
McElfish, Susan/5725 Phillips Ave, Pittsburgh, PA   412-521-6041
McGinnis, Robert/13 Arcadia Rd, Old Greenwich, CT   203-637-5055
McGuire, Arlene Phoebe/The Cambridge #509/Alden Pk,
   Philadelphia, PA   215-844-0754
McIntosh, Jon C/268 Woodward St, Waban, MA   617-964-6292
McManimon, Tom/2700 Route 22, Union, NJ   201-688-2700
McVicker, Charles/4 Willow St, Princeton, NJ   609-924-2660
Meeker, Carlene/24 Shore Dr, Winthrop, MA   617-846-5117
Melgar, Fabian/14 Clover Dr, Smithtown, NY   516-543-7561
Menn, Jennifer J/28-4 Beacon St, Chelsea, MA   617-884-6267
Metcalf, Roger/132 Hendrie Ave, Riverside, CT   203-637-9524
Miles, Elizabeth/185 Goodhill Rd, Weston, CT   203-226-7674
Miller, Warren/PO Box 8, Westport, CT   203-227-7806
Milnazik, Kim/210 Locust St #3F, Philadelphia, PA   215-922-5440
**MISTRETTA, ANDREA/5 BOHNERT PL,
   WALDWICK, NJ (P 245)**   **201-652-5325**
Miyake, Yoshi/185 Goodhill Rd, Weston, CT   203-226-7674
Modell, Frank/PO Box 8, Westport, CT   203-227-7806

ILLUSTRATORS

Mooney, Gerry/64-K Nashville Rd, Bethel, CT	203-798-1108
MOORE, JACK/131 CEDAR LAKE WEST,	
DENVILLE, NJ (P 405)	**201-627-6931**
MORALES, MANUEL/PO BOX 1763,	
BLOOMFIELD, NJ (P 406,407)	**201-429-0848**
MORECRAFT, RON/97 MORRIS AVE,	
DENVILLE, NJ (P 194,195)	**201-627-6728**
Moscowitz, Stephen/1239 University Ave, Rochester, NY	716-442-8433
Moss, Donald/232 Peaceable St, Ridgefield, CT	203-438-5633
Myers, Lou/58 Lakeview Ave, Peekskill, NY	914-737-2307

NO
Nacht, Merle/374 Main St, Weathersfield, CT	203-563-7993
Neibart, Wally/1715 Walnut St, Philadelphia, PA	215-564-5167
NEIDER, ALAN/151 PENN COMMON, MILFORD, CT (P 411)	**203-878-9260**
Newman, Robert/112 Crockett Rd, King of Prussia, PA	215-337-2745
Nix, Jonathon J/Carter Rd, Becket, MA	413-623-5848
Noome, Mike/55 Bulkey Ave, N Westport, CT	203-255-5977
Norman, Marty/5 Radcliff Blvd, Glen Head, NY	516-671-4482
Noyes, David/506 Windsor Dr, Framingham, MA	617-451-6528
Noyse, Janet/118 Woodland Rd, Wyncote, PA	215-572-6975
Oh, Jeffrey/2635 Ebony Rd, Baltimore, MD	301-661-6064
O'Leary, John/547 N 20th St, Philadelphia, PA	215-561-7377
Olsen, Jimmy/50 New York Ave, Clark, NJ	201-388-0967
Olson, Victor/Fanton Meadows, West Redding, CT	203-938-2863
Otnes, Fred/Chalburn Rd, West Redding, CT	203-938-2829
Oughton, Taylor/Jamison, Bucks County, PA	215-598-3246

P
Pack, John/1802 Belmont St NW, Washington, DC	202-293-7750
PALLADINI, DAVID/PO BOX 1228, E HAMPTON, NY (P 54)	**212-983-1362**
PALULIAN, DICKRAN/18 MCKINLEY ST,	
ROWAYTON, CT (P 183)	**203-866-3734**
Papitto, Aurelia/PO Box 1454 GMS, Boston, MA	617-451-5362
Parente, Susan/605 Stage Rd, Monroe, NY	914-782-0360
PARKER, ED ASSOC/9 CARLISLE ST,	
ANDOVER, MA (P 419)	**617-475-2659**
Parry, Ivor A/4 Lorraine Dr, Eastchester, NY	212-889-0707
Passalacqua, David/325 Versa Pl, Sayville, NY	516-589-1663
Pate, Rodney/185 Goodhill Rd, Weston, CT	203-226-7674
PATRICK, PAMELA/410 S UNION ST,	
KENNETT SQUARE, PA (P 420)	**215-444-4375**
Payne, Thomas/11 Colonial Ave, Albany, NY	518-482-1756
PELS, WINSLOW PINNEY/HACK GREEN RD,	
POUND RIDGE, NY (P 424)	**212-570-7098**
Pinkney, Jerry/41 Furnace Dock Rd, Croton-on-Hudson, NY	914-271-5238
Pirk, Kathy/5112 45th ST NW, Washington, DC	202-244-5736
PISANO, AL/21 SKYLINE DR,	
UPPER SADDLE RIVER, NJ (P 425)	**201-327-6716**
Plotkin, Barnett/126 Wooleys Ln, Great Neck, NY	516-487-7457
POLLACK, SCOTT/11 TRINITY PL, HEWLETT, NY (P 427)	**516-295-4026**
Porter, John/5508 Besley Court, Rockville, MD	301-984-3605
Porzio, Ed/131 Bartlett Rd, Winthrop, MA	617-846-3875
Price, George/PO Box 8, Westport, CT	203-227-7806
Provensen, Alice/Meadowbrook Ln Box 171, Staatsburg, NY	914-266-3245
Puccio, Jim/32 Rugg Rd, Allston, MA	617-783-2719

R
Rabl, Lorraine/249 Queen Anne Rd, Bogota, NJ	201-342-4647
RADIOMAYONNAISE/112-A APPLETON ST,	
BOSTON, MA (P 429)	**617-536-5440**
Ramage, Alfred/5 Irwin St #7, Winthrop, MA	617-846-5955
Ravel, Ken/2 Myrtle Ave, Stoney Creek, PA	215-779-2105
Recchia, Dennis & Janet/191 Engle St, Englewood, NJ	201-569-6136
Reeser, Tracy P/254 Andover Rd, Glenmoore, PA	215-942-2597
Regnier, Mark/97 Wachusett, Jamaica Plain, MA	617-522-5295
Reiner, John/27 Commander Ln, Nesconset, NY	516-360-3049
Rera, Lou/340 Linwood Ave, Buffalo, NY	716-885-0015
Reynolds, Bob/4013 N Davis Pl NW, Washington, DC	202-333-0872
Richter, Mische/PO Box 8, Westport, CT	203-227-7806
RICKERD, DAVID/18 UNIVERSITY AVE,	
CHATHAM, NJ (P 194)	**201-635-9513**
RILEY, FRANK/108 BAMFORD AVE,	
HAWTHORNE, NJ (P 127)	**201-423-2659**

RODERICKS, MICHAEL/129 LOUNSBURY RD,	
TRUMBULL, CT (P 432)	**203-268-155**
Rogers, Glenda/318 Lexington Ave, Syracuse, NY	315-478-450
Roman, Irena & John/369 Thom Clapp Rd Box 571,	
Scituate, MA	617-545-651
ROSS, IAN/1010 STATE ST, NEW HAVEN, CT (P 53)	**203-776-588**
ROSS, LARRY/53 FAIRVIEW AVE, MADISON, NJ (P 436)	**201-377-685**
Roth, Gail/185 Goodhill Rd, Weston, CT	203-226-767
Rutherford, Jenny/185 Goodhill Rd, Weston, CT	203-226-767

S
Sahli, Barbara/8212 Flower Ave, Takoma Park, MD	301-585-512
SANDERS, BRUCE/229 BERKELEY #52,	
BOSTON, MA (P 78)	**617-266-385**
Sanderson, Ruth/185 Goodhill Rd, Weston, CT	203-226-767
Santa, Monica/185 Goodhill Rd, Weston, CT	203-226-767
Santore, Charles/138 S 20th St, Philadelphia, PA	215-563-043
Saxon, Charles/PO Box 8, Westport, CT	203-227-780
Schenker, Bob/219 Sugartown Rd #204, Strafford, PA	215-688-655
Schleinkofer, David/344 Crown St, Morrisville, PA	215-295-862
SCHLEMME, ROY/585 CENTER ST, ORADELL, NJ (P 440)	**212-921-973**
Schneider, Rick/260 Montague Rd, Leverett, MA	413-549-070
SCHOFIELD, GLEN/4 HILLSIDE AVE, ROSELAND, NJ (P 441)	**201-226-559**
Schorr, Kathy Staico/PO Box 142, Roxbury, CT	203-266-408
Schorr, Todd/PO Box 142, Roxbury, CT	203-266-408
SCHRECK, JOHN/371 BEACON ST #2,	
BOSTON, MA (P 443)	**617-236-035**
Schroeder, Michael/1327 Walnut St, Reading, PA	215-375-905
Schroeppel, Richard/31 Walnut Hill Rd, Amherst, NH	603-673-099
Seavey, David/2126 Connecticut Ave NW, Washington, DC	202-483-783
Sekeris, Pim/570 Milton St #10, Montreal H2X 1W4, QU	514-844-05
Selwyn, Paul/182 Whitney St, Hartford, CT	203-523-997
Sharpe, Jim/5 Side Hill Rd, Westport, CT	203-226-998
Shaw, Barclay/8 Buena Vista Dr, Hastings-on-Hudson, NY	914-478-026
SHERMAN, OREN/30 IPSWICH #301,	
BOSTON, MA (P 448,449)	**617-437-736**
Shiff, Andrew Z/153 Clinton St, Hopkinton, MA	617-435-360
Simmonds, Oz/236 W Grand St #A5, Elizabeth, NJ	212-254-890
Sims, Blanche/185 Goodhill Rd, Weston, CT	203-226-767
Skibinski, Ray/694 Harrell Ave, Woodbridge, NJ	201-634-302
Smallwood, Steve/2417 3rd St Bsmt, Fort Lee, NJ	201-585-792
Smith, Douglas/405 Washington St #2, Brookline, MA	617-566-381
Smith, Ellen/PO Box 14693, Hartford, CT	203-249-110
SMITH, ELWOOD H/2 LOCUST GROVE RD,	
RHINEBECK, NY (P 452)	**914-876-23**
Smith, Gail Hunter/PO Box 217, Barnegat Light, NJ	609-494-91
SMITH, MARCIA/112 LINDEN ST, ROCHESTER, NY (P 453)	**716-461-93**
Smith, Raymond/222 Willow Ave, Hoboken, NJ	201-653-66
Smith, Susan B/290 Newbury #2F, Boston, MA	617-266-44
Snyder, Emilie/50 N Pine St #107, Marietta, PA	215-426-290
SOILEAU, HODGES/350 FLAX HILL RD,	
NORWALK, CT (P 454)	**203-852-07**
Sokolowski, Ted/RD #2 Box 408, Lake Ariel, PA	717-937-45
Sorensen, Robert/59 Granville Ave, Milford, CT	203-874-62
Soyka, Ed/231 Lafayette Ave, Peekskill, NY	914-737-22
Spanfeller, Jim/Mustato Rd, Katonah, NY	914-232-35
Sparkman, Gene/15 Bradley Lane, Sandy Hook, CT	203-426-00
Sparks, Richard & Barbara/2 W Rocks Rd, Norwalk, CT	203-866-20
Spiak, Sharon/35 Monroe Ave, Dumont, NJ	201-387-93
Spitzmiller, Walter/24 Lee Lane, West Redding, CT	203-938-35
Springer, Sally/317 S Lawrence Ct, Philadelphia, PA	215-925-90
SPROVACH, CRAIG/604 FAIRFIELD AVE,	
STAMFORD, CT (P 459)	**203-327-25**
Stahl, Benjamin F/134 Washington St, S Norwalk, CT	203-838-53
Stasolla, Mario/162-A Spice Bush Ln, Tuxedo, NY	201-676-83
Steig, William/PO Box 8, Westport, CT	203-227-78
Steinberg, Herb/PO Box 65, Roosevelt, NJ	609-448-47
Stevenson, James/PO Box 8, Westport, CT	203-227-78
Stewart, Jonathan/113 South 20th St, Philadelphia, PA	215-561-08
Stirweis, Shannon/31 Fawn Pl, Wilton, CT	203-762-70
Stone, David K/6 Farmview Rd, Port Washington, NY	516-627-70
Syverson, Henry/PO Box 8, Westport, CT	203-227-78
Szabo, Leslie/7 Buck Hill Rd, Westport, CT	203-838-21

Please send us your additions and updates.

TV
Tandem Graphics/5313 Waneta Rd, Bethesda, MD	301-320-5008
TATORE, PAUL/10 WARTBURG PL, VALHALLA, NY (P 50)	**914-769-1061**
Tauss, Herb/S Mountain Pass, Garrison, NY	914-424-3765
Tayler, Dahl (Mr)/120 1st St, Troy, NY	518-274-6379
Thompson, Arthur/39 Prospect Ave, Pompton Plains, NJ	201-835-3534
Thompson, John M/64 Ganung Rd, Ossining, NY	914-762-6487
Thornberg, Bethann/1713 Lanier Pl NW, Washington, DC	202-332-0525
Tiani, Alex/4 Lafayette Court, Greenwich, CT	203-661-7827
Tinkelman, Murray/75 Lakeview Ave W, Peekskill, NY	914-737-5960
TOELKE, CATHLEEN/234 W CANTON ST, BOSTON, MA (P 61)	**617-266-8790**
TOELKE, RON/229 BERKELEY #52, BOSTON, MA (P 77)	**617-266-3858**
Toulmin-Rothe, Ann/49 Richmondville Rd, Westport, CT	203-226-3011
Traub, Patricia/25-30 Aspen St, Philadelphia, PA	215-769-1378
Treatner, Meryl/721 Lombard St, Philadelphia, PA	215-627-2297
TSUI, GEORGE/2250 ELLIOT ST, MERRICK, NY (P 466)	**516-223-8474**
TWO-H STUDIO/45 CORBIN DR, DARIEN, CT (P 239,240)	**203-656-0200**
Van Ryzin, Peter/348 Sound Beach Ave, Old Greenwich, CT	203-637-8076
VARGO, KURT/94 NEW MONMOUTH RD, MIDDLETOWN, NJ (P 52)	**201-671-8679**
Vartanoff, Ellen/6825 Wilson Ln, Bethesda, MD	301-229-3846
Veno, Joe/20 Cutler Rd, Hamilton, MA	617-468-3165
Vernaglia, Michael/1251 Bloomfield St, Hoboken, NJ	201-659-7750
VISKUPIC, GARY/7 WESTFIELD DR, CENTER PORT, NY (P 160)	**516-757-9021**
Vissichelli, Joe/100 Mayfield Ln, Valley Stream, NY	516-872-3867

WYZ
WALCZAK, LARRY/803 PARK AVE, HOBOKEN, NJ (P 472)	**201-798-6176**
WALDMAN, NEIL/47 WOODLANDS AVE, WHITE PLAINS, NY (P 252)	**914-693-2782**
Walker, Norman/37 Stonehenge Rd, Weston, CT	203-226-5812
Wallerstein, Alan/61 Tenth St, Ronkonkoma, NY	516-981-3589
Watson, Karen/100 Churchill Ave, Arlington, MA	617-641-1420
WATTS, MARK/616 IVA LN, FAIRLESS HILLS, PA (P 234)	**215-945-9422**
Weber, Robert/PO Box 8, Westport, CT	203-227-7806
Wehrman, Richard/247 N Goodman St, Rochester, NY	716-271-2280
Weissman, Bari/41 Atkins St, Brighton, MA	617-783-0230
Welkis, Alan/53 Heights Rd, Fort Salonga, NY	516-261-4160
Weller, Linda Boehm/185 Goodhill Rd, Weston, CT	203-226-7674
Whelan, Michael/23 Old Hayrake Rd, Danbury, CT	203-798-6063
Wilcox, David/PO Box 232, Califon, NJ	201-832-7368
Williams, Frank/731 North 24th St, Philadelphia, PA	215-625-2408
Williams, Ted/170 Elder Dr, Macedon, NY	315-986-3770
WILLIGES, MEL/2 HEPWORTH CT, W ORANGE, NJ (P 479)	**201-731-4086**
Wills, Shirley/20 Harding Ave, N Arlington, NJ	201-997-3255
Wilson, Gahan/PO Box 8, Westport, CT	203-227-7806
Wilson, Mary Lou/247 N Goodman St, Rochester, NY	716-271-2280
Witschonke, Alan/28 Tower St #2, Somerville, MA	617-628-5601
Woodman, Bill/PO Box 8, Westport, CT	203-227-7806
Wright, Bob Creative Group Inc/247 North Goodman St, Rochester, NY	716-271-2280
YALOWITZ, PAUL/598 FREEMAN AVE, BRENTWOOD, NY (P 481)	**516-273-7782**
Young, Debby/8 Steephill Rd, Weston, CT	203-227-5672
Young, Robert Assoc/78 North Union St, Rochester, NY	716-546-1973
Young, Wally/8 Steephill Rd, Weston, CT	203-227-5672
Ziegler, Bill/PO Box 8, Westport, CT	203-227-7806

SOUTHEAST

AB
Armstrong, Lynn/7325 Chattahoochie Blf Dr, Atlanta, GA	404-396-0742
Arunski, Joe & Assoc/10433 SW 133rd Pl, Miami, FL	305-387-2130
Azzinaro, Lewis/1908 Holly Ridge Dr #201, McLean, VA	703-893-5483
Bailey, R.C./255 Westward Dr, Miami Springs, FL	305-888-6309
Boone, Joe/ PW Inc/PO Box 99337, Louisville, KY	502-499-9220
Bowles, Aaron/1686 Sierra Woods Ct, Reston, VA	703-471-4019
Bull, Richard/629 N Highland Ave NE #12, Atlanta, GA	404-876-4497
Burke, Gary/14418 NE Third Ct, N Miami, FL	305-893-1998
Butler, Meryl/PO Box 8036, Virginia Beach, VA	804-468-4185

CD
Carey, Mark/1209 Anne Ave, Chesapeake, VA	804-545-2669
Carey, Wayne/532 Hardendorp Ave, Atlanta, GA	404-378-0426
Carter, Zane/1008 N Randolph St #100, Arlington, VA	703-527-7338
Cerny, Paul/610 Wood St, Zephryllis, FL	813-782-4386
Chaffee, Doug/Rt 3 Groveland Dr, Taylors, SC	803-877-9826
Chaisson, Brant/1420 Lee Ave, Houma, LA	504-868-7423
Coastline Studios/2475 Forsyth Rd, Orlando, FL	305-657-6355
CRANE, GARY/523 W 24TH ST, NORFOLK, VA (P 307)	**804-627-0717**
Crunk, Matt/Rte 5 Box 39, Killen, AL	205-757-2020
DAVIS, MICHAEL/1461 ROCK SPRINGS CIR #3, ATLANTA, GA (P 315)	**404-872-5525**
DeBro, James/2725 Hayden Dr, Eastpoint, GA	404-344-2971
Dunlap, Leslie/908 Manor Rd, Alexandria, VA	703-548-4208

FG
Faure, Renee/600 Second St, Neptune Beach, FL	904-246-2781
Findley, John/213 Elizabeth St, Atlanta, GA	404-659-7103
Firestone, Bill/1702 Preston Rd, Alexandria, VA	703-820-1511
FISHER, MIKE/3811 GENERAL PERSHING, NEW ORLEANS, LA (P 336)	**504-827-0382**
FLECK, TOM/ONE PARK PL #120, ATLANTA, GA (P 151)	**404-355-0729**
GAADT, DAVID/2103 TENNYSON DR, GREENSBORO, NC (P 42,43)	**919-288-9727**
George, Eugene/2905 Saint Anne St, New Orleans, LA	504-482-3774
Gordon, Jack/5716 S 2nd St, Arlington, VA	703-820-0145
Gorman, Martha/3057 Pharr Ct Nrth NW #E6, Atlanta, GA	404-261-5632
Graphics Group/6111 PchtreeDunwdy Rd#G101, Atlanta, GA	404-391-9929
Greathead, Ian/2975 Christopher's Court, Marietta, GA	404-952-5067
Guthrie, Dennis/645 Raven Springs Tr, Stone Mtn, GA	404-469-8770

HI
Hamilton, Marcus/12225 Ranburne Rd, Charlotte, NC	704-545-3121
Havaway, Jane/806 Briarcliff Rd, Atlanta, GA	404-872-7284
Henderling, Lisa/800 West Ave #345, Miami Beach, FL	305-531-1771
Herring & Klem/PO Box 48453, Atlanta, GA	404-945-8652
HICKEY, JOHN/3821 ABINGDON CIRCLE, NORFOLK, VA (P 307)	**804-853-2956**
Hicks, Richard Edward/3635 Pierce Dr #76, Chamblee, GA	404-457-8928
Hinojosa, Albino/2101 Mesa Dr, Ruston, LA	318-255-2820
HODGES, MIKE/1151 W PEACHTREE ST NW, ATLANTA, GA (P 214)	**404-892-6303**
HOGENKAMP, JOHANNA/1151 W PEACHTREE ST NW, ATLANTA, GA (P 215)	**404-892-6303**
Hunter, katherine/1120 Scaly Bark Rd #115-D, Charlotte, NC	704-527-4577
HYATT, MITCH/4171 BUCKINGHAM CT, MARIETTA, GA (P 358)	**404-924-1241**
Hyatt, Steven/4171 Buckingham Ct, Marietta, GA	404-924-1241
IMAGE ELECTRONIC INC/2030 POWERS FERRY RD #226, ATLANTA, GA (P 218)	**404-951-9580**
Irvin, Trevor/330 Southerland Terrace, Atlanta, GA	404-377-4754
Ison, Diana/3756 Winding Creek Ln, Charlotte, NC	704-553-2864

JKL
James, Bill/15840 SW 79th Ct, Miami, FL	305-238-5709
Jarvis, David/275 Indigo Dr, Daytona Beach, FL	904-255-1296
Johnson, Pamela R/1415 N Key Blvd, Arlington, VA	703-525-5012
Jones, Jack/104 Ardmore Pl #1, Atlanta, GA	404-355-6357
Kerns, Jeffrey/48 Peachtree Ave, Atlanta, GA	404-233-5158
KILGORE, SUSI/2905 BAY VILLA, TAMPA, FL (P 51)	**813-837-9759**
Lee, Kelly/3511 N 22nd St, Arlington, VA	703-527-4089
LESTER, MIKE/1001 EULALIA RD, ATLANTA, GA (P 38, 39,377)	**404-233-3093**
LEWIS, CHRIS/1115 N VIRGINIA AVE, ATLANTA, GA (P 219)	**404-876-0288**
LOVELL, RICK/2860 LAKEWIND CT, ALPHARETTA, GA (P 383)	**404-442-3943**
Lunsford, Annie/515 N Hudson St, Arlington, VA	301-320-3912

MN
Marks, David/750 Clemont Dr, Atlanta, GA	404-872-1824
MARTIN, DON/5110 S W 80TH ST, MIAMI, FL (P 388)	**305-665-2376**
Matthews, Lu/107 E Cary St, Richmond, VA	804-782-9895
MAYER, BILL/240 FORKNER DR, DECATUR, GA (P 393)	**404-378-0686**
McGary, Richard/180 NE 39th St #125, Miami, FL	305-573-0490
McGurren Weber Ink/104 S Alfred St #C, Alexandria, VA	703-548-0003
MCKELVEY, DAVID/3022 HUNTSHIRE PL, ATLANTA, GA (P 395)	**404-938-1949**

ILLUSTRATORS

McKinney, Deborah/95-50 Regency Sq Blvd, Jacksonville, FL	904-723-6000
McKissick, Randall/905 Rolling View Ln, Columbia, SC	803-798-3688
Moore, Connie Illus/4242 Inverness Rd, Duluth, GA	404-449-9553
Moore, William 'Casey'/4242 Inverness Rd, Duluth, GA	404-449-9553
NELSON, BILL/1402 WILMINGTON AVE,	
RICHMOND, VA (P 87)	**804-358-9637**

OP

Olson, Linda/1 Charter Plaza, Jacksonville, FL	904-723-6000
Overacre, Gary/RD 2, 3802 Vineyard Trace, Marietta, GA	404-973-8878
OVIES, JOE/1900 EMERY ST NW #120,	
ATLANTA, GA (P 36,151)	**404-355-0729**
Pardue, Jack/2307 Sherwood Hall Ln, Alexandria, VA	703-765-2622
Parrish, George/2401 Old Concord Rd, Smyrna, GA	404-435-4189
PASSARELLI, CHARLES/3500 PIEDMONT RD #430,	
ATLANTA, GA (P 151)	**404-262-1209**
Pate, Martin/401 W Peachtree NW, Atlanta, GA	404-221-0700
PENCA, GARY/3184 NW 39TH CT,	
LAUDERDALE LAKES, FL (P 422)	**305-733-5847**
Pittman, Pat/1919 York Dr, Woodbridge, VA	703-491-6867
Profancik, Larry/ PW Inc/PO Box 99337, Louisville, KY	502-499-9220

RS

Rainock, Norman/10226 Purcell Rd, Glen Allen, VA	804-264-8123
Rauchman, Bob/3124 Mary St, Miami, FL	305-445-5628
Rebeiz, Kathryn D/526 Druid Hill Rd, Vienna, VA	703-938-9779
Robinette, John/1147 S Prescott, Memphis, TN	901-452-9853
Robinson, David/112 Michelle St, Garden City, GA	912-964-8135
Romeo, Richard/1066 NW 96th Ave, Ft Lauderdale, FL	305-472-0072
RUDNAK, THEO/1151 W PEACHTREE ST NW,	
ATLANTA, GA (P 220)	**404-892-6303**
SAFFOLD, JOE/719 MARTINA DR NE, ATLANTA, GA (P 221)	**404-231-2168**
Salmon, Paul/5826 Jackson's Oak Ct, Burke, VA	703-250-4943
Sams, B B/PO Box A, Social Circle, GA	404-464-2956
Shelly, Ron/6396 Manor Lane, S Miami, FL	305-667-0154
SOPER, PATRICK/214 STEPHENS, LAFAYETTE, LA (P 455)	**318-233-1635**
Spetseris, Steve/401 W Peachtree NW #1720, Atlanta, GA	404-221-0798
Stanton, Mark/67 Jonesboro St, McDonough, GA	404-957-5966
Stanton, Reggie/411 Park Ave N #11, Winter Park, FL	305-645-1661

TUV

Tull, Bobbi/317 N Howard St, Alexandria, VA	703-370-3451
Turner, Pete/938 Pamlico Dr, Cary, NC	919-467-8466
Ulan, Helen Cerra/4809 Village Dr, Fairfax, VA	703-691-0474
Vaughn, Rob/PO Box 660706, Miami Springs, FL	305-885-1292
Vintson, Sherry/430 Appian Way NE, St Petersburg, FL	813-822-2512
Vondracek, Woody/420 Lincoln Rd #408, Old Miami Beach, FL	305-531-7558

WY

Wasiluck Associates/1333 Tierra Cir, Winter Park, FL	305-678-6964
Webber, Warren/401 W Peachtree NW, Atlanta, GA	404-221-0700
Whitver, Harry K/208 Reidhurst Ave, Nashville, TN	615-320-1795
The Workshop Inc/735 Bismark Rd NE, Atlanta, GA	404-875-0141
Yarnell, David Andrew/PO Box 286, Occoquan, VA	202-690-2987
Young, Bruce/503 Ansley Villa Dr, Atlanta, GA	404-892-6303

MIDWEST

AB

Ahearn, John D/151 S Elm, St Louis, MO	314-781-3389
ALLEN, DAVID/18108 MARTIN #2F, HOMEWOOD, IL (P 261)	**312-798-3283**
Anastas, Nicolette/535 N Michigan Ave, Chicago, IL	312-943-1668
Art Force Inc/21700 NW Hwy #570, Southfield, MI	313-569-1074
Artist Studios/666 Euclid Ave, Cleveland, OH	216-241-5355
Baker, Strandell/233 E Wacker Dr #3609, Chicago, IL	312-664-7525
Behum, Cliff/26384 Aaron Ave, Euclid, OH	216-261-9266
Bemus, Bart/1458 1/2 S High St, Columbus, OH	614-444-0578
Blanchette, Dan/185 N Wabash Ave, Chicago, IL	312-332-1339
Boehm, Roger/126 3rd St, Minneapolis, MN	612-332-0787
Boswick, Steven/3342 Capital, Skokie, IL	312-328-2042
Bowman, Bob/163 Cedarwood Ct, Palatine, IL	312-966-2770
Braught, Mark/629 Cherry St #18, Terre Haute, IN	812-234-6135
Busch, Lonnie/11 Meadow Dr, Fenton, MO	314-343-1330
Butler, Chris/743 N Dearborn, Chicago, IL	312-280-2288
Buttram, Andy/1636 Hickory Glen Dr, Miamisburg, OH	513-859-7428

CD

Call, Ken/520 N Michigan Ave, Chicago, IL	312-644-3017
Carr, Ted/43 E Ohio #1001, Chicago, IL	312-467-6865
Carroll, Michael/1228 E 54th St, Chicago, IL	312-752-6262
Centaur Studios/10 Broadway, St Louis, MO	314-421-6485
Chaisson, Betty/329 NE Park Ave, Claycomo, MO	816-453-3323
Christensen, Corey/405 N Wabash #2614, Chicago, IL	312-822-0560
CIGLIANO, WILLIAM/832 W GUNNISON ST,	
CHICAGO, IL (P 295)	**312-878-1659**
Clay, Steve/245 W North Ave, Chicago, IL	312-280-7945
Clifford, Keesler/6642 West H Ave, Kalamazoo, MI	616-375-0688
Clyne, Dan/535 N Michigan Ave #1416, Chicago, IL	312-943-1660
COBANE, RUSSELL/8291 ALLEN RD, CLARKSTON, MI (P 35)	**313-625-6132**
Cochran, Bobbye/730 N Franklin #403, Chicago, IL	312-943-5912
Collier, John/2309 Willow Creek Ln, Lawrence, KS	913-841-6442
Collins & Lund Studios/1950 Craig Rd, St Louis, MO	314-576-0003
Collins, Britt Taylor/114 Lorraine Rd, Wheaton, IL	312-690-6565
Connelly, Tim/4916 W Cornelia, Chicago, IL	312-794-972-
COSGROVE, DAN/405 N WABASH #4307,	
CHICAGO, IL (P 302)	**312-527-0375**
CRAIG, JOHN/RT 2 BOX 81 TOWER RD,	
SOLDIERS GROVE, WI (P 304)	**608-872-237**
Creative Source Inc/360 N Michigan, Chicago, IL	312-649-977
Crnkovich, Tony/5706 S Narragansett, Chicago, IL	312-586-9690
Csicsko, David/2350 N Cleveland, Chicago, IL	312-935-170
Deal, Jim/2558 W Wilson Ave, Chicago, IL	312-539-608-
DeShetler, Steven A/2914 Allen, St Louis, MO	314-772-8683
DiCianni, Ron/340 Thompson Blvd, Buffalo Grove, IL	312-634-184-
Dinyer, Eric/111 Jefferson Rd, St Louis, MO	314-961-167
Doney, Todd/3830 N Richmond, Chicago, IL	312-463-789
Doyle, Pat/333 N Michigan Ave, Chicago, IL	312-263-206
Duggan, Lee/405 N Wabash #4307, Chicago, IL	312-527-037
Dypold, Pat/26 E Huron St, Chicago, IL	312-337-691
Dzielak, Dennis/5359 S Kolin, Chicago, IL	312-582-550

EF

Eastwood, Peter/221 Traver, Glebn Ellyn, IL	312-469-0228
EATON & IWEN/307 N MICHIGAN, CHICAGO, IL (P 326,327)	**312-332-325**
Eberbach, Andrea/5301 N Delaware, Indianapolis, IN	317-253-042
Elins, Michael/155 N Michigan Ave, Chicago, IL	312-565-003
English, Mark/Rt 3 PO Box 325, Kearney, MO	816-635-443-
Flood, Dick/2210 S Lynn, Urbana, IL	217-328-364
Fruzyna, Frank/435 N Michigan Ave #1832, Chicago, IL	312-644-555

GH

Gerhold/ Smith/13993 Penrod, Detroit, MI	313-835-464
Gieseke, Thomas/7909 W 61st St, Merriam, KS	913-677-459
Goldammer, Ken/405 N Wabash #3611, Chicago, IL	312-836-014
Gonnella, Rick/360 N Michigan Ave, Chicago, IL	312-368-877
Graham, Bill/116 W Illinois, Chicago, IL	312-467-033
GRANING, KEN/1975 CRAGIN DR,	
BLOOMFIELD HILLS, MI (P 37)	**313-851-366**
Groff, David/2265 Avalon Ave, Kettering, OH	513-294-770
Gustafson, Glenn/26 E Huron, Chicago, IL	312-944-568
Hamblin, George/944 Beach St, LaGrange Pk, IL	312-352-178
Hamilton, Laurie/2123 N Clinton St, Chicago, IL	312-975-153
Hammond, Franklin/1179-A W King St #310,	
Toronto M6K 3C5, ON	416-533-443
Handelan-Pedersen/333 N Michigan #1005, Chicago, IL	312-782-683
Harris, Scott/1519 W Sunnyside Ave, Chicago, IL	312-271-847
Hartel, James B/PO Box 20805, Greenfield, WI	414-289-965
HAYNES, MICHAEL/3070 HAWTHORN BLVD,	
ST LOUIS, MO (P 36)	**314-772-315**
Heyden, Yvette/30 E Huron #4005, Chicago, IL	312-787-154
Holladay Prints/PO Box 381, Bettendorf, IA	319-359-341
Howe, Philip/605 Lockerbie St, Indianapolis, IN	317-637-603
Hrabe, Curtis/2944 Greenwood Ave, Highland Park, IL	312-432-463

IJ

Izold, Donald/20475 Bunker Hill Dr, Fairview Park, OH	216-333-998
J H Illustration/1415 W 6th St, Cedar Falls, IA	319-277-247
Jacobsen, Bill/405 N Wabash #1801, Chicago, IL	312-321-955
Jamerson, David/6367 N Guilford Ave, Indianapolis, IN	317-257-875
JAY/15119 WOODLAWN AVE, DOLTON, IL (P 361)	**312-849-567**
Johannes, Greg/360 N Michigan Ave, Chicago, IL	312-649-977

OHNSON, RICK/323 S FRANKLIN, CHICAGO, IL (P 40)	312-987-0935
OHNSTON, DAVID MCCALL/26110 CAROL ST, FRANKLIN, MI (P 134)	313-626-9546
ones, Jan/2332 N Halstead, Chicago, IL	312-929-1851
uenger, Richard/1324 S 9th St, St Louis, MO	314-231-4069
K	
Kahl, Konrad/26039 German Hill, Franklin, MI	313-851-7064
alisch, John W/4201 Levenworth, Omaha, NE	402-734-5064
auffman, George/1232 W 70th Terrace, Kansas City, MO	816-523-0223
ecman, Milan/2730 Somia Dr, Cleveland, OH	216-888-3256
elen, Linda/1922 W Newport, Chicago, IL	312-975-9696
essler, Clifford/6642 West H Ave, Kalamazoo, MI	616-375-0688
rov, Lydia/4008 N Hermitage Ave, Chicago, IL	312-248-8764
scar, George F/24213 Lake Rd, Bay Village, OH	216-871-8325
ock, Carl/311 N Desplaines Ave, Chicago, IL	312-559-0440
ORDIC, VLADIMIR/35351 GROVEWOOD DR, EASTLAKE, OH (P 368)	216-951-4026
rainik, David/4645 N Manor, Chicago, IL	312-539-4475
ramer, Dave/309 A Street, La Porte, IN	219-362-5514
RIEGSHAUSER, SHANNON/12421 W GRAFLEMAN RD, HANNA CITY, IL (P 371)	309-565-7110
ueker, Don/832 S Ballas, St Louis, MO	314-965-6073
L	
Lackner, Paul/29 E Ohio, Chicago, IL	312-565-0030
ambert, John/1911 E Robin Hood Ln, Arlington Heights, IL	312-392-6349
angeneckert, Donald/4939 Ringer Rd, St Louis, MO	314-487-2042
angeneckert, Mark/704 Dover Pl, St Louis, MO	314-752-0199
ANGTON, BRUCE/53145 KINGLET, SOUTH BEND, IN (P 374)	219-277-6137
aurent, Richard/1132 W Columbia Ave, Chicago, IL	312-245-9014
awson, Robert/1523 Seminole, Kalamazoo, MI	616-345-7607
EE, JARED D/2942 OLD HAMILTON RD, LEBANON, OH (P 376)	513-932-2154
ESH, DAVID/6332 GUILFORD AVE, INDIANAPOLIS, IN (P 182)	317-253-3141
tostak, John/7801 Fernhill Ave, Parma, OH	216-351-4966
oveless, Jim/4137 San Francisco, St Louis, MO	314-533-7914
M	
MACNAIR, GREG/7515 WAYNE, UNIVERSITY CITY, MO (P 386)	314-721-3781
agdich, Dennis/1914 N Dayton, Chicago, IL	312-248-6492
aggard, John/1301 Western Ave, Cincinnati, OH	513-721-4434
AHAN, BENTON/PO BOX 66, CHESTERVILLE, OH (P 387)	419-768-2204
anchess, Gregory/233 E Wacker Dr, Chicago, IL	312-565-2701
ayerik, Val/20466 Drake Rd, Strongsville, OH	216-238-9492
ayes, Kevin/1202 Tulsa St, Wichita, KS	316-522-6742
ayse, Steve/506 N Clark, Chicago, IL	312-661-1818
cInturff, Steve/6448 Thompson Rd, Cincinnati, OH	513-741-8639
cMahon, Mark/2620 Highland Ave, Evanston, IL	312-869-6491
eade, Roy/240 Tenth St, Toledo, OH	419-244-9074
ller, Doug/2648 Glen Mawr Ave, Columbus, OH	614-267-6533
ller, William (Bill)/1355 N Sandburg Ter #2002, Chicago, IL	312-787-4093
organ, Leonard/1163 E Ogden Ave #705, Naperville, IL	312-759-3987
unger, Nancy/PO Box 125, Richland, MI	616-629-5184
elson, Fred/3 E Ontario #25, Chicago, IL	312-935-1707
CHOLS, GARRY/1449 N PENNSYLVANIA ST, INDIANAPOLIS, IN (P 415)	317-637-0250
GHTHAWK STUDIO/1250 RIVERBED RD, CLEVELAND, OH (P 37)	216-522-1809
orcia, Ernest/3451 Houston Rd, Waynesville, OH	513-862-5761
ovack, Bob/5356 Huron Rd, Lyndhurst, OH	216-442-0456
PQ	
O'Connell, Mitch/6165 N Winthrop #603, Chicago, IL	312-743-3848
son, Robert A/15215 Buchanan Ct, Eden Prairie, MN	612-934-5767
Malley, Kathy/10350 Komensky, Oak Lawn, IL	312-499-1069
Neill, Brian/17006 Woodbury Ave, Cleveland, OH	216-252-6238
tman, John/535 N Michigan Ave, Chicago, IL	312-266-1417
to, Brian/368 W Huron, Chicago, IL	312-787-6826
ppas, Chris/323 S Franklin, Chicago, IL	312-236-6862
trauskas, Kathy/155 N Michigan Ave, Chicago, IL	312-565-0030
galle Studios Inc/314 N Broadway #1936, St Louis, MO	314-241-4398
t Studios/1370 Ontario St #1430, Cleveland, OH	216-241-6720

Pope, Kevin/2010 W Nichols Rd #D, Arlington Hgts, IL	312-392-9245
Probert, Jean/1022 N Bompart, St Louis, MO	314-968-5076
Quinn, Colleen/535 N Michigan, Chicago, IL	312-943-1668
RS	
Radenstudio/210 W 67th Terr, Kansas City, MO	816-421-5079
Rasmussen, Bonnie/8828 Pendleton, St Louis, MO	314-962-1842
Rawley, Don/7520 Blaisdell Ave S, Richfield, MN	612-866-1023
RAWSON, JON/750 N DEARBORN #2703, CHICAGO, IL (P 230,231)	312-266-4884
Reinert, Kirk/10600 Clifton Blvd #14, Cleveland, OH	216-631-7193
Renaud, Phill/2830 W Leland, Chicago, IL	312-583-2681
Roth, Hy/1300 Ashland St, Evanston, IL	312-491-1937
Ryan, Terry/200 Renaissance #777, Detroit, MI	313-259-4190
Rybka, Stephen/535 N Michigan, Chicago, IL	312-943-1668
Sanford, John/5038 W Berteau, Chicago, IL	312-685-0656
Sauck, Mark/155 N Michigan Ave, Chicago, IL	312-565-0030
Schmelzer, J P/1002 S Wesley Ave, Oak Park, IL	312-386-4005
Schrag, Allan/8530 W Ninth, Wichita, KS	316-722-4585
Schrier, Fred/9058 Little Mtn Rd, Kirtland Hills, OH	216-255-7787
Scibilia, Dom/2902 Franklin Blvd, Cleveland, OH	216-861-2561
SELLARS, JOSEPH/2423 W 22ND ST, MINNEAPOLIS, MN (P 46)	612-377-8766
Seltzer, Meyer Design & Illustration/744 W Buckingham Pl, Chicago, IL	312-348-2885
Sereta, Bruce/3010 Parklane Dr, Cleveland, OH	216-842-9251
Shay, RJ/3301 S Jefferson Ave, St Louis, MO	314-773-9989
Sirrell, Terry/388 E Lambert Dr, Schaumburg, IL	312-980-7047
Skidmore Sahratian Inc/2100 W Big Beaver Rd, Troy, MI	313-643-6000
SLACK, CHUCK/9 CAMBRIDGE LN, LINCOLNSHIRE, IL (P 31)	312-948-9226
Songero, Jay/15119 Woodlawn, Dolton, IL	312-849-5676
SOUKUP, JAMES/ROUTE 1, SEWARD, NE (P 456)	402-643-2339
Speer, Terry/181 Forest St, Oberlin, OH	216-774-8319
Stearney, Mark/405 N Wabash #2809, Chicago, IL	312-644-6669
Stephens Biondi Decicco/230 E Ohio, Chicago, IL	312-944-3340
Storyboard Studio/535 N Michigan Ave, Chicago, IL	312-266-1417
Streff, Michael/2766 Wasson Rd, Cincinnati, OH	513-731-0360
SUMICHRAST, JOZEF/860 N NORTHWOODS, DEERFIELD, IL (P 193)	312-945-6353
T	
Tate, Clark/1120 N LaSalle, Chicago, IL	312-943-5407
Tate, Don/429 W Superior, Chicago, IL	312-440-1444
TAYLOR, DAVID/1449 N PENNSYLVANIA ST, INDIANAPOLIS, IN (P 464)	317-634-2728
Taylor, Richard/155 N Michigan Ave, Chicago, IL	312-565-0030
Terrell, Tim/1929 Plymouth Rd #1012, Ann Arbor, MI	313-663-1999
Thacker, Kat/40335 Plymouth Rd #203, Plymouth, MI	313-455-2765
Theodore, Jim/15735 Pearl Rd, Strongsville, OH	216-238-6188
Thiewes, Sam/111 N Andover Ln, Geneva, IL	312-232-0980
Thomas, Bob/1002 E Washington St, Indianapolis, IN	317-638-1002
Townley, Jon/61 Sunnyside Lane, Columbus, OH	614-268-9717
Triad Productions/4350 Johnson Dr #228, Shawnee Mission, KS	913-432-2821
Trusilo, Jim/535 N Michigan Ave, Chicago, IL	312-943-1668
Tughan, James/1179-A King St W #310, Toronto M6K3C5, ON	416-535-9149
TURGEON, JAMES/233 E WACKER DR #1102, CHICAGO, IL (P 251)	312-861-1039
VW	
Vaccarello, Paul/505 N Lake Shore Dr, Chicago, IL	312-664-2233
Vanderbeek, Don/235 Monteray Ave, Dayton, OH	513-293-5326
Vann, Bill Studio/1706 S 8th St, St Louis, MO	314-231-2322
Vanselow, Holly/1313 W Fletcher, Chicago, IL	312-975-5880
Vuksanovich, Bill & Fran/3224 N Nordica, Chicago, IL	312-283-2138
Walker, John/307 N Michigan Ave #1008, Chicago, IL	312-346-0720
WALKER, KEN/4720 MERCIER ST, KANSAS CITY, MO (P 253)	816-931-7975
Walsh, Cathy/323 S Franklin, Chicago, IL	312-427-6120
Walter, Nancy Lee/PO Box 611, Elmhurst, IL	312-833-3898
Westgate Graphics/1111 Westgate, Oak Park, IL	312-626-7879
Westphal, Ken/7616 Fairway, Prairie Village, KS	913-381-8399
Whitney, Bill/2250 N Lincoln Ave #503, Chicago, IL	312-661-7123
Wickart Brothers/405 N Wabash #1511, Chicago, IL	312-645-0836

Please send us your additions and updates.

Williams, Gordon/1030 Glenmoor Ln, Glendale, MO	314-821-2032
Willson Graphics/100 E Ohio #314, Chicago, IL	312-642-5328
Wimmer, Chuck/5000 Ira Ave, Cleveland, OH	216-651-1724
Wolek, Guy/323 S Franklin, Chicago, IL	312-341-1282
Wolf, Leslie/2350 N Cleveland, Chicago, IL	312-935-1707
The Wozniaks, Elaine & Dorothy/15520 Clifton Blvd, Cleveland, OH	216-226-3565

YZ

Young & Laramore/6367 N Guilford Ave, Indianapolis, IN	317-257-8752
Young, David Jemerson/6367 N Guilford, Indianapolis, IN	317-257-8752
Youssi, John/Rt 1, 220 Powers Rd, Gilberts, IL	312-428-7398
Zadnik, Pat/11900 Edgewater Dr, Cleveland, OH	216-521-6273
Zaresky, Don/9320 Olde Rt 8, Northfield Center, OH	216-467-5917
Zimnicki Design/774 Parkview Ct, Roselle, IL	312-893-2666

SOUTHWEST

ABC

Andrews, Chris/1515 N Beverly Ave, Tucson, AZ	602-325-5126
Archon/2211 S Interregional #308, Austin, TX	512-447-0265
Battes, Greg Design & Illus/2954 Satsuma Dr, Dallas, TX	214-620-7685
Bleck, Cathie/1019 N Clinton, Dallas, TX	214-942-4639
BRAZEAL, LEE LEE/4212 SAN FELIPE, HOUSTON, TX (P 277)	**713-526-2387**
Brown, Rod Design/3 Dal Comm Cmplx #Nexus 20, Irving, TX	214-869-7667
Cherry, Jim/3600 N Hayden Rd #3308, Scottsdale, AZ	602-941-2883
Collier, Steve/5512 Chaucer Dr, Houston, TX	713-522-0205
Connally, Connie/3333 Elm, Dallas, TX	214-742-4302
CORNELIUS, RAY-MEL/4512 SWISS AVE #3, DALLAS, TX (P 57)	**214-826-8988**
Criswell, Ron/703 McKinney Ave #201, Dallas, TX	214-954-4497
CURRY, TOM/309 E LIVE OAK ST, AUSTIN, TX (P 311)	**212-443-8427**

DEF

DEAN, MICHAEL/5512 CHAUCER, HOUSTON, TX (P 318)	**713-527-0295**
Depew, Bob/2755 Rollingdale, Dallas, TX	214-241-9206
Dewy, Jennifer/102 W San Francisco #16, Santa Fe, NM	505-988-2924
DUNNICK, REGAN/1110 LOVETT #202, HOUSTON, TX (P 325)	**713-523-6590**
Durbin, Mike/4034 Woodcraft, Houston, TX	713-667-8129
Durke, Stephen/4907 W Market, Austin, TX	
Eagle, Bruce/1000 W Wilshire #428, Oklahoma City, OK	405-840-3201
Eckles, Jane/6666 Harwin #540, Houston, TX	713-781-5170
Falk, Rusty/707 E Alameda Dr, Tempe, AZ	602-966-1626
FORBES, BART/2706 FAIRMOUNT, DALLAS, TX (P 192)	**214-748-8436**

GHK

Garns, G Allen/3314 East El Moro, Mesa, AZ	602-830-7224
Griffin, David/2706 Fairmount, Dallas, TX	214-742-6746
GRIMES, DON/3514 OAK GROVE, DALLAS, TX (P 345)	**214-526-0040**
Grimes, Rick/2416 1/2 McKinney, Dallas, TX	214-760-9833
Halpern, David/7420 E 70th St, Tulsa, OK	918-252-4973
HIGH, RICHARD/4500 MONTROSE #D, HOUSTON, TX (P 354)	**713-521-2772**
Kirkman, Rick/313 E Thomas Rd #205, Phoenix, AZ	602-279-0119
Kohler, Mark/701 W 7th Ave, Austin, TX	512-476-4283
Kupper, Ketti/6527 Lakewood Blvd, Dallas, TX	214-824-3435

LMP

LAPSLEY, BOB/3707 NOTTINGHAM, HOUSTON, TX (P 47)	**713-667-4393**
Lebo, Narda/4851 Cedar Springs, Dallas, TX	214-528-0375
Lewis, Maurice/3704 Harper St, Houston, TX	713-664-1807
Lindlof, Ed/603 Carolyn Ave, Austin, TX	512-472-0195
Lisieski, Peter/135 Pine St, Nacogdoches, TX	409-564-4244
MacPherson, Kevin/313 E Thomas Rd #205, Phoenix, AZ	602-279-0119
Martin, Larry/3040 Sundial, Dallas, TX	214-521-8700
MCELHANEY, GARY/5205 AIRPORT BLVD #201, AUSTIN, TX (P 394)	**512-451-3986**
McGar, Michael/3330 Irwindell Blvd, Dallas, TX	214-339-0672
PAYNE, CHRIS F/1800 LEAR ST #5, DALLAS, TX (P 179)	**214-421-3993**
Pendleton, Nancy/313 E Thomas Rd #205, Phoenix, AZ	602-279-0119
Peters, Bob/313 E Thomas Rd #205, Phoenix, AZ	602-279-0119
Poli, Kristina/4211 Pebblegate Ct, Houston, TX	713-353-6910

RS

Ricks, Thom/6511 Adair Dr, San Antonio, TX	512-680-65
Roberts, Mark/Art Direction/2127 Banks St, Houston, TX	713-523-23
Robins, Mike/2472 Bolsover, Houston, TX	713-523-53
Ruland, Mike/8946 Long Point Rd, Houston, TX	713-465-24
Salem, Kay/13418 Splintered Oak, Houston, TX	713-469-09
Sketch Pad/2605 Westgate Dr, Arlington, TX	817-469-81
Skiermont, Richard Jr/5905 Gaelic Glen Dr, Oklahoma City, OK	405-721-83
Skistimas, James/7701 N Stemmons Frwy #854, Dallas, TX	214-630-25
Smith, James Noel/1011 North Clinton, Dallas, TX	214-946-42
STEIRNAGLE, MICHAEL/4141 PINNACLE #132, EL PASO, TX (P 460)	**915-533-92**
Strand, David/603 W Garland Ave #206, Garland, TX	214-494-00

TW

TENNISON, JAMES/713 HIGHLAND DR, ARLINGTON, TX (P 204)	**817-861-15**
Warner, Michele/1011 North Clinton, Dallas, TX	214-946-42
Washington, Bill/330 Glenarm, San Antonio, TX	512-734-62
Watford, Wayne/313 E Thomas Rd #205, Phoenix, AZ	602-279-01
Weakley, Mark/105 N Alamo #618, San Antonio, TX	512-222-95
Wells, Steve/754 International #T-38, Houston, TX	713-629-63

ROCKY MOUNTAIN

AC

Anderson, Jon/1465 Ellendale Ave, Logan, UT	801-752-89
Christensen, James C/656 West 550 South, Orem, UT	801-224-62
CUNEO, JOHN/2544 15TH ST, DENVER, CO (P 180)	**303-458-70**

D

DAZZELAND STUDIOS/209 EDISON, SALT LAKE CITY, UT (P 316,317)	**801-355-85**
Dolack, Monte/132 W Front St, Missoula, MT	406-549-32
Droy, Brad/1521 S Pearl, Denver, CO	303-871-07
Duell, Nancy/90 Corona #508, Denver, CO	303-591-93

EFG

ENRIGHT, CINDY/2544 15TH ST, DENVER, CO (P 181)	**303-458-70**
Fujisaki, Pat/5917 S Kenton Way, Englewood, CO	303-698-00
Graphics Studio/219 E 7th St, Denver, CO	303-830-11

H

HARDIMAN, MILES/30 VILLAGE DR, LITTLETON, CO (P 193)	**303-798-91**
Harris, Ralph/PO Box 1091, Sun Valley, ID	208-726-80
HEINER, JOE & KATHY/850 N GROVE DR, ALPINE, UT (P 174)	**801-756-33**
Hinds, Joe/7615 Vance Dr, Arvada, CO	303-424-20
Hull, Richard/776 W 3500 South, Bountiful, UT	801-298-16

LMN

Lediard, Al/2216 Kensington Ave, Salt Lake City, UT	801-328-05
Lyman, Kenvin/209 Edison St, Salt Lake City, UT	801-355-85
Masami/90 Corona #508, Denver, CO	303-778-60
Maughan, William/PO Box 133, Millville, UT	801-752-93
McGowan, Daniel/90 Corona #508, Denver, CO	303-778-60
Meents, Len/Estes Industries, Penrose, CO	303-372-30
Nelson, Will/1517 W Hays, Boise, ID	208-342-75

STV

Sauter, Ron/1032 S York St, Denver, CO	303-698-00
Spira, David/90 Corona #508, Denver, CO	303-778-60
Timmons, Bonnie/90 Corona #508, Denver, CO	303-778-60
Van Schelt, Perry L/6577 Cyclamen Way, W Jordan, UT	801-968-30

W

WELLER, DON/2240 MONARCH DR, PARK CITY, UT (P 71)	**801-649-98**
WHITESIDES, KIM/PO BOX 2189, PARK CITY, UT (P 478)	**801-649-04**
WINBORG, LARRY/464 SOUTH, 275 EAST, FARMINGTON, UT (P 46)	**801-451-53**

WEST

A

Ace Studio/PO Box 332, Oregon House, CA	916-692-1
Aitken, Barbara/6455 La Jolla Blvd #338, La Jolla, CA	619-459-2
Allaire, Michel J/405 Union St #2, San Francisco, CA	415-982-5
Allison, Gene/1808 Stanley Ave, Placentia, CA	714-524-5
Alsina, Gustav/5103 Pico Blvd, Los Angeles, CA	213-939-1

lt, Tim/3099 Wilshire Blvd #870, Los Angeles, CA ... 213 387 8384
vin, John/15942 Londelius, Sepulveda, CA ... 213-279-1775
mit, Emanuel/2822 Denby Ave, Los Angeles, CA ... 213-666-7414
nsel, Richard/7250 Franklin Ave, Los Angeles, CA ... 213-876-4292
nderson, Kevin/1259 Orkney Ln, Cardiff, CA ... 619-753-8410
nderson, Sara/117 W Denny Way, Seattle, WA ... 206-285-1520
nderson, Terry/5902 W 85th Pl, Los Angeles, CA ... 213-645-8469
ndreoli, Rick/467 Fair Dr #207, Costa Mesa, CA ... 714-979-7112
NSLEY, FRANK/1782 FIFTH ST, BERKELEY, CA (P 263) ... **415-644-0585**
rkle, Dave/259 W Orange Grove, Pomona, CA ... 714-865-2967
rshawsky, David/9401 Alcott St, Los Angeles, CA ... 213-276-6058
rtists in Print/Fort Mason Bldg D, San Francisco, CA ... 415-673-6941
rtman Studio IV/4009 Flintlock Way, Anaheim, CA ... 714-974-7395
tkins, Bill/PO Box 1091, Laguna Beach, CA ... 714-499-3857
UGUST, BOB/11147 LA MAIDA,
   N HOLLYWOOD, CA (P 213) ... **818-769-3592**

Backus, Michael/200-A Westminster Ave, Venice, CA ... 213-392-4877
aker, Darcy/7270 Ponto Rd, Carlsbad, CA ... 619-438-1841
AKER, DON/2717 WESTERN AVE, SEATTLE, WA (P 208) ... **206-728-1300**
ANTHIEN, BARBARA/902 MARYLYN CIRCLE,
   PETALUMA, CA (P 264) ... **707-762-1616**
anuelos, Art/111 S Orange St, Orange, CA ... 714-771-4335
anyai, Istvan/1241 9th St #3, Santa Monica, CA ... 213-394-8035
arbee, Joel/209 San Pablo, San Clemente, CA ... 714-498-0067
atcheller, Keith/624 W Cypress Ave, Covina, CA ... 818-331-0439
each, Lou/5312 W 8th St, Los Angeles, CA ... 213-934-7335
eersworth, Roger/618 S Western Ave #201, Los Angeles, CA ... 213-392-4877
eerworth, Roger/200-A Westminster Ave, Venice, CA ... 213-392-4877
eigle, David/5632 Meinhardt Rd, Westminster, CA ... 714-893-7749
ell, Karen/412 N Doheny Dr, Los Angeles, CA ... 213-858-0946
ennett, Mark/13752 Claremont St, Westminister, CA ... 714-897-9873
enzamin, Michele/247 Horizon Ave, Venice, CA ... 213-396-5054
ERGENDORFF, ROGER/17106 SIMS ST #A,
   HUNTINGTON BEACH, CA (P 269) ... **714-840-7665**
ernstein, Sol/649 Encino Vista Dr, Thousand Oaks, CA ... 805-497-7967
ettoli, Delana/737 Vernon Ave, Venice, CA ... 213-396-0296
ingham, Sid/360 1/2 N Mansfield Ave, Los Angeles, CA ... 213-935-4696
rnbaum, Dianne/17301 Elsinore Circle, Huntington Beach, CA ... 714-847-7631
JORKMAN, STEVE/1711 LANGLEY, IRVINE, CA (P 192) ... **714-261-1411**
ackshear, Tom/39 Mary St, San Rafael, CA ... 415-485-1644
air, Barry/PO Box 156, Dana Point, CA ... 714-661-3575
LANK, JERRY/1048 LINCOLN AVE,
   SAN JOSE, CA (P 272,273) ... **408-289-9095**
onder, Ellen/PO Box 5513, Mill Valley, CA ... 415-388-9158
ohn, Richard/595 W Wilson St, Costa Mesa, CA ... 714-548-6669
oyle, Neil/5455 Wilshire Blvd #1212, Los Angeles, CA ... 213-937-4472
adley, Barbara/750 Wildcat Canyon Rd, Berkeley, CA ... 415-673-4200
ingham, Sherry/1440 Bush St, San Francisco, CA ... 415-775-6564
itt, Tracy/4645 Park Blvd, Oakland, CA ... 415-531-6071
oad, David/100 Golden Hinde Blvd, San Rafael, CA ... 415-479-5505
own, Bill & Assoc/4121 Wilshire #315, Los Angeles, CA ... 213-386-2455
own, Charley/716 Montgomery St, San Francisco, CA ... 415-433-1222
own, Dennis/PO Box 16931, Irvine, CA ... 714-832-8090
own, Janis/Rt3 Box 456 #A, Escondido, CA ... 619-743-1795
ROWN, RICK/1502 N MAPLE, BURBANK, CA (P 283) ... **818-842-0726**
oyles, Kathie/1838 El Cerrito Pl #3, Hollywood, CA ... 213-874-1661
ugger, Bob/1830 S Robertson Blvd, Los Angeles, CA ... 213-204-1771
erge, Bill/734 Basin Dr, Topanga, CA ... 213-455-3181
ll, Michael/2350 Taylor, San Francisco, CA ... 415-776-7471
rnside, John E/4204 Los Feliz Blvd, Los Angeles, CA ... 213-665-8913
sacca, Mark/269 Corte Madera Ave, Mill Valley, CA ... 415-381-9048

Callanta, Al/13010 Miller Ave, Norwalk, CA ... 213-921-2369
rroll, Justin/1118 Chautauqua, Pacific Palisades, CA ... 213-450-4197
astillo, Luis/564 Lombard St, San Francisco, CA ... 415-788-2575
tom, Don/638 S Van Ness Ave, Los Angeles, CA ... 213-382-6281
adwick, Paul/5733 Benner St #23, Los Angeles, CA ... 213-254-1820
aney, Bud/7541 Santa Rita Cir #C, Stanton, CA ... 714-898-7012
ang, Warren/1243 Vicente Dr #72, Sunnyvale, CA ... 415-964-1701
HASE, MARGO/120 SYCAMORE AVE,
   LOS ANGELES, CA (P 291) ... **213-537-4421**

Chewning, Randy/360 1/2 N Mansfield Ave, Los Angeles, CA ... 213-935-4696
Chiodo, Joe/2124 Froude St, San Diego, CA ... 619-222-2476
Chorney, Steven/10855 Beckford Ave, Northridge, CA ... 818-985-8181
Clark, Tim/8800 Venice Blvd, Los Angeles, CA ... 213-202-1044
Clarke, Coralie/PO Box 6057, Bonsall, CA ... 619-941-1476
Clenney, Linda/610 22nd St #304, San Francisco, CA ... 415-543-1087
Coconis, Ted/2244 Santa Ana, Palo Alto, CA ... 415-856-9055
Colby, Janet/3589 First Ave, San Diego, CA ... 619-298-4037
Cole, Dick/25 Hotaling Pl, San Francisco, CA ... 415-986-8163
Commander, Bob/412 N Doheny Dr, Los Angeles, CA ... 213-858-0946
The Committee/15468 Ventura Blvd, Sherman Oaks, CA ... 818-986-4420
CONSANI, CHRIS/6376 W 5TH ST,
   LOS ANGELES, CA (P 158) ... **213-934-3395**
Cook, Anne/1857 Mason St, San Francisco, CA ... 415-441-8134
Coppock, Chuck/638 S Van Ness Ave, Los Angeles, CA ... 213-382-6281
Cotter, Debbie/248 Alhambra, San Francisco, CA ... 415-331-9111
Coviello, Ron/1682 Puterbaugh, San Diego, CA ... 619-265-6647
Criss, Keith/4329 Piedmont Ave, Oakland, CA ... 415-547-2528
Critz, Carl/638 S Van Ness Ave, Los Angeles, CA ... 213-382-6281
Cummings, B D/3845 E Casselle, Orange, CA ... 714-633-3322
Curtis, Todd/2046 14th St #10, Santa Monica, CA ... 213-452-0738

DANIELS/1352 HORNBLEND ST, SAN DIEGO, CA (P 200) ... **619-272-8147**
Daniels, Alan/3443 Wade St, Los Angeles, CA ... 213-306-6878
Daniels, Beau/10434 Corfu Ln, Los Angeles, CA ... 213-279-1775
Daniels, Shelley/7247 Margerun Ave, San Diego, CA ... 619-286-8087
Daniels, Stewart/961 Terrace Dr, Oakdale, CA ... 209-847-5596
Darrow, David R/7893-D Rancho Fanita, Santee, CA ... 619-448-5448
Davidson, Kevin/505 S Grand St, Orange, CA ... 714-633-9061
Davis, Jack/3785 Mt Everest Blvd, San Diego, CA ... 619-565-0336
Dean, Bruce/360 1/2 N Mansfield Ave, Los Angeles, CA ... 213-935-4696
Dean, Donald/3960 Rhoda Ave, Oakland, CA ... 415-644-1139
DEANDA, RUBEN/550 OXFORD ST #407,
   CHULA VISTA, CA (P 201) ... **619-427-7765**
Dellorco, Chris/6533 Rubio St, Van Nuys, CA ... 818-994-4859
Deneen, Jim B/3443 Wade St, Los Angeles, CA ... 213-390-9595
Dennewill, Jim/5823 Autry Ave, Lakewood, CA ... 213-920-3895
Densham, Robert S/781 1/2 California Blvd,
   San Luis Obispo, CA ... 805-541-2920
Devaud, Jacques/1830 S Robertson Blvd, Los Angeles, CA ... 213-204-1771
Dietz, James/2203 13th Ave E, Seattle, WA ... 206-325-2857
Diffenderfer, Ed/32 Cabernet Ct, Lafayette, CA ... 415-254-8235
Dismukes, John Taylor/4844 Van Noord, Sherman Oaks, CA ... 818-907-9087
Doe, Bart/3300 Temple St, Los Angeles, CA ... 213-383-9707
Dohrmann, Marsha J/144 Woodbine Dr, Mill Valley, CA ... 415-383-0188
Drake Studios/1556 N Fairfax Ave, Los Angeles, CA ... 213-851-6808
Drake, Bob/1510 Hi-Point, Los Angeles, CA ... 213-931-8690
Drayton, Richard/5018 Dumont Pl, Woodland Hills, CA ... 213-347-2227
Drennon, Tom/916 N Formosa #D, Hollywood, CA ... 213-874-1276
Dudley, Don/PO Box 742, Point Reyes Station, CA ... 415-555-1212
Duffus, Bill/1745 Wagner, Pasadena, CA ... 818-792-7921
DUKE, LAWRENCE W/STAR ROUTE BOX 93,
   WOODSIDE, CA (P 324) ... **415-861-0941**
Duranona, Leo/6340 Lankershim Blvd #105, N Hollywood, CA ... 818-761-0128
Durfee, Tom/25 Hotaling Pl, San Francisco, CA ... 415-781-0527

Eastman, Bryant/14333 Addison St #201, Sherman Oaks, CA ... 818-990-6482
Eckart, Chuck/166 South Park, San Francisco, CA ... 415-552-4252
EDELSON, WENDY/85 S WASHINGTON,
   SEATTLE, WA (P 210) ... **206-625-0109**
Eichenberger, Dave/11607 Clover Ave, Los Angeles, CA ... 213-828-9653
Ellescas, Richard/321 N Martel, Hollywood, CA ... 213-939-7396
Ellmore, Dennis/3245 Orange Ave, Long Beach, CA ... 213-424-9379
Elstad, Ron/18253 Solano River Ct, Fountain Valley, CA ... 714-964-7753
Endicott, James R/Rte 1 Box 27 B, Newberg, OR ... 503-538-5466
Ente, Anke/50 Kings Rd, Brisbane, CA ... 415-467-8109
Ericksen, Marc/1045 Sansome St #306, San Francisco, CA ... 415-362-1214
Erickson, Kernie/Box 2175, Mission Viejo, CA ... 714-831-2818
Etow, Carole/221 17th St #B, Manhattan Beach, CA ... 213-545-0795
Evans, Bill/2030 First Ave #201, Seattle, WA ... 206-623-9459
Evans, Robert/1045 Sansome, San Francisco, CA ... 415-397-5322
Evenson, Stan/1830 S Robertson Blvd #203, Los Angeles, CA ... 213-204-1995

F
Feign, Larry/660 S Glassell St #75, Orange, CA 714-544-4380
Ferrero, Felix/215 Liedesdorff, San Francisco, CA 415-981-1162
Fox, Ronald/2274 237th St, Torrance, CA 213-325-4970
Francuch, George/638 S Van Ness Ave, Los Angeles, CA 213-382-6281
Franks, Bill/638 S Van Ness Ave, Los Angeles, CA 213-382-6281
Fraze, Jon/17081 Kenyon Dr #C, Tustin, CA 714-731-8493
FRAZEE, MARLA/5114 1/2 LA RODA AVE, LOS ANGELES, CA (P 159) 213-258-3846
French, Lisa/489 Norton St, Long Beach, CA 213-423-8741
Fulkerson, Chuck/1671 Longspur Ave, Sunnyvale, CA 408-730-1878
Fulp, Jim/834 Duboce Ave, San Francisco, CA 415-621-5462
Funcich, Tina/14461 Wilson St, Westminster, CA 714-897-6874

G
Gadbois, Brett/1633 N Laurel Ave #23, Los Angeles, CA 213-650-8440
Gage, Susan/5042 Aldama St, Los Angeles, CA 213-655-2126
Gaines, David/2337 Duane St, Los Angeles, CA 213-663-8763
Galloway, Nixon/5455 Wilshire Blvd #1212, Los Angeles, CA 213-937-4472
GARCIA, MANUEL/1352 HORNBLEND ST, SAN DIEGO, CA (P 201) 619-272-8147
Garland, Gil/4928 Hartwick St, Los Angeles, CA 213-933-0610
Garner, Tracy/1830 S Robertson Blvd, Los Angeles, CA 213-204-1771
Garnett, Joe/638 S Van Ness Ave, Los Angeles, CA 213-382-6281
Garo, Harry/7738 E Allen Grove, Downey, CA 213-928-2768
Geary, Rick/2124 Froude St, San Diego, CA 619-222-2476
Gellos, Nancy/20 Armour St, Seattle, WA 206-285-5838
General Graphics/746 Brannan, San Francisco, CA 415-777-3333
George, Jeff/2120 Nelson Ave #C1, Redondo Beach, CA 213-371-0280
Gerrie, Dean/222 W Main St #101, Tuscan, CA 714-838-0234
GIRVIN, TIM DESIGN/911 WESTERN AVE #408, SEATTLE, WA (P 228,229) 206-623-7918
Gisko, Max/90 Gaviota St, San Francisco, CA 415-469-8030
Glad, Deanna/PO Box 3261, Santa Monica, CA 213-393-7464
Glass, Randy/145 N Orange, Los Angeles, CA 213-933-2500
Glassford, Carl/25361 Posada Ln, Mission Viejo, CA 714-895-5623
Gleason, Bob/618 S Western Ave #206, Los Angeles, CA 213-384-3898
Gleeson, Madge/Art Dept/Wstrn Wash Univ, Bellingham, WA 206-676-3000
Gleis, Linda/518 N La Cienga, Los Angeles, CA 213-659-4714
Goddard, John/2774 Los Alisos Dr, Fallbrook, CA 619-728-5473
Gohata, Mark/1492 W 153 St, Gardena, CA 213-327-6595
Goldstein, Howard/7031 Aldea Ave, Van Nuys, CA 818-987-2837
Gomez, Ignacio/812 Kenneth Rd, Glendale, CA 818-243-2838
Gordon, Duane/638 S Van Ness Ave, Los Angeles, CA 213-382-6281
Gordon, Roger/3111 4th St #202, Santa Monica, CA 213-396-2365
Gould, Ron/8039 Paso Robles Ave, Van Nuys, CA 818-345-1436
Graphic Designers Inc/2975 Wilshire Blvd #210, Los Angeles, CA 213-381-3977
Graphicswork/1325 Rincon Rd, Escondido, CA 619-743-8736
Gray, Steve/412 N Doheny Dr, Los Angeles, CA 213-858-0946
Green, Peter/4433 Forman Ave, Toluca Lake, CA 818-760-1011
Gribbitt Ltd/5419 Sunset Blvd, Los Angeles, CA 213-462-7362
Griffith, Linda/13972 Hilo Ln, Santa Ana, CA 714-832-8536
Grim, Elgas/638 S Van Ness Ave, Los Angeles, CA 213-382-6281
Gross, Daerick/318 W 9th St #204, Los Angeles, CA 213-489-1380
Grossman, Myron/8800 Venice Blvd, Los Angeles, CA 213-559-9344
Grove, David/382 Union St, San Francisco, CA 415-433-2100
Guidice, Rick/9 Park Ave, Los Gatos, CA 408-354-7787
Gurvin, Abe/845 Mason Rd, Vista, CA 619-941-1838

H
Hale, Bruce/2451 5th Ave West, Seattle, WA 706-282-1191
Hall, Patricia/5450 Complex St #301, San Diego, CA 619-268-0176
Hamagami, John/7822 Croydon Ave, Los Angeles, CA 213-641-1522
Hamilton, Jack/1040 E Van Bibber Ave, Orange, CA 714-771-5017
Hamilton, Pamela/2956 S Robertson Blvd #9, Los Angeles, CA 213-838-7888
Hammond, Cris/166 South Park, San Francisco, CA 415-552-4252
Hammond, Roger/5455 Wilshire Blvd #1212, Los Angeles, CA 213-937-4472
Hampton, Gerry Inc/PO Box 16304, Irvine, CA 213-431-6979
Harris, Linda/5923 W Pico Blvd, Los Angeles, CA 213-933-7596
Hasenbeck, George/612 Prospect St #401, Seattle, WA 206-283-0980
Hashimoto, Alan/2456 Beverley Ave, Santa Monica, CA 213-396-8529
Hasselle, Bruce/2620 Segerstrom #A, Santa Ana, CA 714-662-5731
Hatzer, Fred/5455 Wilshire Blvd #1212, Los Angeles, CA 213-937-4472

Haydock, Robert/49 Shelley Dr, Mill Valley, CA 415-383-69
HAYNES, BRYAN/1733 ELLINCOURT DR #F, SOUTH PASADENA, CA (P 352) 818-799-79
Hays, Jim/3809 Sunnyside Blvd, Marysville, WA 206-334-75
Hegedus, James C/913 Le Doux, Los Angeles, CA 213-657-19
Heidrich, Tim/14824 Ibex Ave, Norwalk, CA 213-828-96
Heimann, Jim/1548 18th St, Santa Monica, CA 213-828-10
Hendricks, Steve/1050 Elsiemae Dr, Boulder Creek, CA 408-338-66
Henry, James/209 N Venice Blvd #7, Venice, CA 213-306-75
Herrero, Lowell/870 Harrison St, San Francisco, CA 415-543-64
Hicks, Brad/2624 Northlake Ave #41, Altadena, CA 818-794-43
Hill, Glenn/28026 Fox Run Circle, Lake Castaic, CA 805-257-49
Hilliard, Fred/5425 Crystal Springs Dr NE, Bainbridge Island, WA 206-842-60
HILTON-PUTNAM, DENISE/7059-83 PARK MESA WAY, SAN DIEGO, CA (P 198) 619-565-75
Hinton, Hank/6118 W 6th St, Los Angeles, CA 213-938-98
Hitch, J L/260 Newport Center Dr #410, Newport Beach, CA 714-759-09
Hoburg, Maryanne Regal/1695 8th Ave, San Francisco, CA 415-731-18
Hodges, Ken/12401 Bellwood, Los Alamitos, CA 213-431-41
Holmes, Matthew/126 Mering Ct, Sacramento, CA 916-484-60
HOPKINS, CHRISTOPHER/2932 WILSHIRE #202, SANTA MONICA, CA (P 355) 213-828-64
Hopkins/ Sisson Inc/228-R Main St, Venice, CA 213-392-96
Hord, Bob/1760 Monrovia #B-10, Costa Mesa, CA 714-631-38
Hoyos, Andy/360 1/2 N Mansfield Ave, Los Angeles, CA 213-935-46
Hubbard, Roger/7461 Beverly Blvd #405, Los Angeles, CA 213-938-51
Hudson, Dave/2500 E Nutwood Ave #215B, Fullerton, CA 714-879-39
Huhn, Tim/4718 Kester Ave #208, Sherman Oaks, CA 818-986-2
HULSEY, KEVIN/347 SKYEWIAY RD, LOS ANGELES, CA (P 216,217) 818-501-71
HUNT, ROBERT/4376 21ST ST, SAN FRANCISCO, CA (P 356) 415-824-18
Hwang, Francis/999 Town & Country Rd, Orange, CA 714-567-25

IJ
Ikkanda, Richard/2800 28th St #152, Santa Monica, CA 213-450-48
Illustration West/4020 N Palm #207, Fullerton, CA 714-773-91
Irvine, Rex John/6026 Dovetail Dr, Agoura, CA 818-991-25
Jacobi, Kathryn/17830 Osborne St, Northridge, CA 213-396-89
Jenks, Aleta/409 Bryant St, San Francisco, CA 415-495-42
Jenott, John/234 Miller Ave #A, Mill Valley, CA 415-383-2
Jensen, David/1150 Fremont St, San Jose, CA 408-295-59
Johnson, Karen/1600 Beach St #301, San Francisco, CA 415-567-30
Jones, Reginald/197 Zinfandel Ln, St Helena, CA 707-963-75
Jones, Steve/1081 Nowita Pl, Venice, CA 213-396-9
Joy, Pat/247 Alestar #3, Vista, CA 619-726-2
Judd, Jeff/827 1/2 N McCadden Pl, Los Angeles, CA 213-469-03

K
Kabaker, Gayle/1440 Bush St, San Francisco, CA 415-775-65
Kamifuji, Tom/409 Bryant St, San Francisco, CA 415-495-42
Kari, Morgan/3516 Sawtelle Blvd #226, Los Angeles, CA 213-390-13
Karlin, Eugene/Los Angeles, CA 213-459-03
Katayama, Mits/515 Lake Washington Blvd, Seattle, WA 206-324-1
Keefer, Mel/847 5th St #108, Santa Monica, CA 213-395-1
Keeling, Gregg Bernard/659 Boulevard Way, Oakland, CA 415-444-80
Kenyon, Chris/14 Wilmot, San Francisco, CA 415-775-72
Kimble, David/711 S Flower, Burbank, CA 213-849-15
KIMURA, HIRO/6376 W 5TH ST, LOS ANGELES, CA (P 154) 213-934-3
King, Heather/363 Texas St, San Francisco, CA 415-285-7
KITCHELL, JOYCE/1352 HORNBLEND ST, SAN DIEGO, CA (P 199) 619-272-8
Koulian, Jack/442 W Harvard, Glendale, CA 818-956-5
Kramer, Moline/837 S Sycamore, Los Angeles, CA 213-934-6
Kratter, Paul/7461 Beverly Blvd #405, Los Angeles, CA 213-938-5
Kriegler, Richard/2814 Third St, Santa Monica, CA 213-396-9
Kriss, Ron/6671 W Sunset #1519, Los Angeles, CA 213-462-5
Krogle, Bob/11607 Clover Ave, Los Angeles, CA 213-828-9

L
Labadie, Ed/1012 San Rafael Ave, Glendale, CA 818-240-0
Lagerstrom, Wendy/10462 Vanora Dr, Sunland, CA 818-352-5
Lake, Larry/360 1/2 N Mansfield Ave, Los Angeles, CA 213-935-4
Lamb, Dana/PO Box 1091, Yorba Linda, CA 714-996-3
LaRose, Lou/412 N Doheny Dr, Los Angeles, CA 213-858-0

Larson, Ron/940 N Highland Ave, Los Angeles, CA — 213-465-8451
Leader, Lindon/11640 Woodbridge St #106, Studio City, CA — 818-763-3718
Leary, Catherine/1830 S Robertson Blvd, Los Angeles, CA — 213-204-1771
Lee, Warren/88 Meadow Valley Rd, Corte Madera, CA — 415-924-0261
Leech, Richard & Associates/725 Filbert St, San Francisco, CA — 415-981-4840
Leedy, Jeff/209 North St, Sausalito, CA — 415-332-9100
**LEVINE, BETTE/149 N HAMILTON DR #A,
    BEVERLY HILLS, CA (P 27) — 213-653-9765**
Lewis, Dennis/6671 Sunset #1519, Los Angeles, CA — 213-462-5731
Lewis, Louise/2030 First Ave #201, Seattle, WA — 206-623-9459
Lieppman, Jeff/526 Lakeside Ave S #2, Seattle, WA — 206-323-1799
Lindsay, Martin/4469 41st St, San Diego, CA — 619-281-8851
Livingston, Francis/1537 Franklin St #105, San Francisco, CA — 415-776-1531
Lloyd, Gregory/5534 Red River Dr, San Diego, CA — 619-582-3487
Locke, Charles/PO Box 61986, Sunnyvale, CA — 408-734-5298
Lohstoeter, Lori/278 Glen Arm, Pasadena, CA — 818-441-0601
Losch, Diana/Pier 33 N Embarcadero, San Francisco, CA — 415-956-5648
Lozano, Henry Jr/3205 Belle River Dr, Hacienda, CA — 818-330-2095
Lulich, Ted/2420 SW Marigold, Portland, OR — 503-244-6188
Lund, Gary/360 1/2 N Mansfield Ave, Los Angeles, CA — 213-935-4696
Luth, Tom/2506 Spaulding #8, Long Beach, CA — 213-434-5340
Lytle, John/PO Box 5155, Sonora, CA — 209-928-4849

M MacLeod, Lee/200-A Westminster Ave, Venice, CA — 213-392-4877
Maltese, Cristy/PO Box 1347, Ramona, CA — 619-789-0309
Manoogian, Michael/7457 Beck Ave, N Hollywood, CA — 818-764-6114
Manzelman, Judy/9 1/2 Murray Ln, Larkspur, CA — 415-461-9685
Marsh, Cynthia/4434 Matilija Ave, Sherman Oaks, CA — 818-789-5232
Marshall, Craig/28 Abbey St, San Francisco, CA — 415-641-1010
Mattos, John/1546 Grant Ave, San Francisco, CA — 415-397-2138
Mayeda, Kaz/3847 Bentley Ave #2, Culver City, CA — 213-559-6839
McCandlish, Mark Edward/1334 W Foothill Blvd #4D,
    Upland, CA — 714-982-1428
McCargar, Lucy/563 Pilgrim Dr #A, Foster City, CA — 415-363-2130
McConnell, Jim/7789 Greenly Dr, Oakland, CA — 415-569-0852
McCullough, Lendy/5511 Seashore Dr, Newport Beach, CA — 714-642-2244
McDougall, Scott/712 N 62nd St, Seattle, WA — 206-783-1403
McDraw, Brooker/2030 First Ave #201, Seattle, WA — 206-623-9459
McElroy, Darlene/2038 Calvert Ave, Costa Mesa, CA — 714-556-8133
McKee, Ron/5455 Wilshire Blvd #1212, Los Angeles, CA — 213-937-4472
McKiernan, James E/2501 Cherry Ave #310, Signal Hill, CA — 213-427-1953
McMahon, Bob/6820 Independence Ave #31, Canoga Park, CA — 818-999-4127
Mediate, Frank/2975 Wilshire Blvd #210, Los Angeles, CA — 213-381-3977
Megowan, John/3114 1/2 Sherwood Ave, Alhambra, CA — 818-289-5826
Merritt, Norman/5455 Wilshire Blvd #1212, Los Angeles, CA — 213-937-4472
Metz Air Art/2817 E Lincoln Ave, Anaheim, CA — 714-630-3071
**MEYER, GARY/227 W CHANNEL RD,
    SANTA MONICA, CA (P 399) — 213-454-2174**
Mikkelson, Linda S/1624 Vista Del Mar, Hollywood, CA — 213-463-3116
Miller, Steve/5929 Irvine Ave, N Hollywood, CA — 818-985-5610
MILLSAP, DARREL/1744 6TH AVE, SAN DIEGO, CA (P 144) — 619-232-4519
Mitchell, Kathy/828 21st St #6, Santa Monica, CA — 213-828-6331
Mitoma, Tim/1200 Dale Ave #97, Mountain View, CA — 415-965-9734
Moats, George/PO Box 1187, Hanford, CA — 209-584-9026
Monahan, Leo/1624 Vista Del Mar, Los Angeles, CA — 213-463-3116
Montoya, Ricardo/1025 E Lincoln Ave #D, Anaheim, CA — 714-533-0507
Moreau, Alain/1461 1/2 S Beverly Dr, Los Angeles, CA — 213-553-8529
MORSE, BILL/173 18TH AVE, SAN FRANCISCO, CA (P 28) — 415-221-6711
Mouri, Gary/22435 Caminito Pacifico, Laguna Hills, CA — 714-951-8136
**MUKAI, DENNIS/831 PACIFIC ST #5,
    SANTA MONICA, CA (P 38, 39, 246) — 213-452-9060**

N Nasser, Christine/PO Box 3881, Manhattan Beach, CA — 213-318-1066
Navarro, Arlene & Larry/1921 Comstock Ave, Los Angeles, CA — 213-201-4744
Neila, Anthony/270 Sutter St 3rd Fl, San Francisco, CA — 415-956-6344
**NELSON, CRAIG/6010 GRACIOSA DR,
    LOS ANGELES, CA (P 29) — 213-466-6483**
Nelson, Kenton/110 W Ocean #304, Long Beach, CA — 213-491-0847
Nelson, Mike/1836 Woodsdale Ct, Concord, CA — 707-746-0800
Nelson, Susan/2363 N Fitch Mtn Rd, Healdsburg, CA — 707-431-7166
Nesbitt, John/307 1/2 Ruby Ave, Newport Beach, CA — 714-673-0785
Nethery, Susan/1548 18th St, San Mateo, CA — 213-828-1931

Nicholson, Norman/410 Pacific Ave, San Francisco, CA — 415-421-2555
Nikosey, Tom/7417 Melrose Ave, Los Angeles, CA — 213-655-2184
Noble, Larry/10434 Corfu Ln, Los Angeles, CA — 213-279-1775
Nolan, Dennis/579 Beresford Ave, Redwood City, CA — 415-364-0366
Nordell, Dale/515 Lake Washington Blvd, Seattle, WA — 206-324-1199
Nordell, Marilyn/515 Lake Washington Blvd, Seattle, WA — 206-324-1199
Norman, Gary/11607 Clover Ave, Los Angeles, CA — 213-828-9653
Nunez, Manuel/1073 W 9th St, San Pedro, CA — 213-832-2471
Nye, Linda S/10951 Sorrento Valley Rd #1H, San Diego, CA — 619-455-5500
Obrero, Rudy/1830 S Robertson Blvd, Los Angeles, CA — 213-204-1771
O'Brien, Kathy/166 South Park, San Francisco, CA — 415-552-4252
Oden, Richard/631 Cliff Dr, Laguna Blvd, CA — 714-760-7001
Odgers, Jayme/703 S Union, Los Angeles, CA — 213-484-9965
Ohanian, Nancy/22234 Victory Blvd #6303, Woodland Hills, CA — 818-247-0135
O'Mary, Tom/8418 Menkar Rd, San Diego, CA — 619-578-5361
O'Neil, Sharon/409 Alberto Way #6, Los Gatos, CA — 408-354-3816
**OSBORNE, JACQUELINE/101 MIDDLEFIELD RD,
    PALO ALTO, CA (P 418) — 415-326-2276**

PQ Pace, Julie/339 S Mariposa Ave, Los Angeles, CA — 213-480-0867
Page, Frank/10434 Corfu Ln, Los Angeles, CA — 213-279-1775
Palombi, Peter/19811 Quiet Surf Cir, Huntington Beach, CA — 714-536-5850
Pansini, Tom/16222 Howland Ln, Huntington Bch, CA — 714-847-9329
Paris Productions/2207 Garnet, San Diego, CA — 619-272-4992
Parkinson, Jim/6170 Broadway Terrace, Oakland, CA — 415-547-3100
Parmentier, Henri/10462 Vanora Dr, Sunland, CA — 818-352-5173
Passey, Kim/3443 Wade St, Los Angeles, CA — 213-306-6878
Pavia, Cathy/1830 S Robertson Blvd, Los Angeles, CA — 213-204-1771
Peck's Builders Art/17865 Skypark Cir #K, Irvine, CA — 714-261-6233
**PECK, EVERETT/1352 HORNBLEND ST,
    SAN DIEGO, CA (P 197) — 619-272-8147**
Pederson, Sharleen/7742 Redland St #H3036,
    Playa Del Rey, CA — 213-306-7847
**PERINGER, STEPHEN/6046 LAKESHORE DR SO,
    SEATTLE, WA (P 209) — 206-725-7779**
Peterson, Barbara/2629 W Northwood, Santa Ana, CA — 714-546-2786
Peterson, Eric/270 Termino Avenue, Long Beach, CA — 213-438-2785
Peterson, Julie/2547 Anza St, San Francisco, CA — 415-221-0238
Phillips, Barry/1318 1/2 S Beverly Glen, Los Angeles, CA — 213-275-6524
Phister, Suzanne/248 Alhambra, San Francisco, CA — 415-922-4304
Platz, Henry III/15922 118th Pl NE, Bothell, WA — 206-488-9171
Platz, Rusty/515 Lake Washington Blvd, Seattle, WA — 206-324-1199
Pluym, Todd Vander/425 Via Anita, Redondo Beach, CA — 213-378-5559
Podevin, J F/223 South Kenmore #4, Los Angeles, CA — 213-739-5083
Pound, John/2124 Froude St, San Diego, CA — 619-222-2476
Precision Illustration/10434 Corfu Ln, Los Angeles, CA — 213-279-1775
Prochnow, Bill/1717 Union, San Francisco, CA — 415-673-0825
Puchalski, John/412 N Doheny Dr, Los Angeles, CA — 213-858-0946
Putnam, Jamie/10th and Parker, Berkeley, CA — 415-549-2500
Pyle, Chuck/146 10th Ave, San Francisco, CA — 415-751-8087
Quarnstrom, Doris/19681 Lancewood Plaza, Yorba Linda, CA — 714-970-2271

R Rand, Ted/515 Lake Washington Blvd, Seattle, WA — 206-324-1199
Ray, Christian/2022 Jones St, San Francisco, CA — 415-928-0457
Ray, Greg/824 Providencia Ave E, Burbank, CA — 818-845-2375
Raymond, T/1010 Urania Ave, Leucadia, CA — 619-753-3341
Redmond, Russell/1744 Sixth Ave, San Diego, CA — 619-232-7093
Richardson, Rich/5851 Antigua Blvd, San Diego, CA — 619-268-0033
**RIESER, BILL/419 VIA LINDA VISTA,
    REDONDO BEACH, CA (P 89) — 213-373-4762**
Rinaldi, Linda/17734 Miranda St, Encino, CA — 818-881-1578
Robbins, George/2700 Neilson Way #1423, Santa Monica, CA — 213-392-4439
Robles, Bill/5455 Wilshire Blvd #1212, Los Angeles, CA — 213-937-4472
**RODRIGUEZ, ROBERT/1548 18TH ST,
    SANTA MONICA, CA (P 193) — 213-828-2840**
Rogers, Mike/7461 Beverly Blvd #405, Los Angeles, CA — 213-938-5177
**ROGERS, PAUL/6376 W 5TH ST,
    LOS ANGELES, CA (P 156, 157) — 213-934-3395**
Roman, Thom/PO Box 584, Cypress, CA — 714-220-2858
Rother, Sue/1537 Franklin St #103, San Francisco, CA — 415-441-8893
Rowe, Ken/36325 Panorama Dr, Yucaipa, CA — 714-797-7030
Rutherford, John/55 Alvarado Ave, Mill Valley, CA — 415-383-1788

ILLUSTRATORS CONT'D.

Please send us your additions and updates.

ILLUSTRATORS

S
Saint John, Bob/1036 S 6th Ave, Arcadia, CA — 818-447-0375
**SAKAHARA, DICK/28826 CEDARBLUFF DR,
RANCHO PALOS VERDES, CA (P 155)** — **213-541-8187**
Salk, Larry/7461 Beverly Blvd #405, Los Angeles, CA — 213-938-5177
Sanford, James/1153 Oleander Rd, Lafayette, CA — 415-284-9015
Sano, Kazu/105 Stadium Ave, Mill Valley, CA — 415-381-6377
Scanlan, David/145 N Orange, Los Angeles, CA — 213-933-2500
Scanlon, Dave/2523 Valley Dr, Manhattan Beach, CA — 213-545-0773
Schaar, Bob/23282 Morobe Cr, Laguna Niguel, CA — 714-831-9845
Schields, Gretchen/708 Montgomery St, San Francisco, CA — 415-558-8851
Schilens, Tim/1372 Winston Ct, Upland, CA — 714-623-4999
Schockner, Jan/412 N Doheny Dr, Los Angeles, CA — 213-858-0946
Schumacher, Michael/2030 First Ave #201, Seattle, WA — 206-623-9459
Scribner, Jo Anne L/3314 N Lee, Spokane, WA — 509-484-3208
Shannon, Tom/17291 Marken Ln, Huntington Bch, CA — 714-842-1602
Shehorn, Gene/1672 Lynwood Dr, Concord, CA — 415-687-4516
Shepherd, Roni/1 San Antonio Pl, San Francisco, CA — 415-421-9764
Shields, Bill/2231 Pine St, San Francisco, CA — 415-346-0376
Sigwart, Forrest/1033 S Orlando Ave, Los Angeles, CA — 213-655-7734
Simmons, Russ/1555 S Brockton Ave #5, Los Angeles, CA — 213-820-7477
Sizemore, Ted/10642 Vanora Dr, Sunland, CA — 818-352-5173
Sky Pie Graphics/240 S Helix, Solana Beach, CA — 714-755-8692
Smith, J Peter/PO Box 69559, Los Angeles, CA — 213-464-1163
Smith, John C/2030 First Ave #201, Seattle, WA — 206-623-9459
Smith, Kenneth/3545 El Caminito St, La Crescenta, CA — 818-248-2531
Smith, Terry/10642 Vanora Dr, Sunland, CA — 818-352-5173
Snyder, Teresa & Wayne/4291 Suzanne Dr, Pittsburg, CA — 406-549-6772
Sobel, June/706 Marine St, Santa Monica, CA — 213-392-2842
Solvang-Angell, Diane/515 Lake Washington Blvd, Seattle, WA — 206-324-1199
South, Randy/48 Second Ave 4th Fl, San Francisco, CA — 415-543-1170
Spear, Jeffrey A/1111 Euclid St #302, Santa Monica, CA — 213-395-3939
Spear, Randy/4325 W 182nd St #20, Torrance, CA — 213-370-6071
Specht/Watson Studio/1252 S LaCienega Blvd,
Los Angeles, CA — 213-652-2682
Speidel, Sandy/14 Wilmot, San Francisco, CA — 415-775-7276
Spencer, Joe/11201 Valley Spring Ln, Studio City, CA — 818-760-0216
Spohn, Cliff/3216 Bruce Dr, Fremont, CA — 415-651-4597
Sprattler, Rob/1947 El Arbolita Dr, Glendale, CA — 818-249-3022
Starkweather, Teri/4633 Galendo St, Woodland Hills, CA — 818-992-5938
Steele, Robert/14 Wilmot, San Francisco, CA — 415-923-0741
Stehrenberger, Mark/10434 Corfu Ln, Los Angeles, CA — 213-279-1775
Stein, Mike/4340 Arizona, San Diego, CA — 619-295-2455
Stepp, Don/275 Marguerita Ln, Pasadena, CA — 818-799-0263
**STERMER, DUGALD/1801 FRANKLIN ST #404,
SAN FRANCISCO, CA (P 249)** — **415-441-4384**
Stevenson, Kay/410 S Griffith Park Dr, Burbank, CA — 818-845-4069
Stewart, Barbara/1640 Tenth Ave #5, San Diego, CA — 619-238-0083
Stewart, Walt/PO Box 621, Sausalito, CA — 415-868-0481
Stout, William G/812 S LaBrea, Hollywood, CA — 213-936-6342
Strange, Jedd/1951 Abbott St, San Diego, CA — 619-224-7730
Studio/922 Grand Ave, San Diego, CA — 619-272-4801
Suvityasiri, Sarn/1811 Leavenworth St, San Francisco, CA — 415-928-1602

TV
Tanenbaum, Robert/5505 Corbin Ave, Tarzana, CA — 818-345-6741
Taylor, C Winston/17008 Lisette St, Granada Hills, CA — 818-363-5761
Thomas, Anne/2400 E 42nd Ave #403R, Seattle, WA — 206-329-5489
Thomas, Debra/6307 Lake Shore Dr, San Diego, CA — 619-698-5135
Thon, Bud/410 View Park Ct, Mill Valley, CA — 415-383-3299
Tilley, Debbie/944 Virginia Ln, Escondido, CA — 619-481-3251
Tomita, Tom/148 N Catalina Ave #5, Pasadena, CA — 818-796-4213

Tompkins, Tish/1660 Redcliff St, Los Angeles, CA — 213-662-166
Triffet, Kurt/758 E Colorado #202, Pasadena, CA — 818-440-952
Truesdale Art & Design/5482 Complex St #112,
San Diego, CA — 619-268-102
Tsuchiya, Julie/409 Bryant St, San Francisco, CA — 415-495-427
Tucker, Ezra/4634 Woodman Ave #202, Sherman Oaks, CA — 818-905-075
Turner, Charles/3880 Begonia St, San Diego, CA — 619-453-671
Vance, Jay/676 Lafayette Park Place, Los Angeles, CA — 213-387-117
Vandervoort, Gene/3201 S Ramona Dr, Santa Ana, CA — 714-549-319
Vanle, Jay/638 S Van Ness Ave, Los Angeles, CA — 213-382-628
Vargas, Kathy/5082 Tasman Dr, Huntington Beach, CA — 213-721-596
Varon, Russell/18371 Warren Ave, Tustin, CA — 714-832-659
Vigon, Jay/708 S Orange Grove Ave, Los Angeles, CA — 213-937-035
Vinson, W T/4118 Vernon, Glen Avon, CA — 714-685-769
Vogelman, Jack H/1314 Dartmouth Dr, Glendale, CA — 818-243-320
Voss, Tom/525 West B St #G, San Diego, CA — 619-238-167

W
Wack, Jeff/3614 Berry Dr, Studio City, CA — 818-508-034
Walden, Craig/515 Lake Washington Blvd, Seattle, WA — 206-324-119
Walstead, Curt/610 S Wilton Pl #2, Los Angeles, CA — 213-382-362
Waters Art Studio/1820 E Garry St #207, Santa Ana, CA — 714-250-446
**WATSON, RICHARD JESSE/PO BOX 1470,
MURPHYS, CA (P 476)** — **209-728-270**
Watts, Stan/3896 San Marcus Ct, Newbury Park, CA — 805-499-474
Westlund Design Assoc/5410 Wilshire Blvd #503,
Los Angeles, CA — 213-938-521
Weston, Will/135 S LaBrea, Los Angeles, CA — 213-854-366
Wexler, Ed/4701 Don Pio Dr, Woodland Hills, CA — 818-888-385
Whidden Studios/11772 Sorrento Vlly Rd #260, San Diego, CA — 619-455-177
**WHITE, CHARLES WILLIAM/11543 HESBY ST,
NORTH HOLLYWOOD, CA (P 254)** — **818-985-353**
Wicks, Ren/5455 Wilshire Blvd #1212, Los Angeles, CA — 213-937-447
**WILLARDSON + ASSOC/103 W CALIFORNIA,
GLENDALE, CA (P 173)** — **818-242-568**
Williams, John A/1091 N Pershing #2, San Bernadino, CA — 714-885-71
Wilson, Dick/11607 Clover Ave, Los Angeles, CA — 213-828-968
Wilson, Rowland/33871 Calle Acordarse,
San Juan Capistrano, CA — 714-240-80
Wilson, Terry/2110 Orange, Costa Mesa, CA — 714-646-67
Winston-Davis, Jeannie/412 N Doheny Dr, Los Angeles, CA — 213-858-09
**WITUS, EDWARD/2932 WILSHIRE BLVD #202,
SANTA MONICA, CA (P 480)** — **213-828-65**
**WOLFE, BRUCE/206 EL CERRITO AVE,
PIEDMONT, CA (P 226,227)** — **415-655-78**
Wolfe, Corey/2120 W 240th St, Lomita, CA — 213-534-19
Wolin, Ron/3977 Oeste Ave, North Hollywood, CA — 818-984-07
Woodward, Teresa/544 Paseo Miramar, Pacific Palisades, CA — 213-459-23
Wright, Jonathan/1838 El Cerrito Pl #3, Hollywood, CA — 213-874-16

XYZ
Xavier, Roger/23200 Los Codona Ave, Torrance, CA — 213-375-16
Yamada, Jane/1243 Westerly Terr, Los Angeles, CA — 213-663-62
Yamada, Tony/1243 Westerly Terr, Los Angeles, CA — 213-663-62
Yenne, Bill/576 Sacramento, San Francisco, CA — 415-989-24
Yeomans, Jeff/820 Deal Ct #C, San Diego, CA — 619-488-25
Zaslavsky, Morris/228 Main St Studio 6, Venice, CA — 213-399-36
Zebot, George/PO Box 4295, Laguna Beach, CA — 714-499-50
**ZICK, BRIAN/3251 PRIMERA AVE,
LOS ANGELES, CA (P 175)** — **213-855-88**
Zippel, Arthur/2110 E McFadden #D, Santa Ana, CA — 714-835-84
Zito, Andy/135 S La Brea Ave, Los Angeles, CA — 213-931-11
Zitting, Joel/2404 Ocean Pk Blvd Ste A, Santa Monica, CA — 213-452-70

GRAPHIC DESIGNERS

NEW YORK CITY

A
AKM Associates	212-687-7636
Abramson, Michael R Studio	212-683-1271
Adams, Gaylord Design	212-684-4625
Album Graphics Inc	212-489-0793
Aliman, Elie	212-925-9621
Allied Graphic Arts	212-730-1414
American Express Publishing Co	212 382 5600
Anagraphics Inc	212-279-2370
Ancona Design Atelier	212-947-8287
Anspach Grossman Portugal	212-692-9000
Antler & Baldwin Graphics	212-751-2031
Antupit and Others Inc	212-686-2552
Appelbaum Company	212-752-0679
Apteryx Ltd	212-972-1396
Art Department	212-391-1826
The Art Farm Inc	212-688-4555
Art Plus Studio	212-564-8258
Associated Industrial Design Inc	212-624-0034
Athey, Diane	212-787-7415

B
BN Associates	212-682-3096
Balasas, Cora	718-633-7753
Bantam Books Inc	212-765-6500
Barmache, Leon Design Assoc Inc	212-752-6780
Barnett Design Group	212-677-8830
Barry, Jim	212-873-6787
Becker Hockfield Design Assoc	212-505-7050
Bell, James Graphic Design Inc	212-929-8855
Bellows, Amelia	212-777-7012
Berger, Barry David	212-734-4137
Besalel, Ely	212-759-7820
Bessen & Tully, Inc	212-838-6406
Binns, Betty Graphic Design	212-679-9200
Biondo, Charles Design Assoc	212-867-0760
Birch, Colin Assoc Inc	212-223-0499
Bloch, Graulich & Whelan, Inc	212-687-8375
Bloker Group	212-686-1132
Bonnell Design Associates Inc	212-921-5390
Bordnick & Assoc	212-563-1544
Botero, Samuel Assoc	212-935-5155
Bradbury Heston Ward Inc	212-308-4800
Bradford, Peter	212-982-2090
Branin, Max	212-254-9608
Braswell, Lynn	212-222-8761
Breth, Jill Marie	212-781-8370
Brochure People	212-696-9185
Brodsky Graphics	212-684-2600
Brown, Alastair Assoc	212-221-3166
Brown, Kim	212-567-5671
Buckley Designs Inc	212-861-0626
Burdick, Joshua Assoc Inc	212-696-4440
Burns, Tom Assoc Inc	212-594-9883
By Design	212-684-0388
The Byrne Group	212-889-0502

C
CCI Art Inc	212-687-1552
CAIN, DAVID (P 236)	**212-691-5783**
Cannan, Bill & Co Inc	212-563-1004
Caravello Studios	212-620-0620
Carnase, Inc	212-679-9880
Cetta, Al	212-989-9696
Chajet Design Group Inc	212-684-3669
Chang, Ivan	212-777-6102
Chapman, Sandra S	718-855-7396
Charles, Irene Assoc	212-765-8000
Chermayeff & Geismar Assoc.	212-532-4499
Chu, H L & Co Ltd	212-889-4818
Church, Wallace Assoc	212-755-2903
Ciffer, Jill	212-691-7013

Cohen, Norman Design	212-679-3906
Composto, Mario Assoc	212-682-3420
Condon, J & M Assoc	212-242-7811
Corchia Woliner Assoc	212-977-9778
Corpographics, Inc.	212-483-9065
Corporate Annual Reports Inc.	212-889-2450
Corporate Graphics Inc	212-599-1820
Cosgrove Assoc Inc	212-889-7202
Cotler, Sheldon Inc	212-719-9590
Cousins, Morison S & Assoc	212-751-3390
Crane, Eileen	212-644-3850
Crane, Susan Inc	212-260-0580
Csoka/Benato/Fleurant Inc	212-242-6777
Cuevas, Robert	212-661-7149
Curtis Design Inc.	212-685-0670

D
DMCD	212-682-9044
Daniel Design	212-889-0071
Danne & Blackburn Inc.	212-371-3250
Davis-Delaney-Arrow Inc	212-686-2500
DeHarak, Rudolph	212-929-5445
Delgado, Lisa	212-685-5925
Delphan Company	212-371-6700
DeMartin-Marona-Cranstoun-Downes	212-682-9044
Design Alliance	212-799-0095
Design Derivatives Inc	212-751-7650
Design Influence Inc	212-840-2155
Designframe	212-924-2426
The Designing Women	212-864-0909
Diamond Art Studio	212-685-6622
Diane Adzema	212-982-5657
DICKENS, HOLLY (P 17)	**212-682-1490**
DiComo, Charles & Assoc	212-689-8670
DiFranza Williamson Inc	212-832-2343
Dinand, Pierre Design	212-751-3086
DiSpigna, Tony	212-674-2674
Displaycraft	718-784-8186
Domino, Bob	212-935-0139
Donovan & Green Inc	212-755-0477
DORET, MICHAEL (P 322,323)	**212-929-1688**
Douglas, Barry Designs Ltd	212-734-4137
Drate, Spencer	212-620-4672
Dreyfuss, Henry Assoc	212-957-8600
Dubins, Milt Designer Inc	212-691-0232
Dubrow, Oscar Assoc	212-688-0698
Duffy, William R	212-682-6755
Dwyer, Tom	212-986-7108

E
Edelman Studios Inc	212-505-9020
Edge, Dennis Design	212-679-0927
Eichinger, Inc	212-421-0544
Eisenman and Enock	212-431-1000
Ellies, Dave Industrial Design Inc	212-679-9305
Emerson, Wajdowicz	212-807-8144
Environetics Inc	212-759-3830
Environment Planning Inc	212-661-3744
Erikson Assoc.	212-688-0048
Etc Graphics, Inc	212-889-8777
Etheridge, Palombo, Sedewitz	212-944-2530
Eucalyptus Tree Studio	212-226-0331

F
FDC Planning & Design Corp	212-355-7200
Failing, Kendrick G Design	212-677-5764
Falkins, Richard Design	212-840-3045
Farmlett Barsanti Inc	212-691-9398
Farrell, Bill	212-562-8931
Feucht, Fred Design Group Inc	212-682-0040
Filicori, Mauro Visual Communications	212-677-0065
Fineberg Associates	212-734-1220
Florville, Patrick Design Research	718-475-2278
Flying Eye Graphics	212-725-0658
Forman, Yale Designs Inc	212-799-1665

GRAPHIC DESIGNERS

FREEMAN, IRVING (P 339)	**212-674-6705**
Friday Saturday Sunday Inc	212-260-8479
Friedlandor, Ira	212-580-9800
Frye Assoc	212-986-5454
Fulgoni, Louis	212-243-2959
Fulton & Partners	212-695-1625
G GL & C Advertising Design Inc.	212-683-5811
GALE, CYNTHIA (P 341)	**212-860-5429**
Gale, Robert A Inc	212-535-4791
Gardner, Beau Assoc Inc	212-832-2426
Gatter Inc	212-687-4821
Gentile Studio	212-986-7743
George, Hershell	212-925-2505
Gerstman & Meyers Inc.	212-586-2535
Gianninoto Assoc, Inc.	212-759-5757
Giber, Lauren	212-473-2062
Giovanni Design Assoc.	212-725-8536
Gips & Balkind & Assoc	212-421-5940
Gladstein, Renee	212-873-0257
Gladych, Marianne	212-925-9712
Glaser, Milton	212-8C0-3161
Glusker Group	212-757-4438
Goetz Graphics	212-679-4250
Goldman, Neal Assoc	212-687-5058
Gorbaty, Norman Design	212-684-1665
Gorman, W Chris Assoc	212-696-9377
Graphic Art Resource Assoc	212-929-0017
The Graphic Expression Inc.	212-759-7788
Graphics 60 Inc.	212-687-1292
Graphics Institute	212-887-8670
Graphics by Nostradamus	212-581-1362
Graphics for Industry	212-889-6202
Graphics to Go	212-889-9337
Gray, George	212-873-3607
Green, Douglas	212-752-6284
Griffler Designs	212-794-2625
Grimmett, Douglas	212-777-1099
Grossberg, Manuel	212-620-0444
Grunfeld Graphics Ltd	212-431-8700
Gucciardo & Shapokas	212-683-9378
H H G Assoc Inc	212-221-3070
HBO Studio Productions Inc	212-477-8600
Haas, Arie	212-382-1677
Halle, Doris	212-321-2671
Halversen, Everett	718-438-4200
Handler Group Inc	212-391-0951
Harris-Gorbaty Assoc Inc	212-684-1665
Haydee Design Studio	212-242-3110
Hecker, Mark Studio	212-620-9050
Heimall, Bob Inc	212-245-4525
Heiney, John & Assoc	212-686-1121
Herbick, David	718-852-6450
Holden, Cynthia	212-222-4214
Holland, DK	212-789-3112
Holzsager, Mel Assoc Inc	212-741-7373
Hooper, Ray Design	212-924-5480
Hopkins, Will	212-580-9800
Horvath & Assoc Studios Ltd	212-741-0300
Hub Graphics	212-421-5807
Human Factors/Industrial Design Inc	212-730-8010
IJ IGC Graphics	212-689-5148
ISD Incorporated	212-751-0800
Image Communications Inc	212-807-9677
Infield & D'Astolfo	212-924-9206
Inkwell Inc	212-279-2066
Inner Thoughts	212-674-1277
Intersight Design Inc	212-696-0700
Jaffe Communications, Inc	212-697-4310
Johnson, Dwight	718-834-8529
Johnston, Shaun & Susan	212-663-4686
Jonson Pedersen Hinrichs & Shakery	212-889-9611
K KLN Publishing Services Inc	212-686-8200
Kacik Design	212-753-0031
Kaeser & Wilson Design	212-563-2455
Kahn, Al Group	212-580-3517
Kahn, Donald	212-889-8898
Kallir Phillips Ross Inc.	212-878-3700
Kass Communications	212-868-3133
Kass, Milton Assoc Inc	212-874-0418
Kaye Graphics	212-889-8240
Keithley & Assoc	212-807-8388
Kleb Associates	212-246-2841
Ko Noda and Assoc International	212-759-4044
Kollberg-Johnson Assoc Inc	212-686-3648
Koons, Irv Assoc	212-752-4130
L LCL Design Assoc Inc	212-758-2600
Lacy, N Lee	212-532-6200
Lake, John	212-644-3855
The Lamplight Group	212-682-6272
Landi-Rosiak Inc	212-661-3630
LEBBAD, JAMES A (P 375)	**212-679-2231**
Lee & Young Communications	212-689-4000
Lefkowith Inc.	212-758-8551
Leo Art Studio	212-736-8780
Lesley-Hille Inc	212-677-7571
Lester & Butler	212-889-0571
Levine, Gerald	212-986-1061
Levine, William V & Assoc	212-683-7171
Lichtenberg, Al Graphic Art	212-865-4311
Lieberman, Ron	212-947-0651
Liebert Studios Inc	212-686-4521
Lika Association	212-490-3661
Lind Brothers Inc	212-924-9281
Lippincott & Margulies Inc	212-832-3000
LITTLE APPLE ART (P 380)	**718-499-7045**
Lopez, Dick Inc	212-599-2332
Loukin, Serge Inc	212-255-5661
Lubliner/Saltz	212-679-9810
Luckett Slover & Partners	212-620-9710
Lukasiewicz Design Inc	212-581-3360
Lundgren, Ray Graphics	212-370-1620
Luth & Katz Inc	212-644-5710
M M & Co Design Group	212-243-0000
Maddalone, John	212-807-6016
Maggio, Ben Assoc Inc	212-697-8660
Maggio, J P Design Assoc Inc	212-725-9690
Maleter, Mari	718-726-7100
Mantel Koppel & Scher Inc	212-683-0800
Marchese, Frank	212-988-6200
Marciuliano Inc	212-697-0700
Marckrey Design Group Inc	212-475-2800
Marcus, Eric	718-789-1100
Marino, Guy Graphic Design	212-935-1100
Mauro, C L & Assoc Inc	212-868-3900
Mauro, Frank Assoc Inc	212-719-5500
Mayo-Infurna Design	212-888-7878
McDonald, B & Assoc	212-869-9700
McGhie Assoc Inc	212-661-2900
McGovern & Pivoda	212-840-2900
Meier Adv	212-355-6400
Mentkin, Robert	212-534-5100
Merrill, Abby Studio Inc	212-753-7575
The Midnight Oil	212-582-9000
Millenium Design	212-986-4500
The Miller Organization Inc	212-685-7770
Miller, Irving D Inc	212-755-4000
Mirenburg, Barry	718-885-0800
Mitchell, E M Inc	212-986-5500

Please send us your additions and updates.

Mizerek Design	212-900-5702
Modular Marketing Inc	212-581-4690
Mont, Howard Assoc Inc	212-683-4360
Montoya, Juan Design Corp	212-242-3622
Morris, Dean	212-420-0673
Moshier, Harry & Assoc	212-873-6130
Moskof & Assoc	212-333-2015
Mossberg, Stuart Design Assoc	212-873-6130
Muir, Cornelius, Moore	212-687-4055
Murro, A & Assoc Inc	212-691-4220
Murtha Desola Finsilver Fiore	212-832-4770
N N B Assoc Inc	212-684-8074
Nelson, George & Assoc Inc	212-777-4300
Nemser & Howard, Inc	212-832-9595
New American Graphics	212-532-3551
Newman, Harvey Assoc	212-391-8060
Nicholson Design	212-206-1530
Nightingale, Gordon	212-685-9263
NITZBURG, ANDREW (P 80)	**212-686-3514**
Nobart NY Inc	212-475-5522
Noneman & Noneman Design	212-473-4090
North, Charles W Studio	212-242-6300
Notovitz & Perrault Design Inc	212-686-3300
Novus Visual Communications Inc	212-689-2424
O Oak Tree Graphics Inc	212-398-9355
Offenhartz, Harvey Inc	212-751-3241
Ohlsson, Eskil Assoc Inc	212-758-4412
Ong & Assoc	212-355-4343
O'Reilly, Robert Graphic Studio	212-832-8992
Orlov, Christian	212-873-2381
Oz Communications Inc	212-686-8200
P Page Arbitrio Resen Ltd	212-421-8190
Pahmer, Hal	212-889-6202
Palladino, Tony	212-751-0068
Parshall, C A Inc	212-947-5971
Parsons School of Design	212-741-8900
Patel, Harish Design Assoc	212-686-7425
Pellegrini & Assoc	212-686-4481
Pencils Portfolio Inc	212-355-2468
Penpoint Studio Inc	212-243-5435
Penraat Jaap Assoc	212-873-4541
Performing Dogs	212-260-1880
Perlman, Richard Design	212-599-2380
Perlow, Paul	212-758-4358
Peters, Stan Assoc Inc	212-684-0315
Peterson Blythe & Cato	212-557-5566
Pettis, Valerie	212-683-7382
Plumb Design Group Inc	212-673-3490
Podob, Al	212-697-6643
Pop Shots Corporate Design	212-489-1070
Prendergast, J W & Assoc Inc	212-687-8805
Primary Design Group	212-219-1000
Profile Press Inc	212-736-2044
Projection Systems International	212-682-0995
PushPin Lubalin Peckolick	212-674-8080
R **QUON, MIKE DESIGN OFFICE (P 428)**	**212-226-6024**
RC Graphics	212-755-1383
RD Graphics	212-889-5612
Rafkin Rubin Inc	212-869-2540
Rapecis Assoc Inc	212-972-1775
Ratzkin, Lawrence	212-279-1314
Regn-Califano Inc	212-239-0380
Robinson, Mark	718-638-9067
Rogers, Ana	212-741-4687
Rogers, Richard Inc	212-685-3666
ROMERO, JAVIER (P 435)	**212-206-9175**
Rosenthal, Herb & Assoc Inc	212-685-1814
Ross Design Assoc Inc	212-206-0044

Ross/Pento Inc	212-757-5604
Royce Graphics	212-239-1990
Russell, Anthony Inc	212-255-0650
S SCR Design Organization	212-752-8496
Sabanosh, Michael	212-947-8161
Saiki Design	212-679-3523
Sakin, Sy	212-688-3141
Saks, Arnold	212-861-4300
Salisbury & Salisbury Inc	212-575-0770
Salpeter, Paganucci, Inc	212-683-3310
Saltzman, Mike Group	212-929-4655
Sandgren Associates Inc	212-679-4650
Sawyer, Arnie Studio	212-685-4927
Saxton Communications Group	212-953-1300
Say It In Neon	212-691-7977
Schaefer-Cassety Inc	212-840-0175
SchaefferBoehm, Ltd	212-947-4345
Schechter Group Inc	212-752-4400
Schecterson, Jack Assoc Inc	212-889-3950
Schumach, Michael P	718-445-1587
Schwartz, Robert & Assoc	212-689-6482
Scott, Louis Assoc	212-674-0215
Serge Loukin Inc	212-255-5651
Shapiro, Ellen Graphic Design	212-221-2625
Shareholder Graphics	212-661-1070
Shareholders Reports	212-686-9099
Sherin & Matejka Inc	212-686-8410
Sherowitz, Phyllis	212-532-8933
Shreeve, Draper Design	212-675-7534
Siegel & Gale Inc	212-730-0101
Silberlicht, Ira	212-595-6252
Silverman, Bob Design	212-371-6472
Singer, Paul Design	718-449-8172
SLOAN, WILLIAM (P 450)	**212-226-8110**
Smith, Edward Design	212-255-1717
SMITH, LAURA (P 322,323)	**212-206-9162**
Sochynsky, Ilona	212-686-1275
Solay/Hunt	212-840-3313
Sorvino, Skip	212-580-9638
St Vincent Milone & McConnells	212-921-1414
Stillman, Linda	212-410-3225
Stuart, Gunn & Furuta	212-689-0077
Studio 42	212-354-7298
The Sukon Group, Inc	212-986-2290
Swatek and Romanoff Design Inc	212-807-0236
Systems Collaborative Inc	212-608-0584
T Tapa Graphics	212-243-0176
Tauss, Jack George	212-279-1658
Taylor & Ives	212-244-0750
Taylor, Stan Inc	212-685-4741
Teague, Walter Dorwin Assoc	212-557-0920
Tercovich, Douglas Assoc Inc	212-838-4800
Theoharides Inc	212-838-7760
Thompson Communications	212-685-4400
Three	212-988-6267
Tobias, William	212-741-1712
Tower Graphics Arts Corp	212-421-0850
Tribich, Jay Design Assoc	212-679-6016
Tscherny, George Design	212-734-3277
Tunstull Studio	718-875-9356
Turner/Miller	212-371-3035
UV Ultra Arts Inc	212-679-7493
Vecchio, Carmine	212-683-2670
Viewpoint Graphics	212-685-0560
Vignelli Assoc.	212-593-1416
Visible Studio Inc	212-683-8530
Visual Accents Corp	212-777-7766
Visual Development Corp	212-532-3202

GRAPHIC DESIGNERS (side tab)

W

Wajdowicz, Jurek	212-807-8144
Waldman, Veronica	212-260-3552
Waters, John Assoc Inc	212-807-0717
Waters, Pamela Studio Inc	212-620-8100
Webster, Robert Inc	212-677-2966
Weed, Eunice Assoc Inc	212-725-4933
Weeks & Toomey	212-564-8260
Whelan Design Office	212-691-4404
The Whole Works	212-575-0765
Wijtvliet, Ine	212-684-4575
Wilke, Jerry	212-689-2424
Wilke/Davis Assoc Inc	212-532-5500
Withers, Bruce Graphic Design	212-599-2388
Wizard Graphics Inc	212-686-8200
Wolf, Henry Production Inc	212-472-2500
Wolff, Rudi Inc	212-873-5800
Wood, Alan	212-889-5195
Works	212-696-1666

YZ

Yoshimura-Fisher Graphic Design	212-431-4776
Young Goldman Young Inc	212-697-7820
Zazula, Hy Inc	212-581-2747
Zeitsoff, Elaine	212-580-1282
Zimmerman & Foyster	212-674-0259

NORTHEAST

A

Action Incentive/Rochester, NY	716-427-2410
Adam Filippo & Moran/Pittsburgh, PA	412-261-3720
Advertising Design Assoc Inc/Baltimore, MD	301-752-2181
Alber Associates/Philadelphia, PA	215-969-4293
Another Color Inc/Washington, DC	202-328-1414
Aries Graphics/Manchester, NH	603-668-0811
Art Service Assoc Inc/Pittsburgh, PA	412-391-0902
Art Services Inc/Washington, DC	202-526-5607
Art Staff & Co/Potomac, MD	301-983-0531
The Artery/Baltimore, MD	301-752-2979
Arts and Words/Washington, DC	202-463-4880
Artwork Unlimited Inc/Washington, DC	202-638-6996
Autograph/Annapolis, MD	301-268-3300
The Avit Corp/Fort Lee, NJ	201-886-1100

B

Bain, S Milo/Hartsdale, NY	914-946-0144
Bally Design Inc/Carnegie, PA	412-276-5454
Banks & Co/Boston, MA	617-262-0020
Barancik, Bob/Philadelphia, PA	215-893-9149
Barton-Gillet/Baltimore, MD	301-685-3626
Bedford Photo-Graphic Studio/Bedford, NY	914-234-3123
Belser, Burkey/Washington, DC	202-462-1482
Bennardo, Churik Design Inc/Pittsburgh, PA	412-963-0133
Berns & Kay Ltd/Washington, DC	202-387-7032
Beveridge and Associates, Inc/Washington, DC	202-337-0400
Blum, William Assoc/Boston, MA	617-232-1166
Bogus, Sidney A & Assoc/Melrose, MA	617-662-6660
Bomzer Design Inc/Boston, MA	617-227-5151
Bookmakers/Westport, CT	203-226-4293
Booth, Margot/Washington, DC	202-244-0412
Boscobel Advertising, Inc/Laurel, MD	301-953-2600
Boulanger Associates Inc/Armonk, NY	914-273-5571
Bradick Design & Methods Inc/Guys Mills, PA	814-967-2332
Brady, John Design Consultants/Pittsburgh, PA	412-227-9300
Breckenridge Designs/Washington, DC	202-833-5700
Bressler, Peter Design Assoc/Philadelphia, PA	215-925-7100
Bridy, Dan/Pittsburgh, PA	412-288-9362
Brier, David/E Rutherford, NJ	201-896-8476
Brown and Craig Inc/Baltimore, MD	301-837-2727
Buckett, Bill Assoc/Rochester, NY	716-546-6580
Burke & Michael Inc/Pittsburgh, PA	412-321-2301
Byrne, Ford/Philadelphia, PA	215-564-0500

C

Cable, Jerry Design/Madison, NJ	201-966-012●
Cabot, Harold & Co Inc/Boston, MA	617-426-760●
Calingo, Diane/Kensington, MD	301-949-355●
Cameron Inc/Boston, MA	617-338-440●
Captain Graphics/Boston, MA	617-367-100●
Carlson, Tim/Brookline, MA	617-566-733●
Carmel, Abraham/Peekskill, NY	914-737-143●
Case/Washington, DC	202-328-590●
Casey Mease Inc/Wilmington, DE	302-655-210●
Chaparos Productions Limited/Washington, DC	202-289-483●
Charysyn & Charysyn/Westkill, NY	518-989-672●
Chase, David O Design Inc/Skaneateles, NY	315-685-571●
Chronicle Type & Design/Washington, DC	202-828-351●
Clark, Dave/Riva, MD	301-956-416●
Coblyn & Schillig/Washington, DC	202-363-192●
Colopy Dale Inc/Pittsburgh, PA	412-332-670●
Communications Graphics Group/Rockville, MD	301-279-915●
Concept Packaging Inc/Ft Lee, NJ	201-224-576●
Consolidated Visual Center Inc/Tuxedo, MD	301-772-730●
Cook & Shanosky Assoc/Princeton, NJ	609-921-020●
Creative Communications Center/Pennsauken, NJ	609-665-205●
The Creative Dept/Philadelphia, PA	215-988-039●
Creative Presentations Inc/Washington, DC	202-737-715●
Crozier, Bob & Assoc/Washington, DC	202-638-713●
Curran & Connors Inc/Jericho, NY	516-433-660●

D

D J C Design Assoc/Washington, DC	202-965-604●
Dakota Design/King of Prussia, PA	215-265-125●
Dale, Terry/Washington, DC	202-244-386●
Daroff Design Inc/Philadelphia, PA	215-636-990●
D'Art Studio Inc/Boston, MA	617-482-444●
Dawson Designers Associates/Assonet, MA	617-644-294●
DeCesare, John/Darien, CT	203-655-605●
DeMartin-Marona-Cranstoun-Downes/Wilmington, DE	302-654-527●
Design Associates/Arlington, VA	703-243-771●
Design Center Inc/Boston, MA	617-542-125●
Design Communication Collaboration/Washington, DC	202-833-908●
Design Communications/Bethesda, MD	301-986-887●
Design Group of Boston/Boston, MA	617-437-108●
Design Technology Corp/Billerica, MA	617-272-889●
Design Trends/Valhalla, NY	914-948-090●
Design for Medicine Inc/Philadelphia, PA	215-925-710●
Designworks Inc/Watertown, MA	617-926-628●
DiFiore Associates/Pittsburgh, PA	412-471-060●
Dimensional Design & Fabrication/Rochester, NY	716-473-170●
Dimmick, Gary/Pittsburgh, PA	412-321-722●
Dohanos, Steven/Westport, CT	203-227-354●
Downing, Allan/Needham, MA	617-449-478●
Drafting and Design Studio/Columbia, MD	301-730-559●
Duffy, Bill & Assoc/Washington, DC	202-965-221●

E

Edigraph Inc/Katonah, NY	914-232-37●
Educational Media/Graphics Division/Washington, DC	202-625-22●
Egress Concepts/Katonah, NY	914-232-84●
Environetics DC Inc/Washington, DC	202-466-71●
Erickson, Peter/Maynard, MA	617-897-64●
Eucalyptus Tree Studio/Baltimore, MD	301-243-02●
Evans Garber & Paige/Utica, NY	315-733-23●
Evans, Timothy Graphics/Washington, DC	202-293-02●

F

Fader Jones & Zarkades/Boston, MA	617-267-77●
Falcone & Assoc/Chatham, NJ	201-635-29●
Fall, Dorothy Graphic Design/Washington, DC	202-338-20●
Fannell Studio/Boston, MA	617-267-08●
Fitzpatrick & Associates/Silver Springs, MD	301-946-46●
Forum Inc/Fairfield, CT	203-259-56●
Fossella, Gregory Assoc/Boston, MA	617-267-49●
Fowler, Cynthia/Silver Spring, MD	301-445-12●
Fraser, Robert & Assoc Inc/Baltimore, MD	301-685-37●
Fresh Produce/Lutherville, MD	301-821-18●
Friday Design Group Inc/Washington, DC	202-965-96●

Please send us your additions and updates.

Froelich Advertising Service/Mahwah, NJ	201-529-1707

G

Galasso, Gene Assoc Inc/Silver Spring, MD	202-439-1282
Gasser, Gene/Chatham, NJ	201-635-6020
Gateway Studios/Pittsburgh, PA	412-471-7224
Glass, Al/Washington, DC	202-333-3993
Glickman, Frank Inc/Boston, MA	617-524-2200
Glidden, Thea & Assoc/Baltimore, MD	301-523-5903
Good, Peter Graphic Design/Chester, CT	203-526-9597
Graham Associates Inc/Washington, DC	202-833-9057
Grant Marketing Assoc./Conshohocken, PA	215-834-0550
The Graphic Suite/Pittsburgh, PA	412-661-6699
Graphic Workshop/Emerson, NJ	201-967-8500
Graphicenter/Washington, DC	202-544-0333
Graphics By Gallo/Washington, DC	202-234-7700
Graphics Plus Corp/St Malden, MA	617-321-7500
Graphicus Corp/Baltimore, MD	301-727-5553
Grear, Malcolm Designers Inc/Providence, RI	401-331-5656
Greenfield, Peggy/Foxboro, MA	617-543-6644
Gregory & Clyburne/New Canaan, CT	203-966-8343
Groff, Jay Michael/Silver Spring, MD	301-565-0431
Groff-Long Associates/Bethesda, MD	301-654-0279
Group Four Inc/Avon, CT	203-678-1570

H

Hain, Robert Assoc/Scotch Plains, NJ	201-322-1717
Hammond Design Assoc/Milford, NH	603-673-5253
Harrington-Jackson/Boston, MA	617-536-6164
Harvey, Ed/Washington, DC	703-671-0880
Hegemann Associates/Nyack, NY	914-358-7348
Herbick & Held/Pittsburgh, PA	412-321-7400
Herbst Lazar Rogers & Bell Inc/Lancaster, PA	717-291-9042
Herman & Lees/Cambridge, MA	617-876-6463
Hillmuth, James/Washington, DC	202-244-0465
Holl, RJ/ Art Directions/Wales, MA	413-267-5024
Holloway, Martin/Springfield, NJ	201-376-6737
Hough, Jack Inc/Norwalk, CT	203-846-2666
The Hoyt Group/Waldwick, NJ	201-652-6300
Hrivnak, James/Silver Spring, MD	301-681-9090
HUERTA, GERARD/DARIEN, CT (P 239)	**203-656-0505**
Huyysen, Roger/Darien, CT	203-656-0200

J

Image Consultants/Burlington, MA	617-273-1010
Innovations & Development Inc/Ft Lee, NJ	201-944-9317
Irish Graphics/Boston, MA	617-247-4168
Jain, Marcel/Visual Concepts/Greenwich, CT	203-869-1928
Jaeger Design Studio/Washington, DC	202-785-8434
Jarrin Design Inc/Pound Ridge, NY	914-764-4625
Jensen, R S/Baltimore, MD	301-727-3411
Johnson & Simpson Graphic Design/Newark, NJ	201-624-7788
Johnson Design Assoc/Acton, MA	617-263-5345
Johnson, Charlotte/Washington, DC	202-544-7936
Jones, Tom & Jane Kearns/Washington, DC	202-232-1921

K

KBH Graphics/Baltimore, MD	301-539-7916
Kahana Associates/Jenkintown, PA	215-887-0422
Katz-Wheeler Design/Philadelphia, PA	215-567-5668
Kaufman, Henry J & Assoc Inc/Washington, DC	202-333-0700
Keaton Design/Washington, DC	202-547-4422
Kell & Chaddick/Silver Spring, MD	202-585-4000
Ketchum International/Pittsburgh, PA	412-456-3693
King-Casey Inc/New Canaan, CT	203-966-3581
Kim, Matt & Assoc/Avon, CT	203-678-1222
Klotz, Don/Wilton, CT	203-762-9111
Knox, Harry & Assoc/Washington, DC	202-833-2305
Kostanecki, Andrew Inc/New Canaan, CT	203-966-1681
Kovanen, Erik/Wilton, CT	203-762-8961
Kramer/Miller/Lomden/Glossman/Philadelphia, PA	215-545-7077
Krohne, David/Washington, DC	202-265-2371
Krone Graphic Design/Lemoyne, PA	717-774-7431

L

LAM Design Inc/White Plains, NY	914-948-4777
LaGrone, Roy/Somerset, NJ	201-463-4515
Landoroman, Myra/Malaga, NJ	609-694-1011
Langdon, John/Wenonah, NJ	609-468-7868
Lange, Erwin G/Wenonah, NJ	609-468-7868
Lapham/Miller Assoc/Andora, MA	617-367-0110
Latham Brefka Associates/Boston, MA	617-536-8787
Lausch, David Graphics/Baltimore, MD	301-235-7453
Lebowitz, Mo/N Bellemore, NY	516-826-3397
Leeds, Judith K Studio/West Caldwell, NJ	201-226-3552
Lenney, Ann/Washington, DC	202-667-1786
Leotta Designers Inc/Conshohocken, PA	215-828-8820
Lester Associates Inc/West Nyack, NY	914-358-6100
Levinson Zaprauskis Assoc/Philadelphia, PA	215-248-5242
Lewis, Hal Design/Philadelphia, PA	215-563-4461
Lion Hill Studio/Baltimore, MD	301-837-6218
Lizak, Matt/N Smithfield, RI	401-766-8885
Lussier, Mark/E Norwalk, CT	203-852-0363

M

M&M Graphics/Baltimore, MD	301-747-4555
MDB Communications Inc/Rockville, MD	301-279-9093
MacIntosh, Rob Communication/Boston, MA	617-267-4912
Macey Noyes Inc/Stanford, CT	914-941-7120
Maglio, Mark/Plainville, CT	203-793-0771
Mahoney, Ron/Pittsburgh, PA	412-261-3824
Major Assoc/Baltimore, MD	301-752-6174
Mandala/Philadelphia, PA	215-923-6020
Marcus, Sarna/Amazing Graphic Design/Bethesda, MD	301-951-7044
Mariuzza, Pete/Briarcliff Manor, NY	914-769-3310
Martucci Studio/Boston, MA	617-266-6960
Mason, Kim/Washington, DC	202-646-0118
Media Concepts/Boston, MA	617-437-1382
Media Loft/Minneapolis, MN	612-831-0226
Melanson, Donya Assoc/Boston, MA	617-482-0421
Micolucci, Nicholas Assoc/King of Prussia, PA	215-265-3320
Miho, J Inc/Redding, CT	203-938-3214
Milcraft/Annandale, NJ	201-735-8632
Mitchell & Company/Washington, DC	202-342-6025
Mitchell & Webb Inc/Boston, MA	617-262-6980
Morlock Graphics/Tuson, MD	301-825-5080
Moss, John C/Chevy Chase, MD	301-320-3912
Mossman Art Studio/Baltimore, MD	301-243-1963
Mueller & Wister/Philadelphia, PA	215-568-7260
Muller-Munk, Peter Assoc/Pittsburgh, PA	412-261-5161
Myers, Gene Assoc/Pittsburgh, PA	412-661-6314

NO

Nason Design Assoc/Boston, MA	617-266-7286
National Photo Service/Fort Lee, NJ	212-860-2324
Navratil Art Studio/Pittsburgh, PA	412-471-4322
Nimeck, Fran/South Brunswick, NJ	201-821-8741
Nolan & Assoc/Washington, DC	202-363-6553
North Charles Street Design Org./Baltimore, MD	301-539-4040
Odyssey Design Group/Washington, DC	202-783-6240
Ollio Studio/Pittsburgh, PA	412-281-4483
Omnigraphics/Cambridge, MA	617-354-7444
On Target/Riverside, CT	203-637-8300
One Harvard Sq Design Assoc/Cambridge, MA	617-876-9673

P

Paganucci, Bob/Montvale, NJ	201-391-1752
Paine/ Bluett/ Paine Inc/Bethesda, MD	301-493-8445
Paragraphics Inc./White Plains, NY	914-948-4777
Parks, Franz & Cox, Inc/Washington, DC	202-797-7568
Parry, Ivor A/Eastchester, NY	914-961-7338
Pasinski, Irene Assoc/Pittsburgh, PA	412-683-0585
Patazian Design Inc/Boston, MA	617-262-7848
Peck, Gail M/Washington, DC	202-667-7448
Perspectives In Communications/Washington, DC	202-667-7448
Pesanelli, David Assoc/Washington, DC	202-363-4760
Petty, Daphne/Washington, DC	202-667-8222
Phillips Design Assoc/Boston, MA	617-787-5757
Picture That Inc/Newtown Square, PA	215-353-8833
Planert, Paul Design Assoc/Pittsburgh, PA	412-621-1275
Plataz, George/Pittsburgh, PA	412-322-3177
Plumridge Artworks/Bethesda, MD	301-530-9624

Porter, Al/Graphics Inc/Washington, DC	202-244-0403
Prelude to Print/Rockville, MD	301-984-1488
Presentation Associates/Washington, DC	202-333-0080
Prestige Marking & Coating Co/Stamford, CT	203-329-0384
Production Studio/Port Washington, NY	516-944-6688
Publication Services Inc/Stamford, CT	203-348-7351

R
RKM Inc/Washington, DC	202-364-0148
RSV/Boston, MA	617-262-9450
RZA Inc/Westwood, NJ	201-664-4543
Ralcon Inc/West Chester, PA	215-692-2840
Rand, Paul Inc/Weston, CT	203-227-5375
Redtree Associates/Washington, DC	202-628-2900
Research Planning Assoc/Philadelphia, PA	215-561-9700
Rieb, Robert/Westport, CT	203-227-0061
Ringel, Leonard Lee Graphic Design/Kendall Park, NJ	201-297-9084
Rinnisana Communications/Silver Spring, MD	301-587-1505
Ritter, Richard Design Inc/Berwyn, PA	215-296-0400
Romax Studio/Stamford, CT	203-324-4260
Rosborg Inc/Newton, CT	203-426-3171
Roth, J H Inc/Peekskill, NY	914-737-6784
Rubin, Marc Design Assoc/Breesport, NY	607-739-0871
Rule-Master Design/Englewood, NJ	201-567-4265

S
Sanchez/Philadelphia, PA	215-564-2223
Schneider Design/Baltimore, MD	301-467-2611
Schoenfeld, Cal/Fairfield, NJ	201-575-7335
Schwartz, Adler Graphics Inc/Baltimore, MD	301-433-4400
Selame Design Associates/Newton Lower Falls, MA	617-969-6690
Shapiro, Deborah/Jersey City, NJ	201-432-5198
Simpson Booth Designers/Cambridge, MA	617-661-2630
Smarilli Graphics Inc/Mechanicsburg, PA	717-697-8094
Smith, Agnew Moyer/Pittsburgh, PA	412-322-6333
Smith, Doug/Larchmont, NY	914-834-3997
Smith, Gail Hunter/Barnegat Light, NJ	609-494-9136
Smith, Tyler Art Direction/Providence, RI	401-751-1220
Snowden Associates Inc/Washington, DC	202-362-8944
Sparkman & Bartholomew/Washington, DC	202-785-2414
Stansbury Ronsaville Wood Inc/Annapolis, MD	301-261-2046
Star Design Inc/Moorestown, NJ	609-235-8150
Steel Art Co Inc/Allston, MA	617-566-4079
Stettler, Wayne Design/Philadelphia, PA	215-235-1230
Stockman & Andrews Inc/E Providence, RI	401-438-0694
Stolt, Jill Design/Rochester, NY	716-461-2594
Stuart, Neil/Mahopac, NY	914-618-1662
The Studio Group/Washington, DC	202-332-3003
Studio Six Design/Springfield, NJ	201-379-5820
Studio Three/Philadelphia, PA	215-665-0141

T
Takajian, Asdur/N Tarrytown, NY	914-631-5553
Taylor, Pat/Washington, DC	202-338-0962
Telesis/Baltimore, MD	301-235-2000
Tetrad Inc/Annapolis, MD	301-268-8680
Thompson, Bradbury/Riverside, CT	203-637-3614
Thompson, George L/Reading, MA	617-944-6256
TOELKE, CATHLEEN/BOSTON, MA (P 61)	**617-266-8790**
Torode, Barbara/Philadelphia, PA	215-732-6792
Town Studios Inc/Pittsburgh, PA	412-471-5353
Troller, Fred Assoc Inc/Rye, NY	914-698-1405

V
Van Der Sluys Graphics Inc/Washington, DC	202-265-3443
VanDine, Horton, McNamara, Manges Inc/Pittsburgh, PA	412-261-4280
Vance Wright Adams & Assoc/Pittsburgh, PA	412-322-1800
Vinick, Bernard Assoc Inc/Hartford, CT	203-525-4293
Viscom Inc/Baltimore, MD	301-764-0005
Visual Research & Design Corp/Boston, MA	617-536-2111
The Visualizers/Pittsburgh, PA	412-488-0944

W
Warkulwiz Design/Philadelphia, PA	215-546-0880
Wasserman's, Myron Graphic Design Group/Philadelphia, PA	215-922-4545
Weadock, Rutka/Baltimore, MD	301-563-2100
Weitzman & Assoc/Bethesda, MD	301-652-7035
Weymouth Design/Boston, MA	617-542-2647
White, E James Co/Alexandria, VA	703-750-3680
Wickham & Assoc Inc/Washington, DC	202-296-4866
Wilke, Jerry Design/Croton-On-Hudson, NY	914-271-6760
Willard, Janet Design Assoc/Allison Park, PA	412-486-8100
Williams Associates/Lynnfield, MA	617-599-1818
Wilsonwork Graphic Design/Washington, DC	202-332-9010
Wright, Kent M Assoc Inc/Sudbury, MA	617-443-9900

YZ
Yeo, Robert/Hoboken, NJ	201-659-327
Yurdin, Carl Industrial Design Inc/Port Washington, NY	516-944-781
Zeb Graphics/Washington, DC	202-293-168
Zmiejko & Assoc Design Agcy/Freeland, PA	717-636-230

SOUTHEAST

A
Ace Art/New Orleans, LA	504-861-2222
Alphabet Group/Atlanta, GA	404-892-6500
Alphacom Inc/N Miami, FL	305-949-5588
Anderson & Santa Inc/Ft Lauderdale, FL	305-561-055
Art Services/Atlanta, GA	404-892-2105
Arts & Graphics/Annandale, VA	703-941-2560
Arunski, Joe & Assoc/Miami, FL	305-387-2130
The Associates Inc/Arlington, VA	703-534-3940
Aurelio & Friends Inc/Miami, FL	305-385-072

B
Baskin & Assoc/Alexandria, VA	703-836-331
Bender, Diane/Arlington, VA	703-521-1000
Blair Incorporated/Bailey's Crossroads, VA	703-820-901
Bodenhamer, William S Inc/Miami, FL	305-253-9284
Bonner Advertising Art/New Orleans, LA	504-895-7930
Bono Mitchell Graphics/Arlington, VA	703-276-061
Bowles, Aaron/Reston, VA	703-471-4010
Brimm, Edward & Assoc/Palm Beach, FL	305-655-1050
Brothers Bogusky/Miami, FL	305-891-3643
Bugdal Group/Miami, FL	305-264-186
Burch, Dan Associates/Louisville, KY	502-895-488

C
Carlson Design/Gainesville, FL	904-373-315
Chartmasters Inc/Atlanta, GA	404-262-761
Communications Graphics Inc/Atlanta, GA	404-231-903
Cooper-Copeland Inc/Atlanta, GA	404-892-347
Creative Design Assoc/Lake Park, FL	305-845-612
Creative Services Inc/New Orleans, LA	504-943-084
Creative Services Unlimited/Naples, FL	813-262-020
Creative Technologies Inc/Annandale, VA	703-256-744

DEF
Design Consultants Inc/Falls Church, VA	703-241-232
Design Inc/Fairfax, VA	703-273-505
Design Workshop Inc/Miami, FL	305-884-630
Designcomp/Vienna, VA	703-938-182
Emig, Paul E/Arlington, VA	703-522-592
First Impressions/Tampa, FL	813-224-045
Foster, Kim A/Miami, FL	305-642-180
From Us Advertising & Design/Atlanta, GA	404-373-037

G
Garrett Lewis Johnson/Atlanta, GA	404-221-070
Gerbino Advertising Inc/Ft Lauderdale, FL	305-776-505
Gestalt Associates, Inc/Alexandria, VA	703-683-112
Get Graphic Inc/Vienna, VA	202-938-182
Graphic Arts Inc/Alexandria, VA	703-683-430
Graphic Consultants Inc/Arlington, VA	703-536-837
Graphics 4/Ft Lauderdale, FL	305-764-147
Graphics Associates/Atlanta, GA	404-873-585
Graphics Group/Atlanta, GA	404-391-992
Graphicstudio/N Miami, FL	305-893-101
Great Incorporated/Alexandria, VA	703-836-602
Gregg, Bill Advertising Design/Miami, FL	305-854-765
Group 2 Atlanta/Atlanta, GA	404-355-319

GRAPHIC DESIGNERS

Please send us your additions and updates.

H		
Haikalis, Stephanie/Alexandria, VA	703-998-8695	
Hall Graphics/Coral Gables, FL	305-443-8346	
Hall, Stephen Design Office/Louisville, KY	502-584-5030	
Hannau, Michael Ent. Inc/Hialeah, FL	305-887-1536	
Hauser, Sydney/Sarasota, FL	813-388-3021	
Helms, John Graphic Design/Memphis, TN	901-363-6589	

IJK		
Identitia Incorporated/Tampa, Fl	813-221-3326	
Jensen, Ruport & Assoc Inc/Atlanta, GA	404-092-0650	
Johnson Design Group Inc/Arlington, VA	703-525-0808	
Jordan Barrett & Assoc/Miami, FL	305-667-7051	
Kelly & Co Graphic Design Inc/St Petersburg, FL	813-327-1009	
Kjeldsen, Howard Assoc Inc/Atlanta, GA	404-266-1897	
Klickovich Graphics/Louisville, KY	502-459-0295	

LM		
Lowell, Shelley Design/Atlanta, GA	404-636-9149	
Mabrey Design/Sarasota, FL	813-957-1063	
Marks, David/Atlanta, GA	404-872-1824	
Maxine, J & Martin Advertising/McLean, VA	703-356-5222	
McGurren Weber Ink/Alexandria, VA	703-548-0003	
MediaFour Inc/Falls Church, VA	703-573-6117	
Michael, Richard S/Knoxville, TN	615-584-3319	
Miller, Hugh K/Orlando, FL	305-293-8220	
Moore, William 'Casey'/Duluth, GA	404-449-9553	
Morgan-Burchette Assoc/Alexandria, VA	703-549-2393	
Morris, Robert Assoc Inc/Ft Lauderdale, FL	305-973-4380	
Muhlhausen, John Design Inc/Atlanta, GA	404-393-0743	

P		
PL&P Advertising Studio/Ft Lauderdale, FL	305-776-6505	
PRB Design Studio/Winter Park, FL	305-671-7992	
Parallel Group Inc/Atlanta, GA	404-261-0988	
Pertuit, Jim & Assoc Inc/New Orleans, LA	504-568-0808	
Platt, Don Advertising Art/Hialeah, FL	305-888-3296	
Point 6/Ft Lauderdale, FL	305-563-6939	
Polizos, Arthur Assoc/Norfolk, VA	804-622-7033	
Positively Main St Graphics/Sarasota, FL	813-366-4959	
Pre-Press Studio Design/Alexandria, VA	703-548-9194	
Prep Inc/Arlington, VA	703-979-6575	
Price Weber Market Comm Inc/Louisville, KY	502-499-9220	
Promotion Graphics Inc/N Miami, FL	305-891-3941	

QR		
Quantum Communications/Arlington, VA	703-841-1400	
Rasor & Rasor/Cary, NC	919-467-3353	
Rebeiz, Kathryn Dereki/Vienna, VA	703-938-9779	
Reinsch, Michael/Hilton Head Island, SC	803-842-3298	
Revelations Studios, Inc./Orlando, Fl	305-896-4240	
Rodriguez, Emilio Jr/Miami, FL	305-235-4700	

S		
Sager Assoc Inc/Sarasota, FL	813-366-4192	
Salmon, Paul/Burke, VA	703-250-4943	
Schulwolf, Frank/Coral Gables, FL	305-665-2129	
Seay, Jack Design Group/Norcross, GA	404-447-4840	
Showcraft Designworks/Clearwater, FL	813-586-0061	
Sirrine, J E/Greenville, SC	803-298-6000	
Supertype/Hialeah, FL	305-885-6241	

TUV		
Tash, Ken/Falls Church, VA	703-237-1712	
Thayer Dana Industrial Design/Monroe, VA	804-929-6359	
Thomas, Steve Design/Charlotte, NC	704-332-4624	
Turpin Design Assoc./Atlanta, GA	404-320-6963	
Unique Communications/Herndon, VA	703-471-1406	
Varisco, Tom Graphic Design Inc/New Orleans, LA	504-949-2888	
Visualgraphics Design/Tampa, FL	813-877-3804	

W		
Walton & Hoke/Falls Church, VA	703-538-5727	
Wells Squire Assoc Inc/Ft Lauderdale, FL	305-763-8063	
Whitver, Harry K Graphic Design/Nashville, TN	615-320-1795	
Winner, Stewart Inc/Louisville, KY	502-583-5502	
Wood, Tom/Atlanta, GA	404-262-7424	
The Workshop Inc/Atlanta, GA	404-875-0141	

MIDWEST

A		
Aarons, Allan Design/Northbrook, IL	312-291-9800	
Ades, Leonards Graphic Design/Northbrook, IL	312-564-8863	
Advertising Art Studios Inc/Milwaukee, WI	414-276-6306	
Album Graphics/Melrose Park, IL	312-344-9100	
Allied Design Group/Chicago, IL	312-743-3330	
Anderson Studios/Chicago, IL	312-922-3039	
Anderson, I K Studios/Chicago, IL	312-664-4536	
Architectural Signing/Chicago, IL	312-871-0100	
Art Forms Inc/Cleveland, OH	216-361-3855	
Arvind Khatkate Design/Chicago, IL	312-337-1478	

B		
Babcock & Schmid Assoc/Bath, OH	216-666-8826	
Bagby Design/Chicago, IL	312-861-1288	
Bal Graphics Inc/Chicago, IL	312-337-0325	
Bali Design Ltd/Chicago, IL	312-642-6134	
Banka Mango Design Inc/Chicago, IL	312-467-0059	
Bartels & Cartsens/St Louis, MO	314-781-4350	
Beda Ross Design/Chicago, IL	312-944-2332	
Benjamin, Burton E Assoc/Highland Park, IL	312-432-8089	
Berg, Don/Milwaukee, WI	414-276-7828	
Bieger, Walter Assoc/Arden Hills, MN	612-636-8500	
Blake, Hayward & Co/Evanston, IL	312-864-9800	
Blau-Bishop & Assoc/Chicago, IL	312-321-1420	
Boelter Industries Inc/Minneapolis, MN	612-831-5338	
Boller-Coates-Spadero/Chicago, IL	312-787-2798	
Bowlby, Joseph A/Chicago, IL	312-922-0890	
Bradford-Cout Graphic Design/Skokie, IL	312-539-5557	
Brooks Stevens Assoc Inc/Mequon, WI	414-241-3800	
Busch, Lonnie/Fenton, MO	314-343-1330	

C		
CMO Graphics/Chicago, IL	312-527-0900	
Campbell Art Studio/Cincinnati, OH	513-221-3600	
Campbell Creative Group Inc/Milwaukee, WI	414-351-4150	
Carter, Don W/ Industrial Design/Kansas City, MO	816-356-1874	
Centaur Studios Inc/St Louis, MO	314-421-6485	
Chartmasters Inc/Chicago, IL	312-787-9040	
Chestnut House/Chicago, IL	312-822-9090	
Claudia Janah Designs Inc/Chicago, IL	312-726-4560	
Clifford, Keesler/Kalamazoo, MI	616-375-0688	
Combined Services Inc/Minneapolis, MN	612-339-7770	
Container Corp of America/Chicago, IL	312-580-5500	
Contours Consulting Design Group/Bartlett, IL	312-837-4100	
Coons/Beirise Design Associate/Cincinnati, OH	513-751-7459	

D		
Day, David Design & Assoc/Cincinnati, OH	513-621-4060	
DeBrey Design/Minneapolis, MN	612-935-2292	
DeGoede & Others/Chicago, IL	312-951-6066	
Dektas Eger Inc/Cincinnati, OH	513-621-7070	
Design Alliance Inc/Cincinnati, OH	513-621-9373	
Design Consultants/Chicago, IL	312-642-4670	
Design Factory/Overland Park, KS	913-383-3085	
The Design Group/Madison, WI	608-274-5393	
Design Group Three/Chicago, IL	312-337-1775	
Design Mark Inc/Indianapolis, IN	317-872-3000	
Design Marks Corp/Chicago, IL	312-327-3669	
Design North Inc/Racine, WI	414-639-2080	
The Design Partnership/Minneapolis, MN	612-338-8889	
Design Planning Group/Chicago, IL	312-943-8400	
Design Train/Cincinnati, OH	513-761-7099	
Design Two Ltd/Chicago, IL	312-642-9888	
Dezign House III/Cleveland, OH	216-621-7777	
Di Cristo & Slagle Design/Milwaukee, WI	414-273-0980	
Dickens Design Group/Chicago, IL	312-222-1850	
DICKENS, HOLLY/CHICAGO, IL (P 17)	**312-346-1777**	
Dimensional Designs Inc/Indianapolis, IN	317-637-1353	
Doty, David Design/Chicago, IL	312-348-1200	
Dresser, John Design/Libertyville, IL	312-362-4222	
Dynamic Graphics Inc/Peoria, IL	309-688-9800	

Please send us your additions and updates.

E

Eaton and Associates/Minneapolis, MN	612-871-1028
Egger/Assoc Inc/Park Ridge, IL	312-296-9100
Ellies, Dave IndustrialDesign Inc/Columbus, OH	614-488-7995
Elyria Graphics/Elyria, OH	216-365-9384
Emphasis 7 Communications/Chicago, IL	312-951-8887
Engelhardt Design/Minneapolis, MN	612-377-3389
Environmental Graphics Inc/Indianapolis, IN	317-634-1458
Epstein & Assoc/Cleveland, OH	216-421-1600
Eurographics/Chicago, IL	312-951-5110

F

Falk, Robert Design Group/St Louis, MO	314-531-1410
Feldkamp-Malloy/Chicago, IL	312-263-0633
Ficho & Corley Inc/Chicago, IL	312-787-1011
Final Draft Graphic Art/Cleveland, OH	216-861-3735
Fleishman-Hillard, Inc/St Louis, MO	314-982-1700
Fleming Design Office/Minneapolis, MN	612-830-0099
Flexo Design/Chicago, IL	312-321-1368
Ford & Earl Assoc Inc/Warren, MI	313-536-1999
Forsythe-French Inc/Kansas City, MO	816-561-6678
Frederiksen Design/Villa Park, IL	312-343-5882
Frink, Chin, Casey Inc/Minneapolis, MN	612-333-6539

G

Gellman, Stan Graphic Design Studio/St Louis, MO	314-361-7676
Gerhardt and Clements/Chicago, IL	312-337-3443
Glenbard Graphics Inc/Carol Stream, IL	312-653-4550
Goldsholl Assoc/Northfield, IL	312-446-8300
Goldsmith Yamasaki Specht Inc/Chicago, IL	312-266-8404
Goodwin, Arnold/Chicago, IL	312-787-0466
Goose Graphics/Minneapolis, MN	612-333-3502
Gournoe, M Inc/Chicago, IL	312-787-5157
Graphic Corp/Des Moines, IA	515-247-8500
Graphic House Inc/Detroit, MI	313-259-7790
Graphic Productions/Chicago, IL	312-236-2833
Graphic Specialties Inc/Minneapolis, MN	612-722-6601
Graphica Corp/Troy, MI	313-649-5050
Graphics Group/Chicago, IL	312-782-7421
Graphics-Cor Associates/Chicago, IL	312-332-3379
Greenberg, Jon Assoc Inc/Berkley, MI	313-548-8080
Greenlee-Hess Ind Design/Mayfield Village, OH	216-461-2112
Greiner, John & Assoc/Chicago, IL	312-644-2973
Grusin, Gerald Design/Chicago, IL	312-944-4945

H

Handelan-Pedersen/Chicago, IL	312-782-6833
Hans Design/Northbrook, IL	312-272-7980
Harley, Don E Associates/West St Paul, MN	612-455-1631
Herbst Lazar Rogers & Bell Inc/Chicago, IL	312-822-9660
Higgins Hegner Genovese Inc/Chicago, IL	312-644-1882
Hirsch, David Design Group Inc/Chicago, IL	312-329-1500
Hirsh Co/Skokie, IL	312-267-6777
Hoekstra, Grant Graphics/Chicago, IL	312-641-6940
Hoffar, Barron & Co/Chicago, IL	312-922-0890
Hoffman-York Inc/Milwaukee, WI	414-259-2000
Horvath, Steve Design/Milwaukee, WI	414-271-3992

I

IGS Design Div of Smith Hinchman & Grylls/Detroit, MI	313-964-3000
ISD Incorporated/Chicago, IL	312-467-1515
Identity Center/Schaumburg, IL	312-843-2378
Indiana Design Consortium/Lafayette, IN	317-423-5469
Industrial Technological Assoc/Cleveland, OH	216-349-2900
Ing, Victor Design/Morton Grove, IL	312-965-3459
Intelplex/Maryland Hts, MO	314-739-9996

J

J M H Corp/Indianapolis, IN	317-639-2535
James, Frank Direct Marketing/Clayton, MO	314-726-4600
Jansen, Ute/Chicago, IL	312-922-5048
Johnson, Stan Design Inc/Brookfield, WI	414-783-6510
Johnson, Stewart Design Studio/Milwaukee, WI	414-265-3377
Jones, Richmond Designer/Chicago, IL	312-935-6500
Joss Design Group/Chicago, IL	312-828-0055

K

KDA Industrial Design Consultants Inc/Addison, IL	312-495-9466
Kaulfuss Design/Chicago, IL	312-943-2161
Kearns, Marilyn/Chicago, IL	312-645-1888
Keller Lane & Waln/Chicago, IL	312-782-7421
Kovach, Ronald Design/Chicago, IL	312-461-9888
Krupp, Merlin Studios/Minneapolis, MN	612-871-6611

L

LVK Associates Inc/St Louis, MO	314-534-2104
Lange, Jim Design/Chicago, IL	312-228-2089
Larson Design/Minneapolis, MN	612-835-2271
Lehrfeld, Gerald/Chicago, IL	312-944-0651
Lenard, Catherine/Chicago, IL	312-248-6937
Lerdon, Wes Assoc/Columbus, OH	614-486-8188
Lesniewicz/Navarre/Toledo, OH	419-243-7131
Lipson Associates Inc/Northbrook, IL	312-291-0500
Lipson Associates Inc/Cincinnati, OH	513-961-6225
Liska & Assoc/Chicago, IL	312-943-5910
Loew, Dick & Assoc/Chicago, IL	312-787-9032
Logelman, Dick/Chicago, IL	312-565-2386
Lubell, Robert/Toledo, OH	419-531-2267

M

Maddox, Eva Assoc Inc/Chicago, IL	312-670-0092
Manning Studios Inc/Cincinnati, OH	513-621-6959
Market Design/Cleveland, OH	216-771-0300
Marsh, Richard Assoc Inc/Chicago, IL	312-236-1331
McCoy, Steven/Omaha, NB	402-554-1416
McDermott, Bill Graphic Design/St Louis, MO	314-962-6286
McGuire, Robert L Design/Kansas City, MO	816-523-9164
McMurray Design Inc/Chicago, IL	312-527-1555
Media Corporation/Columbus, OH	614-488-7767
Minnick, James Design/Chicago, IL	312-527-1864
Moonink Inc/Chicago, IL	312-565-0040
Murrie White Drummond Leinhart/Chicago, IL	312-943-5995

NO

Naughton, Carol & Assoc/Chicago, IL	312-454-1888
Nobart Inc/Chicago, IL	312-427-9800
Nottingham-Spirk Design Inc/Cleveland, OH	216-231-7830
Oak Brook Graphics, Inc/Elmhurst, IL	312-832-3200
Obata Design/St Louis, MO	314-241-1710
Osborne-Tuttle/Chicago, IL	312-565-1910
Oskar Designs/Evanston, IL	312-328-1734
Our Gang Studios/Omaha, NB	402-341-4965
Overlock Howe Consulting Group/St Louis, MO	314-533-4484

P

Pace Studios/Lincolnwood, IL	312-676-9770
Painter/Cesaroni Design, Inc/Glenview, IL	312-724-8840
Palmer Design Assoc/Wilmette, IL	312-256-7448
Paramount Technical Service Inc/Cleveland, OH	216-585-2550
Perman, Norman/Chicago, IL	312-642-1348
Phares Associates Inc/Birmingham, MI	313-645-919-
Pinzke, Herbert Design/Chicago, IL	312-528-227
Pitt Studios/Cleveland, OH	216-241-6721
Polivka-Logan Design/Minnetonka, MN	612-474-112-
Porter-Matjasich/Chicago, IL	312-670-4355
Powell/Kleinschmidt Inc/Chicago, IL	312-726-2201
Pride and Perfomance/St Paul, MN	612-646-480
Prodesign Inc/Plymouth, MI	612-476-120
Purviance, George Marketing Comm/Clayton, MO	314-721-276
Pycha and Associates/Chicago, IL	312-944-367

QR

Quality Graphics/Akron, OH	216-375-528
Qually & Co Inc/Chicago, IL	312-944-023
RHI Inc/Chicago, IL	312-467-129
Ramba Graphics/Lakewood, OH	216-228-513
Red Wing Enterprises/Chicago, IL	312-951-044
Redmond, Patrick Design/St Paul, MN	612-292-985
Reed Design Assoc Inc/Madison, WI	608-238-190
Reed, Stan/Madison, WI	608-238-190
Richardson/Smith Inc/Worthington, OH	614-885-345
Roberts Webb & Co/Chicago, IL	312-861-006
Robinson, Thompson & Wise/Overland Park, KS	913-451-947

Ross & Harvey/Chicago, IL	312-407-1290
Roth, Randall/Chicago, IL	312-467-0140
Rotheiser, Jordan I/Highland Park, IL	312-433-4288

S Samata Assoc/West Dundee, IL 312-428-8600

Sargent, Ann Design/Minneapolis, MN	612-870-9995
Savlin/ Williams Assoc/Evanston, IL	312-328-3366
Schlatter Group Inc/Battle Creek, MI	616-964-0898
Schmidt, Wm M Assoc/Harper Woods, MI	313-881-8075
Schultz, Ron Design/Chicago, IL	312-528-1853
Scott, Jack/Chicago, IL	312-922-1467
Seltzer, Meyer Design & Illustration/Chicago, IL	312-348-2885
Sherman, Roger Assoc Inc/Dearborn, MI	313-582-8844
Simanis, Vito/St Charles, IL	312-584-1683
Simons, I W Industrial Design/Columbus, OH	614-451-3796
Skolnick, Jerome/Chicago, IL	312-944-4568
Slavin Assoc Inc/Chicago, IL	312-944-2920
Smith, Glen The Co/Minneapolis, MN	612-871-1616
Source Inc/Chicago, IL	312-236-7620
Space Design International Inc/Cincinnati, OH	513-241-3000
Spatial Graphics Inc/Milwaukee, WI	414-545-4444
Stepan Design/Mt Prospect, IL	312-364-4121
Strandell Design Inc/Chicago, IL	312-861-1654
Strizek, Jan/Chicago, IL	312-664-4772
Stromberg, Gordon H Visual Design/Chicago, IL	312-275-9449
Studio One Graphics/Livonia, MI	313-522-7505
Studio One Inc/Minneapolis, MN	612-831-6313
Swoger Grafik/Chicago, IL	312-943-2491
Synthesis Concepts/Chicago, IL	312-787-1201

TU T & Company/Chicago, IL 312-463-1336

Tassian, George Org/Cincinnati, OH	513-721-5566
Taylor & Assoc/Des Moines, IA	515-276-0992
Tepe Hensler & Westerkamp/Cincinnati, OH	513-241-0100
Thorbeck & Lambert Inc/Minneapolis, MN	612-871-7979
TURGEON, JAMES/CHICAGO, IL (P 251)	**312-861-1039**
Underwood, Muriel/Chicago, IL	312-236-8472
Unicom/Milwaukee, WI	414-354-5440

V Vallarta, Frederick Assoc Inc/Chicago, IL 312-944-7300

Vanides-Mlodock/Chicago, IL	312-663-0595
Vann, Bill Studio/St Louis, MO	314-231-2322
Vista Three Design/Minneapolis, MN	612-920-5311
Visual Image Studio/St Paul, MN	612-644-7314

WXZ Wallner Harbauer Bruce & Assoc/Chicago, IL 312-787-6787

Weber Conn & Riley/Chicago, IL	312-527-4260
Weiss, Jack Assoc/Evanston, IL	312-866-7480
Widmer, Stanley Assoc Inc/Staples, MN	218-894-3466
Winbush Design/Chicago, IL	312-527-4478
Wooster + Assoc/Winnetka, IL	312-726-7944
Worrel, W Robert Design/Minneapolis, MN	612-340-1300
Zeno/Chicago, IL	312-327-1989
Zender and Associates/Cincinnati, OH	513-561-8496

SOUTHWEST

A

3D/International/Houston, TX	713-871-7000
Worthwhile Place Comm/Dallas, TX	214-946-1348
&M Associates Inc/Phoenix, AZ	602-263-6504
ckerman & McQueen/Oklahoma City, OK	405-843-9451
he Ad Department/Ft Worth, TX	817-335-4012
d-Art Studios/Ft Worth, TX	817-335-9603
dvertising Inc/Tulsa, OK	918-747-8871
rnold Harwell McClain & Assoc/Dallas, TX	214-521-6400
t Associates/Irving, TX	214-258-6001

BC

Beals Advertising Agency/Oklahoma City, OK	405-848-8513
he Belcher Group Inc/Houston, TX	713-271-2727
rooks & Pollard Co/Little Rock, AR	501-375-5561
entral Advertising Agency/Fort Worth, TX	817-390-3011

Chandler, Jeff/Dallas, TX	214-946-1348
Chesterfield Interiors Inc/Dallas, TX	214-747-2211
Clark, Betty & Assoc/Dallas, TX	214-980-1685
Coffee Design Inc/Houston, TX	713-780-0571
Cranford/ Johnson & Assoc/Little Rock, AR	501-376-6251

DEF Design Bank/Austin, TX 512-445-7584

Design Enterprises, Inc/El Paso, TX	915-594-7100
Designmark/Houston, TX	713-626-0953
Ellies, Dave Industrial Design Inc/Dallas, TX	214-742-8654
Executive Image/Dallas, TX	214-733-0496
Fedele Creative Consulting/Dallas, TX	214-528-3501
First Marketing Group/Houston, TX	713-626-2500
Friesenhahn, Michelle/San Antonio, TX	512-822-3325

G GKD/Oklahoma City, OK 405-943-2333

The Goodwin Co/El Paso, TX	915-584-1176
Gore, Fred M & Assoc/Dallas, TX	214-521-5844
Graphic Designers Group Inc/Houston, TX	713-622-8680
Graphics Hardware Co/Phoenix, AZ	602-242-4687
Graphics Intrnl Adv & Dsgn/Fort Worth, TX	817-731-9941
GRIMES, DON/DALLAS, TX (P 345)	**214-526-0040**
Grimm, Tom/Dallas, TX	214-526-0040

HIK Harrison Allen Design/Houston, TX 713-771-9274

Hill, Chris/Houston, TX	713-523-7363
Hood Hope & Assoc/Tulsa, OK	918-250-9511
ISD Incorporated/Houston, TX	713-236-8232
Konig Design Group/San Antonio, TX	512-824-7387

LMNO Lowe Runkle Co/Oklahoma City, OK 405-848-6800

Mantz & Associates/Dallas, TX	214-521-7432
McCulley, Mike/Euless, TX	214-528-4889
McGrath, Michael Design/Richardson, TX	214-644-4358
Morales, Frank Design/Dallas, TX	214-827-2101
Neumann, Steve & Friends/Houston, TX	713-629-7501
Owens & Assoc Advertising Inc/Phoenix, AZ	602-264-5691

PRS Pirtle Design/Dallas, TX 214-522-7520

Reed Melnichek Gentry/Dallas, TX	214-634-7337
The Richards Group/Dallas, TX	214-987-2700
Strickland, Michael & Co/Houston, TX	713-961-1323
Sullivan, Jack Design Group/Phoenix, AZ	602-271-0117
Suntar Designs/Prescott, AZ	602-778-2714

TVW Total Designers/Houston, TX 713-688-7766

Varner, Charles/Dallas, TX	214-744-0148
WW3 Papagalos/Phoenix, AZ	602-279-2933
Weekley & Penny Inc/Houston, TX	713-529-4861
Winius Brandon/Bellaire, TX	713-666-1765
Witherspoon/Fort Worth, TX	817-335-1373

ROCKY MOUNTAIN

Ampersand Studios/Denver, CO	303-388-1211
Arnold Design Inc/Denver, CO	303-832-7156
The Art Directors Club of Denver/Denver, CO	303-831-9251
Barnstorm Studios/Colorado Springs, CO	303-630-7200
Blanchard, D W & Assoc/Salt Lake City, UT	801-484-6344
Chen, Shih-chien/Edmonton T6L5K2, AB	403-462-8617
CommuniCreations/Denver, CO	303-759-1155
Consortium West/Concept Design/Salt Lake City, UT	801-278-4441
Cuerden Advertising Design/Denver, CO	303-321-4163
Design Center/Salt Lake City, UT	801-532-6122
Duo Graphics/Ft Collins, CO	303-463-2788
Entercom/Denver, CO	303-393-0405
General Graphics/Denver, CO	303-832-5258
Gibby, John Design/Layton, UT	801-544-0736
Graphic Concepts Inc/Salt Lake City, UT	801-359-2191
Malmberg & Assoc/Aurora, CO	303-699-9364
Markowitz & Long/Boulder, CO	303-449-7394
Matrix International Inc/Denver, CO	303-388-9353

GRAPHIC DESIGNERS CONT'D.

Please send us your additions and updates.

Multimedia/Denver, CO	303-777-5480
Okland Design Assoc/Salt Lake City, UT	801-484-7861
Radetsky Design Associates/Denver, CO	303-629-7375
Tamburello, Michael Communications/Littleton, CO	303-733-0128
Tandem Design Group Inc/Denver, CO	303-831-9251
Taylor, Robert W Design Inc/Boulder, CO	303-443-1975
Three B Studio & Assoc/Denver, CO	303-777-6359
Visual Communications/Littleton, CO	303-773-0128
Visual Images Inc/Denver, CO	303-388-5366
Walker Design Associates/Denver, CO	303-773-0426
Weller Institute for Design/Park City, UT	801-649-9859
Wilson, Cheryl/Boulder, CO	303-444-0979
Woodard Racing Graphics Ltd/Boulder, CO	303-443-1986
Worthington, Carl A Partnership/Boulder, CO	303-443-7271

WEST

A
A & H Graphic Design/Rancho Bernardo, CA	619-486-0777
ADI/Los Angeles, CA	213-254-7131
AGI/Los Angeles, CA	213-462-0821
Ace Design/Sausalito, CA	415-332-9390
Adfiliation/Eugene, OR	503-687-8262
Advertising Design & Production Service/San Diego, CA	619-483-1393
Advertising/Design Assoc/Walnut Creek, CA	415-421-7000
Allied Artists/San Francisco, CA	415-421-1919
Antisdel Image Group/Santa Clara, CA	408-988-1010
Art Zone/Honolulu, HI	808-537-6647
Artists In Print/San Francisco, CA	415-673-6941
Artmaster Studios/San Fernando, CA	213-365-7188
Artworks/Los Angeles, CA	213-380-2187
Asbury Tucker & Assoc/Long Beach, CA	213-595-6481
Aurora Borealis/San Francisco, CA	415-392-2971

B
Bailey, Robert Design Group/Portland, OR	503-228-1381
Banuelos Design/Orange, CA	714-771-4335
Barile & Garnas Design/Oakland, CA	415-339-8360
Barnes, Herb Graphics/S Pasadena, CA	213-682-2420
Basic Designs Inc/Sausalito, CA	415-388-5141
Bass, Yager and Assoc/Hollywood, CA	213-466-9701
Bean, Carolyn Associates Inc/San Francisco, CA	415-957-9573
Beggs Langley Design/Palo Alto, CA	415-327-5275
Belew, Tandy/San Francisco, CA	415-543-7377
Bennett, Douglas Design/Seattle, WA	206-324-9966
Bennett, Ralph Assoc/Van Nuys, CA	213-782-3224
Bhang, Samuel Design Assoc/Los Angeles, CA	213-382-1126
Blazej, Rosalie Graphics/San Francisco, CA	415-586-3325
Blik, Ty/San Diego, CA	619-299-4227
Bloch & Associates/Santa Monica, CA	213-450-8863
Boelter, Herbert A/Burbank, CA	213-845-5055
Boyd, Douglas Design/Los Angeles, CA	213-655-9642
Bright & Associates, Inc/Los Angeles, CA	213-658-8844
Briteday Inc/Mountain View, CA	415-968-5668
Brookins, Ed/Studio City, CA	213-766-7336
Brosio Design/San Diego, CA	619-226-4322
Brown, Bill/Los Angeles, CA	213-386-2455
Brown, Steve/Northridge, CA	213-349-0785
Burns & Associates Inc/San Francisco, CA	415-567-4404
Burridge Design/Santa Barbara, CA	805-965-8023
Burridge, Robert/Santa Barbara, CA	805-964-2087
Business Graphics/Los Angeles, CA	213-467-0292
Busse and Cummins/San Francisco, CA	415-957-0300

C
CAG Graphics/Van Nuys, CA	213-901-1077
Camozzi, Teresa/San Francisco, CA	415-392-1202
Carlson, Keith Advertising Art/San Francisco, CA	415-397-5130
Carre Design/Santa Monica, CA	213-395-1033
Cassidy Photographic Design/Santa Clara, CA	408-735-8443
Catalog Design & Production Inc/San Francisco, CA	415-468-5500
Chan Design/Santa Monica, CA	213-393-3735
Chandler Media Productions/Irvine, CA	714-261-6183
Chapman Productions/Los Angeles, CA	213-460-4302

Chartmasters Inc/San Francisco, CA	415-421-6591
CHASE, MARGO/LOS ANGELES, CA (P 291)	**213-537-4421**
Churchill, Steven/San Diego, CA	619-560-1225
Clark, Tim/Los Angeles, CA	213-202-1044
Coak, Steve/Altadena, CA	818-797-5477
The Coakley Heagerty Co/Santa Clara, CA	408-249-6242
Coates Advertising/Portland, OR	503-241-1124
Cognata Associates Inc/San Francisco, CA	415-931-3800
Communication Design/San Diego, CA	619-455-5500
Conber Creations/Portland, OR	503-288-2938
Conversano, Henry & Assoc/Oakland, CA	415-547-6890
Corporate Comms Group/Marina Del Rey, Ca	213-821-9086
Corporate Graphics/San Francisco, CA	415-474-2888
Crawshaw, Todd Design/San Francisco, CA	415-956-3169
Creative Consultant/Venice, CA	213-399-3875
Cronan, Michael Patrick/San Francisco, CA	415-543-6745
Crop Mark/Los Angeles, CA	213-388-3142
Cross, James/Los Angeles, CA	213-474-1484
Crouch + Fuller Inc/Del Mar, CA	619-450-9200

D
Dahm & Assoc Inc/Torrance, CA	213-320-0460
Dancer Fitzgerald & Sample/San Francisco, CA	415-981-6250
Danziger, Louis/Los Angeles, CA	213-935-1251
Davis, Pat/Sacramento, CA	916-442-9025
Dawson, Chris/Los Angeles, CA	213-937-5867
Dayne, Jeff The Studio/Portland, OR	503-222-7144
Daystar Design/La Mesa, CA	619-463-5014
Dellaporta Adv & Graphic/Santa Monica, CA	213-394-0023
DeMaio Graphics & Advertising/Reseda, CA	818-785-6551
Design & Direction/Torrance, CA	213-320-0822
Design Corps/Los Angeles, CA	213-651-1422
Design Direction Group/Pasadena, CA	213-792-4765
Design Element/Los Angeles, CA	213-656-3293
Design Graphics/Los Angeles, CA	213-749-7347
Design Office/San Francisco, CA	415-543-4760
Design Projects Inc/Encino, CA	213-995-0303
Design Vectors/San Francisco, CA	415-391-0399
The Design Works/Los Angeles, CA	213-477-3577
Design/Graphics/Portland, OR	503-227-7247
Designage/Newport Beach, CA	714-852-1585
The Designory Inc/Long Beach, CA	213-432-5707
Detanna Advertising Design/Beverly Hills, CA	213-852-0808
Dimensional Design/N Hollywood, CA	213-769-569-
Diniz, Carlos/Los Angeles, CA	213-387-117-
Doane, Dave Studio/Orange, CA	714-548-7285
Doerfler Design/La Jolla, CA	619-455-0506
Dowlen, James/Santa Rosa, CA	707-576-7286
Dupre Design/Coronado, CA	619-435-8368
Dyer-Cahn/Los Angeles, CA	213-937-4100
Dyna-Pac/San Diego, CA	619-560-011

EF
Earnett McFall & Assoc/Seattle, WA	206-364-495
Ehrig & Assoc/Seattle, WA	206-623-666
Engle, Ray/Los Angeles, CA	213-381-500
Exhibit Design Inc/San Mateo, CA	415-342-306
Farber, Melvyn Design Group/Santa Monica, CA	213-829-266
Finger, Julie Design Inc/Los Angeles, CA	213-653-054
Five Penguins Design/Burbank, CA	213-841-557
Floyd Design & Assoc/Lafayette, CA	415-563-050
Flying Colors/San Francisco, CA	415-563-050
Follis, Dean/Los Angeles, CA	213-735-128
Fox, BD & Friends Advertising Inc/Hollywood, CA	213-464-013
Frazier, Craig/San Francisco, CA	415-863-961
Frey, Karin/San Francisco, CA	415-552-717
Furniss, Stephanie Design/San Rafael, CA	415-488-469

G
Garner, Glenn Graphic Design/Seattle, WA	206-323-778
Garnett, Joe Design/Illus/Los Angeles, CA	213-279-153
Georgopoulos/Imada Design/Los Angeles, CA	213-933-642
Gerber Advertising Agency/Portland, OR	503-221-010
Gillian/Craig Assoc/San Francisco, CA	415-558-898
GIRVIN, TIM DESIGN/SEATTLE, WA (P 228,229)	**206-623-791**

Please send us your additions and updates.

Glickman, Abe Design/Van Nuys, CA	213-989-3223
The Gnu Group/Sausalito, CA	415-332-8010
Gohata, Mark/Gardena, CA	213-327-6595
Gotschalk's Graphics/San Diego, CA	619-578-5094
Gould & Assoc/W Los Angeles, CA	213-208-5577
Graformation/N Hollywood, CA	213-985-1224
Graphic Data/Pacific Beach, CA	714-274-4511
Graphic Designers Inc/Los Angeles, CA	213-381-3977
Graphic Designs by Joy/Newport Beach, CA	714-642-0271
Graphic Ideas/San Diego, CA	619 299 3433
Greiman, April/Los Angeles, CA	213-462-1771
Guido, Jeff/Los Angeles, CA	213-858-5906

H
Hale, Dan Ad Design Co/Woodland Hills, CA	213-347-4021
Hardbarger, Dave Design/Oakland, CA	415-655-4928
Harper and Assoc/Bellevue, WA	206-462-6486
Harrington and Associates/Los Angeles, CA	213-876-5272
Harte-Yamashita & Forest/Los Angeles, CA	213-884-1727
Hauser, S G Assoc Inc/Woodland Hills, CA	213-884-1727
Helgesson, Ulf Ind Dsgn/Woodland Hills, CA	213-883-3772
Hernandez, Daniel/Whittier, CA	213-696-0607
Hornall Anderson Design Works/Seattle, WA	206-467-5800
Hosick, Frank Design/Seattle, WA	206-789-5535
Hubert, Laurent/Menlo Park, CA	415-321-5182
Humangraphic/San Diego, CA	619-299-0431
Hyde, Bill/Foster City, CA	415-345-6955

IJ
Imag'Inez/San Francisco, CA	415-398-3203
Image Stream/Los Angeles, CA	213-933-9196
ImageMakers/Santa Barbara, CA	805-965-8546
Imagination Creative Services/Santa Clara, CA	408-988-8696
Imagination Graphics/Santa Ana, CA	714-662-3114
J J & A/Burbank, CA	213-849-1444
Jaciow Design Inc/Mountain View, CA	415-962-8860
Jaciow Kelley Org/Menlo Park, CA	415-327-8210
Jerde Partnership/Los Angeles, CA	213-413-0130
Johnson Rodger Design/Rolling Hills, CA	213-377-8860
Johnson, Paige Graphic Design/Palo Alto, CA	415-327-0488
Joly Major Product Design Group/San Francisco, CA	415-641-1933
Jones, Steve/Venice, CA	213-396-9111
Jonson Pedersen Hinrichs & Shakery/San Francisco, CA	415-981-6612
Juett Dennis & Assoc/Los Angeles, CA	213-385-4373

K
K S Wilshire Inc/Los Angeles, CA	213-879-9595
KLAC Metro Media/Los Angeles, CA	213-462-5522
Kageyama, David Designer/Seattle, WA	206-622-7281
Keating, Kate Assoc/San Francisco, CA	415-398-6611
Keser, Dennis/San Francisco, CA	415-387-6448
Kessler, David Photographics/Hollywood, CA	213-462-6043
Klein/Los Angeles, CA	213-278-5600
Klein, Larry Designer/San Carlos, CA	415-595-1332
Kleiner, John A Graphic Design/Santa Monica, CA	213-747-0604
Kuey, Patty/Yorba Linda, CA	714-970-5286
Kuwahara, Sachi/Los Angeles, CA	213-937-8360

L
Lacy, N Lee Assoc Ltd/Los Angeles, CA	213-852-1414
LaFleur Design/Sausalito, CA	415-332-3725
Lancaster Design/Santa Monica, CA	213-450-2999
Landes & Assoc/Torrance, CA	213-540-0907
Landor Associates/San Francisco, CA	415-955-1200
Larson, Ron/Los Angeles, CA	213-465-8451
Laurence-Deutsch Design/Los Angeles, CA	213-937-3521
Leipzig, Dale/Huntington Beach, CA	714-847-1240
Leong, Russel Design Group/Palo Alto, CA	415-321-2443
Lesser, Joan/Etcetera/Los Angeles, CA	213-450-3977
Levine & Company, Steve Levine/Venice, CA	213-399-9336
Logan Carey & Rehag/San Francisco, CA	415-543-7080
Loveless, J R Design/Santa Ana, CA	714-754-0886
Lum, Darell/Monterey Park, CA	213-613-2538
Lumel-Whiteman Assoc/North Hollywood, CA	213-769-5332
Lumel-Whiteman Assoc/Monterey Park, CA	213-613-2538

M
Maddu, Patrick & Co/San Diego, CA	619-238-1340
Manhattan Graphics/Manhattan Beach, CA	213-376-2778
Manwaring, Michael Office/San Francisco, CA	415-421-3595
Marketing Tools/Encinitas, CA	619-942-6042
Marra, Ann Graphic Design/Portland, OR	503-227-5207
Matrix Design Consultants/Los Angeles, CA	213-487-6300
Matthews, Robert/Campbell, CA	408-378-0878
McKee, Dennis/San Francisco, CA	415-673-0852
Media Services Corp/San Francisco, CA	415-928-3033
Meek, Kenneth/Pasadena, CA	213-449-9722
Mikkelson, Linda S/Hollywood, CA	213-463-3116
Miller, Marcia/Ingelwood, CA	213-677-4171
Miura Design/Torrance, CA	213-320-1957
Mize, Charles Advertising Art/San Francisco, CA	415-421-1548
Mizrahi, Robert/Buena Park, CA	714-527-6182
Mobius Design Assoc/Los Angeles, CA	213-937-0331
Molly Designs Inc/Irvine, CA	714-768-7155
Monahan, Leo/Los Angeles, CA	213-463-3116
Mortensen, Gordon/Santa Barbara, CA	805-962-5315
Murphy, Harry & Friends/Mill Valley, CA	415-383-8586
Murray/Bradley Inc/Seattle, WA	206-622-7082

N
N Graphic/San Francisco, CA	415-863-3392
Naganuma, Tony K Design/San Francisco, CA	415-433-4484
Nagel, William Design Group/Palo Alto, CA	415-328-0251
New Breath Productions/Los Angeles, CA	213-876-3491
New Concepts Industrial Design Corp/Seattle, WA	206-633-3111
Nicholson Design/San Diego, CA	619-235-9000
Nicolini Associates/Oakland, CA	415-531-5569
Niehaus, Don/Los Angeles, CA	213-279-1559
Nine West/Pasadena, CA	213-799-2727
Nordenhook Design/Newport Beach, CA	714-752-8631

OP
Odgers, Jayme/Los Angeles, CA	213-484-9965
Olson Design Inc/Del Mar, CA	619-450-9200
Orr, R & Associates Inc/El Toro, CA	714-770-1277
Osborn, Michael Design/San Francisco, CA	415-495-4292
Oshima, Carol/Covina, CA	213-966-0796
Pacific Rim Design/Vancouver V5V2K9, BC	604-879-6689
Package Deal/Tustin, CA	714-731-2301
Pease, Robert & Co/Alamo, CA	415-820-0404
Peddicord & Assoc/Santa Clara, CA	408-727-7800
Persechini & Co/Beverly Hills, CA	213-657-6175
Petzold & Assoc/Portland, OR	503-221-1800
Pihas Schmidt Westerdahl Co/Portland, WA	503-228-4000
Ponce de Leon Design/Costa Mesa, CA	714-957-8920
Popovich, Mike c/o Pacific Graphic Assoc/City of Industry, CA	213-336-6958
Powers Design International/Newport Beach, CA	714-645-2265
Primo Angeli Graphics/San Francisco, CA	415-974-6100

QR
The Quorum/Clinton, WA	206-522-6872
RJL Design Graphics/Fremont, CA	415-657-2038
Ray, Mark/Dixville, CA	805-323-8333
Regis McKenna Inc/Palo Alto, CA	415-494-2030
Reid, Scott/Santa Barbara, CA	805-963-8926
Reineck & Reineck/San Francisco, CA	415-566-3614
Reineman, Richard Industrial Design/Newport Beach, CA	714-673-2485
Reis, Gerald & Co/San Francisco, CA	415-543-1344
Rickabaugh Design/Portland, OR	503-223-2191
Ritola, Roy Inc/San Francisco, CA	415-788-7010
Roberts, Eileen Design/Carlsbad, CA	619-439-7800
Robinson, David & Assoc/San Diego, CA	714-298-2021
Rogow & Bernstein Dsgn & Fabrication/Los Angeles, CA	213-936-9916
Rolandesign/Woodland Hills, CA	213-346-9752
Runyan, Richard Design/West Los Angeles, CA	213-477-8878
Runyan, Robert Miles & Assoc/Playa Del Rey, CA	213-823-0975
Rupert, Paul Designer/San Francisco, CA	415-391-2966

S
Sackheim, Morton Enterprises/Beverly Hills, CA	213-652-0220
San Diego Art Prdctns/San Diego, CA	619-239-5523
Sanchez, Michael Assoc/Pasadena, CA	213-793-4017

Please send us your additions and updates.

Sandvick, John Studios/Los Angeles, CA	213-685-7148
Sant'Andrea, Jim West Inc/Compton, CA	213-979-9100
Schaefer, Robert Television Art/Hollywood, CA	213-462-7877
Schorer, R Thomas/Palos Verdes, CA	213-377-0207
Schwab, Michael Design/San Francisco, CA	415-546-7559
Schwartz, Clem & Bonnie Graphic Design/San Diego, CA	619-291-8878
Scroggin & Fischer Advertising/San Francisco, CA	415-391-2694
See Design & Production Inc/Salem, OR	503-393-1733
Seigle Rolfs & Wood Inc/Honolulu, HI	808-524-5080
Seiniger & Assoc/Los Angeles, CA	213-653-8665
Sellers, Michael Advertising/San Francisco, CA	415-781-7200
Shaw, Michael Design/Manhattan Beach, CA	213-545-0516
Shenon, Mike/Palo Alto, CA	415-326-4608
Shoji Graphics/Los Angeles, CA	213-384-3091
Shuman, Sharon Designer/Los Angeles, CA	213-837-6998
Sidjakov, Nicholas/San Francisco, CA	415-931-7500
Siege, Gretchen/Seattle, WA	206-623-9459
Signworks Inc/Seattle, WA	206-525-2718
Smidt, Sam/Palo Alto, CA	415-327-0707
The Smith Group/Portland, OR	503-224-1905
Sorensen, Hugh Industrial Design/Brea, CA	714-529-8493
Soyster & Ohrenschall Inc/San Francisco, CA	415-956-7575
Spangler Leonhardt/Seattle, WA	206-624-0551
Spear, Jeffrey A/Santa Monica, CA	213-395-3939
Spivey, William Design Inc/Newport Beach, CA	714-752-1203
The Stansbury Company/Beverly Hills, CA	213-273-1138
Steinberg, Bruce/San Francisco, CA	415-864-0739
Stephenz, The Group/Campbell, CA	408-379-4883
Strong, David Design Group/Seattle, WA	206-447-9160
The Studio/San Francisco, CA	415-928-4400
Sugi, Richard Design & Assoc/Los Angeles, CA	213-385-4169
Sullivan & Assoc/Los Angeles, CA	213-384-3331
Superior Graphic Systems/Long Beach, CA	213-433-7421
Sussman & Prejza/Santa Monica, CA	213-829-3337
T Tartak, Donald H Design/Los Angeles, CA	213-477-3571
Thomas & Assoc/Santa Monica, CA	213-451-8502
Thomas, Greg/Los Angeles, CA	213-479-8477
Thomas, Keith M Inc/Santa Ana, CA	714-979-3051
Thompson, Larry Design/San Bernadino, CA	714-885-4976
Trade Marx/Seattle, WA	206-623-7676
Tribotti Design/Sherman Oaks, CA	213-784-6101
Trygg Stefanic Advertising/Los Altos, CA	415-948-3493
Tycer Fultz Bellack/Palo Alto, CA	415-856-1600
UV Unigraphics/San Francisco, CA	415-398-8232
Valentino Graphic Design/Thousand Oaks, CA	805-495-9933
VanHamersveld Design/Los Angeles, CA	213-656-3815
VanNoy & Co Inc/Los Angeles, CA	213-386-7312
Vanderbyl Design/San Francisco, CA	415-543-8447
Vanderwielen Designs/Irvine, CA	714-851-8078
Vantage Advertising & Marketing Assoc/San Leandro, CA	415-352-3640
Vicom Associates/San Francisco, CA	415-391-8700
Vigon, Larry/Los Angeles, CA	213-394-6502
Village Design/Irvine, CA	714-857-9048
Visual Resources Inc/Los Angeles, CA	213-851-6688
Voltec Associates/Los Angeles, CA	213-467-2106
W Walton, Brenda/Sacramento, CA	916-456-5833
Webster, Ken/Orinda, CA	415-254-1098
Weideman and Associates/North Hollywood, CA	213-769-8488
Wertman, Chuck/San Francisco, CA	415-433-4452
West End Studios/San Francisco, CA	415-434-0380
West, Suzanne Design/Palo Alto, CA	415-324-8068
White, Ken Design/Los Angeles, CA	213-467-4681
Whitely, Mitchell Assoc/San Francisco, CA	415-398-2920
Wilkerson, Haines/Manhattan Beach, CA	213-372-3325
Wilkins & Peterson Graphic Design/Seattle, WA	206-624-1695
WILLARDSON + ASSOC/GLENDALE, CA (P 173)	**818-242-5688**
Williams & Ziller Design/San Francisco, CA	415-621-0330
Williams, Leslie/Norwalk, CA	213-864-4135
Williamson & Assoc Inc/Los Angeles, CA	213-836-0143
Winters, Clyde Design/San Francisco, CA	415-391-5643
Woodward, Teresa/Pacific Palisades, CA	213-459-2317
Workshop West/Beverly Hills, CA	213-278-1370
YZ Yamaguma & Assoc/San Jose, CA	408-279-0500
Yanez, Maurice & Assoc/Los Angeles, CA	213-462-1309
Young & Roehr Adv/Portland, OR	503-297-4501
Yuguchi Krogstad/Los Angeles, CA	213-383-6915
Zamparelli & Assoc/Pasadena, CA	818-799-4370
Zolotow, Milton/Westwood, CA	213-453-4885